T0328811

A Theory of Fairness and Social Welfare

The definition and measurement of social welfare have been a vexed issue for the past century. This book makes a constructive, easily applicable proposal and suggests how to evaluate the economic situation of a society in a way that gives priority to the worse-off and that respects each individual's preferences over his or her own consumption, work, leisure, and so on. This approach resonates with the current concern to go "beyond the GDP" in the measurement of social progress. Compared to technical studies in welfare economics, this book emphasizes constructive results rather than paradoxes and impossibilities, and shows how one can start from basic principles of efficiency and fairness and end up with concrete evaluations of policies. Compared to more philosophical treatments of social justice, this book is more precise about the definition of social welfare and reaches conclusions about concrete policies and institutions only after a rigorous derivation from clearly stated principles.

Marc Fleurbaey is a Research Director of the National Center for Scientific Research (CNRS) and serves on the staff of CERSES, the joint research entity of the CNRS and the Université Paris Descartes. He first worked at INSEE, taught subsequently at the Universities of Cergy-Pontoise and Pau, and as of 2011 is a professor at Princeton University. Professor Fleurbaey is a research associate at CORE at the Université Catholique de Louvain, at Sciences-Po in Paris, and at IDEP in Marseilles, and a visiting professor at the London School of Economics. He is a former editor of the journal *Economics and Philosophy* (Cambridge University Press) and is currently a managing editor of *Social Choice and Welfare*. He is the author, editor, or coeditor of seven books, including *Fairness, Responsibility, and Welfare* (2008), and *Justice, Political Liberalism, and Utilitarianism: Themes from Harsanyi and Rawls* (with Maurice Salles and John Weymark, Cambridge University Press, 2008). His papers on normative and public economics have appeared in leading journals such as *Econometrica*, the *Journal of Political Economy*, and the *Journal of Economic Theory*.

François Maniquet is Professor of Economics at CORE at the Université Catholique de Louvain, Belgium, and teaches part time at the University of Warwick, UK. He served as an FNRS research associate at the University of Namur, Belgium, until 2005. Professor Maniquet has been a visiting scholar at several research centers, including the Institute for Advanced Study in Princeton, New Jersey, in 2001–2002. He was awarded the Social Choice and Welfare Prize in 2004, and he received the Koç Prize for the best paper in the *Review of Economic Design* that same year. Professor Maniquet has published papers on welfare economics, public economics, game theory, and political economics in eminent journals such as *Econometrica, Review of Economic Studies*, the *Journal of Economic Theory*, and the *American Journal of Political Science*. He is currently one of the editors of the Cambridge University Press journal *Economics and Philosophy*. Professor Maniquet was recently awarded the Francqui Prize, the highest scientific distinction in Belgium.

Econometric Society Monographs

Other titles in the series:

G. S. Maddala, *Limited dependent and qualitative variables in econometrics*, 978 0 521 24143 4, 978 0 521 33825 7

Gerard Debreu, *Mathematical economics: Twenty papers of Gerard Debreu*, 978 0 521 23736 9, 978 0 521 33561 4

Jean-Michel Grandmont, *Money and value: A reconsideration of classical and neoclassical monetary economics*, 978 0 521 25141 9, 978 0 521 31364 3

Franklin M. Fisher, *Disequilibrium foundations of equilibrium economics*, 978 0 521 37856 7

Andreu Mas-Colell, *The theory of general equilibrium: A differentiable approach*, 978 0 521 26514 0, 978 0 521 38870 2

Truman F. Bewley, Editor, *Advances in econometrics – Fifth World Congress* (Volume I), 978 0 521 46726 1

Truman F. Bewley, Editor, *Advances in econometrics – Fifth World Congress* (Volume II), 978 0 521 46725 4

Hervé Moulin, *Axioms of cooperative decision making*, 978 0 521 36055 5, 978 0 521 42458 5

L. G. Godfrey, *Misspecification tests in econometrics: The Lagrange multiplier principle and other approaches*, 978 0 521 42459 2

Tony Lancaster, *The econometric analysis of transition data*, 978 0 521 4378 9

Alvin E. Roth and Marilda A. Oliviera Sotomayor, Editors, *Two-sided matching: A study in game-theoretic modeling and analysis*, 978 0 521 43788 2

Wolfgang Härdle, *Applied nonparametric regression*, 978 0 521 42950 4

Jean-Jacques Laffont, Editor, *Advances in economic theory – Sixth World Congress* (Volume I), 978 0 521 48459 6

Jean-Jacques Laffont, Editor, *Advances in economic theory – Sixth World Congress* (Volume II), 978 0 521 48460 2

Halbert White, *Estimation, inference and specification*, 978 0 521 25280 5, 978 0 521 57446 4

Christopher Sims, Editor, *Advances in econometrics – Sixth World Congress* (Volume I), 978 0 521 44459 0, 978 0 521 56610 0

Christopher Sims, Editor, *Advances in econometrics – Sixth World Congress* (Volume II), 978 0 521 44460 6, 978 0 521 56609 4

Roger Guesnerie, *A contribution to the pure theory of taxation*, 978 0 521 62956 0

David M. Kreps and Kenneth F. Wallis, Editors, *Advances in economics and econometrics – Seventh World Congress* (Volume I), 978 0 521 58983 3

David M. Kreps and Kenneth F. Wallis, Editors, *Advances in economics and econometrics – Seventh World Congress* (Volume II), 978 0 521 58982 6

David M. Kreps and Kenneth F. Wallis, Editors, *Advances in economics and econometrics – Seventh World Congress* (Volume III), 978 0 521 58013 7, 978 0 521 58981 9

Donald P. Jacobs, Ehud Kalai, and Morton I. Kamien, Editors, *Frontiers of research in economic theory: The Nancy L. Schwartz Memorial Lectures, 1983–1997*, 978 0 521 63222 5, 978 0 521 63538 7

A. Colin Cameron and Pravin K. Trivedi, *Regression analysis of count data*, 978 0 521 63201 0, 978 0 521 63567 7

Steinar Strom, Editor, *Econometrics and economic theory in the 20th century: The Ragnar Frisch Centennial Symposium*, 978 0 521 63323 9, 978 0 521 63365 9

Continued on page following the index

A Theory of Fairness and Social Welfare

Marc Fleurbaey
CERSES, Université Paris Descartes

François Maniquet
CORE, Université Catholique de Louvain

CAMBRIDGE
UNIVERSITY PRESS

CAMBRIDGE
UNIVERSITY PRESS

University Printing House, Cambridge CB2 8BS, United Kingdom

One Liberty Plaza, 20th Floor, New York, NY 10006, USA

477 Williamstown Road, Port Melbourne, VIC 3207, Australia

4843/24, 2nd Floor, Ansari Road, Daryaganj, Delhi - 110002, India

79 Anson Road, #06-04/06, Singapore 079906

Cambridge University Press is part of the University of Cambridge.

It furthers the University's mission by disseminating knowledge in the pursuit of education, learning and research at the highest international levels of excellence.

www.cambridge.org
Information on this title: www.cambridge.org/9780521715348

© Marc Fleurbaey and François Maniquet 2011

First published 2011

A catalogue record for this publication is available from the British Library

Library of Congress Cataloging in Publication data
Fleurbaey, Marc.
A theory of fairness and social welfare / Marc Fleurbaey, François Maniquet.
   p.   cm. – (Econometric society monographs)
Includes bibliographical references and index.
ISBN 978-0-521-88742-7 (hardback) – ISBN 978-0-521-71534-8 (paperback)
1. Social justice.   2. Welfare economics.   3. Fairness.   I. Maniquet,
François, 1965–   II. Title.
HM671.F573   2011
330.15′56–dc22   2011006792

ISBN 978-0-521-88742-7 Hardback
ISBN 978-0-521-71534-8 Paperback

To Christine and Hélène,
and Hélène, Elise, Antonin, and Timothée

Contents

Preface

The idea of the line of research presented in this book emerged from a conversation in the French foothills of the Pyrenees in April 1996. The prevailing separation between the theory of social choice, the theory of fair allocation, and public economics seemed to call for a unified approach that would construct social preferences similar to the first, relying on fairness concepts from the second, and derive policy conclusions for the third. It took more time than we expected to transform this idea into a recognized theory, and we are pleased to acknowledge the support and constructive influence of many colleagues and friends. The late Louis Gevers, who had worked himself at the intersection of social choice and fair allocation, was the first to express interest and provide encouragements. Our debt to him is immense. Peter Hammond, Philippe Mongin, Juan de Diós Moreno-Ternero, Erwin Ooghe, Erik Schokkaert, Yves Sprumont, Kotaro Suzumura, and Koichi Tadenuma were very helpful at different stages of our work and became coauthors and partners in this research. We are also deeply indebted to Eric Maskin, John Roemer, and John Weymark, who commented on and discussed several of our early works on this topic. Their support was both helpful and encouraging. The interest shown by students who made their own contribution to this direction of research, Efthymios Athanasiou and Giacomo Valletta, was a great reward. The confirmation that a variety of empirical applications were possible came thanks to the fruitful collaboration with Koen Decancq, Brigitte Dormont, Michel Fouquin, Guillaume Gaulier, Stéphane Luchini, Juan de Diós Moreno-Ternero, Christophe Muller, Esther Regnier, and Erik Schokkaert, and the support of CEPII, the French Ministry of Social Affairs, the Junta de Andalucía, and the Foundation of Risk. We also benefited a great deal from the influence, through their work and through stimulating conversation, of Serge Kolm, Hervé Moulin, and William Thomson, as well as Dilip Abreu, Claude d'Aspremont, Tony Atkinson, Salvador Barberà, Charles Blackorby, Walter Bossert, Antoine d'Autume, Angus Deaton, David Donaldson, Rodolphe Dos Santos Ferreira, Lionel Fontagné, Nicolas Gravel, Faruk Gul, Michel Le Breton, Kevin Roberts, Amartya Sen, Alain Trannoy, and Bertil Tungodden.

This manuscript benefited from many sorts of help. The first chapters owe much to the hospitality of Nuffield College, Oxford, and later chapters to a Lachmann fellowship at the London School of Economics and Political Science, London, and a sabbatical semester at Northwestern University, Evanston. The final preparation of the manuscript was greatly enhanced by a CORE Prize and the focused settings of Louvain-la-Neuve. Summer schools at the Urrutja Foundation, San Sebastian, the University of Hitotsubashi, Tokyo, and the Universities of Málaga, Siena, Strasbourg, and Rouen, provided opportunities for presentation and discussions. Detailed written comments were generously provided by Juan de Diós Moreno-Ternero and Giacomo Valletta, as well as by a reading group comprising Paolo Brunori, Karen Decancq, Koen Decancq, Xavier Jara, Marco Mantovani, Erwin Ooghe, Paolo Piacquadio, Christelle Sapata, and Stéphane Zuber. Two referees made very helpful suggestions and provided detailed remarks that improved the text substantially. The interest expressed, and advice provided, by the two editors who handled the manuscript, Matt Jackson and George Mailath, is also gratefully acknowledged. Scott Parris, from Cambridge University Press, gave us much help with his characteristic enthusiasm. Our colleagues at CERSES and CORE deserve many thanks for providing a supportive environment. Last, but not least, our families have not only accepted absences and absent-mindedness, but also steadily supported our interest in fairness and social justice. We dedicate this book to them.

Introduction

The evaluation of allocations of resources, distributions of well-being, and public policies is a pervasive need in economics and a frequent activity of economists. This is, however, generally considered a difficult and hazardous exercise. The danger is not just the risk of mixing value judgments and factual assessments. It is also, perhaps primarily, the risk of getting lost in the morass of the controversies and impossibility theorems of the field that one can broadly call normative economics. However, the development of this field in the past century has been impressive, and has provided very powerful analytical tools. In particular, the theory of social choice and the theory of fair allocation have, separately, proposed an array of promising concepts and methods. In this book we put the concepts of these two theories to use and propose a general theory of social criteria for economic allocation problems.

In a nutshell, then, this book studies the elaboration of criteria for the evaluation of social and economic situations, and the application of such criteria to the search for optimal public policies. Several broad objectives are assigned to the criteria developed in our analysis.

First, the criteria should be sufficiently comprehensive so when they declare one situation to be preferable to another, there is a sense in which this evaluation takes account of all relevant considerations and is not merely a judgment that the considered situation is better in only one respect. More specifically, the idea is that the criteria should incorporate principles of efficiency as well as principles of equity. Restricting attention to efficiency only, or to equity only, would not provide very useful criteria in our opinion.[1] A related tenet of this requirement of comprehensiveness is that the criteria must be individualistic in the sense of taking account of every individual situation in its own right, and of giving due consideration to every individual's perspective on his or her own position. Criteria that rely directly on global quantities of the population without grounding this on an assessment of every individual situation are therefore excluded from the outset, although, obviously, it will be considered

---

[1] See, e.g., Arrow (1963) for a criticism of pure efficiency criteria.

quite valuable when, from a properly individualistic criterion, we are sometimes able to derive simple criteria based on global data.

Second, the criteria should be fine-grained enough to be useful in most contexts of public decision making and institutional design. Criteria that simply point to the optimal solution in some special context of implementation are not sufficient from this standpoint.[2] We are looking for sufficiently precise rankings of all the options that may be on the agenda in various economic and political contexts. This may be slightly more than what is really needed in practice, because decision makers need to know only what the optimal option is in their particular context, not how to rank all the suboptimal options or the infeasible options. Given the great variety of possible contexts, however, and, in particular, having in mind that the job of public decision makers is mostly to evaluate imperfect reforms in characteristically suboptimal situations, we think that the most convenient kind of criterion is a fine-grained ranking of all options that may be on the agenda in some possible context.

Finally, because we think of applications in public economics, the criteria must be relevantly applicable to the evaluation of social and economic situations – that is, primarily, the evaluation of conflicts of interest between individuals in the allocation of economic resources. We believe that for such applications, general abstract criteria will not sufficiently take account of the ethically relevant features of individuals' interests. More precisely, requirements of fairness are sometimes general, but are also often particular to the situation at hand. Fairness in the distribution of unproduced commodities is not the same as fairness in production, and fairness in the production of a private good is not the same as that for a public good. As a consequence, the main focus here is on economic models of resource allocation, rather than on abstract models of political or collective decision, although some words will be said on the latter. What qualifies as a fair solution to one specific allocation problem, however, may depend on how related problems are solved. For instance, the solutions to the public good problem discussed in Chapter 8 make sense only if the income distribution itself is fair.

One defining feature of our analysis throughout this book is that individual situations are not described initially by interpersonally comparable measures of utility or well-being. It is part of our theory to construct interpersonal comparisons on the basis of *ordinal noncomparable preferences* over bundles of resources. Moreover, we put special emphasis on cases in which preferences are heterogeneous. Some words of explanation are needed about this particular feature of our approach.

---

[2] In a more philosophical context, Sen (2009) emphasizes that, in view of the imperfections of the societies with which analysts and decision makers are grappling, it is important to rank the social alternatives instead of merely delineating a perfectly just but unattainable society as is done in many theories of justice.

Following Robbins and Samuelson,[3] an important stream of economic analysis has embraced the view that utility cannot easily be compared across individuals, and that interpersonal utility comparisons always involve value judgments with little or no objective basis. In this vein, many economists adopted the ethical assumption that interpersonal comparisons should be made in terms of mental states (such as happiness) and the empirical assumption that mental states are not observable. They therefore deleted utility numbers from their analyses as much as technically possible, focusing on ordinal preferences. The ordinal approaches to welfare economics that are based on the Pareto efficiency criterion and its extensions through compensation tests, including the theory of fair allocation, that somehow emerged from the theory of general equilibrium, have been motivated by such skepticism about interpersonal comparisons of utility.

Although our approach is compatible with this traditional defiance about utilities, we do not endorse the views just described. The behaviorist presumption that mental states, unlike choices of objects and consumption bundles, are not observable has now fallen into disrepute. Mental states such as happiness are amenable to some kind of objective measurement, or are likely to become so in the near future. It is true, nonetheless, that individuals' various goals in life, and their corresponding achievements, are essentially incommensurable, so measuring satisfaction (a complex judgment that is quite distinct from simple mental states such as happiness or even the feeling of being satisfied) in a meaningful and interpersonally comparable way is problematic. If interpersonal comparisons had to be made in terms of satisfaction, there would indeed be a serious difficulty whenever individual preferences are heterogeneous, as in our models.

More important, however, the ethical assumption that interpersonal comparisons should be made in terms of mental states, which owes much to the utilitarian tradition, is now under heavy criticism. Many authors, especially Rawls (1971, 1982), Dworkin (2000), and Sen (1992), have argued that for the evaluation of social and economic allocations, a focus on subjective or mental states is not appropriate. They argue that social justice deals primarily with the distribution of resources and means of flourishing (including personal characteristics that may be registered as internal resources) rather than the distribution of subjective satisfaction. The way in which individuals obtain degrees of satisfaction from given amounts of resources or capabilities should, in this view, be considered a matter of personal responsibility. We adopt this view in this book, and the metric of interpersonal comparisons that will be used here will be primarily a resource metric.[4] However, unlike Rawls and Sen, we do

---

[3] See Robbins (1932), Samuelson (1947), and, for a historical synthesis on the origins of positivism in economics, Hammond (1991).

[4] To be precise, we should say that comparisons are made in our work in terms of the objects of individual preferences. In our economic models, such objects are resources. But if the objects

not accept the idea that a simple index that disregards individual subjectivity can be used, because we consider it important to take account of individual preferences to allocate resources appropriately. Comparisons must be made in terms of a personalized measure of the value of resources, and devising such a measure is an essential task in our work.

In summary, our approach in terms of ordinal noncomparable preferences over bundles of resources is compatible with several important ethical views, not just with the positivist tradition of ordinalism that has been influential in economics. Obviously, being able to devise social criteria on the sole basis of data that can be extracted from observable demand behavior, or even less, as we shall see, is indeed a practical advantage. But this advantage does not determine our methodology.

The topic of this book can, then, be more technically described as the aggregation of conflicting individual preferences into a consistent social ranking. Admittedly, we are a far cry from achieving the ultimate goal of devising a set of criteria for the evaluation of general social and economic situations, where by "general" we mean a complete description of societies in all dimensions and all details. What we provide here is a series of analyses for simple contexts depicted by tractable models.

The first chapter of this book maps out the field of welfare economics and social choice theory and explains how our approach relates to, and supplements, the existing approaches. Social choice theory has been dubbed the "science of the impossible," and we explain in particular why, in our view, there is much room for interesting possibilities. It is now well known that obtaining possibility results has to do with the information that is used by the criteria. The fourth chapter examines the informational basis of our approach with greater detail, after some general results of the approach have been presented in the second and third chapters.

Our focus in the first part of the book is the canonical model of distribution of unproduced goods. This model is simple but useful as a basic tool for the analysis of multidimensional problems. Some of the results we obtain with it are recurrent in all contexts. Moreover, it is sufficiently abstract to be versatile, and some results can be easily transposed to other contexts – for instance, when goods are replaced by functionings in the description of individual situations.

The second and third chapters present two basic results that are pervasive in our approach, as they come up in some way or other in all economic models that have been studied so far. The first basic result is a conflict between the idea of reducing resource inequalities across individuals and the Pareto principle. This efficiency–equality tension is due to the fact that with heterogeneous preferences, resource inequalities do not always obviously translate into inequalities in the relevant interpersonally comparable measure.

---

of preferences are "functionings" or "capabilities," comparisons are made in functionings or capabilities, as explained in Chapter 7. Our approach is therefore immune to Sen's charge against Rawls and Dworkin that focusing on resources is "fetishistic."

The second basic result is that the combination of the Pareto principle and some mild requirements that impose a minimal inequality aversion (namely, it must be positive, or even simply nonnegative) force the social criteria to actually have an infinite aversion to inequality, as in the maximin criterion. The literature on social welfare contains justifications of the maximin and the leximin criteria that involve rather strong egalitarian requirements, in the one-dimensional context when individual well-being is measured by an interpersonally comparable index of income or utility. The different justification we obtain here hinges on the multidimensional context of multiple goods being allocated among individuals.

The second part of the book examines the particular social rankings that can be defined for the model of distribution of unproduced goods. It considers, in turn, the case of divisible goods and the case of indivisibles. The third part introduces production, for the relatively simple case in which one output is produced with one input, such as labor. We do, however, examine in detail the case of unequal skills, which is particularly relevant for applications to public economics. As alluded to previously, the main value of defining fine-grained rankings of all allocations is the possibility of giving policy advice under any restriction of the set of feasible allocations. A particularly relevant context of application is provided by incentive constraints that arise when the public authority has imperfect information about individual characteristics. We show, in particular, how the social rankings obtained can be used for the evaluation of income tax schedules, when the population is heterogeneous in both skill levels and preferences about leisure and consumption, and such characteristics are private knowledge. This study of production deals with what is technically described as the production of a private good, but we also examine the problem of production of a public good, which is also relevant to public economics. An example of application to public good funding in the second-best context (i.e., when individuals may misrepresent their willingness to pay for the public good) is provided.

In the second and third parts of the book we adopt the same methodology, which consists of defining efficiency and equity requirements and determining what kind of social rankings satisfy these requirements. Once a social ranking is obtained, it can be used for the evaluation of public policies; in the last part of the book, we focus particularly on the translation of the ranking of allocations into a ranking of policies, for standard tax-and-transfer instruments.

We end this introduction with a caveat. This is a work in normative economics, in which we derive social criteria from basic ethical principles and apply them to policy issues. We consider that the role of the economist in this kind of analysis is to establish the link between value judgments and policy conclusions, not to use the authority of expertise to promote personal prejudice. As an illustration of this stance, we often end up considering different criteria that rely on alternative ethical principles. We do not endorse each and every criterion that is proposed here, which would be inconsistent, and we refrain, as much as we can, from expressing definite preferences when several criteria are on the table. Of course, we exercised some judgment in the selection of the basic principles, retaining (or focusing on) those that appear reasonable for current prevailing views. All in all, we find support in Samuelson's defense of welfare economics:

> It is a legitimate exercise of economic analysis to examine the consequences of various value judgments, whether or not they are shared by the theorist (1947, p. 220).

How to read this book. The bulk of the argument in this book requires only some minimal mathematical competence, and our hope is that it is accessible to most economists. However, economic allocations are complex objects and our proofs often involve the examination of several different allocations that differ from each other in all sorts of ways. As a consequence, many of the long and tedious proofs of our results have been relegated to the appendix, in which case the main text contains only an intuitive explanation of the logic of the argument. Among other things, the index lists all the axioms that are used in the search of social criteria, to make it easy to locate their first appearance in the book. The same has been done for the mathematical notations.

General notations. The set of real numbers (respectively, non-negative, positive real numbers) is $\mathbb{R}$ (respectively, $\mathbb{R}_+$, $\mathbb{R}_{++}$) the set of natural integers (respectively, relative, positive integers) is $\mathbb{N}$ (respectively, $\mathbb{Z}$, $\mathbb{Z}_{++}$), the set of rational numbers (respectively, positive rational numbers) is $\mathbb{Q}$ (respectively, $\mathbb{Q}_{++}$).

Vector inequalities are denoted $\geq, >, \gg$. Weak (respectively, strict) set inclusion is denoted $\subseteq$ (respectively, $\subsetneq$).

The cardinality of set A is denoted $|A|$. The set A^B is the set of mappings from B to A. The (Minkowski) addition of sets is defined as $A + B = \{x \mid \exists (a, b) \in A \times B, \ x = a + b\}$.

An ordering is a reflexive and transitive binary relation on a set. The subset of maximal elements of a set A for an ordering R is denoted $\max|_R A$.

PART I

BASICS

This first part of this book is an introduction to the approach that is developed. Its first aim is to help the reader understand where the approach lies in the broad field of normative economics; the first chapter reviews the various subdomains of the field to highlight the main differences. Its main point is to show that our approach is the only one that combines various features that are scattered in various classical approaches. Fundamentally, this approach opens a working space at the intersection of social choice theory and fair allocation theory. Like the former, it constructs rankings of all possible alternatives; like the latter, it involves fairness principles about resource allocation rather than interpersonal comparisons of utility; like both theories, it puts the Pareto principle, the ideal of respecting individual preferences, first in the order of priorities. The expression "fair social choice" is often used as a name for the approach.[1]

The second and third chapters introduce general results that appear to be common to all models that have been studied so far. These results are striking and somewhat counterintuitive. The first is that there is a tension between the Pareto principle and the deceptively simple idea that an agent who has more in all dimensions than another, such as one who consumes more of all commodities, is necessarily better off and should transfer some of the surplus to the other agent. The idea that "having more in all dimensions" is an obvious situation of advantage has been flagged by Sen (1985, 1992) as a partial but robust solution to the problem of indexing well-being in a multidimensional context. This seems indeed very natural, but our approach, because it involves respecting individual preferences, implies that it must sometimes happen that the better-off agent is the one who has less in all dimensions. As we will explain, this is in fact much less counterintuitive than it seems when individual preferences are taken into account.

The second result is that, once again because of the multidimensional context and the respect of individual preferences, a minimal degree of inequality aversion in the social criterion implies that one must actually give absolute priority to the worst-off. This is surprising because it appears easy to use individual

---

[1] It is more transparent but less entertaining than the alternative name "welfair economics."

utility functions with a certain degree of concavity to obtain a finite preference, in the social ordering, for equality in resources. As it turns out, it is not easy at all. The construction of such utility functions is so difficult and informationally demanding that the only "simple" approach consists of adopting the absolute priority for the worst-off. As illustrated several times in this book, this does not mean that this approach is only for radicals. Giving absolute priority for the worst-off is compatible with many possible ways of identifying the worst-off. As we will show, even free-market libertarians can see their ideas reflected in particular social criteria developed along this vein.

The fourth and last chapter of this part may be skipped by the reader who is more interested in applications than in theoretical underpinnings. It examines the informational requirements of our approach. In the theory of social choice, following Sen (1970), it has become classical to analyze the problem of finding possibility results as a problem about the information that is used in the construction of social preferences. This is justified, and in Chapter 4 we show how our possibility results are linked to the fact that our social preferences involve certain kinds of interpersonal comparisons. However, they do not perform interpersonal comparisons of utility but instead compare resource bundles or, more precisely, indifference curves (or sets, in more than two dimensions). We also examine in that chapter other aspects of information that are important in understanding the approach, such as the fact that social preferences may depend in a limited way on the feasible set.

CHAPTER 1

A Contribution to Welfare Economics

1.1 INTRODUCTION

Social welfare and fairness are concepts with a venerable history in economic theory. In this chapter, we situate the approach that is developed in this book within the field of welfare economics. The simplest way to do this is to compare it with the various existing approaches in the field. For each of them, we list the main features that are shared with our approach, and explain why we keep them. We also present the main differences and explain and justify why we have to, or choose to, depart from those classical approaches. We hope that this short overview clarifies how our undertaking can contribute to the development of some of these subfields.

This discussion relies on a simple example. Assume that a positive quantity of several divisible private goods must be distributed to a population of agents, each of whom has personal preferences over his or her own consumption.[1] We discuss each classical subfield of welfare economics, as well as our approach, in this simple framework.

The preferences are assumed to be well-behaved and self-centered (i.e., without consumption externalities). What we call an *economy* is a population with a profile of preferences and a social endowment to be distributed. Formally, we consider that there are ℓ goods (with $\ell \geq 2$). The social endowment of goods is denoted $\Omega \in \mathbb{R}_{++}^{\ell}$. The population is a nonempty finite set N.

Each agent i in N has a preference relation R_i, which is a complete ordering over bundles z_i belonging to agent i's consumption set $X = \mathbb{R}_+^{\ell}$. For two bundles $x, y \in X$, we write $x R_i y$ to denote that agent i is at least as well off at x as at y. The corresponding strict preference and indifference relations are denoted P_i and I_i, respectively. We restrict attention to preferences that are continuous (i.e., for all $x \in X$, the sets $\{y \in X \mid y R_i x\}$ and $\{y \in X \mid x R_i y\}$ are closed), monotonic (i.e., for two bundles $x, y \in X$, if $x \geq y$, then $x R_i y$ and

---

[1] This canonical model has a long tradition in welfare economics. In the more recent literature, it is examined by Arrow (1963), Kolm (1972), Varian (1974), Moulin and Thomson (1988), and Moulin (1990, 1991), among many others.

3

if $x \gg y$, then $x\ P_i\ y$), and convex (i.e., for two bundles $x, y \in X$, if $x\ R_i\ y$ then $\lambda x + (1 - \lambda) y\ R_i\ y$ for all $\lambda \in [0, 1]$). Let $\mathcal{R}$ denote the set of such preferences.

An economy is denoted $E = (R_N, \Omega)$, where $R_N = (R_i)_{i \in N}$ is the profile of preferences for the whole population. Let $\mathcal{E}$ denote the class of all economies satisfying the preceding conditions. An *allocation* is a list of bundles $z_N = (z_i)_{i \in N} \in X^N$.[2] It is *feasible* for E if

$$\sum_{i \in N} z_i \leq \Omega.$$

We denote the set of feasible allocations for E by $Z(E)$. As we see in the following sections, each subfield of welfare economics addresses different questions in this model, and offers specific ways of solving them.

1.2   THEORY OF FAIR ALLOCATION

The theory of fair allocation (for a survey, see Thomson 2010), pioneered by Kolm (1968, 1972) and Varian (1974), looks for ways of allocating resources that are efficient, in the sense of Pareto, and fair. It turns out that, typically, fairness does not receive a unique interpretation in resource allocation models. As a consequence, the theory aims to identify all possible ways of capturing intuitions of fairness, define axioms that encapsulate these intuitions, and look at allocation rules that satisfy the axioms. An *allocation rule* is a correspondence S that associates to each economy E, in a domain $\mathcal{D} \subseteq \mathcal{E}$, a subset $S(E)$ of the feasible allocations.

The two allocation rules that have received the most attention are the egalitarian Walrasian and the egalitarian-equivalent rules. The first one, which we denote S^{EW}, selects all the allocations arising as competitive equilibrium allocations from an equal division of the social endowment of goods. The individual budget delineated by the endowment $\omega_i \in X$ and market prices $p \in \mathbb{R}^\ell_+$ is defined as

$$B(\omega_i, p) = \{z_i \in X \mid p z_i \leq p \omega_i\}.$$

Allocation rule 1.1 Egalitarian Walrasian (S^{EW})
For all $E = (R_N, \Omega) \in \mathcal{E}$,

$$S^{EW}(E) = \left\{ z_N \in Z(E) \mid \exists p \in \mathbb{R}^\ell_+, \forall i \in N,\ z_i \in \max|_{R_i} B\left(\frac{\Omega}{|N|}, p \right) \right\}.$$

A feasible allocation z_N for an economy $E \in \mathcal{E}$ is *(Pareto) efficient* if there is no feasible z'_N such that $z'_i\ R_i\ z_i$ for all $i \in N$ and $z'_i\ P_i\ z_i$ for some $i \in N$. Let $P(E)$ denote the set of efficient allocations for E. We can now define the second allocation rule. It selects all the Pareto efficient allocations having the

---

[2] The notation X^N is simpler than $X^{|N|}$ and is just as correct, as X^N is the set of mappings from N to X.

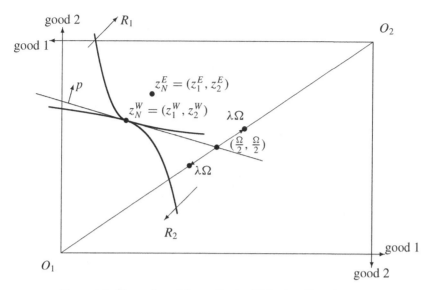

Figure 1.1. Illustration of the egalitarian Walrasian allocation rule

property that each agent is indifferent between his or her bundle and a fraction
of the social endowment, the same for all agents.

Allocation rule 1.2 Egalitarian-Equivalent (S^{EE})
For all $E = (R_N, \Omega) \in \mathcal{E}$,

$$S^{EE}(E) = \{z_N \in P(E) \mid \exists \lambda \in \mathbb{R}_+, \forall i \in N, \ z_i \ I_i \ \lambda\Omega\}.$$

Figures 1.1 and 1.2 illustrate these allocation rules in the Edgeworth box.
We have $N = \{1, 2\}$; preferences R_1, R_2 are represented by two indifference
curves for each agent. The allocations represented in the figures are selected
by the allocation rules defined earlier: $z_N^W = (z_1^W, z_2^W) \in S^{EW}(E)$ and $z_N^E = (z_1^E, z_2^E) \in S^{EE}(E)$.

Our theory has much in common with the theory of fair allocation, and we
consider that we are mainly contributing to that theory. First, the (sometimes
implicit) central ethical objective on which the theory is grounded is that of
resource equality. In the simple model we use in this chapter, as well as in
any other resource allocation model studied from that fairness point of view,
if allocating goods equally were always possible and compatible with Pareto
efficiency, then no other solution would be looked for. As explained in the
introduction, we believe that equality of resources can be a key objective of a
theory of fairness and social welfare, following the argument of Rawls' and
other philosophers that social justice is a matter of allocating resources rather
than subjective satisfaction or happiness.

Our work can be seen as an application of this approach in economic theory,
to the limited extent that the models we study in this book are very partial
descriptions of societies and that agents' preferences are a crude description

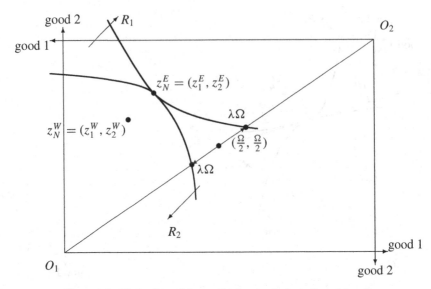

Figure 1.2. Illustration of the egalitarian-equivalent allocation rule

of their conceptions of a good life. On the other hand, our simple models are already sufficiently rich to prove that the seemingly simple notion of equality of resources can receive several interpretations, all of which are axiomatically justified.

The main difference between the theory of fair allocation in its current shape and our contribution is that a solution to a resource allocation problem in the former is an allocation rule, whereas in the latter it is a social ordering function. Let us explain this key point. When one studies allocation rules, the objective is limited to identifying the optimal allocations for each economy in a given domain, optimality being defined by a combination of efficiency and fairness axioms. In our approach, we look for *social ordering functions* (SOFs), which specify, for each economy, a complete ranking of the corresponding allocations.[3] Formally, a *social ordering* (for economy $E = (R_N, \Omega)$) is a complete ordering over the set X^N of allocations. A SOF **R** associates every economy E in some domain $\mathcal{D} \subseteq \mathcal{E}$ with a social ordering $\mathbf{R}(E)$. For $z_N, z'_N \in X^N$, we write $z_N \, \mathbf{R}(E) \, z'_N$ to denote that allocation z_N is at least as good as z'_N in E. The corresponding strict social preference and social indifference relations are denoted $\mathbf{P}(E)$ and $\mathbf{I}(E)$, respectively.

Let us illustrate this notion. The following example of a SOF also relies on the concept of egalitarian-equivalence and applies the leximin criterion to

---

[3] Tadenuma, Thomson, and other authors have studied complete allocation rankings based on fairness properties. They are precursors of the approach presented in this book. The rankings they obtain, however, all fail to satisfy the Pareto axioms on which we insist in the next chapters. See Chaudhuri (1986), Diamantaras and Thomson (1991), Tadenuma (2002, 2005), and Tadenuma and Thomson (1995).

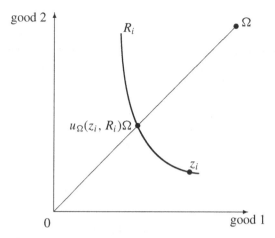

Figure 1.3. Computation of $u_\Omega(z_i, R_i)$

specific individual indices. The general definition of the leximin criterion is the following: for two vectors of real numbers a_N, a'_N, one says that a_N is better than a'_N for the leximin criterion, which will be denoted here by

$$a_N \geq_{lex} a'_N,$$

when the smallest component of a_N is not lower than the smallest component of a'_N, and if they are equal, the second smallest component is not lower, and so forth.

The specific individual indices to which the leximin criterion is applied by the SOF are defined as follows. They evaluate every agent's bundle by the fraction of Ω to which this agent is indifferent.[4] Indices of this sort are actually standard "utility" representations of individual preferences.[5] Formally, let us define the function $u_\Omega(z_i, R_i)$ by the condition

$$u_\Omega(z_i, R_i) = \lambda \Leftrightarrow z_i \, I_i \, \lambda\Omega.$$

We propose to call it the Ω-*equivalent* utility function, as it measures the proportional share of Ω that would give agent i the same satisfaction as with z_i. Figure 1.3 illustrates this notion.

When the leximin criterion is applied to Ω-equivalent utilities, one obtains the Ω-equivalent leximin SOF:

Social ordering function 1.1 Ω-Equivalent Leximin ($\mathbf{R}^{\Omega lex}$)
For all $E = (R_N, \Omega) \in \mathcal{E}$, $z_N, z'_N \in X^N$,

$$z_N \, \mathbf{R}^{\Omega lex}(E) \, z'_N \Leftrightarrow (u_\Omega(z_i, R_i))_{i \in N} \geq_{lex} \left(u_\Omega(z'_i, R_i)\right)_{i \in N}.$$

---

[4] This "egalitarian-equivalent" SOF was introduced by Pazner and Schmeidler (1978b), and, with an approach that is closer to ours, by Pazner (1979). The general idea of egalitarian-equivalence can be traced back at least to Kolm (1968), who attributes it to Lange (1936).

[5] See, e.g., Debreu (1959), Kannai (1970).

Of course, an allocation rule can be technically assimilated to a simple SOF for which the optimal allocations are socially strictly preferred to the nonoptimal ones, and for which all allocations are socially indifferent in each of these two classes. Such a SOF is obviously too coarse for many applications in which the fully optimal allocations cannot be obtained. Moreover, it violates the weak Pareto requirement, according to which an allocation is strictly better than another one as soon as each agent strictly prefers a bundle in the former allocation to the one in the latter. The SOFs we study in this book, such as the Ω-equivalent leximin, all satisfy this requirement.

Axiom 1.1 Weak Pareto
For all $E = (R_N, \Omega) \in \mathcal{D}$, and $z_N, z'_N \in X^N$, if $z_i\, P_i\, z'_i$ for all $i \in N$, then $z_N\, \mathbf{P}(E)\, z'_N$.

We think that SOFs may play a crucial role in the study of social fairness, after we take the implementation issue into account. Indeed, it is often the case that the set of allocations among which the policymaker must choose is so narrow that it does not contain any of the optimal allocations. Such constraints may come from asymmetries of information and, hence, incentive considerations (associated to the revelation of preferences). They may also be associated with the very nature of the problem. This is the case, for instance, if a status quo exists and the solution needs to be looked for in a neighborhood of it, or if the tools that the policymaker can resort to are limited – for instance, to linear taxation. Having a complete ranking of the allocations and maximizing it always leads to a well-defined solution (provided the set of implementable allocations is compact and the social ordering is continuous[6]) no matter which constraints turn out to be the binding ones.

Let us assume, for instance, that the social choice must be made among the set of allocations containing equal division and the allocations that can be obtained from it through trade at fixed price $\overline{p}$. Figure 1.4 illustrates, in a two-agent economy, the allocation $(\overline{z}_1^E, \overline{z}_2^E)$ that maximizes $\mathbf{R}^{\Omega \text{lex}}$ (both agents are indifferent between the bundle $\overline{z}_i^E$ they get and $\overline{\lambda}\Omega$, whereas all other allocations in the $\overline{p}$ trade line assign bundles that at least one agent finds worse than $\overline{\lambda}\Omega$). Observe that $(\overline{z}_1^E, \overline{z}_2^E)$ is inefficient and does not correspond to the first-best allocation for $\mathbf{R}^{\Omega \text{lex}}$.

In the following chapters, we give examples of applications of SOF maximization processes in the framework of second-best theory (that is, when the only constraint is that preferences or skills are the private information of the agents).

One may argue, however, that building SOFs is too demanding a task, as an extension of the allocation rule approach can be sufficient. Indeed, if the

---

[6] Continuity of the social ordering is actually not necessary. It is enough if the ordering can be constructed as the lexicographic composition of continuous orderings. Many SOFs that appear here, indeed, aggregate indices of well-being in a leximin way, and they are, therefore, lexicographic compositions of continuous orderings.

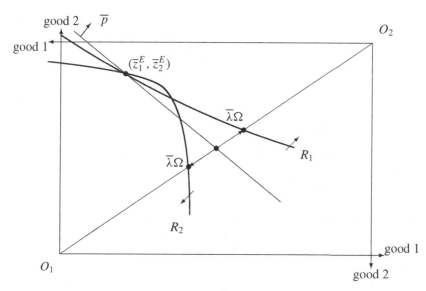

Figure 1.4. Best allocation for $\mathbf{R}^{\Omega\text{lex}}$ when only trade at fixed price $\overline{p}$ is possible

domain of problems for which an allocation rule is required to select optimal allocations is enlarged to include all problems that are likely to be faced by the policymaker (that is, all first-best and second-best problems, all possible reforms, and so on), then an allocation rule is as useful as a SOF.

Even if the preceding argument is perfectly valid, the social ordering approach remains justified, for the following reasons. First, as is well known from decision theory, as soon as the domain of problems is sufficiently rich, defining a consistent allocation rule is equivalent to defining a SOF. Second, from a technical point of view, studying an allocation rule in such a rich domain of problems requires identifying the set of feasible allocations in a sufficiently precise way, which may be infeasible (as is often the case when one looks at incentive constraints; an exception is Maniquet and Sprumont 2010). Focusing our attention on SOFs, therefore, guarantees the consistency of the policy recommendations that can arise from social welfare maximization under several kinds of constraints and simplifies our task.

Let us complete this section by pointing out another key aspect of the theory of fair allocation that is retained here – namely, its informational basis. Consider, for instance, $\mathbf{R}^{\Omega\text{lex}}$, which applies the leximin criterion to Ω-equivalent utilities. These "utilities," however, are mere indices representing ordinal and noncomparable preferences R_i. To make this clear, imagine that instead of starting our analysis at the level of preferences, we had introduced exogenous utility functions (measuring subjective satisfaction, for instance) $u_i : X \to \mathbb{R}$, and defined the set $\mathcal{U}$ of all utility functions representing continuous, monotonic, and convex preferences. In this alternative framework, an economy would be a list $E = (u_N, \Omega) \in \mathcal{U}^N \times \mathbb{R}^{\ell}_{++}$. In such a setting, our approach would simply ignore the properties of such utility functions other than the underlying preferences – that is, it would seek SOFs that satisfy the following axiom.

Axiom 1.2 Ordinalism and Noncomparability
For all $E = (u_N, \Omega)$, $E' = (u'_N, \Omega) \in \mathcal{D}$, *and* $z_N, z'_N \in X^N$, *if for all* $i \in N$ *there exists an increasing function* $g_i : \mathbb{R} \to \mathbb{R}$ *such that for all* $x \in X$, $u'_i(x) = g_i(u_i(x))$, *then* $z_N \mathbf{R}(E) z'_N \iff z_N \mathbf{R}(E') z'_N$.

Ordinalism follows from the fact that any utility function can be replaced by any strictly increasing transformation of it, so only the ranking of bundles matters. Noncomparability follows from the fact that those transformations of utility functions can differ among agents (we may have as many g_i functions as agents), so no common meaning can be attributed to utility levels or utility differences, in particular. Under ordinalism and noncomparability we do not lose any generality by defining economies directly in terms of preferences R_i.

At this point, we want to discuss an important clarification. Broadly speaking, the notions of well-being used by economists belong to three families. In the first family, well-being is measured in a way that does not take the individuals' subjective point of view into account. Examples include wealth and life expectancy. We can, of course, assume that doing better in these dimensions is better for the individuals, but how they trade off these dimensions against other components of well-being is not part of the picture. In the second family, all the attention is on subjective feelings or judgments. How agents trade off different dimensions of well-being is now taken into account, to the extent that nothing else enters the picture. Examples include happiness, subjective satisfaction, or utility. Our approach belongs to a third family. Individual preferences on how to trade off dimensions are respected, but we build indices of well-being in terms of quantities of resources that agents use to reach a given level of satisfaction. We return to this issue in Section 1.4.

1.3 ARROVIAN SOCIAL CHOICE THEORY

Contrary to the theory of fair allocation, Arrovian social choice looks for fine-grained rankings of the allocations. As explained earlier, our approach displays this feature as well.

The main difference between Arrovian social choice and our approach comes from the axioms we impose. The key axiom in the Arrovian tradition is the following independence requirement.[7] A SOF $\mathbf{R}$ satisfies this requirement if and only if the ranking between two allocations depends only on the individual preferences about these two allocations.

---

[7] It was called "independence of irrelevant alternatives" by Arrow (1963), a normative name that we do not retain, as it is controversial whether the concerned alternatives are indeed irrelevant.

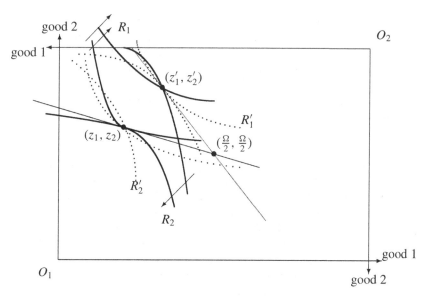

Figure 1.5. Independence of irrelevant alternatives requires $z_N R(E) z'_N \Leftrightarrow z_N R(E') z'_N$

Axiom 1.3 Arrow Independence
For all $E = (R_N, \Omega)$, $E' = (R'_N, \Omega) \in \mathcal{D}$, and z_N, $z'_N \in X^N$, if R_i and R'_i coincide on $\{z_i, z'_i\}$ for all $i \in N$, then $z_N \mathbf{R}(E) z'_N \Longleftrightarrow z_N \mathbf{R}(E') z'_N$.

We illustrate the consequences of imposing Arrow independence in Figure 1.5. By monotonicity of preferences, agent 1 always prefers z'_1 to z_1, and agent 2 z_2 to z'_2. By Arrow independence, this implies that $z_N = (z_1, z_2)$ and $z'_N = (z'_1, z'_2)$ need to be ordered the same way independently of the preferences. In the economy $E = (R_N, \Omega)$, z_N is a competitive allocation from equal division; that is, $z_N \in S^{EW}(E)$, whereas z'_N is an inefficient allocation. In the economy $E' = (R'_N, \Omega)$, on the other hand, $z'_N \in S^{EW}(E)$ and z_N is inefficient. It may look reasonable to use this information to rank z_N above z'_N in E, and z'_N above z_N in E'. Arrow independence prevents us from doing so.

The key objective of Arrovian social choice is to combine Arrow independence with Pareto axioms. If the domain $\mathcal{D}$ over which the SOF is defined contains, for instance, all the profiles of continuous, monotonic and convex preferences, Arrow independence and weak Pareto lead to dictatorship (Bordes and Le Breton 1989). Dictatorship means that there is an individual who imposes his or her strict preferences P_i to the social ordering for all profiles in the domain. More precisely, fixing N and Ω, there is an individual $i \in N$ such that for all $R_N \in \mathcal{R}^N$, all $z_N, z'_N \in \left(\mathbb{R}^\ell_+ \setminus \{0\} \right)^N$, $z_i P_i z'_i \Rightarrow z_N \mathbf{P}(E) z'_N$. This is, obviously, in contradiction with resource equality, as this agent's monotonic preferences will then be satisfied at the expense of all the others.

The literature on Arrovian social choice in economic domains (that is, domains in which trade or production opportunities are explicitly modeled and preferences are typically restricted to be self-centered and satisfy conditions of continuity, monotonicity, and convexity) has focused on identifying the domains of economies over which Arrow's negative result is reproduced. The general picture is that the domain restrictions consistent with the nature of the allocation problems are not sufficient to escape Arrow's impossibility, or, when Arrow's impossibility is avoided, to be consistent with any minimal objective of resource equality.

We depart from Arrovian social choice by shifting the emphasis from Arrow independence to resource equality properties. We agree that saving on the information needed to make social judgments is important. In particular, the social preference between two alternatives should depend only on information that is, in some way, linked to these alternatives. We do not accept, however, to make it more important than allocating resources fairly. Our strategy, later in the book (starting in Chapter 3), will therefore be to look at possible weakenings of Arrow independence compatible with our objective of resource equality. For instance, the Ω-equivalent leximin defined in the previous section satisfies the requirement that the ranking between two allocations depends only on the individual indifference curves at these two allocations.

This discussion gives us the opportunity to make the following clarification point. We believe that any attempt to give axiomatic foundations to welfare economics refers, explicitly or implicitly, to a hierarchy of the norms that are taken into account. The hierarchy adopted in this book is the following: the norm that is given priority is efficiency; none of the SOFs studied here would recommend a Pareto inferior allocation. Our second norm is resource equality. As it will be clear in the following chapters, many axioms capture the ideal of resource equality, and one ultimately must make a selection among them. Our third norm is informational simplicity or parsimony, and the weakenings of Arrow independence belong to this category.

Consequently, our strategy will always be to begin with a discussion of resource equality axioms, to check whether they are compatible with Pareto axioms, and, when necessary, to identify the trade-offs between them. We do not claim that the hierarchy adopted here is the only reasonable one, but we hope it is sufficiently reasonable to serve as a useful guide for the development of an attractive approach.

To conclude this section, let us mention an important consequence of the fact that we give priority to resource equality axioms over informational parsimony axioms: we allow our ranking of the allocation to depend on the available resources (which is captured by the fact that the SOFs have $E = (R_N, \Omega)$ and not only R_N as their argument), whereas the Arrovian approach to social choice excludes this possibility, making a radical distinction between the objectives (the satisfaction of the population) and the constraints (the feasible set of allocations). Again, it would be better if, at the end, we obtained SOFs that do not depend on this kind of information (and, sometimes, this will be achieved), but we are not ready to drop our resource equality objective because of such informational parsimony considerations.

1.4 WELFARISM

Welfarism is the social ethics according to which social welfare comes from an appropriate aggregation of individual welfare indices. If one understands the notion of "welfare index" in a broad sense, few social criteria fall out of this category. In particular, the $\mathbf{R}^{\Omega \text{lex}}$ SOF is welfarist, as it applies the leximin criterion to welfare indices corresponding to Ω-equivalent utilities. Most of the SOFs analyzed in this book are welfarist in a similar way.

An important branch of social choice theory has sprung out of Arrow's impossibility by introducing exogenous interpersonally comparable utility functions (for recent surveys, see Bossert and Weymark 2004 and d'Aspremont and Gevers 2002). It has explained the links between certain types of aggregation and certain types of interpersonal comparisons. The sum-utilitarian criterion, for instance, requires that welfare indices be cardinally measurable and that, at least, the unit of welfare measure be comparable. An egalitarian criterion such as the leximin, on the other hand, requires the utility levels to be comparable.

In comparison, our approach satisfies ordinalism and noncomparability, as explained in the previous section, and, instead of taking welfare indices as exogenous data, it proposes to construct well-being indices out of ordinal and noncomparable preferences. Moreover, the particular well-being indices used in the various SOFs studied in this book are derived from specific fairness axioms, thereby obtaining an ethical justification. In this way, the interpersonal comparisons performed in our approach embody specific value judgments in an explicit and transparent way.

In summary, for a broad interpretation of welfarism, our approach is welfarist but, rather than leaving the definition of welfare to an outside analysis, it offers specific proposals about how to define and measure the individual well-being indices.

As soon as individual welfare is, as is often the case, defined in a more specific sense that is directly tied to a subjective notion of well-being, such as the level of satisfaction or happiness, it is clear that our approach should then be branded as non-welfarist. The individual indices that serve in the SOFs of this book are indices of resource value rather than of subjective well-being.

Two opposite objections might be raised at this point. One could first object to our approach that our emphasis on resource equality should lead us to drop preferences altogether. Our reply is that we want to allocate resources to allow agents to follow their view of the good life, and a better satisfaction of one agent's preferences means that this agent has moved closer to what he or she thinks is a good life. Consequently, there is no reason to waste individuals' opportunities to achieve their goals, and this is precisely why Pareto efficiency should be kept.

The opposite objection is that by focusing on resource equality, our approach falls prey to "resource fetishism" (Sen 1985) and neglects the inequalities that individuals may endure in their abilities to make use of resources to their own benefit. The answer to this objection, which takes inspiration from Dworkin's theory, is that it is an easy extension of our approach to take account of personal abilities as internal resources over which individuals may have preferences as well, jointly with external resources. This extension is not studied in this book, but it has been the topic of another book (Fleurbaey 2008).[8]

Finally, let us mention some further differences between most welfarist theories and our approach. First, our theory is less ambitious, as we aim only at giving recommendations for specific allocation problems, whereas welfarist solutions are generally presented as readily applicable to any kind of social choice problem. Second, as we prove at length in the following chapters, it turns out that not all aggregation processes are compatible with our approach. More specifically, we must reach the conclusion that, when combining the axioms in which we are interested, only the leximin aggregation method (or, at least, some aggregation method compatible with the maximin) is acceptable.

1.5 MULTIDIMENSIONAL INEQUALITY AND WELFARE DOMINANCE

In the model that serves as the illustrative tool of this chapter, there are quantities of ℓ goods to be allocated among agents. In the special case where $\ell = 1$, we are left with a situation in which all preferences coincide: more is better than less. This is the classical model of the theory of inequality measurement. This theory aims to provide complete rankings over the set of distribution vectors, and reducing inequality is identical to allocating resources equally.

The classical theory of inequality measurement has been extended recently to take multiattribute situations into account – that is, to build orderings over allocations of several goods based on the ideal of resource equality. Our approach has exactly the same objective. The only, but essential, difference relates to the way preferences are taken into account. What is key in the theory of SOFs is that individual preferences are allowed to differ among agents, and we impose Pareto axioms. This feature is not shared by the approaches to be described now.

The first approach, which may be called the *dominance approach*, assumes that there exists a function measuring how quantities of the good to allocate are transformed into utility, and this function is the same for all individuals (e.g., Atkinson and Bourguignon 1982). In this approach, the utility function used to evaluate quantities of resources can be interpreted in two ways. In one interpretation, it represents individual preferences, which must then be assumed to be identical. In another interpretation, it consists of an index chosen by the evaluator, and reflects the evaluator's ethical choice about, for instance,

---

[8] See also the survey by Fleurbaey and Maniquet (2010).

how an increase in some resources allocated to a relatively poor agent trades off against a decrease in some other resource allocated to a relatively richer agent.

The key feature of the dominance approach is that an allocation of resources, z_N, is said to be better than another one, z'_N, if the sum of the individual utilities at the former is larger than the corresponding sum at the latter independent of which utility function is chosen to evaluate the individual bundles. More precisely, for a given set $\mathcal{U}$ of admissible utility functions, an allocation is said to dominate another if its sum of utilities is greater for each and every utility function in that set.

Axiom 1.4 Dominance with respect to $\mathcal{U}$
For all $E = (R_N, \Omega) \in \mathcal{D}$, and $z_N, z'_N \in X^N$,

$$z_N \, \mathbf{R}(E) \, z'_N \iff \forall u \in \mathcal{U}, \quad \sum_{i \in N} u(z_i) \geq \sum_{i \in N} u(z'_i).$$

An immediate consequence of this definition is that the resulting ordering will be partial. In the one-dimensional context, it coincides with the generalized Lorenz criterion stated by Shorrocks (1983) when $\mathcal{U}$ is the set of increasing concave functions. Another major difference from our approach is the fact that the same index is used to evaluate the bundle of all the agents, whereas we take as a starting point that individuals may have different preferences and that these preferences should be respected.

Related approaches focus on inequality measurement rather than welfare. One seeks direct generalizations of the Lorenz criterion.[9] Another approach constructs inequality indices. In some of these indices, no index of individual well-being appears at all. The emphasis is on how unequally each good is distributed and how the inequalities in the distribution of each good should be aggregated. For instance, consider the following multidimensional generalization of the Gini coefficient (Gajdos and Weymark 2005). Two allocations are compared in the following way. For each allocation, first, the Gini mean[10] of the distribution of each good is computed separately, and, second, the geometric mean of these means is computed. The allocation with the largest geometric mean is socially preferred to the other.

To define this SOF formally, we need to introduce the following notation. For $E = (R_N, \Omega) \in \mathcal{D}$, $z_N \in X^N$ and $k \in \{1, \ldots, \ell\}$, let $\widetilde{z}_k \in \mathbb{R}^N_+$ denote the permutation vector of $(z_{ik})_{i \in N}$ where the components are in decreasing order: $\widetilde{z}_{1k} \geq \widetilde{z}_{2k} \geq \ldots \geq \widetilde{z}_{|N|k}$.

---

[9] See, e.g., Kolm (1977), Koshevoy (1995).

[10] The Gini mean of a distribution is the weighted arithmetic mean where the weights are determined by the rank of the corresponding component in the distribution of that good among agents.

Social ordering function 1.2 Multidimensional Gini ($\mathbf{R}^{MG}$)
For all $E = (R_N, \Omega) \in \mathcal{E}$, $z_N, z'_N \in X^N$,

$$z_N \, \mathbf{R}^{MG}(E) \, z'_N \Leftrightarrow \prod_{k=1}^{\ell} \left(\frac{1}{|N|^2} \sum_{i=1}^{|N|} (2i - 1)\widetilde{z}_{ik} \right)^{\frac{1}{\ell}}$$

$$\geq \prod_{k=1}^{\ell} \left(\frac{1}{|N|^2} \sum_{i=1}^{|N|} (2i - 1)\widetilde{z}'_{ik} \right)^{\frac{1}{\ell}}.$$

Contrary to the results that can be derived from the dominance approach, this SOF provides us with a complete ranking of the allocations. Another feature of this approach is that it does not use any information regarding individual preferences (except the fact that more is better). Therefore, the $\mathbf{R}^{MG}$ SOF satisfies Arrow independence but violates the Pareto principle. Consequently, the approach is justified only in contexts in which no information on preferences can be obtained, or when the evaluator has good reasons to disregard the information that can be obtained.

In conclusion, the main contribution of our approach to the study of multidimensional inequality is to put individual preferences at the heart of the theory and to study inequality under a strict application of the Pareto principle. On the other hand, we share with this literature the key concern of resource equality, and, as it will become clear in the following chapters, we borrow from this literature some crucial properties of inequality aversion.

1.6   BERGSON–SAMUELSON SOCIAL WELFARE FUNCTIONS

Arrovian social choice theory has developed mainly as an attempt to make sense of the social welfare functions introduced by Bergson (1938) and further discussed, clarified, and vindicated by Samuelson (1947). Conceptually, a Bergson–Samuelson social welfare function is a representation tool for a SOF that satisfies the Pareto principle. Consequently, it can be written as a social welfare function of individual utilities, as follows:

Axiom 1.5 Bergson–Samuelson Social Welfare Function
For all $E = (R_N, \Omega) \in \mathcal{D}$, there exists a function $W : \mathbb{R}^N \to \mathbb{R}$ and, for each $i \in N$, a utility function $u_i : X \to \mathbb{R}$ representing R_i such that for all $z_N, z'_N \in X^N$, $z_N \, \mathbf{R}(E) \, z'_N \iff W\left((u_i(z_i))_{i \in N} \right) \geq W\left((u_i(z'_i))_{i \in N} \right).$

An important feature of this axiom is that the functions W and u_i can be picked arbitrarily, provided the ordering obtained with the composite function $W\left((u_i(z_i))_{i \in N} \right)$ corresponds to $\mathbf{R}(E)$. The function W is not a fixed social welfare function meant to be applied to exogenous and arbitrary utilities. As emphasized by Samuelson:

> There are an infinity of equally good indicators... which can be used. Thus, if one of these is written as $\bar{W} = W(u_1, \ldots, u_n)$, and if we were to change from one set of cardinal indices of individual utility to another set $(u'_1, \ldots, u'_n)$, we should simply change the form of the function W so as to leave all social decisions invariant. (1947, p. 228, with adapted notation).

This makes it possible for a SOF that is representable in this way to satisfy ordinalism and noncomparability, as Bergson and Samuelson were keen to insist. There was a controversy on such a possibility a few decades ago, which was triggered by the mistaken belief of some commentators that the W function was meant to be fixed and that the utility functions were exogenous.[11]

Not many of the SOFs we define and study in this book can be represented by Bergson–Samuelson functions, but this is only because they involve the leximin criterion, which is not representable by a function. For instance, a maximin variant of the Ω-equivalent leximin SOF defined in Section 1.2 is representable by a Bergson–Samuelson social welfare function, with W as the min function, and, in $E = (R_N, \Omega) \in \mathcal{D}$, $u_i(z_i) = u_\Omega(z_i, R_i)$. In this light, our work can be viewed as a contribution to the Bergson–Samuelson tradition.

The relationship between our approach and the Bergson–Samuelson tradition is more than a formal one. The original objective of Bergson, indeed, was to construct objects that could be used to evaluate societies from a fairness point of view:

> The optimum income distribution... is not determined by an empirical comparison of marginal social welfare per dollar among different households. Rather, it is determined by the rule of equity, which itself defines social welfare in the sphere of income distribution (1938, p. 66).

Unfortunately, neither Bergson nor Samuelson provided hints as to what the "rule of equity" could be. We believe that the Bergson–Samuelson tradition can be developed in three ways. First, it is not sufficient to find examples of Bergson–Samuelson functions (as Samuelson [1977] did, for instance); it is also important to provide an axiomatic basis for them to elucidate their ethical underpinnings. Second, because of Samuelson's reluctance to consider cross-economy axioms such as Arrow independence, it is generally believed that the Bergson–Samuelson approach is a "single-profile" approach. Nonetheless, SOFs that are representable by Bergson–Samuelson functions can satisfy cross-economy robustness properties. In particular, there is a specific weakening of Arrow's independence property that is needed to obtain reasonable

---

[11] A detailed study of this controversy was made by Fleurbaey and Mongin (2005).

Bergson–Samuelson SOFs. This point has already been made in the literature (by Hansson [1973], Mayston [1974], and Pazner [1979]), but is not well known. Third, properly justified Bergson–Samuelson functions can be used to reach original policy conclusions in public economics. Although public economics is often made with not very precise social welfare functions, we believe that more precise conclusions can be obtained with the more specific social criteria that emerge from a sufficiently rich axiomatic analysis. In this book we propose several second-best analyses and devote one full chapter to the optimal income taxation problem.

It should be clear now why we see our approach as part of welfare economics, and we do hope to contribute to the revival of a field that has received too little attention in the past decades.

1.7   COST–BENEFIT ANALYSIS

Cost–benefit analysis is one of the oldest branches of welfare economics. Its aim is to evaluate social policy, and it refers specifically to willingness to pay in a market economy. One can distinguish three variants of cost–benefit analysis. The oldest variant is based on Marshallian consumer surplus and producer surplus in partial equilibrium analysis. This has been refined for the general equilibrium approach by replacing the Marshallian surplus by compensating and equivalent variations or by the related Kaldor–Hicks–Scitovsky compensation tests. Finally, most specialists now advocate using something similar to a Bergson–Samuelson social welfare function to avoid the problems raised by the older approaches. The old approaches, however, remain in use in much of the applied work done in evaluation units of governments throughout the world, as well as in branches of normative economics such as industrial policy and international economic policy.

As the Bergson–Samuelson approach has already been discussed in the previous section, let us focus here on compensating and equivalent variations. In the context of our example, the typical question would be to assess the change from a market equilibrium (z_N, p) corresponding to endowments ω_N, to another market equilibrium (z'_N, p') corresponding to endowments ω'_N. This reveals an immediate difference with the objective of a SOF: here, the ranking of allocations need not be complete.

The compensating variation for agent $i \in N$ is defined by

$$p'\omega'_i - \min \left\{ p'x \mid x \, R_i \, z_i \right\},$$

which can be interpreted as the amount agent i would be willing to pay in the final state to move from z_i to z'_i. This agent's equivalent variation is defined by

$$\min \left\{ px \mid x \, R_i \, z'_i \right\} - p\omega_i,$$

corresponding to the payment the agent would accept, in the initial state, to forgo the move from z_i to z'_i.

The change is socially acceptable in that approach if, over all agents, the sum of the compensating (or equivalent) variations is positive. Informally, a reform is implemented if there exists a way for those who gain to strictly compensate those who lose, to leave no one worse off than in the initial allocation. This is a kind of utilitarian point of view in which gains and losses are measured and compared in monetary terms, and where the essential feature is that compensation be possible, should it be implemented or not.

There are two classical problems with this approach.[12] First, such criteria are not transitive. This occurs because the reference prices that serve to evaluate the changes depend on the pair of allocations to be compared. Second, it is ethically dubious to consider that virtual compensation of losers can justify a reform. Suppose the losers are mostly among the poorest of the population, and the gainers are among the richest. It then seems shocking to declare the change to be good simply because compensation is possible, even if the compensation will never be implemented.

Our approach seeks to remedy these two problems, first by constructing transitive orderings and second by putting enough inequality aversion to avoid sacrificing the worse-off in this way. What our approach has in common with cost–benefit analysis, however, is the focus on resource valuation as opposed to subjective utility. In both approaches, ordinal noncomparable preferences are the main informational ingredient about individual well-being.

To illustrate how the cost–benefit criteria can be minimally changed to come close to our approach, observe that the sum of compensating or equivalent variations evaluates a particular allocation z_N by computing

$$\sum_{i \in N} \min \left\{ p^* x \mid x \, R_i \, z_i \right\},$$

where p^* is the reference price vector (either the final or the initial prices, for compensating or equivalent variations, respectively). As we will see in Chapter 5, an interesting ordering in our approach consists in evaluating an allocation by the formula

$$\max_{p : p\Omega = 1} \min_{i \in N} \min \{ px \mid x \, R_i \, z_i \}.$$

In this formula we see that the sum over all $i \in N$ is replaced by the maximin criterion, whereas the moving reference price is replaced by a reference price that is specific to the allocation but does not depend on which other allocation the allocation z_N is compared to. These two changes alleviate the problems that plague the sum of compensating or equivalent variations. In a sense, our approach can be viewed as correcting the flaws of cost–benefit analysis.

---

[12] Criticisms of compensating or equivalent variations, or of the related compensation tests, can be found in Arrow (1963), Boadway and Bruce (1984), and Blackorby and Donaldson (1990), among many other references.

1.8   MONEY-METRIC UTILITIES

For a fixed reference price p^*, the expression

$$m_i(z_i) = \min \left\{ p^* x \mid x \, R_i \, z_i \right\}$$

is a utility representation of agent i's preferences, a "money-metric" utility. Samuelson and Swamy (1974) and Samuelson (1974) proposed to use this number as the key ingredient of a quantity index that is convenient for tracking individual well-being accurately, in contrast with standard indices such as the Laspeyres, Paasche, or Fisher quantity indices, which do not respect individual preferences in general.

Once this number has been put on the table, it is tempting to incorporate it in a social welfare function to evaluate allocations:

$$W(m_1(z_1), \ldots, m_n(z_n)).$$

This has not been proposed by Samuelson, who was particularly adamant against summing up money-metric utilities across individuals, but the idea has been promoted by many authors – in particular, by Deaton and Muellbauer (1980) and King (1983). As should be clear by now, our own approach is very close to this idea, although it encompasses many variants of it.

This idea attracted much criticism and its popularity quickly declined. Three main critiques seem to have been influential. The first critique is that the money-metric utility does not incorporate sufficient information about subjective welfare, as it depends only on ordinal noncomparable preferences. "A variation of one's intensities of pleasure or welfare cannot, therefore, find any reflection in this numbering system as long as the ordering remains unchanged" (Sen 1979, p. 11).

This criticism may have gained momentum from the fact that money-metric utilities have often been presented as a "monetary measure of subjective welfare," clearly an oxymoron. It is much more sensible to defend the notion as depicting "the objective circumstances- the constraints-faced by each individual" (Deaton and Muellbauer 1980, p. 225), which is well in line with our own focus on resource equality.

A second critique is that a social welfare function W whose arguments are money-metric utilities $m_i(z_i)$ may fail to be quasiconcave in commodity consumptions z_N, even when individual preferences are convex and W is quasiconcave (Blackorby and Donaldson, 1988). This appears incompatible with a minimal preference for equality. For instance, consider a two-agent population in which both individuals have the same direct utility function over two-commodity bundles (x, y): $u_i(x, y) = \min \{x, y + 1\}$. This is illustrated in Figure 1.6. Take reference prices $p = (1, 1)$ and consider the allocation in which both individuals consume the bundle $(1, 1)$. Their money-metric utility is then equal to 1. Now introduce some inequality, letting individual 1 consume $(1 - \delta, 1)$ and individual 2 consume $(1 + \delta, 1)$ for a small $\delta > 0$. Then individual 1's money-metric utility is $1 - \delta$, whereas individual 2's money-metric

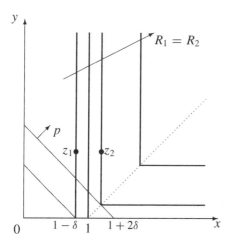

Figure 1.6. A social welfare function with money-metric utilities fails to be quasi-concave

utility is $1 + 2\delta$. For δ small enough, any differentiable and symmetric social welfare function bearing on money-metric utilities will declare this change to be an improvement:

$$dW = -\frac{\partial W}{\partial m_1}\delta + \frac{\partial W}{\partial m_2}2\delta > 0$$

if $\frac{\partial W}{\partial m_1} = \frac{\partial W}{\partial m_2}$, as should be the case for a symmetrical social welfare function because the two individuals are equally well-off in the initial situation. The problem disappears only if one takes the maximin or the leximin criterion instead of a social welfare function with finite inequality aversion. We will see in Chapter 3 how this observation can be generalized and, instead of undermining the approach, can serve to justify the maximin or the leximin as aggregation criteria.

The third criticism, developed by Roberts (1980) and Slesnick (1991), is that the m_i function depends on the reference vector p^*, and that, if one wants to be able to perform interpersonal comparisons or social evaluations that are independent of the reference, severe restrictions are required (e.g., identical homothetic preferences). When individual preferences are different from one individual to another, with crossing indifference curves, the mere ranking of individuals simply cannot be independent of p^*. What we argue in our approach is that references need not be arbitrary but can be selected on the ground of specific fairness considerations. In this light, it appears unduly demanding – perhaps even ethically inappropriate – to seek evaluations that are independent of the reference.

In conclusion, we believe that none of the criticisms raised against money-metric utilities is decisive. There seems to be an interesting conceptual area that is jointly close to the theory of fair allocation, social choice theory, and various

Table 1.1. *Comparison of the Main Approaches*

	SOF	Pareto	Resource Equality	Ordinal Noncomparability
Fair allocation	−	+	+	+
Arrovian social choice	+	+	−	+
Welfarism (broad)	+	?	?	?
Welfarism (subjective)	+	+	−	−
Dominance	(incomplete)	−	+	+
Multidimensional inequality indices	+	−	+	+
Bergson–Samuelson	+	+	?	+
Cost–benefit	(incomplete & intransitive)	+	−	+
Money-metric utility	+	+	?	+
Fair SOFs (this book)	+	+	+	+

Legend: + : yes; − : no; ? : undetermined.

branches of welfare economics such as the Bergson–Samuelson approach, cost–benefit analysis, and money-metric utilities. Our thesis in this book is that this area is more fertile than has been considered.

1.9   CONCLUSION

This quick general view of the main fields of welfare economics has identified four key items that allow us to compare our approach with those fields: whether the objective defines a complete and fine-grained ordering, whether possibly different preferences are taken into account and respected, whether the emphasis is put on resource equality, and whether the informational basis of the social judgments satisfy the ordinalism noncomparability requirement. How each field behaves with respect to these items is summarized in Table 1.1. A question mark in a cell means that the approach leaves this issue unspecified.

These comparisons allow us to characterize our approach as follows: we study SOFs that are consistent with the Pareto principle and satisfy fairness properties, while sticking to ordinal and noncomparable information on individual preferences. The underlying view of a just society is one in which resources are allocated among agents in such a way that the value they attach to bundles of resources is equalized.

With this work, we especially hope to convey two key messages:

- Welfare economics is not caught in a dilemma between impossibility and interpersonal comparisons of subjective utility.
- Considerations of fairness (interpreting justice in terms of resource equality) are useful to address second-best policy problems.

CHAPTER 2

Efficiency versus Equality

2.1 INTRODUCTION

The evaluation of allocations of resources in a given context should depend on the characteristics of the context – in particular, the preferences of the population. This is why the object of our study is a *social ordering function* (SOF), which specifies, for each economy in an admissible domain, a complete ranking of the corresponding allocations. As stated in the introduction, we study social ordering functions in distribution models, with divisible or indivisible goods, as well as in production models of a private or a public good. This study is developed in Parts II and III. In this work, fairness is interpreted as resource equality, but there are different ways of specifying this notion – in particular, in relation to the specific features of the environment, so the social ordering functions that end up being selected do not have much in common. Some partial results, however, turn out to be general in the sense that they have their counterparts in each of the studied models.

In this first part of the book, we present and discuss these general and basic results. They provide two insights into the possibilities and limitations surrounding the construction of social ordering functions. The first concerns the way in which resource equality requirements need to be defined to be compatible with basic efficiency principles. The second lesson concerns the degree of inequality aversion that is compatible with efficiency and informational simplicity requirements. The model we rely on to present these general results is the canonical "fair division" model, which was introduced in the previous chapter and is also the topic of a more specific analysis of social ordering functions in Part II of this book. The fact that this model is rather abstract, but at the same time contains the main ingredients of economic allocation models that pertain to our analysis (multiple goods, heterogeneous individual preferences) social ordering functions, makes it quite suitable for the presentation of general findings on.

The topic of this chapter is the way in which resource equality requirements may clash with the Pareto principle when they are defined without sufficient precaution. In particular, requiring that a transfer of resources from agent

j to agent k be a social improvement, whenever j is assigned more of all commodities than k, turns out to be incompatible with standard versions of the Pareto principle. This means that "consuming more of all commodities than another agent" is not sufficient for an agent to be unambiguously identified as better off than the other agent in the ethically appropriate sense. In this chapter, we present this result formally (Section 2.2) and we analyze several ways of modifying the equality requirement to recover compatibility with the Pareto principle (Section 2.3).

2.2 RESOURCE EQUALITY VERSUS PARETO EFFICIENCY

The idea of resource equality has a well-established tradition in the theory of fair allocation, in which it finds a variety of expressions: equality of budgets, no-envy (no agent should prefer another's bundle), egalitarian-equivalence (every agent should be indifferent to a reference bundle), lower bounds (e.g., every agent should be at least as well off as at equal split), solidarity (every agent should be affected in the same direction when general parameters such as resources or population size change), and so forth.[1] Here we deal with orderings, so the idea of the "optimality" of resource equality must be translated into the "betterness" of inequality reduction. This naturally leads us to consider the Pigou–Dalton transfer principle[2] as a starting point.

The transfer principle is standardly formulated in the one-dimensional framework of income distributions. It then says that a transfer from one agent to another with lower income reduces inequality, or increases social welfare, provided it does not reverse their ranking, or at least provided the transfer does not exceed the initial gap between them. We must adapt this to our multidimensional framework with multiple goods.

The version of the Pigou–Dalton principle that we retain focuses on transfers of positive bundles of resources from an agent to another, such that, even after the transfer, the recipient consumes less of every good than the donor. More precisely, Axiom 2.1 says that if a transfer of positive quantities of each good is made from j to k, with the other agents being unaffected, and after the transfer j still consumes more of every good than k, the final allocation is at least as good as the initial allocation.

Axiom 2.1 Transfer
For all $E = (R_N, \Omega) \in \mathcal{D}$, and $z_N, z'_N \in X^N$, if there exist $j, k \in N$, and $\Delta \in \mathbb{R}^{\ell}_{++}$ such that

$$z_j - \Delta = z'_j \gg z'_k = z_k + \Delta$$

and for all $i \neq j, k$, $z_i = z'_i$, then $z'_N \mathbf{R}(E) z_N$.

---

[1] For recent surveys, see Moulin and Thomson (1997) and Thomson (2001).
[2] From Pigou (1912) and Dalton (1920).

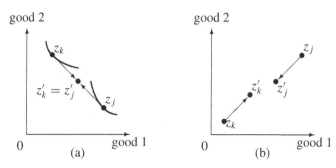

Figure 2.1. Pigou–Dalton transfers

All the (positive and negative) results of this book involving transfer axioms would remain valid if the transfer axioms combined the requirement that z'_j dominate z'_k with the additional restriction that Δ should be a certain fraction $\lambda \in (0, 1/2)$ of $z_j - z_k$:

$$z'_j = z_j - \lambda \left(z_j - z_k \right) \gg z'_k = z_k + \lambda \left(z_j - z_k \right).$$

We forget this additional restriction for simplicity of presentation only. In the literature on multidimensional inequality, it is common to consider the larger class of Pigou–Dalton transfers defined by the formula

$$z'_j = z_j - \lambda \left(z_j - z_k \right), \quad z'_k = z_k + \lambda \left(z_j - z_k \right),$$

for $\lambda \in [0, 1]$. No requirement is made about $z_j > z_k$, so these complex Pigou–Dalton transfers may go in opposite directions for different dimensions. For instance, in a two-good economy, if $z_j = (1, 3)$ and $z_k = (3, 1)$, a complex Pigou–Dalton transfer, in which j is a recipient in the first dimension and a donor in the second, may yield $z'_j = z'_k = (2, 2)$. As it may happen that $z_j \, P_j \, z'_j$ and $z_k \, P_k \, z'_k$, such transfers may go against both individual preferences. (See Figure 2.1(a) for an illustration.) The clash with the Pareto axioms is then immediate.

This kind of problem can be avoided if, as in the axiom of transfer defined previously, the transfer is performed only between two agents who are ranked in the same way in all dimensions – that is, when one consumes more of every good than the other, and the transfer involves a positive amount of every good going from the richer to the poorer. In that case, the agent who receives the transfer is bound to benefit from it, whereas the donor is bound to have a reduced satisfaction (see Figure 2.1(b)). The transfer cannot then directly go against unanimous preferences.

Unfortunately, the Pigou–Dalton principle, as embodied in the axiom of transfer, does conflict with efficiency.

Theorem 2.1 *On the domain $\mathcal{E}$, no SOF satisfies* weak Pareto *and* transfer.

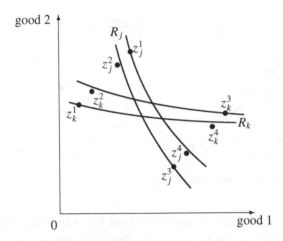

Figure 2.2. Proof of Theorem 2.1

The simple proof is illustrated in Figure 2.2. Four allocations are represented in a two-agent economy. Agent j is "richer" than agent k in allocations 1 and 2, whereas the converse is true in the other allocations. Weak Pareto requires that $z_N^1 \mathbf{P}(E) z_N^4$, because z_i^4 is below the indifference curve containing z_i^1, for $i = j, k$. Similarly, $z_N^3 \mathbf{P}(E) z_N^2$. On the other hand, transfer requires $z_N^2 \mathbf{R}(E) z_N^1$ and $z_N^4 \mathbf{R}(E) z_N^3$, which creates a cycle.

The example used to prove the theorem involves well-chosen preferences. One can prove, however, that for every economy in which not all agents have the same preferences, it is impossible to construct a social ordering of allocations satisfying weak Pareto and transfer.[3]

There is a similar problem with a transfer axiom that restricts attention to reducing inequality of budgets at unchanged prices.[4] It is very tempting to think that when agents have unequal budgets and this inequality is reduced (without altering market prices), the situation is improved. Things are, again, not so simple. This provides a way to slightly strengthen Theorem 2.1. One can observe that Theorem 2.1 still holds when transfer is replaced by the logically weaker axiom stating that for all $E = (R_N, \Omega) \in \mathcal{D}$, and $z_N, z_N' \in X^N$, if there exist $j, k \in N$, and $\Delta \in \mathbb{R}_{++}^\ell$, $p \in \mathbb{R}_{++}^\ell$ such that

$$z_j \in \max|_{R_j} B\left(z_j, p\right), \; z_k \in \max|_{R_k} B\left(z_k, p\right),$$

$$z_j' \in \max|_{R_j} B\left(z_j', p\right), \; z_k' \in \max|_{R_k} B\left(z_k', p\right),$$

$$z_j - \Delta = z_j' \gg z_k' = z_k + \Delta$$

and for all $i \neq j, k, z_i = z_i'$, then $z_N' \mathbf{R}(E) z_N$.

---

[3] See Fleurbaey and Trannoy (2003). Brun and Tungodden (2004) prove a similar single-profile result with a different transfer condition, which involves

$$z_k' \geq z_j > z_j' > z_k,$$

implying that the receiver gets more than the donor.

[4] This is from Gibbard (1979).

In other words, even assuming additionally that agents choose their bundles in budgets and that the transfer does not alter prices, the idea that reducing inequality is good may conflict with efficiency. The proof is a simple adaptation of Figure 2.2 (one only must bend the indifference curves to equalize the marginal rates of substitutions of j and k in allocations z_N^1 and z_N^2, as well as in z_N^3 and z_N^4).

This first set of results is undoubtedly bad news, as the axioms involved seem so basic. This questions the intuition that when an agent is above another in all dimensions, he or she is undoubtedly better off. There is a paradox here. Any monotonic preference relation values a greater bundle more, so when an agent has more of every good than another, all agents are unanimous in considering that this agent has a better bundle. But, as shown in Figure 2.2, all agents may also be indifferent between this allocation and another in which they all consider that, because this agent now has less of every good, his or her bundle is less valuable.[5] There is a tension between different facets of the idea of respecting unanimous preferences.

There are two possible ways out of the impossibility. One can weaken or forget the efficiency requirements, or adopt weaker versions of the transfer principle. We follow the latter route, because we find it worthwhile to explore the extent to which fairness considerations can be taken into account while retaining the Pareto principle. As it turns out, much can be done along this vein, and this provides the material for this book.

The alternative route might also be worth exploring, but it has a lesser priority, in our opinion, because in the simple settings of distribution and production that we study in this model, the Pareto principle seems hard to relinquish. A criterion violating this principle will sometimes, maybe often, lead to selecting inefficient allocations; such situations are inherently unstable because agents can find other allocations that make every agent better off. Moreover, whereas it is relatively easy to formulate weaker versions of the transfer principle, as done in the next section, it seems harder to weaken the Pareto axioms without abandoning the Pareto principle altogether.[6]

In this chapter, we stress the conflict between the Pareto principle and the transfer principle, but it is worth noting that the problem does not come from the inequality aversion embodied in the transfer principle. One can have similar difficulties with axioms reflecting only a principle of impartiality, for instance. Consider a two-agent economy. Out of impartiality, one might consider requiring

$$(z_1, z_2)\, \mathbf{I}(E)\,(z_2, z_1),$$

but this obviously clashes with the Pareto principle because it may be that, for instance, (z_1, z_2) is unanimously preferred to (z_2, z_1).

---

[5] Our focus here is the problem of evaluating allocations for a given population. One can also directly study the problem of making interpersonal comparisons and obtain an alternative formulation of the same difficulty. Who is better off when indifference curves cross? On this "indexing problem," see Fleurbaey (2007a) and Pattanaik and Xu (2007).

[6] See, however, Sprumont (2006). See also the Pareto efficiency axiom in Section 4.4.

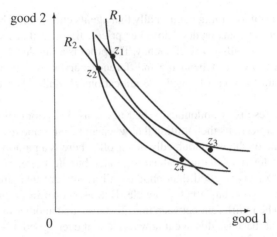

Figure 2.3. Impartiality versus Pareto

The conflict with Pareto would remain even if one restricted the application of this indifference requirement to the case in which $z_1 \gg z_2$, so (z_1, z_2) cannot be unanimously preferred to (z_2, z_1). In Figure 2.3, one sees that weak Pareto implies that $(z_1, z_2) \, \mathbf{P}(E) \, (z_3, z_4)$ and $(z_4, z_3) \, \mathbf{P}(E) \, (z_2, z_1)$. It is therefore impossible to also have $(z_1, z_2) \, \mathbf{I}(E) \, (z_2, z_1)$ and $(z_3, z_4) \, \mathbf{I}(E) \, (z_4, z_3)$, even though $z_1 \gg z_2$ and $z_3 \gg z_4$.

2.3 ACCOMMODATING EQUALITY

In this section, we present two main ways to escape the impossibility by weakening transfer. The first one consists of restricting application of the transfer principle to particular regions of the space of goods.

Take the well-known principle that, in fair division, no agent should receive a bundle that is worse, for the agent's preferences, than an equal split of the available resources (Steinhaus 1948, Moulin 1996). This suggests applying the transfer principle to cases in which the relatively rich agent is one who gets a bundle he or she strictly prefers to an equal split, and the relatively poor agent prefers an equal split to the bundle he or she gets. It is clear that the ranking of the agents according to this criterion cannot be affected as one moves along indifference curves, which allows us to escape the impossibility. We actually consider a simpler restriction, namely, focusing on cases in which bundles physically dominate or are dominated by an equal split. In this way, the resulting requirement no longer needs to refer to preferences. See Figure 2.4 for an illustration.

We can now formulate the axiom saying that if a transfer of positive quantities of each good is made from j to k, all other agents being unaffected, and after the transfer j still consumes more than his or her per capita share while k

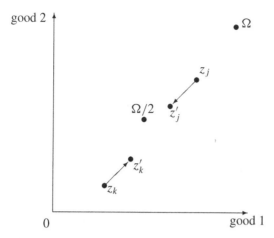

Figure 2.4. Equal-split transfer

still consumes less, then the after-transfer allocation is at least as good as the initial allocation.

Axiom 2.2 Equal-Split Transfer
For all $E = (R_N, \Omega) \in \mathcal{D}$, and $z_N, z'_N \in X^N$, if there exist $j, k \in N$, and $\Delta \in \mathbb{R}^{\ell}_{++}$ such that

$$z_j - \Delta = z'_j \gg \frac{\Omega}{|N|} \gg z'_k = z_k + \Delta$$

and for all $i \neq j, k$, $z_i = z'_i$, then $z'_N \mathbf{R}(E) z_N$.

A related way of carving out a region of the space in which the transfer principle is applied consists of referring to bundles that are proportional to the social endowment. Let us say that an allocation $z_N \in X^N$ is *proportional* for $E = (R_N, \Omega)$ if for all $i \in N$, $z_i = \lambda_i \Omega$ for some $\lambda_i \in \mathbb{R}_+$. We denote the set of proportional allocations for E by $\Pr(E)$. Proportional allocations delineate a simple setting in which all interpersonal comparisons, as well as transfers between agents, can be conceived directly in terms of fractions of the social endowment. Again, restricting the application of the transfer principle to proportional allocations prevents the ranking of agents into richer and poorer from varying (technically, it prevents us from using Pareto indifference to move along the indifference surfaces and apply the axiom twice). Again, no information on preferences is necessary to formulate the axiom. Figure 2.5 illustrates this kind of transfer.

In a nutshell, the following axiom is identical to transfer except that it restricts attention to the case in which all individual bundles in the initial and final allocations are proportional to Ω.

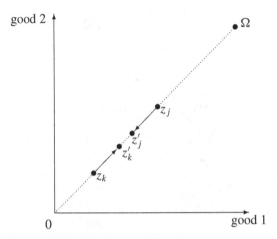

Figure 2.5. Proportional-allocations transfer

Axiom 2.3 Proportional-Allocations Transfer
For all $E = (R_N, \Omega) \in \mathcal{D}$, *and* $z_N, z'_N \in \mathrm{Pr}(E)$, *if there exist* $j, k \in N$, *and*
$\Delta \in \mathbb{R}^{\ell}_{++}$ *such that*

$$z_j - \Delta = z'_j \gg z'_k = z_k + \Delta$$

and for all $i \neq j, k$, $z_i = z'_i$, *then* $z'_N \, \mathbf{R}(E) \, z_N$.

One can, of course, generalize this approach and consider allocations in which bundles are proportional to any arbitrary reference bundle. The argument underlying Theorem 2.1, however, indicates that it is hopeless to simultaneously satisfy two transfer axioms referring to two different (nonproportional) reference bundles. Only one direction of proportionality can be chosen. Why, then, focus on the direction of the social endowment Ω rather than any other reference bundle? The same kind of argument as in Theorem 2.1, again, shows that any other direction would entail a conflict with equal-split transfer. Even more dramatically, perhaps, any other fixed direction would make it impossible to satisfy the following basic axiom jointly with the transfer axiom.[7] Axiom 2.4 says that when the simple equal split of Ω is efficient, then it should be among the allocations that are optimal for $\mathbf{R}(E)$ in $Z(E)$.

Axiom 2.4 Equal-Split Selection
For all $E = (R_N, \Omega) \in \mathcal{D}$, *if* $(\Omega / |N|, \dots, \Omega / |N|) \in P(E)$, *then*

$$(\Omega / |N|, \dots, \Omega / |N|) \in \max|_{\mathbf{R}(E)} Z(E).$$

Another way of escaping the impossibility is by restricting application of the transfer principle to pairs of agents having the same preferences. Technically,

---

[7] This discussion is generalized in Theorem 4.1.

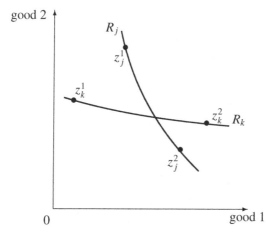

Figure 2.6. No-envy versus Pareto

this prevents any crossing of indifference curves as in the above figures. Ethically, the fact that agents have the same preferences guarantees not only that both prefer the bundle with more of every good, but also that this unanimous (among the two concerned agents) ranking of bundles extends to all Pareto indifferent allocations. There is, then, no doubt at all about who has a more or a less valuable position. Contrary to the preceding axioms, the preferences of the agents now play a role. The following axiom, then, is identical to transfer but for the fact that agents j and k, between whom the transfer takes place, must have identical preferences.

Axiom 2.5 Transfer among Equals
For all $E = (R_N, \Omega) \in \mathcal{D}$, and $z_N, z'_N \in X^N$, if there exist $j, k \in N$ such that $R_j = R_k$ and $\Delta \in \mathbb{R}^\ell_{++}$ such that

$$z_j - \Delta = z'_j \gg z'_k = z_k + \Delta,$$

and for all $i \neq j, k$, $z_i = z'_i$, then $z'_N \mathbf{R}(E) z_N$.

The justification of this axiom can also refer to the concept of equity as *no-envy*, a key notion in the theory of fair allocation.[8] Agent k envies agent j in z_N whenever $z_j P_k z_k$. At the allocations z_N and z'_N considered in the preceding axiom, k envies j and moreover, as they have identical preferences, k would envy j at any Pareto indifferent allocation.

The no-envy concept is a selection concept adapted to allocation rules and does not easily apply to SOFs in the multidimensional context, for the same sort of reason as the Pigou–Dalton transfer. Indeed, when indifference curves cross, as in Figure 2.6 (compare with Figure 2.2), an allocation in which agent

---

[8] The seminal references are Kolm (1972) and Varian (1974). For a recent survey, see Arnsperger (1994).

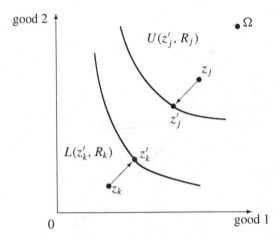

Figure 2.7. Nested-contour transfer

k envies agent j, such as z_N^1 in the figure, can be Pareto equivalent to another allocation, such as z_N^2, in which j envies k. It is then difficult to decide who, among j and k, should be given priority on the basis of the no-envy concept. In particular, it is incompatible with Pareto axioms to require an allocation to be preferred to another when they differ in terms of the number or presence of envy occurrences.[9]

The situation is not problematic, however, when indifference curves do not cross, as in Figure 2.7. In such a case, when one agent envies another, this remains true for all other allocations that are Pareto equivalent to this one. This noncrossing property can be obtained when preferences are not exactly identical; this suggests another axiom of transfer, which is stronger than transfer among equals. Instead of requiring that the preferences of j and k be identical, it simply requires that their indifference curves through their bundles in z_N and z_N' be nested and thereby do not cross. The condition that indifference curves of the donor and recipient do not cross after (and, as a result, before) the transfer can be formally written as having an empty intersection of the former's upper contour and the latter's lower contour sets (see Figure 2.7).

The (closed) upper and lower contour sets will be denoted

$$U(z_i, R_i) = \{x \in X \mid x \, R_i \, z_i\},$$

$$L(z_i, R_i) = \{x \in X \mid z_i \, R_i \, x\}.$$

Axiom 2.6 then says that a transfer from j to k, the other agents being unaffected, such that after the transfer j's upper contour set is still disjoint from k's lower contour set, produces an allocation that is at least as good as the initial allocation.

---

[9] See Tadenuma (2002) and Suzumura (1981a,b).

Axiom 2.6 Nested-Contour Transfer
For all $E = (R_N, \Omega) \in \mathcal{D}$, and $z_N, z'_N \in X^N$, if there exist $j, k \in N$, and $\Delta \in \mathbb{R}^\ell_{++}$ such that

$$z_j - \Delta = z'_j \gg z'_k = z_k + \Delta,$$
$$U(z'_j, R_j) \cap L(z'_k, R_k) = \emptyset$$

and for all $i \neq j, k$, $z_i = z'_i$, then $z'_N \, \mathbf{R}(E) \, z_N$.

A third way of weakening transfer may be considered. Let an allocation z_N be called *balanced* when $\sum_{i \in N} z_i = \Omega$, and let $\bar{Z}(E)$ denote the set of balanced allocations in economy E. One sees that in Figure 2.2, it cannot be the case that both z^1 (or z^2) and z^3 (or z^4) are feasible and balanced. Restricting the requirement to balanced allocations may therefore seem to be another way out of the impossibility, but it is not, if the economy has at least three agents. Consider the following axiom, which is identical to transfer but for the fact that the initial and final allocations must be balanced.

Axiom 2.7 Balanced-Allocations Transfer
For all $E = (R_N, \Omega) \in \mathcal{D}$, and $z_N, z'_N \in \bar{Z}(E)$, if there exist $j, k \in N$, and $\Delta \in \mathbb{R}^\ell_{++}$ such that

$$z_j - \Delta = z'_j \gg z'_k = z_k + \Delta$$

and for all $i \neq j, k$, $z_i = z'_i$, then $z'_N \, \mathbf{R}(E) \, z_N$.

One then obtains the following result. Let $\mathcal{E}^3$ denote the subdomain of $\mathcal{E}$ containing the economies with a population of size $|N| \geq 3$.

Theorem 2.2 *On the domain $\mathcal{E}^3$, no SOF satisfies* weak Pareto *and* balanced-allocations transfer.

Figure 2.8 illustrates the argument. One sees that $z^1_N \, \mathbf{P}(E) \, z^5_N$ and $z^3_N \, \mathbf{P}(E) \, z^2_N$ by weak Pareto. On the other hand, balanced-allocations transfer implies $z^2_N \, \mathbf{R}(E) \, z^1_N$, $z^4_N \, \mathbf{R}(E) \, z^3_N$ and $z^5_N \, \mathbf{R}(E) \, z^4_N$, which produces a cycle.

We conclude this analysis in the following statement that the relevant transfer axioms are not only separately, but also jointly, compatible with weak Pareto and even with the stronger axiom of strong Pareto. Strong Pareto requires an allocation to be weakly preferred to another whenever all agents weakly prefer it. It also requires strict preference as soon as at least one agent displays strict preference.

Axiom 2.8 Strong Pareto
For all $E = (R_N, \Omega) \in \mathcal{D}$, and $z_N, z'_N \in X^N$, if $z_i \, R_i \, z'_i$ for all $i \in N$, then $z_N \, \mathbf{R}(E) \, z'_N$; if, in addition, $z_i \, P_i \, z'_i$ for some $i \in N$, then $z_N \, \mathbf{P}(E) \, z'_N$.

Theorem 2.3 *On the domain $\mathcal{E}$, the Ω-equivalent leximin $\mathbf{R}^{\Omega \text{lex}}$ satisfies* strong Pareto, equal-split transfer, proportional-allocations transfer, equal-split selection, transfer among equals, *and* nested-contour transfer.

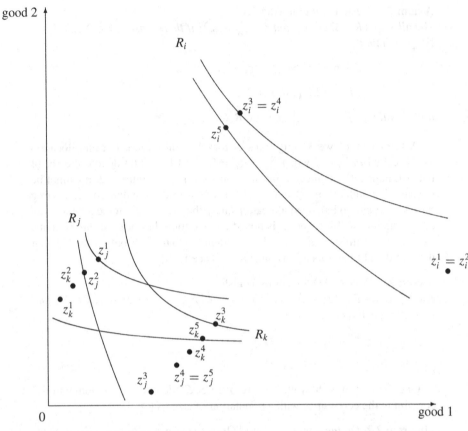

Figure 2.8. Proof of Theorem 2.2

Note that the Ω-equivalent leximin $\mathbf{R}^{\Omega\text{lex}}$ satisfies the transfer axioms in a strong way, as the posttransfer allocation is deemed strictly better than the pretransfer allocation.

Finally, it is worthwhile comparing $\mathbf{R}^{\Omega\text{lex}}$ to two other SOFs that will serve as useful examples in this book. Let us first define these two SOFs. The first one is another kind of Ω-equivalent SOF.[10] It relies on the same valuation of individual bundles, but applies the Nash-product social welfare function instead of the leximin criterion. This is less strongly egalitarian.[11]

---

[10] It is inspired from a family of SOFs proposed by Eisenberg (1961) and Milleron (1970). These authors are less specific about the utility indices to be used, because they focus on the case of homothetic individual preferences. In their particular context, any choice of a homogeneous utility representation of individual preferences yields the same social ordering. See Chapter 6 for a study of this particular subdomain.

[11] As it is defined here, this SOF is not good at evaluating allocations in which $z_j \, I_j \, 0$ for some $j \in N$, since $\prod_{i \in N} u_\Omega(z_i, R_i) = 0$ for such allocations, no matter what happens to agents $i \neq j$. One can, for instance, refine the definition in the following way. Let $D(z_N) = \{i \in N \mid z_i \, I_i \, 0\}$.

Social ordering function 2.1 Ω-Equivalent Nash ($\mathbf{R}^{\Omega Nash}$)
For all $E = (R_N, \Omega) \in \mathcal{E}$, $z_N, z_N' \in X^N$,

$$z_N \, \mathbf{R}^{\Omega Nash}(E) \, z_N' \Leftrightarrow \prod_{i \in N} u_\Omega(z_i, R_i) \geq \prod_{i \in N} u_\Omega(z_i', R_i).$$

The other example orders allocations with respect to the coefficient of resource utilization. This coefficient measures the level of efficiency of an allocation.[12] It is equal to the scalar $\lambda \in [0, 1]$ such that a fraction λ of the resources would have been just enough to provide the same satisfaction level to all agents – that is, if, in an economy with resources limited to a fraction λ of the current resources, there exists a Pareto efficient allocation that is Pareto indifferent to the current allocation (i.e., all agents are indifferent between the two).[13] Recall that $P(E)$ denotes the set of Pareto efficient allocations for economy E.

Social ordering function 2.2 Resource Utilization ($\mathbf{R}^{RU}$)
For all $E = (R_N, \Omega) \in \mathcal{E}$, $z_N, z_N' \in X^N$, *and* $\lambda, \lambda' \in \mathbb{R}_+$ *such that there exist* $z_N^* \in P(R_N, \lambda\Omega)$ *and* $z_N^{*\prime} \in P\left(R_N, \lambda'\Omega\right)$ *with* $z_i \, I_i \, z_i^*$ *and* $z_i' \, I_i \, z_i'^*$ *for all* $i \in N$,

$$z_N \, \mathbf{R}^{RU}(E) \, z_N' \Leftrightarrow \lambda \geq \lambda'.$$

The computation of λ is illustrated in Figure 2.9 with the Edgeworth box. Computing λ is equivalent to moving agent 2's origin O_2 down the ray $O_1 O_2$ until agent 2's indifference curve (which moves down correspondingly) is tangent to agent 1's. Once this is obtained, the new origin for agent 2 represents precisely $\lambda\Omega$.

All the Pareto efficient allocations are considered socially equivalent by this ordering function, and they are socially preferred to any inefficient allocation. Obviously, this SOF incorporates only efficiency considerations and disregards distributional issues. An interesting feature of the resource utilization SOF is that, contrary to $\mathbf{R}^{\Omega lex}$, it does not involve the intermediate computation of specific utility representations of individual preferences. However, it can be defined in terms of sums of money-metric utilities, for endogenous prices. Indeed, it ranks allocations in the same way as the expression

$$\max_{p:p\Omega=1} \sum_{i \in N} \min \{px \mid x \, R_i \, z_i\}.$$

Then:

$$z_N \, \mathbf{R}^{\Omega Nash}(E) \, z_N' \Leftrightarrow |D(z_N)| < |D(z_N')|$$

$$\text{or} \left[|D(z_N)| = |D(z_N')| \text{ and } \prod_{i \notin D(z_N)} u_\Omega(z_i, R_i) \geq \prod_{i \notin D(z_N')} u_\Omega(z_i', R_i) \right].$$

---

[12] The coefficient of resource utilization was introduced by Debreu (1951).

[13] When one ranks all allocations, including the infeasible, one will of course have $\lambda > 1$ for some of them.

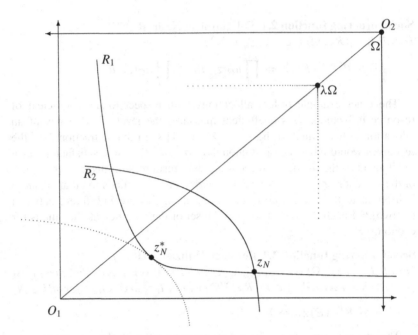

Figure 2.9. $\mathbf{R}^{\mathrm{RU}}$ in the Edgeworth box

This fact is proved as follows. Let $z_N^* \in P(R_N, \lambda\Omega)$. If p such that $p\Omega = 1$ is a supporting price vector for z_N^*,[14] and let $z_N \in X^N$ be Pareto indifferent to z_N^*. One has $\min\{px \mid x\, R_i\, z_i\} = \min\{px \mid x\, R_i\, z_i^*\} = pz_i^*$ for all $i \in N$ and $\sum_i z_i^* = \lambda\Omega$, so

$$\sum_{i\in N} \min\{px \mid x\, R_i\, z_i\} = p \sum_i z_i^* = \lambda.$$

For any arbitrary price vector p' such that $p'\Omega = 1$, any $i \in N$, one has

$$\min\{p'x \mid x\, R_i\, z_i\} = \min\{p'x \mid x\, R_i\, z_i^*\} \le p'z_i^*,$$

so

$$\sum_{i\in N} \min\{p'x \mid x\, R_i\, z_i\} \le p' \sum_i z_i^* = \lambda,$$

implying in turn that

$$\lambda = \max_{p:p\Omega=1} \sum_{i\in N} \min\{px \mid x\, R_i\, z_i\}.$$

---

[14] The vector p supports allocation z_N when for all $i \in N$, z_i is a best bundle for R_i in the set $\{x \in X \mid px \le pz_i\}$.

Table 2.1. *Properties Satisfied by the Three SOFs*

	$\mathbf{R}^{RU}$	$\mathbf{R}^{\Omega\text{lex}}$	$\mathbf{R}^{\Omega\text{Nash}}$
Strong Pareto	+	+	+
Transfer	−	−	−
Equal-split transfer	−	+	−
Proportional-allocations transfer	−	+	+
Equal-split selection	+	+	−
Transfer among equals	−	+	−
Nested-contour transfer	−	+	−

The relationship between efficiency and the sum of money-metric utility functions was critically commented on by Samuelson with his characteristically sharp style:

> Whatever the merits of the money-metric utility concept developed here, a warning must be given against its misuse. Since money can be added across people, those obsessed by Pareto-optimality in welfare economics as against interpersonal equity may feel tempted to add money-metric utilities across people and think that there is ethical warrant for maximizing the resulting sum. That would be an illogical perversion, and any such temptation should be resisted. (1974, p. 1266)

Let us now briefly examine what axioms, among those introduced so far, are satisfied by the three SOFs $\mathbf{R}^{RU}$, $\mathbf{R}^{\Omega\text{lex}}$, and $\mathbf{R}^{\Omega\text{Nash}}$. As Table 2.1 shows, $\mathbf{R}^{RU}$, unsurprisingly, has a bad record with respect to transfer axioms. More surprisingly, perhaps, $\mathbf{R}^{\Omega\text{Nash}}$ does not perform very well either in terms of resource equality. It does satisfy proportional-allocations transfer, but not the others – not even equal-split selection (which is satisfied by $\mathbf{R}^{RU}$). This suggests that a strong aversion to inequality may, paradoxically, be necessary to satisfy minimally egalitarian requirements. This will be the topic of the next chapter.

2.4 CONCLUSION

All the fairness requirements defined in this chapter work as follows. By comparing the bundles of resources agents get, it is possible to identify pairs of agents such that one is relatively richer than the other. Then, a transfer of resources from the richer to the poorer is a strict (or weak) social improvement. Such requirements are compatible with efficiency axioms only if there is an unambiguous way to identify who is relatively rich and who is relatively poor. This may require looking at the preferences of the agents, as in transfer among equals or nested-contour transfer, or relating the bundles that agents receive to the total amount of available resources, as in equal-split transfer or proportional-allocations transfer.

It is already clear from the preceding discussion how a SOF can be defined without comparing individual utilities. The SOFs considered here compare bundles of resources, or, more precisely, indifference sets; this is the additional information that makes it possible to stick to ordinal noncomparable information about preferences. Theorem 2.1 gives a warning against hasty comparisons of bundles when one wants the SOF to obey the Pareto principle. It is not too surprising that the Pareto principle reduces the scope for immediate comparisons of objective situations.

One may find it frustrating that this undermines what Sen (1992) dubbed the "intersection approach," namely, the idea that when an agent's bundle is unanimously considered better than another's bundle by the population's preferences, this should be endorsed by the social criterion by giving priority to the agent with the dominated bundle. Our results imply this intuitive idea is deceptive.

This is, however, much less paradoxical than it seems at first glance. On the contrary, one may even argue that it makes perfect sense. When the Pareto principle is respected, what matters is not simply the amount of resources agents receive, but also how they value them compared with alternative bundles. Formally, the Pareto principle requires us to disregard bundles of resources and focus exclusively on the agents' indifference sets. When the indifference curves of two agents cross, it is not obvious who is the better off, even though one of them may consume more of every commodity than the other. This is not unreasonable at all, especially if one thinks of more concrete settings. Those who consume more and work less are not necessarily better off if their willingness to work is larger and their labor time is somehow constrained, those who have a higher income and less sickness may be actually worse off because they find it harder to cope with their health problems, and so on.

In conclusion, it is possible to rely on ordinal noncomparable individual preferences to define consistent resource-egalitarian and Paretian social criteria, but it is important to realize that this may require taking account of preferences in a somewhat comprehensive way.

CHAPTER 3

Priority to the Worst-Off

3.1 INTRODUCTION

Chapter 2 described the tension between efficiency and resource equality. From this, one could worry that imposing the Pareto principle will restrict the scope of egalitarian requirements excessively. This chapter dispels such worries. On the contrary, the combination of the egalitarian axioms proposed in Chapter 2 with Pareto requirements has strong egalitarian consequences. More precisely, a small aversion to inequality may, when combined with Pareto axioms, justify a strong aversion to inequality under some circumstances. A preliminary intuition for this fact can be obtained by observing that an agent may be indifferent between making a small donation in one region of the consumption space and a large donation in another region, as illustrated in Figure 3.1.

In this figure, allocation (z_j^2, z_k^2) is obtained from allocation (z_j^1, z_k^1) by making a transfer from j to k: this transfer is balanced in the sense that what j gives equals what k receives. For both agents, however, this is equivalent to going from (z_j^3, z_k^3) to (z_j^4, z_k^4), in which the transfer made between j and k is a "leaky-bucket" transfer, in which the recipient gets less than is given by the donor.

Now, consider the situation depicted in Figure 3.2. In this case, it is impossible to compare (z_j, z_k) with (z_j', z_k') by reference to a single balanced transfer. A leaky-bucket transfer appears necessary here. The transfer axioms introduced in the previous chapter, by themselves, justify only balanced transfers. In this chapter, nonetheless, we show that such axioms may actually justify all leaky-bucket transfers, in the sense that they may imply that the social ordering function must display an infinite aversion to inequality. This holds when, in addition to Pareto axioms, certain requirements of independence and separability (to be defined subsequently) are imposed on the social ordering function.

The chapter is structured as follows. The next section examines how to combine the axiom of transfer among equals with the Pareto principle, showing how an infinite inequality aversion is hard to avoid. Sections 3.3 and 3.4 repeat the exercise for nested-contour transfer and equal-split transfer.

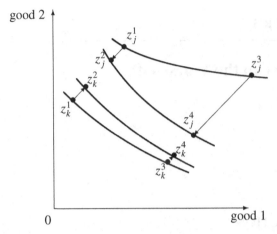

Figure 3.1. Justifying a leaky-bucket transfer

3.2 ABSOLUTE PRIORITY TO THE WORST-OFF

Consider the following strengthening of transfer among equals. Instead of considering that some amount of resources is transferred from j to k, we consider that some amount of resources is taken out of j's bundle and some other, possibly much smaller, amount of resources is added to k's bundle (as in Figure 3.2). If we still require the resulting allocation to be socially at least as good as the initial one, this means that we give absolute priority to the worst-off, accepting any possible loss of resources in the transfer.[1] This axiom is called *priority among equals*, but the word "priority" here is a shortcut for "absolute priority for the worse-off in the relevant pair of agents."[2] We later define similar "priority" axioms, with the same convention.

Axiom 3.1 Priority among Equals
For all $E = (R_N, \Omega) \in \mathcal{D}$, and $z_N, z'_N \in X^N$, if there exist $j, k \in N$ such that $R_j = R_k$,

$$z_j \gg z'_j \gg z'_k \gg z_k,$$

and for all $i \neq j, k$, $z_i = z'_i$, then $z'_N \, \mathbf{R}(E) \, z_N$.

---

[1] A similar "equity" condition was introduced by Hammond (1976) for the context of utilities. It says that if $u_j > u'_j \geq u'_k > u_k$, and $u'_i = u_i$ for all $i \neq j, k$, then $(u'_i)_{i \in N}$ is at least as good as $(u_i)_{i \in N}$.

[2] Parfit (1991) introduced the word "priority" to cover the whole span of degrees of priority, from very low to infinite. His main intention was to distinguish views that focus on the worst-off out of a concern for the badly-off from those that are inspired by aversion to inequality per se. We do not dwell on this distinction here, and our transfer (and priority) axioms can be motivated from both standpoints.

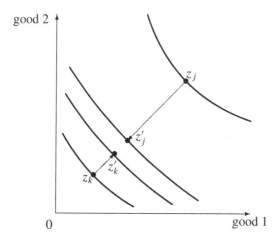

Figure 3.2. A leaky-bucket transfer

Incidentally, if a SOF satisfies strong Pareto and priority among equals, then it must consider that the posttransfer allocation is strictly better than the pretransfer allocation, and not just at least as good. Indeed, consider an allocation z_N'' such that

$$z_j \gg z_j' \gg z_j'' \gg z_k' \gg z_k'' \gg z_k,$$

and for all $i \neq j, k$, $z_i'' = z_i$. By priority among equals, $z_N'' \mathbf{R}(E) z_N$ and by strong Pareto, $z_N' \mathbf{P}(E) z_N''$, implying $z_N' \mathbf{P}(E) z_N$ by transitivity.

We now present a particular situation in which, combined with strong Pareto, transfer among equals may justify the leaky-bucket transfer depicted in Figure 3.2 by a sequence of transfers that are all balanced. In fact, we make use of Pareto indifference, a weaker axiom than strong Pareto, which says that two allocations are equally good if all agents are indifferent between the bundles they consume at these two allocations.

Axiom 3.2 Pareto Indifference
For all $E = (R_N, \Omega) \in \mathcal{D}$, and $z_N, z_N' \in X^N$, if $z_i I_i z_i'$ for all $i \in N$, then $z_N \mathbf{I}(E) z_N'$.

Consider Figure 3.3, in which, compared with Figure 3.2, some additional indifference curves have been drawn. Because there is no crossing of indifference curves in this figure, it is possible that these curves belong to one and the same preference ordering; we will indeed assume that agents j and k have the same preferences, so transfer among equals can be applied.

By virtue of transfer among equals, indeed, one sees that $z_N^2 \mathbf{R}(E) z_N^1$ and $z_N^4 \mathbf{R}(E) z_N^3$. Pareto indifference, however, also requires $z_N \mathbf{I}(E) z_N^1$, $z_N^2 \mathbf{I}(E) z_N^3$, and $z_N^4 \mathbf{I}(E) z_N'$. Putting together these relations, by transitivity one concludes that $z_N' \mathbf{R}(E) z_N$. The leaky-bucket transfer has been proved

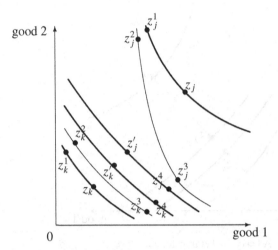

Figure 3.3. From transfer among equals to absolute priority

equivalent to a sequence of balanced transfers and Pareto equivalent changes and is thereby vindicated.

This reasoning depends crucially on the particular shape of the intermediate indifference curves (the thin curves) drawn in Figure 3.3. For other configurations, it would generally be impossible to produce a leaky-bucket transfer out of a sequence of balanced transfers and Pareto equivalent changes. However, it would be cumbersome if the ranking of two allocations such as z_N, z_N' had to depend on other indifference curves than those observed at these allocations.

The independence axiom that we now introduce requires the ranking to disregard such "irrelevant" indifference curves. More precisely, it says that the social ranking of two allocations should remain unaffected by a change in individual preferences that does not modify the agents' indifference sets at the bundles they receive in these two allocations.[3] Let the indifference set of i at z_i be defined as $I(z_i, R_i) = \{x \in X \mid x \, I_i \, z_i\}$.

Axiom 3.3 Unchanged-Contour Independence
For all $E = (R_N, \Omega)$, $E' = (R_N', \Omega) \in \mathcal{D}$, and $z_N, z_N' \in X^N$, if for all $i \in N$,

$$I(z_i, R_i') = I(z_i, R_i) \text{ and } I(z_i', R_i') = I(z_i', R_i),$$

then $z_N \, \mathbf{R}(E) \, z_N' \Leftrightarrow z_N \, \mathbf{R}(E') \, z_N'$.

This axiom is weaker than Arrow independence because it makes it possible to use more information about individual preferences than pairwise preferences

---

[3] A similar property was introduced by Hansson (1973) in the abstract voting model, and was adapted to the context of fair division by Pazner (1979).

about z_i, z_i'. Chapter 4 contains a detailed discussion of independence axioms in social choice. For the time being, let us observe that unchanged-contour independence is, unlike Arrow independence, satisfied by a wide range of social criteria. The three SOFs presented as examples in the previous chapters ($\mathbf{R}^{\Omega\text{lex}}$, $\mathbf{R}^{\Omega\text{Nash}}$, and $\mathbf{R}^{RU}$) do satisfy it. It is also satisfied by cost–benefit criteria based on sums of compensating or equivalent variations.[4] It is satisfied by the fair allocation solutions[5] when they are redefined as SOFs. For instance, consider the SOF that simply ranks all envy-free and efficient allocations above all others, or the SOF that ranks all egalitarian Walrasian allocations above all others. Both satisfy unchanged-contour independence.

The fact that this axiom is widely satisfied does not justify it, but suggests that it is connected to basic principles. Simplicity is one such basic principle. Unchanged-contour independence makes the evaluation of allocations simpler; things could be very complex otherwise.

Apart from simplicity, there is also the question of relevance. If one considers that agents should assume responsibility for their preferences, then one may argue that changes in preferences do not justify any additional claim on resources. If this logic is pushed too far, one is left with the objective of allocating resources without taking preferences into account at all. We clearly do not want to go that far, as the Pareto principle is at the top of our hierarchy of values (see Section 1.3). Consequently, our way of capturing the ethical value of responsibility for one's preferences is to impose axioms of independence with respect to changes in preferences that are still compatible with Pareto (and fairness) axioms.

More specifically, what matters for the evaluation of an allocation, arguably, is what agents think of the bundle they have, and how it compares with other bundles. It does not seem to matter so much how, in detail, agents rank bundles that are worse than theirs, or better than theirs, apart from the fact that the latter rank above the former. When agents experience changes of preferences within their lower or their upper contour sets, without affecting the content of these sets themselves, one may say that there is no reason that this should be a public matter justifying a reallocation of resources. For instance, in a market economy, when the indifference curve does not change, the agent's choice in his or her budget set does not change either.

Under unchanged-contour independence, such a strongly egalitarian requirement as priority among equals turns out to be implied by transfer among equals and Pareto indifference. We can now state the result. Unless this is absolutely obvious, we also check at the end of the proofs that the axioms are necessary for the result, in the sense that counterexamples can be found if any of them is dropped.

---

[4] See Section 1.7.
[5] See Section 1.2.

Theorem 3.1 *On the domain* $\mathcal{E}$, *if a SOF satisfies* Pareto indifference,[6] transfer among equals, *and* unchanged-contour independence, *then it satisfies* priority among equals.

Proof. The argument is a direct development of the explanations given about Figure 3.3. Let **R** satisfy Pareto indifference, transfer among equals, and unchanged-contour independence. Let $E = (R_N, \Omega) \in \mathcal{E}$, $z_N, z'_N \in X^N$ and $j, k \in N$ be such that $R_j = R_k$, $z_j \gg z'_j \gg z'_k \gg z_k$, and for all $i \neq j, k$, $z_i = z'_i$.

First case: there exist $x \in U(z_j, R_j)$, $x' \in L(z'_j, R_j)$ such that $x \not\succ x'$. Let $R'_j = R'_k \in \mathcal{R}$, $z^1_j, z^2_j, z^3_j, z^4_j, z^1_k, z^2_k, z^3_k, z^4_k \in X$, $\Delta \in R^\ell_{++}$ be constructed in such a way that for $i \in \{j, k\}$,

$$I(z_i, R'_i) = I(z_i, R_i), \ I(z'_i, R'_i) = I(z'_i, R_i),$$

$$z^1_i \, I'_i \, z_i, \ z^3_i \, I'_i \, z^2_i, \ z'_i \, I'_i \, z^4_i,$$

and

$$z^2_j = z^1_j - \Delta \gg z^2_k = z^1_k + \Delta,$$

$$z^4_j = z^3_j - \Delta \gg z^4_k = z^3_k + \Delta.$$

This construction is illustrated in Figure 3.3. The thick curves represent indifference curves for $R_j = R_k$ as well as for $R'_j = R'_k$, whereas the thin curves are indifference curves for $R'_j = R'_k$.

Let $E' = ((R_{N\setminus\{j,k\}}, R'_j, R'_k), \Omega) \in \mathcal{E}$. By Pareto indifference,

$$(z_{N\setminus\{j,k\}}, z^1_j, z^1_k) \, \mathbf{I}(E') \, z_N.$$

By transfer among equals,

$$(z_{N\setminus\{j,k\}}, z^2_j, z^2_k) \, \mathbf{R}(E') \, (z_{N\setminus\{j,k\}}, z^1_j, z^1_k).$$

By Pareto indifference,

$$(z_{N\setminus\{j,k\}}, z^3_j, z^3_k) \, \mathbf{I}(E') \, (z_{N\setminus\{j,k\}}, z^2_j, z^2_k).$$

By transfer among equals,

$$(z_{N\setminus\{j,k\}}, z^4_j, z^4_k) \, \mathbf{R}(E') \, (z_{N\setminus\{j,k\}}, z^3_j, z^3_k).$$

By Pareto indifference, $z'_N \, \mathbf{I}(E') \, (z_{N\setminus\{j,k\}}, z^4_j, z^4_k)$. By transitivity, $z'_N \, \mathbf{R}(E') \, z_N$. By unchanged-contour independence, $z'_N \, \mathbf{R}(E) \, z_N$.

Second case: there are no $x \in U(z_j, R_j)$, $x' \in L(z'_j, R_j)$ such that $x \not\succ x'$. Then let $z^*_j, z^*_k \in X$ be such that $z_j \gg z^*_j \gg z'_j$ and $z'_k \gg z^*_k \gg z_k$, and

---

[6] There is a variant of Theorem 3.1, Lemma A.1 (proved in the appendix), that involves weak Pareto instead of Pareto indifference. It does not imply priority among equals, but a variant of it in which "for all $i \neq j, k, z_i = z'_i$" is replaced by "for all $i \neq j, k, z'_i \, P_i \, z_i$." Similar variants can also be constructed for the next results of this chapter.

such that there exist $x \in U(z_j, R_j)$, $x^* \in L(z_j^*, R_j)$ such that $x \not\succ x^*$, as well as $x^{**} \in U(z_j^*, R_j)$, $x' \in L(z_j', R_j)$ such that $x^{**} \not\succ x'$. By the argument of the first case, one shows that $(z_{N\setminus\{j,k\}}, z_j^*, z_k^*) \mathbf{R}(E) z_N$ and that $z_N' \mathbf{R}(E) (z_{N\setminus\{j,k\}}, z_j^*, z_k^*)$. By transitivity, $z_N' \mathbf{R}(E) z_N$.

Finally, let us check that every axiom is necessary for the conclusion of the theorem.

1. Drop Pareto indifference. A counterexample is $\mathbf{R}^{p\text{sum}}$, defined as follows, for a given $p \in \mathbb{R}_{++}^\ell$. For all $E = (R_N, \Omega) \in \mathcal{E}$, $z_N \mathbf{R}^{p\text{sum}}(E) z_N'$ iff $\sum_{i \in N} p z_i \geq \sum_{i \in N} p z_i'$.
2. Drop transfer among equals. Take $\mathbf{R}^{\Omega\text{sum}}$, defined as follows. For all $E = (R_N, \Omega) \in \mathcal{E}$, $z_N \mathbf{R}^{\Omega\text{sum}}(E) z_N'$ iff $\sum_{i \in N} u_\Omega(z_i, R_i) \geq \sum_{i \in N} u_\Omega(z_i', R_i)$.
3. Drop unchanged-contour independence. Let $\mathcal{E}^{IL}$ denote the class of economies in which agents have identical linear preferences, and for every linear R, let $u(., R)$ be a linear representation of R. Consider $\mathbf{R}^{IL}$ defined as follows. It coincides with $\mathbf{R}^{\Omega\text{lex}}$ on $\mathcal{E} \setminus \mathcal{E}^{IL}$, whereas for all $E = (R_N, \Omega) \in \mathcal{E}^{IL}$, $z_N \mathbf{R}^{IL}(E) z_N'$ iff $\sum_{i \in N} u(z_i, R_i) \geq \sum_{i \in N} u(z_i', R_i)$. ∎

Transfer among equals is, alone, compatible with a zero inequality aversion. For instance, it is satisfied by the (non-Paretian) SOF that ranks allocations according to the value of total consumption, $p_0 \sum_i z_i$, for some fixed price vector p_0. The preceding result then produces absolute inequality aversion from axioms that are each, separately, compatible with no aversion to inequality at all. This kind of result draws much from the multidimensional framework of this model, and has no counterpart in the theory of social choice or the theory of inequality measurement dealing with one-dimensional measures of well-being.

Theorem 3.1 is valid with a weaker version of transfer among equals restricted to transfers Δ that are proportional to $z_j - z_k$. As alluded to in Section 1.8, this result generalizes the observation made by Blackorby and Donaldson (1988) that a differentiable increasing and symmetric social welfare function bearing on money-metric utilities may fail to be quasiconcave in z_N. This is shown as follows.

By construction, such a social welfare function satisfies unchanged-contour independence and strong Pareto. If $R_j = R_k$ and $z_j \gg z_k$, permuting z_j and z_k gives an equivalent allocation by symmetry, and a convex combination of the permuted allocation and the initial allocation amounts to making a transfer from j to k. Under quasiconcavity, this posttransfer allocation should be at least as good as the initial one, implying that the weaker version of transfer among equals described in the beginning of this paragraph would be satisfied as well. However, as such a differentiable social welfare function does not give absolute priority to the worst-off, by our result it cannot satisfy (the weak version of) transfer among equals and therefore it cannot be quasiconcave in z_N.

3.3 FROM NESTED-CONTOUR TRANSFER
TO ABSOLUTE PRIORITY

As we saw in Section 2.3, nested-contour transfer is stronger than transfer among equals because it allows transfers between agents with noncrossing indifference curves even when they have different preferences. Consider the following strengthening of nested-contour transfer, which gives absolute priority to the worse-off by allowing leaky-bucket transfers.

Axiom 3.4 Nested-Contour Priority
For all $E = (R_N, \Omega) \in \mathcal{D}$, and $z_N, z'_N \in X^N$, if there exist $j, k \in N$ such that

$$z_j \gg z'_j \gg z'_k \gg z_k,$$

$$U(z'_j, R_j) \cap L(z'_k, R_k) = \emptyset$$

and for all $i \neq j, k$, $z_i = z'_i$, then $z'_N \, \mathbf{R}(E) \, z_N$.

When, at two allocations, two agents have noncrossing indifference curves (i.e., four noncrossing curves altogether), if one does not know the rest of their indifference maps, one must consider it possible that they actually have identical preferences throughout. As a consequence, under unchanged-contour independence, which forces one to consider all possibilities concerning the rest of the indifference map, a transfer between agents with nested indifference curves must be treated as a transfer between agents with identical preferences. Under unchanged-contour independence, therefore, priority among equals implies nested-contour priority (similarly, transfer among equals implies nested-contour transfer). One can then immediately state the following corollary to Theorem 3.1.

Corollary 3.1 *On the domain $\mathcal{E}$, if a SOF satisfies Pareto indifference, transfer among equals, and unchanged-contour independence, then it satisfies nested-contour priority.*

There is another way in which nested-contour transfer, combined with Pareto indifference, can imply an infinite inequality aversion. Consider the situation depicted in Figure 3.4. In addition to agents j and k, some other agent l is considered, with two of this agent's indifference curves. These three agents may have different preferences, but it is important that no crossing occurs between the curves of the figure.

The bundles represented on the figure are such that

$$z_l^1 - z_l^2 = \frac{1}{4}\left(z'_k - z_k\right) \text{ and } z_l^4 - z_l^3 = \frac{1}{4}\left(z_j - z'_j\right).$$

This is important because it makes the following reasoning possible. Start from allocation (z_j, z_k, z_l^1). By nested-contour transfer, the allocation $(z_j, z_k + (z_l^1 - z_l^2), z_l^2)$ is better. It is Pareto equivalent to $(z_j, z_k + (z_l^1 - z_l^2), z_l^3)$. By nested-contour transfer again, the allocation $(z_j - (z_l^4 - z_l^3),$

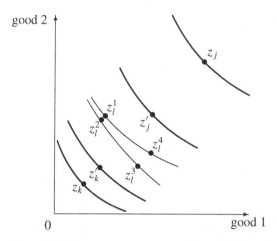

Figure 3.4. From nested-contour transfer to absolute priority

$z_k + (z_l^1 - z_l^2), z_l^4)$ is better than the previous one. It is Pareto equivalent to $(z_j - (z_l^4 - z_l^3), z_k + (z_l^1 - z_l^2), z_l^1)$.

In this last allocation, agent l is back at z_l^1, whereas the net operation between j and k is a leaky-bucket transfer, because $z_l^4 - z_l^3 \gg z_l^1 - z_l^2$. Repeat this sequence of transfers and Pareto equivalent changes three more times. One then ends up with allocation

$$(z_j - 4\left(z_l^4 - z_l^3\right), z_k + 4\left(z_l^1 - z_l^2\right), z_l^1),$$

which is equal to (z'_j, z'_k, z_l^1). In this configuration, then, we are able to deduce from nested-contour transfer and Pareto indifference that (z'_j, z'_k, z_l^1) is at least as good as (z_j, z_k, z_l^1). A sequence of balanced transfers and Pareto equivalent changes, once again, eventually produces a leaky-bucket transfer.

In this case, what is important is the presence of agent l with appropriate indifference curves in the relevant area between z'_j and z'_k. Should the evaluation of the change from (z_j, z_k) to (z'_j, z'_k) depend on the presence of a third agent with special preferences? This violates the principle of separability, according to which a change of allocation concerning a subpopulation should not depend on the rest of the population, which is not affected.

This principle of separability can be formalized in the following axiom, which states that modifying the parameters describing an unconcerned agent (i.e., this agent's bundle and/or preferences) does not modify the social ordering of the two allocations under consideration.

Axiom 3.5 Separability
For all $E = (R_N, \Omega) \in \mathcal{D}$, and $z_N, z'_N \in X^N$, if there is $i \in N$ such that $z_i = z'_i$, then for all $R'_i \in \mathcal{R}$ such that $E' = \left(\left(R_{N\setminus\{i\}}, R'_i\right), \Omega\right) \in \mathcal{D}, z''_i \in X$,

$$z_N \, \mathbf{R}(E) \, z'_N \Leftrightarrow \left(z_{N\setminus\{i\}}, z''_i\right) \mathbf{R}(E') \left(z'_{N\setminus\{i\}}, z''_i\right).$$

There are similar axioms in welfare economics[7] and in social choice,[8] requiring that agents who are indifferent between two alternatives do not influence social preferences over these alternatives. The separability principle can be related to the principle of subsidiarity, saying that unconcerned agents should not influence a particular decision. As Fleming colorfully put it,

> [I]n considering policies affecting inhabitants of this planet we do not feel hampered by our ignorance regarding states of mind which prevail among the inhabitants of Mars. (1952, p. 372)

Note, however, that separability is not satisfied by important SOFs. The resource utilization SOF, for instance, violates it, as does a Walrasian SOF, introduced in Chapter 5. Therefore, in a sense, separability is more restrictive and less compelling than unchanged-contour independence.

A similar result to Corollary 3.1 can be obtained with separability instead of unchanged-contour independence. As is not surprising from the preceding discussion around Figure 3.4, it requires a minimum of three agents in the population.

Theorem 3.2 *On the domain $\mathcal{E}^3$, if a SOF satisfies* Pareto indifference, nested-contour transfer, *and* separability, *then it satisfies* nested-contour priority.

Proof. The argument relies directly on the reasoning made around Figure 3.4. Let **R** satisfy Pareto indifference, nested-contour transfer, and separability. Let $E = (R_N, \Omega) \in \mathcal{E}^3$, $z_N, z'_N \in X^N$, $j, k \in N$ be such that $z_j \gg z'_j \gg z'_k \gg z_k$, $U(z'_j, R_j) \cap L(z'_k, R_k) = \emptyset$, and for all $i \neq j, k, z_i = z'_i$. Let $\Delta_j = z_j - z'_j$ and $\Delta_k = z'_k - z_k$.

Let $l \in N$, $l \neq j, k$, $R'_l \in \mathcal{R}$, $z_l^1, z_l^2, z_l^3, z_l^4 \in X$, and $m \in \mathbb{Z}_{++}$ be defined in such a way that $z_l^1 I'_l z_l^4$, $z_l^2 I'_l z_l^3$, $z_l^1 = z_l^2 + \frac{\Delta_k}{m}$, $z_l^4 = z_l^3 + \frac{\Delta_j}{m}$, $U(z_l^2, R'_l) \cap L(z'_k, R_k) = \emptyset$, $U(z'_j, R_j) \cap L(z_l^1, R'_l) = \emptyset$, and $z'_j \gg z_l^t \gg z'_k$ for all $t \in \{1, 2, 3, 4\}$. This construction is illustrated in Figure 3.4 with $m = 4$.

Let $E' = \left(\left(R_{N \setminus \{l\}}, R'_l \right), \Omega \right) \in \mathcal{E}$. By nested-contour transfer,

$$\left(z_{N \setminus \{k,l\}}, z_k + \frac{\Delta_k}{m}, z_l^2 \right) \mathbf{R}(E') \left(z_{N \setminus \{l\}}, z_l^1 \right).$$

By Pareto indifference,

$$\left(z_{N \setminus \{k,l\}}, z_k + \frac{\Delta_k}{m}, z_l^3 \right) \mathbf{I}(E') \left(z_{N \setminus \{k,l\}}, z_k + \frac{\Delta_k}{m}, z_l^2 \right).$$

By nested-contour transfer,

$$\left(z_{N \setminus \{j,k,l\}}, z_j - \frac{\Delta_j}{m}, z_k + \frac{\Delta_k}{m}, z_l^4 \right) \mathbf{R}\left(E' \right) \left(z_{N \setminus \{k,l\}}, z_k + \frac{\Delta_k}{m}, z_l^3 \right).$$

[7] See, in particular, Fleming (1952).
[8] Key references are Sen (1970) and d'Aspremont and Gevers (1977).

By Pareto indifference,

$$\left(z_{N\setminus\{j,k,l\}}, z_j - \frac{\Delta_j}{m}, z_k + \frac{\Delta_k}{m}, z_l^1\right) \mathbf{I}\left(E'\right)\left(z_{N\setminus\{j,k,l\}}, z_j - \frac{\Delta_j}{m}, z_k + \frac{\Delta_k}{m}, z_l^4\right).$$

To sum up, using transitivity,

$$\left(z_{N\setminus\{j,k,l\}}, z_j - \frac{\Delta_j}{m}, z_k + \frac{\Delta_k}{m}, z_l^1\right) \mathbf{R}\left(E'\right)\left(z_{N\setminus\{l\}}, z_l^1\right).$$

Repeating the argument m times and using transitivity again,

$$\left(z_{N\setminus\{j,k,l\}}, z_j - \Delta_j, z_k + \Delta_k, z_l^1\right) \mathbf{R}\left(E'\right)\left(z_{N\setminus\{l\}}, z_l^1\right).$$

Because $z_{N\setminus\{j,k,l\}} = z'_{N\setminus\{j,k,l\}}$, $z_j - \Delta_j = z'_j$, $z_k + \Delta_k = z'_k$, one obtains

$$\left(z'_{N\setminus\{l\}}, z_l^1\right) \mathbf{R}\left(E'\right)\left(z_{N\setminus\{l\}}, z_l^1\right).$$

By separability, $z'_N \mathbf{R}(E) z_N$.

Finally, let us check that every axiom is necessary for the conclusion of the theorem. The examples below are defined in the proof of Theorem 3.1.

1. Drop Pareto indifference. Take $\mathbf{R}^{p\text{sum}}$.
2. Drop nested-contour transfer. Take $\mathbf{R}^{\Omega\text{sum}}$.
3. Drop separability. Take $\mathbf{R}^{IL}$. ∎

There is no counterpart of this result for transfer among equals, as one can find SOFs satisfying strong Pareto, transfer among equals, and separability, but not priority among equals.[9]

3.4 FROM EQUAL-SPLIT TRANSFER TO ABSOLUTE PRIORITY

In a similar way as for transfer among equals and nested-contour transfer, we can strengthen the equal-split transfer axiom by requiring that a transfer given to an agent consuming strictly less than an equal split be a social improvement, whatever the amount of resources drawn from a donor who gets strictly more than an equal split (see Figure 3.5).

Axiom 3.6 Equal-Split Priority
For all $E = (R_N, \Omega) \in \mathcal{D}$, and $z_N, z'_N \in X^N$, if there exist $j, k \in N$ such that

$$z_j \gg z'_j \gg \frac{\Omega}{|N|} \gg z'_k \gg z_k$$

and for all $i \neq j, k$, $z_i = z'_i$, then $z'_N \mathbf{R}(E) z_N$.

---

[9] Here is an example. For any economy $E = (R_N, \Omega)$, partition N into $I(E)$ and $J(E)$, where $I(E)$ is the subset of agents with linear preferences and $J(E)$ is the complement. If $I(E) = N$, the SOF evaluates an allocation by the sum $\sum_{i \in N} u_\Omega(z_i, R_i)$. Otherwise, it applies the leximin criterion to the vector $(u_\Omega(z_j, R_j) + \sum_{i \in I(E)} u_\Omega(z_i, R_i))_{j \in J(E)}$.

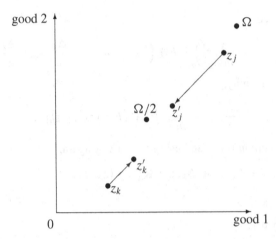

Figure 3.5. Equal-split priority

Theorem 3.3 *On the domain $\mathcal{E}$, if a SOF satisfies* strong Pareto, equal-split transfer, *and* unchanged-contour independence, *then it satisfies* equal-split priority.

The logic of the proof, which is relegated to the appendix, is similar to the proof of Theorem 3.1. However, the constraint that the bundle $\Omega/|N|$ be in between the bundles of the donor and recipient makes a construction as in Figure 3.3 impossible, in general, in one step (the thin indifference curve at z_j^2, z_j^3, in this figure cannot in general be close to the thick indifference curves at z_j^2, z_j^3 when these points are required to dominate $\Omega/|N|$). The argument then requires a few additional steps.

Unchanged-contour independence cannot be replaced by separability in Theorem 3.3, because one can find SOFs satisfying strong Pareto, equal-split transfer, and separability, but not equal-split priority (e.g., utilitarian SOFs that add up utilities computed in such a way that marginal utility for bundles below $\Omega/|N|$ is always greater than some fixed value, whereas marginal utility for bundles above $\Omega/|N|$ is always smaller than this value). There is, however, a similar result involving a stronger separability axiom. This axiom is defined as follows. It states that when an agent has the same bundle in two allocations, the ranking of these two allocations should remain the same if this agent were simply absent from the economy (whereas Ω remains the same). The difference between this axiom and separability is small; in this book, the SOFs that are studied and satisfy the latter also satisfy the former.

Axiom 3.7 Separation
For all $E = (R_N, \Omega) \in \mathcal{D}$ with $|N| \geq 2$, and $z_N, z_N' \in X^N$, if there is $i \in N$ such that $z_i = z_i'$, then

$$z_N \, \mathbf{R}(E) \, z_N' \Leftrightarrow z_{N \setminus \{i\}} \, \mathbf{R}(R_{N \setminus \{i\}}, \Omega) \, z_{N \setminus \{i\}}'.$$

We also need to introduce a replication axiom, requiring that in a replicated economy – that is, an economy obtained by "cloning" each agent a given number of times and multiplying the available resources by the same number – replicated allocations should be ranked exactly as in the initial economy. Some notation is needed to make this statement precise. If r is a positive integer, an economy $E' = (R_{N'}, \Omega')$ is an r-replica of $E = (R_N, \Omega)$ if $\Omega' = r\Omega$ and there exists a mapping $\gamma : N' \to N$ such that for all $i \in N$, $\left| \gamma^{-1}(i) \right| = r$ and for all $j \in \gamma^{-1}(i)$, $R_j = R_i$. This implies, in particular, that $\left| N' \right| = r \left| N \right|$.[10] We use a similar terminology for allocations and for preference profiles. Thus, the allocation $z_{N'} \in X^{N'}$ is an r-replica of z_N if there exists a mapping $\gamma : N' \to N$ such that for all $i \in N$, $\left| \gamma^{-1}(i) \right| = r$ and for all $j \in \gamma^{-1}(i)$, $z'_j = z_i$; the profile $R_{N'}$ is an r-replica of R_N if there exists a mapping $\gamma : N' \to N$ such that for all $i \in N$, $\left| \gamma^{-1}(i) \right| = r$ and for all $j \in \gamma^{-1}(i)$, $R'_j = R_i$.

Axiom 3.8 Replication
For all $E = (R_N, \Omega) \in \mathcal{D}$, $z_N, z'_N \in X^N$, and $r \in \mathbb{Z}_{++}$, if $E' = \left(R_{N'}, \Omega' \right) \in \mathcal{D}$ is an r-replica of E, then $z_N \mathbf{R}(E) z'_N \Leftrightarrow z_{N'} \mathbf{R}\left(E'\right) z'_{N'}$.

Theorem 3.4 *On the domain $\mathcal{E}$, if a SOF satisfies* Pareto indifference, equal-split transfer, separation, *and* replication, *then it satisfies* equal-split priority.

The basic idea of the proof, provided in the appendix, is the same as for Theorem 3.2, but there is a difficulty owing to the fact that the added agent (agent l in the proof of Theorem 3.2) must now be below $\Omega/|N|$ when he or she receives a transfer from agent j, and above $\Omega/|N|$ when he or she donates to agent k. It is impossible, with monotonic preferences, to move agent l from one situation to the other by Pareto indifference. This is why replication comes into play. By Lemma 4.1 proved in Chapter 4, separation and replication together imply that the SOF is insensitive to multiplying Ω by a positive rational number q. Then one can locate $q\Omega$ wherever suitable to make the application of equal-split transfer legitimate.

There is no result of this sort with proportional-allocations transfer, as this axiom is satisfied by $\mathbf{R}^{\Omega \text{Nash}}$, which also satisfies strong Pareto, unchanged-contour independence, separation, and replication. The fact that proportional-allocations transfer does not imply a strong inequality aversion can be understood by noting that it has a purely one-dimensional content, applying to allocations with bundles on a given line. The results of this chapter rely on the multidimensional setting in which the other transfer axioms operate.

---

[10] A permutation of the agents' preferences creates a 1-replica of the economy. The replication axiom therefore implies anonymity. It is possible to define weaker forms of the replication requirement that do not imply anonymity. Nothing important depends on this in our analysis.

3.5 CONCLUSION

The main conclusion of this chapter is that as soon as one accepts axioms limiting the information that can be used to compare two allocations, such as unchanged-contour independence or separability, one is led to an extreme form of egalitarianism. Increasing the amount of resources allocated to the worst-off is always good for society, no matter how much is taken from the better-off agents. This conclusion will be reproduced in the subsequent chapters. Almost all the SOFs we will define and characterize are of the maximin or leximin type. As explained in this chapter, this results from our willingness to take agents' preferences into account and at the same time to seek some mild degree of resource equality.

This confirms and generalizes the observation made at the end of the previous chapter. The resource utilization SOF $\mathbf{R}^{RU}$ involves the summation operator and is concerned only with efficiency. The Ω-equivalent Nash SOF $\mathbf{R}^{\Omega\text{Nash}}$ relies on the product but fails to satisfy the most basic equity axioms. In this first series of examples, only the Ω-equivalent leximin SOF $\mathbf{R}^{\Omega\text{lex}}$ combines efficiency and equity concerns in a satisfactory way. We now know that, in general, studying fairness in (multidimensional) models in which both resources and preferences matter yields social criteria that are necessarily of the maximin or leximin type.[11]

Not all results in this book, however, will deal with such extreme criteria; we will see that certain "moderate" SOFs, such as $\mathbf{R}^{\Omega\text{Nash}}$, have interesting properties in particular contexts.

More important, however, we will also see that the class of leximin SOFs contain a great variety of social criteria, because there remains a wide array of possibilities about the way in which individual indices of resources are computed. Our approach appears sufficiently flexible to incorporate various notions of needs, rights, and personal responsibilities and liabilities, which may substantially affect the distributional conclusions based on such criteria. Under the appropriate assumptions about how individual situations are evaluated, it is even possible for a maximin SOF to advocate laisse-faire policies (see, in particular, Chapters 7 and 10).

Therefore we do not think that the apparently restrictive conclusions of these first two chapters are bad news. It is, on the contrary, quite helpful to know the answer to the question, "How should individual indices be aggregated?" The crucial question that remains to be addressed, and on which policy conclusions will dramatically depend, is, "How should individual indices be defined?"

It is also worth noting that SOFs that focus on the worst-off are easier to implement under incentive constraints (the so-called second-best context), as it will be illustrated in Chapters 5, 8, 9 and 11, without leading to extreme conclusions (in Chapter 11, for instance, we show that even a moderate amount

---

[11] In the one-dimensional model, all degrees of inequality aversion are compatible with the Pigou–Dalton transfer principle. See Chakravarty (1990) for a general presentation.

of redistribution is compatible with leximin SOFs). Indeed, with such SOFs, the policymaker must only forecast the impact of redistribution on the worst-off and need not evaluate the global impact of policy on the whole distribution, except to check whether the policy is feasible.

CHAPTER 4

The Informational Basis of Social Orderings

4.1 INTRODUCTION

This chapter seeks to clarify some features of social ordering functions that may appear intriguing to the specialist of social choice theory or of fair allocation theory. The reader who is more interested in the applications of the approach may skip this chapter. Three issues are examined, which all have to do with the informational basis of SOFs.

The first issue is connected to the fact that we define SOFs as functions $\mathbf{R}(R_N, \Omega)$ instead of functions $\mathbf{R}(R_N)$. It may appear strange that the ranking of allocations should vary as a function of the available resources, as if an ethical objective could depend on feasibility constraints. Section 4.2 explains why this dependence is important for obtaining some results, although it is not essential to the notion of the SOF in general.

Section 4.3 examines how our theory relates to the theory of social choice in economic environments. We already mentioned in Chapter 3 that our SOFs satisfy a weaker axiom of independence – namely, unchanged-contour independence – than Arrow's famous independence of irrelevant alternatives. Relaxing Arrow's independence axiom is the key ingredient that enables us to obtain possibility results. In Section 4.3 we examine how the possibility results are affected when one varies the quantity of information that is used, through various axioms of independence.

Finally, Section 4.4 compares the theory of SOFs to the theory of fair allocation, in which allocation rules, instead of SOFs, are the subject. We argue that the difference between the two objects is thinner than usually thought, and that the informational basis is similar in both theories.

4.2 THE FEASIBLE SET

Many of the SOFs studied in this book depend on Ω, and therefore depend on (some of) the feasibility constraints bearing on the economy. This may seem somehow in contradiction with the celebrated Arrow program of social choice theory, which allegedly consists of two separate steps. The first step constructs a social preference ordering for every profile of individual preference orderings. The second step derives a social choice function that selects a subset of alternatives in terms of the optimization of social preferences within every possible set of feasible social alternatives. The first step, then, is meant to determine the uniform social objective *before* the set of feasible social alternatives is revealed. The second step is meant to determine the rational social choice *after* the set of feasible social alternatives is revealed.

In Section 5.4, second-best applications are presented, in which the best allocations are determined under feasibility and incentive-compatibility constraints. Such constraints delineate a smaller set of attainable allocations than the feasible set $Z(E)$, and the precise set of attainable allocations may vary depending on preferences and endowments. These second-best applications partly respect the Arrow program because the same SOF is applied independently of the particular set of attainable allocations that is at hand.

However, a more purist application of the Arrow program would exclude any consideration of feasibility from the definition of social preferences. It seems to us that this purist approach can be accommodated in our framework simply by requiring SOFs to satisfy the following axiom, which says that social ordering should depend only on R_N and not on anything else, specifically Ω. It is called *independence of the feasible set*:[1]

Axiom 4.1 Independence of the Feasible Set
For all $E = (R_N, \Omega)$, $E' = (R_N, \Omega') \in \mathcal{D}$, and $z_N, z'_N \in X^N$, $z_N \, \mathbf{R}(E) \, z'_N \Leftrightarrow z_N \, \mathbf{R}(E') \, z'_N$.

The analysis of Chapter 2 showed that egalitarian axioms formulated without restriction to particular regions of the consumption set conflict with the Pareto principle. Some of the restrictions, such as those referring to equal split, involve the social endowment Ω. This observation suggests that imposing independence of the feasible set entails some costs with respect to the fairness properties of the SOF – in particular, those relating to equal split. For instance, none of the three SOFs of Table 2.1 satisfies independence of the feasible set.

This does not mean that a SOF satisfying independence of the feasible set cannot have some good properties. For instance, consider the Ω_0-equivalent leximin SOF, which relies on a fixed reference bundle Ω_0 for any economy. This SOF satisfies strong Pareto, nested-contour priority (and therefore nested-contour transfer, transfer among equals, and priority among equals) and the secondary axioms (unchanged-contour independence, separation and replication). It does not, however, satisfy the equal-split axioms and related axioms bearing on proportional allocations. Actually, we have the following impossibility.

---

[1] Note that Ω may not be the only variable that directly determines the actual feasible agenda in some contexts (e.g., incentive-compatibility constraints or pure political constraints may also play a role).

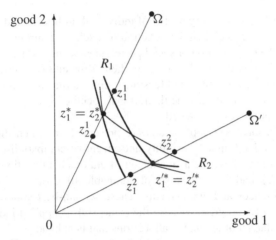

Figure 4.1. Proof of Theorem 4.1

Theorem 4.1 *On the domain $\mathcal{E}$, no SOF satisfies* weak Pareto, equal-split selection, *and* independence of the feasible set.

Proof. Let $N = \{1, 2\}$ and $E = (R_N, \Omega)$, $E' = (R_N, \Omega') \in \mathcal{E}$. This is illustrated in Figure 4.1, which displays two allocations z_N^1, z_N^2, in addition to two equal-split allocations $z_N^*, z_N'^*$, which are efficient in E and E', respectively. By independence of the feasible set, there is a social ordering R over X^N such that $R = \mathbf{R}(E) = \mathbf{R}(E')$. By equal-split selection, $z_N^* \, R \, z_N^1$. By weak Pareto, $z_N^2 \, R \, z_N^*$. By equal-split selection, $z_N'^* \, R \, z_N^2$. By transitivity, $z_N'^* \, R \, z_N^1$. However, by weak Pareto, $z_N^1 \, P \, z_N'^*$, which is a contradiction. ∎

By the same argument, one shows that no SOF can satisfy weak Pareto, independence of the feasible set, and select egalitarian Walrasian allocations (in the sense that $\max|_{\mathbf{R}(E)} Z(E) \cap S^{EW}(E) \neq \emptyset$) in every economy $E \in \mathcal{E}$. The same holds about egalitarian-equivalent allocations $S^{EE}(E)$.[2]

Such impossibilities suggest that independence of the feasible set is not so uncontroversial as it appears at first glance. In our framework, we restrict attention to $\Omega \in \mathbb{R}_{++}^{\ell}$ with positive quantities of all goods, but it may enhance our intuitive understanding of this issue to momentarily extend the analysis to the case in which some goods may be absent. Consider the problem of distributing bread and water to a given population. When there is no water, a particular ranking of allocations of bread will be formed. According to independence of the feasible set, this ranking should be retained even if water becomes available. This is questionable, for the following reason. In absence of water, presumably some simple egalitarian ranking would seem reasonable for the allocation of bread. When water is available, however, the allocation of bread could

---

[2] See Fleurbaey and Maniquet (2008b).

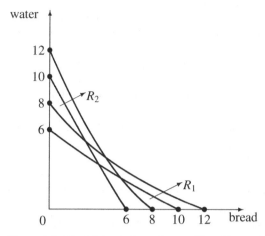

Figure 4.2. Combining independence of feasible set with Pareto

legitimately take account of how much individuals are willing to substitute water for bread.

The problem becomes acute, indeed, under Pareto axioms. For simplicity, consider a population with two agents, with allocations and preferences illustrated in Figure 4.2. Assume for instance that, for the allocations of bread (good 1) only, in absence of water, giving 10 to agent 1 and 8 to agent 2 is better than giving 12 and 6, respectively:

$$((10, 0), (8, 0)) \; \mathbf{R}(E) \; ((12, 0), (6, 0)). \tag{4.1}$$

Now suppose that individual preferences are such that

$$(10, 0) \; I_1 \; (0, 6), \quad (12, 0) \; I_1 \; (0, 8),$$

$$(6, 0) \; I_2 \; (0, 10), \quad (8, 0) \; I_2 \; (0, 12).$$

By independence of the feasible set, the preceding ranking of allocations of bread should be retained even when water is available. Now, in view of the agents' preferences, Pareto indifference and (4.1) entail that

$$((0, 6), (0, 12)) \; \mathbf{R}(E) \; ((0, 8), (0, 10)).$$

By independence of the feasible set, this ranking of allocations of water should be retained even when there is no bread.

This shows that independence of the feasible set is very restrictive in such a context. It prevents social preferences from taking account of the relative scarcity of goods, and from focusing on the appropriate parts of individual preferences. For instance, if one thinks that an egalitarian Walrasian allocation is a good social objective, it makes little sense to look for social preferences that are independent of the relative scarcity of goods, as individual situations must be evaluated in terms of budgets, and the relative prices of goods will depend on total supply.

With this argument, we believe we have shown that it is reasonable to make recommendations that depend on the total endowment.[3] Formally, this means that a change in total endowment may affect the social ranking of allocations. We do not believe, however, that every ingredient that affects the set of feasible allocations should be allowed to affect the social ranking. Let us consider information constraints. In the income taxation problem, for instance, labor time is sometimes observable and sometimes not. Making the social ranking depend on these constraints means, in that case, that the social ranking to maximize may be different, should labor time be observable or not. That does not sound legitimate to us.

Even as far as Ω is concerned, one may argue that the direction of Ω is relevant, but its size is not. Only the relative scarcity of the goods matters. We must emphasize, in this respect, that the SOFs studied in this book are generally insensitive to multiplication of Ω by a scalar. Let us encapsulate this idea as an axiom stating that a proportional expansion of the social endowment has no effect on the ranking of any pair of allocations.

Axiom 4.2 Independence of Proportional Expansion
For all $E = (R_N, \Omega)$, $E' = (R_N, \lambda\Omega) \in \mathcal{D}$ *with* $\lambda > 1$, *and* $z_N, z'_N \in X^N$,
$z_N \, \mathbf{R}(E) \, z'_N \Leftrightarrow z_N \, \mathbf{R}(E') \, z'_N$.

In particular, the social orderings obtained with any of the SOFs from Table 2.1 satisfy this axiom. According to the preceding discussion, it is not the feasibility set per se that appears relevant, but the relative scarcity of goods as reflected in the direction of Ω. The size of Ω itself does not seem to matter so much in this argument.

The idea that the SOF should be insensitive to multiplications of Ω by a scalar can actually be related to some of the axioms already introduced – namely, separation and replication. These axioms together imply that the social ordering should be independent of multiplication of Ω by a rational number.

Lemma 4.1 *If a SOF* $\mathbf{R}$ *satifies separation and replication, then for all* $E = (R_N, \Omega) \in \mathcal{E}$ *and all rational numbers* $q \in \mathbb{Q}_{++}$,

$$\mathbf{R}(R_N, q\Omega) = \mathbf{R}(E).$$

Proof. Let $\mathbf{R}$ be defined on $\mathcal{E}$.

Step 1. First we claim that if $\mathbf{R}$ satisfies separation and replication, it satisfies the following property: For all $E = (R_N, \Omega) \in \mathcal{E}$, and $z_N, z'_N \in X^N, r \in \mathbb{Z}_{++}$, if $E' = (R_{N'}, \Omega) \in \mathcal{E}$ is such that $R_{N'}$ is an r-replica of R_N, then

$$z_N \mathbf{R}(E) z'_N \Leftrightarrow z_{N'} \mathbf{R}(E') z'_{N'}.$$

---
[3] We come back on that issue in Section 7.3.

Let $E = (R_N, \Omega) \in \mathcal{E}$. Let $R_{N'}$ be an r-replica of R_N. Consequently, $R_{N'}$ can be decomposed into $(R_{N^1}, R_{N^2}, \ldots, R_{N^r})$ such that R_{N^s} is a 1-replica of R_N for each $s \in \{1, \ldots, r\}$. By replication,

$$z_N \mathbf{R}(E) z'_N \Leftrightarrow z_{N^s} \mathbf{R}(R_{N^s}, \Omega) z'_{N^s}.$$

Let $z^0_{N'}, z^1_{N'}, z^2_{N'}, \ldots, z^r_{N'} \in X^{N'}$ be defined by: $z^0_{N^s} = z_N$ for all $s \in \{1, \ldots, r\}$, and $z^t_{N^s} = z'_N$ if $s \leq t$ whereas $z^t_{N^s} = z_N$ if $s > t$, for $t \in \{1, \ldots, r\}$. That is,

$$z^0_{N'} = (z_N, \ldots, z_N),$$

$$z^1_{N'} = (z'_N, z_N, \ldots, z_N),$$

$$z^2_{N'} = (z'_N, z'_N, z_N, \ldots, z_N),$$

$$\vdots$$

$$z^r_{N'} = (z'_N, \ldots, z'_N).$$

One has $z^0_{N'} = z_{N'}$ and $z^r_{N'} = z'_{N'}$. By separation, for all $s \in \{1, \ldots, r\}$,

$$z^{s-1}_{N'} \mathbf{R}(E') z^s_{N'} \Leftrightarrow z_{N^s} \mathbf{R}(R_{N^s}, \Omega) z'_{N^s}.$$

Applying this last relationship $s - t$ times, we get, for $0 \leq t < s \leq r$,

$$z^t_{N'} \mathbf{R}(E') z^s_{N'} \Leftrightarrow z_N \mathbf{R}(E) z'_N.$$

In particular, for $t = 0$ and $s = r$, we get the desired result.

Step 2. To complete the proof, let $E = (R_N, \Omega) \in \mathcal{E}$. Let $z_N, z'_N \in X^N$, and $p, q \in \mathbb{Z}_{++}$. Let R_{N^p} be a p-replica of R_N. By replication,

$$z_N \mathbf{R}(E) z'_N \Leftrightarrow z_{N^p} \mathbf{R}(R_{N^p}, p\Omega) z'_{N^p}.$$

By Step 1,

$$z_{N^p} \mathbf{R}(R_{N^p}, p\Omega) z'_{N^p} \Leftrightarrow z_N \mathbf{R}(R_N, p\Omega) z'_N.$$

Let R_{N^q} be a q-replica of R_N. By the previous claim, again,

$$z_N \mathbf{R}(R_N, p\Omega) z'_N \Leftrightarrow z_{N^q} \mathbf{R}(R_{N^q}, p\Omega) z'_{N^q}.$$

Finally, by replication,

$$z_{N^q} \mathbf{R}(R_{N^q}, p\Omega) z'_{N^q} \Leftrightarrow z_N \mathbf{R}\left(R_N, \frac{p}{q}\Omega\right) z'_N.$$

Gathering the relationships, we obtain the desired outcome. ∎

We conclude this section with a discussion of our general approach, in relation to feasibility. As explained in Chapter 1, the social orderings we study rank all allocations in X^N – the feasible as well as the infeasible. This is justified because the relevant feasibility constraints (resources, incentives, politics) may vary depending on the context, and, in particular, this allows us to formulate and discuss the independence of the feasible set axiom and similar axioms in a convenient way.

It is possible, however, to modify the framework a little and restrict the social orderings to bear only on $Z(E)$, which is, in any given economy E, and more precisely for any given Ω, the greatest feasible set under any circumstance. There is not much to be gained by this restriction, as there is no difficulty in defining social orderings that rank infeasible allocations as well. From the technical point of view, however, this restriction is interesting because it reduces the set of allocations that can be constructed in the proofs of characterization theorems. This raises the (not purely technical) question of whether other kinds of SOFs would then become admissible.

We doubt that this is the case. Indeed, even if a SOF ranks only allocations in $Z(E)$, one can formulate a variant of independence of proportional expansion applying to feasible allocations and stating that the multiplication of Ω by a scalar greater than 1 should not alter the initial ranking over the set $Z(E)$. If this axiom is added to the axioms considered so far, then all the allocations considered in the proofs of our results can be rendered feasible by multiplying Ω by a sufficiently large λ. Then all the proofs go through and the results remain valid. This implies that the new SOFs obtained in a framework in which only $Z(E)$ is ordered would violate this axiom and be very sensitive not only to the direction of Ω, but also to its size. It is not easy to find arguments that would justify this.

It is worth noting another interesting property of $\mathbf{R}^{\Omega\text{lex}}$. To rank two allocations z, z' from $Z(E)$, one needs to know only the Ω-equivalent utilities – that is, the bundles $\lambda_i \Omega$ and $\lambda_i' \Omega$ such that for all i, $\lambda_i \Omega \ I_i \ z_i$ and $\lambda_i' \Omega \ I_i \ z_i'$. When $z, z' \in Z(E)$, necessarily $\lambda_i, \lambda_i' \leq 1$, implying that for all i, $\lambda_i \Omega$ and $\lambda_i' \Omega$ are "feasible" in the sense that they belong to feasible allocations (even if the allocations $(\lambda_i \Omega)_{i \in N}$ and $(\lambda_i' \Omega)_{i \in N}$ themselves may not be feasible). As a consequence, to rank z, z', it is then sufficient to know individual preferences over feasible bundles. The $\mathbf{R}^{\Omega\text{lex}}$ SOF is independent of individual preferences over infeasible bundles. This property is also satisfied by $\mathbf{R}^{\Omega\text{Nash}}$ and $\mathbf{R}^{RU}$ but is not satisfied by all the SOFs studied in this book – in particular, it is not satisfied by the Walrasian SOF introduced in the next chapter. An axiom of independence of preferences over infeasible bundles is introduced in Section 6.5, and related ideas of independence of preferences are discussed in more detail in the next section.

4.3 INFORMATION ON PREFERENCES

In Chapter 3, we introduced unchanged-contour independence, an axiom limiting the relevant information about preferences to the indifference sets at the allocations under consideration. The main SOFs studied in this book satisfy this axiom, which therefore appears perfectly compatible with efficiency and with fairness requirements. This is a good property because, as was explained in Section 3.2, it substantially simplifies the evaluation of allocations and because it goes well with the idea that individual preferences are a personal responsibility and should not be relied on more than needed.

Can we use even less information about preferences without sacrificing too much about efficiency or fairness? The theory of social choice famously started with the much stronger Arrow independence, as recalled in Section 1.3. Arrow's theorem proves that this condition forces one to either abandon efficiency (weak Pareto) or to abandon impartiality between agents.[4] If one abandons efficiency, one can, for instance, use an index U_0, independent of R_N, in a SOF $\mathbf{R}$ defined by:

$$z_N \, \mathbf{R}(E) \, z_N' \Leftrightarrow (U_0(z_i))_{i \in N} \geq_{lex} \left(U_0(z_i') \right)_{i \in N} .$$

If one keeps weak Pareto, the theorem says that one must drop impartiality in a severe way, because there must be a *dictator* – namely, an agent i_0 such that for all $E = (R_N, \Omega) \in \mathcal{D}$, and $z_N, z_N' \in (X \setminus \{0\})^N$, one has $z_N \, \mathbf{P}(E) \, z_N'$ whenever $z_{i_0} \, P_{i_0} \, z_{i_0}'$. A proof of this statement for the present model can be found in Bordes and Le Breton (1989). For instance, a SOF $\mathbf{R}$ satisfying Arrow independence and strong Pareto can be defined in the following way:

$$z_N \, \mathbf{I}(E) \, z_N' \Leftrightarrow z_i \, I_i \, z_i' \text{ for all } i \in N,$$

$$z_N \, \mathbf{P}(E) \, z_N' \Leftrightarrow z_i \, P_i \, z_i' \text{ for some } i \in N \text{ and } z_j \, I_j \, z_j' \text{ for all } j < i.$$

In this SOF, there is a sequence of dictators such that agent i's strict preference decides only when the agents of higher authority (taken to be $j < i$ in this example) are indifferent.

It is transparent that Arrow independence is logically stronger than unchanged-contour independence, and Arrow's theorem shows that it is too strong because it requires too much sacrifice either on efficiency or on fairness. It is, in fact, very intuitive that this condition is not compelling. For instance, in axioms such as transfer among equals or nested-contour transfer, one needs to check that indifference curves do not cross for the transfer to be recommended, and one cannot do so if the only information usable, as required by Arrow independence, is that the recipient would like to obtain the transfer, whereas the donor would rather not donate.

At this stage, a natural question is what happens when the information about preferences that can be used in the evaluation is intermediate between pairwise preferences (as with Arrow independence) and indifference sets (as with unchanged-contour independence). Whereas under Arrow independence the information that can be used to rank two allocations involves preferences over two bundles for every agent (one bundle for each allocation), the information that is actually used by a SOF such as $\mathbf{R}^{\Omega \text{lex}}$ involves only four bundles (two for each allocation, the actual bundle and the "equivalent" bundle). This is much less than the quantity of information allowed by unchanged-contour

---

[4] See Le Breton and Weymark (2002) for a survey of Arrovian social choice theory in economic domains.

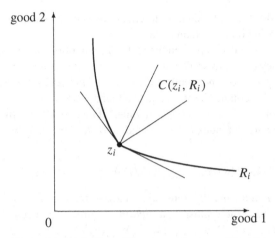

Figure 4.3. Definition of the supporting cone $C(z_i, R_i)$

independence. Therefore the key issue is not the quantity of information, but where in the consumption set this information comes from. This point is clearly illustrated in the following paragraphs.

Starting from Arrow independence, let us introduce additional information that is "local"– that is, close to the actual bundles consumed. A first step consists of introducing information about marginal rates of substitution. As we do not assume differentiability, we will rely on supporting cones defined as follows. $C(z_i, R_i)$ is the cone of price vectors that support the upper contour set for R_i at z_i:

$$C(z_i, R_i) = \{p \in \mathbb{R}^\ell \mid \forall q \in X, \ pq = pz_i \Rightarrow z_i \, R_i \, q\}.$$

This definition is illustrated in Figure 4.3. As preferences $R_i \in \mathcal{R}$ are assumed to be monotonic, one has $C(z_i, R_i) \subseteq \mathbb{R}^\ell_+$. The following axiom says that the ranking of two allocations should not be affected by a change of individual preferences if individual preferences on the corresponding bundles remain unchanged, with unchanged supporting cones (in particular, with unchanged marginal rates of substitution for the case of differentiable preferences).

Axiom 4.3 Unchanged-Cone Independence
For all $E = (R_N, \Omega)$, $E' = (R'_N, \Omega) \in \mathcal{D}$, and $z_N, z'_N \in X^N$, if for all $i \in N$, R_i and R'_i agree on $\{z_i, z'_i\}$ and

$$C(z_i, R_i) = C(z_i, R'_i),$$
$$C(z'_i, R_i) = C(z'_i, R'_i),$$

then $z_N \, \mathbf{R}(E) \, z'_N \Leftrightarrow z_N \, \mathbf{R}(E') \, z'_N$.

As it turns out, this condition entails the same dictatorial result as Arrow independence. The proof of this is tedious,[5] but we can illustrate the problem by focusing on anonymity, which is a stronger requirement of impartiality than nondictatorship, but still very compelling. It requires the social ordering to be invariant when preferences and bundles are permuted across agents. Let $z_{\pi(N)}$ denote $\left(z_{\pi(i)}\right)_{i \in N}$.

Axiom 4.4 Anonymity
For all $E = (R_N, \Omega) \in \mathcal{D}$, all $z_N, z'_N \in X^N$, all permutations $\pi : N \to N$, $z_N \mathbf{R}(E) z'_N \Leftrightarrow z_{\pi(N)} \mathbf{R}(R_{\pi(N)}, \Omega) z'_{\pi(N)}$.

The proof that anonymity and weak Pareto are incompatible under some independence condition has a typical structure. First, observe that anonymity implies the following axiom, saying that permuting the bundles of two agents with identical preferences yields a new allocation that is just as good as the initial allocation.

Axiom 4.5 Anonymity among Equals
For all $E = (R_N, \Omega) \in \mathcal{D}$, all $j, k \in N$, and $z_N, z'_N \in X^N$, if $R_j = R_k$ and $(z'_j, z'_k) = (z_k, z_j)$ while $z'_i = z_i$ for all $i \neq j, k$, then $z_N \mathbf{I}(E) z'_N$.

Suppose one can find a two-agent economy $E = ((R_1, R_2), \Omega)$ and an allocation $z_N = (a, b)$ with $a > b$ such that given the information about preferences at (a, b) and at (b, a) that can be used under the independence axiom, one could assume as well that the agents have the same preferences. More precisely, this sentence means the following: there is R_0 such that, under the independence axiom, $\mathbf{R}(E)$ and $\mathbf{R}((R_0, R_0), \Omega)$ must agree on how to rank (a, b) and (b, a). Observe that as $a > b$, individual preferences over such bundles are always the same when they are strictly monotonic. Therefore, when preferences are strictly monotonic, applying the independence condition simply requires checking some extra condition such as, in the case of unchanged-cone independence, equality of supporting cones at a and b for R_1, R_2, and R_0. In the case of Arrow independence, no extra condition needs to be checked.

By anonymity among equals, $(a, b) \mathbf{I}((R_0, R_0), \Omega) (b, a)$. Therefore, by independence, $(a, b) \mathbf{I}(E) (b, a)$.

Introduce another allocation $z'_N = (a', b')$, in some other region of X, such that $a' \gg b'$ and, again, such that given the information about preferences at (a', b') and at (b', a') that can be used under the independence axiom, one could assume as well that the agents have the same preferences. By the same reasoning as done previously, this implies that $(a', b') \mathbf{I}(E) (b', a')$.

The reason z'_N was said to belong to some other region of X is that one needs to assume the following pattern of preferences: $a' P_1 a P_1 b P_1 b'$ and $a P_2 a' P_2 b' P_2 b$. This requires that there is no domination between bundles of

---

[5] See Fleurbaey et al. (2005a).

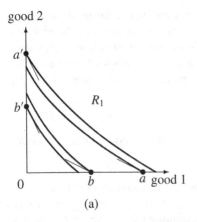
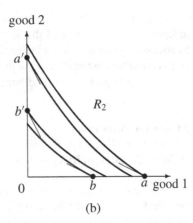

Figure 4.4. Individual preferences

z_N and bundles of z'_N. Under this preference profile, weak Pareto implies that $(a', b') \mathbf{P}(E)(a, b)$ and $(b, a) \mathbf{P}(E)(b', a')$. Recapitulating, one has

$$(a, b) \mathbf{I}(E)(b, a) \mathbf{P}(E)(b', a') \mathbf{I}(E)(a', b') \mathbf{P}(E)(a, b),$$

which is impossible.

Figure 4.4 illustrates a possible profile of preferences that produces this outcome when unchanged-cone independence (this also works for Arrow independence) is considered and requires equal supporting cones between R_1 and R_2 at each of the four bundles. Let us write down the result.

Theorem 4.2 *On the domain $\mathcal{E}$, no SOF satisfies* weak Pareto, anonymity, *and* unchanged-cone independence.

It is transparent that the same impossibility result would be obtained with an even weaker independence condition requiring to have R_N and R'_N coincide on some vicinity of fixed size surrounding the bundles; that is,

$$V_\varepsilon(x) = \{q \in X \mid \|q - x\| \leq \varepsilon\},$$

where $\|\cdot\|$ denotes the Euclidean norm and $\varepsilon > 0$.[6] The bundles a, b, a', b' must then be located sufficiently far from one another so the regions $V_\varepsilon(a)$, $V_\varepsilon(b)$, $V_\varepsilon(a')$, $V_\varepsilon(b')$ do not overlap and contain portions of indifference sets that can be connected in various ways to have the pattern of preferences required for the proof. This new independence condition is not logically stronger than unchanged-contour independence because it involves information about other indifference sets than the indifference sets containing the four bundles.

Another direction of weakening Arrow independence is obtained by considering the sets of allocations that one can obtain from the allocations by certain operations. Two examples will be presented here. The first one is reminiscent of

---

[6] Although Arrow's dictatorship result is preserved with unchanged-cone independence, it no longer holds true for this new axiom. See Fleurbaey et al. (2005a) for details.

the condition mentioned at the end of the previous section, referring to feasible bundles. For a given pair of allocations z_N, z'_N, let $F(z_N, z'_N)$ denote the set of bundles that can be obtained from resources used in z_N or z'_N. In the following expression, $a \vee b = (\max\{a_k, b_k\})_k$.

$$F(z_N, z'_N) = \left\{ q \in X \mid q \leq \sum_{i \in N} z_i \vee \sum_{i \in N} z'_i \right\}.$$

To fix ideas, let us write down the corresponding axiom, which says that the ranking of two allocations is unchanged when individual preferences remain unchanged over all bundles that could be distributed to an individual with resources sufficient to make both z_N and z'_N feasible.

Axiom 4.6 Unchanged-F-Set Independence
For all $E = (R_N, \Omega)$, $E' = (R'_N, \Omega) \in \mathcal{D}$, *and* $z_N, z'_N \in X^N$, *if for all* $i \in N$, R_i *and* R'_i *agree on* $F(z_N, z'_N)$, *then* $z_N \, \mathbf{R}(E) \, z'_N \Leftrightarrow z_N \, \mathbf{R}(E') \, z'_N$.

This axiom is not strictly weaker than the previous ones because information about supporting cones or vicinities may involve bundles that do not belong to $F(z_N, z'_N)$. Nonetheless it should seem rather weak because it involves potentially large sets over which information about preferences is relevant. As a matter of fact, the dictatorship result still holds with this axiom. Observe that Figure 4.4 also illustrates how to apply this axiom in a very simple way to prove a variant of Theorem 4.2: when (a, b), and therefore (b, a), belong to an axis, the feasible bundles involve only one good.

An even weaker axiom consists of considering the whole subspace of bundles using the same commodities as z_N and z'_N. Let

$$S(z_N, z'_N) = \left\{ q \in X \mid q_k = 0 \text{ if } \sum_{i \in N} z_{ik} + \sum_{i \in N} z'_{ik} = 0 \right\}.$$

Axiom 4.7 Unchanged-Subspace Independence
For all $E = (R_N, \Omega)$, $E' = (R'_N, \Omega) \in \mathcal{D}$, *and* $z_N, z'_N \in X^N$, *if for all* $i \in N$, R_i *and* R'_i *agree on* $S(z_N, z'_N)$, *then* $z_N \, \mathbf{R}(E) \, z'_N \Leftrightarrow z_N \, \mathbf{R}(E') \, z'_N$.

This axiom is quite natural: it requires ignoring individual preferences over commodities that are not used in z_N, z'_N to rank these two allocations. Arrow himself, trying to defend Arrow independence, ended up defending something that is closer to unchanged-subspace independence than to Arrow independence:

> Suppose that there are just two commodities, bread and wine. A distribution, deemed equitable by all, is arranged, with the wine-lovers getting more wine and less bread than the abstainers. Suppose now that all the wine is destroyed. Are the wine-lovers entitled, because of that fact, to more than an equal share of bread? The answer is, of course, a value judgment. My own feeling is that tastes for unattainable alternatives should have nothing to do with the decision among the attainable ones; desires in conflict with reality are not entitled to consideration. (1963, p. 73)

With this axiom, the dictatorship result no longer holds, but Theorem 4.2 is immediately extended, and once again Figure 4.4 provides the relevant illustration, with the two axes playing the role of subspaces.

In these cases, when the dictatorship implication no longer holds, the SOFs that satisfy the properties are still substantially dictatorial. This can be viewed when one defines a dictator as follows: For a given population N, agent $i \in N$ is a *dictator on* $(\mathcal{D}, Y)$ if for all $R_N \in \mathcal{D}$, all $z_N, z'_N \in Y$, $z_N \, \mathbf{P}(E) \, z'_N$ whenever $z_i \, P_i \, z'_i$. With this definition, the larger $\mathcal{D}$ and Y for a given dictator, the more dictatorial the rule. For instance, letting $\mathcal{E}^N$ denote the subset of $\mathcal{E}$ corresponding to population N, weak Pareto and Arrow independence do not imply the existence of a dictator on $\left(\mathcal{E}^N, X^N\right)$ but only on $\left(\mathcal{E}^N, (X \setminus \{0\})^N\right)$.[7]

Let a subset of commodities $K \subseteq \{1, \dots, \ell\}$ be called sufficient for R_i if for $x_i \in X$, there is $y_i \in X$ such that $y_{ik} = 0$ for all $k \notin K$ and $y_i \, R_i \, x_i$. In other words, K is sufficient if the agent can always reach any arbitrarily high level of satisfaction with the consumption of commodities from K only. Let $\mathcal{R}^*$ denote the subset of $\mathcal{R}$ containing strictly monotonic preferences and $\mathcal{E}^*$, $\mathcal{E}^{*N}$ the corresponding subdomains. Fix the population N (with $|N| \geq 2$) and let $\mathcal{D}^*_N$ denote the set of preference profiles for which a strict subset of $\{1, \dots, \ell\}$ (possibly specific to the profile) is sufficient for all $i \in N$, and $\overline{Y}_N$ denotes the set of allocations that do not use all commodities:

$$\mathcal{D}^*_N = \left\{ R_N \in \left(\mathcal{R}^*\right)^N \mid \exists K \subsetneq \{1, \dots, \ell\}, \forall i \in N, \ K \text{ is sufficient} \right\},$$

$$\overline{Y}_N = \left\{ z_N \in X^N \mid \sum_i z_i \notin \mathbb{R}^\ell_{++} \right\}.$$

On Figure 4.4, the preferences could be such that every commodity is sufficient, because the indifference curves meet each axis, and the allocations under consideration do not use all commodities.

Fleurbaey and Tadenuma (2007, Theorem 1) give the following result showing that even though there is no dictator on $\left(\mathcal{E}^N, (X \setminus \{0\})^N\right)$, there is still a lot of dictatorship under unchanged-subspace independence.

Theorem 4.3 *If a SOF defined on $\mathcal{E}^*$ satisfies weak Pareto and unchanged-subspace independence, then for all N with $|N| \geq 2$ there is $i \in N$ who is a dictator on $\left(\mathcal{D}^*_N, (X \setminus \{0\})^N\right)$ and on $\left(\mathcal{E}^{*N}, \overline{Y}_N\right)$.*

A similar result relative to independence defined with respect to vicinities around the bundles has yet to be established.

The negative results in this section all have a common feature. They involve an independence axiom that forces the evaluation to rely only on information about preferences that is local in a certain sense. This is quite clear for Arrow

---

[7] Consider the SOF such that for every N there are $i, j \in N$ such that for all $E = (R_N, \Omega)$, all $z_N, z'_N \in X^N$, $z_N \, \mathbf{P}(E) \, z'_N$ if $z_j > z'_j = 0$; if either $z_j = z'_j = 0$ or $z_j, z'_j > 0$, $z_N \, \mathbf{R}(E) \, z'_N$ iff $z_i \, R_i \, z'_i$. For this SOF, for every N, there i who is a dictator on $\left(\mathcal{E}^N, (X \setminus \{0\})^N\right)$ but not on $\left(\mathcal{E}^N, X^N\right)$. It satisfies weak Pareto and Arrow independence.

independence or unchanged-cone independence. It is also true for unchanged-F-set independence and unchanged-subspace independence, even though these axioms accept information about preferences over whole sets or subspaces, because the particular sets or subspaces under consideration are specific to the allocations under consideration.

In contrast, unchanged-contour independence, for which possibility results are obtained, makes it possible to use information about the indifference set that is arbitrarily extended in the commodity space. Recall, however, that SOFs such as $\mathbf{R}^{\Omega \text{lex}}$ do not need more information than preferences about bundles $x \leq \Omega$ to rank feasible allocations. In conclusion, the lesson that the construction of attractive SOFs requires nonlocal information must not be exaggerated.

The problem becomes more serious for SOFs that satisfy independence of the feasible set. If one wants to construct a SOF that depends only on preferences and not at all on the available resources, then the preceding results imply that one must accept the possibility that the ranking of two particular allocations may depend on properties of the individual indifference sets at these allocations that are arbitrarily remote from the bundles consumed in these allocations. For instance, in a two-good economy, the fixed-reference SOF $\mathbf{R}^{\Omega_0 \text{lex}}$, for $\Omega_0 = (1, 1)$, will always check the location of indifference curves at bundles on the 45° line to rank allocations, even when these allocations contain only one good, or contain thousands of units more in one commodity than in the other. We consider that this observation reinforces the view that independence of the feasible set is not a compelling requirement.

4.4 ALLOCATION RULES AS SOCIAL ORDERING FUNCTIONS

The requirement of nonlocal information about preferences vanishes when the Pareto axiom is weakened, as shown in this section. The topic of this section is not, however, the weakening of Pareto axioms, but the comparison of the SOFs studied in this book with the allocation rules that one finds in the theory of fair allocation.

The theory of fair allocation has often been contrasted with the theory of social choice because the latter has delivered mostly impossibility theorems, whereas the former contains many positive results in the form of characterizations of nice allocation rules. An intuitive but deceptive explanation for this contrast is that the theory of social choice seeks orderings of all allocations, whereas the theory of fair allocation is satisfied with the selection of a small subset of optimal allocations.

This explanation is not satisfactory, in fact, because a selection of a subset of allocations can be formally[8] associated with a complete ordering classifying

---

[8] We do not mean that the objective of the theory of fair allocation rules is to identify two-tier orderings, but simply that looking for allocation rules is formally equivalent to looking for two-tier orderings.

all allocations into two tiers: the optimal allocations and the rest. To understand why the theory of fair allocation succeeds when the theory of social choice fails, one must confront the allocation rules and the complete orderings they generate to the axioms of social choice. The only plausible explanation is that some of the axioms of the impossibility theorems of social choice are not satisfied by the allocation rules.

Recall that an allocation rule S associates every economy E in its domain with a nonempty subset $S(E) \subseteq Z(E)$. The two-tier SOF generated by S can be denoted $\mathbf{R}_S$ and is defined as follows: $z_N \, \mathbf{R}_S(E) \, z'_N$ if and only if $z_N \in S(E)$ or $z'_N \notin S(E)$. One therefore has $z_N \, \mathbf{P}_S(E) \, z'_N$ if and only if $z_N \in S(E)$ and $z'_N \notin S(E)$. The two prominent allocation rules of the theory of fair allocation are, as recalled in Section 1.2, the egalitarian Walrasian rule S^{EW}, which selects the competitive equilibria in which all agents have equal budgets, and the egalitarian-equivalent rule S^{EE}, which selects the allocations z_N such that $z_N \in P(E)$ and there is λ such that for all $i \in N$, $z_i \, I_i \, \lambda\Omega$. There is a variant of this rule that is based on a fixed Ω_0 that does not depend on E. Let us confront these SOFs to the core impossibility theorem of social choice theory, namely, Arrow's impossibility. This theorem has three ingredients: weak Pareto, Arrow independence, and nondictatorship.

The SOFs $\mathbf{R}_{S^{EW}}$ and $\mathbf{R}_{S^{EE}}$ are obviously not dictatorial – actually, no two-tier SOF can be dictatorial, because the dictator imposes his or her strict preferences over the SOF, which implies that the SOF must have more than two tiers. Therefore, the theory of fair allocation satisfies the nondictatorship requirement automatically.

For a similar reason, however, no two-tier SOF can satisfy weak Pareto. From such a SOF, one can at most require that the allocations it selects in $Z(E)$ be Pareto efficient. This requirement can be formulated as an axiom for any kind of SOF:

Axiom 4.8 Pareto Efficiency
For all $E \in \mathcal{D}$, $\max|_{\mathbf{R}(E)} Z(E) \subseteq P(E)$.

This weakening of Pareto reflects the fact that allocation rules only select a subset of allocations and do not seek to rank all allocations in a more precise way.[9]

Arrow independence can be satisfied by a two-tier SOF, but is not satisfied by those associated with the prominent allocation rules of the theory of fair allocation. In Section 1.3 this was illustrated for the egalitarian Walrasian

---

[9] In a discussion in Section 1.2, we argued that defining allocation rules is as demanding a task as defining social ordering functions when one enlarges the domain of problems for which a selection of optimal allocations is requested. Similarly, the axiom of Pareto efficiency can be strengthened by enlarging the domain of problems. At the extreme, if we enlarge the domain to all compact subsets Z of $Z(e)$, then Pareto efficiency becomes equivalent to weak Pareto.

allocation rule.[10] A similar illustration can be made for the egalitarian-equivalent allocation rule.

More generally, no reasonable allocation rule will satisfy Arrow independence. Indeed, on the subdomain $\mathcal{E}^*$ of economies with strictly monotonic preferences, Wilson's (1972) theorem (as extended by Bordes and Le Breton 1989 to economic environments) states that a SOF satisfying Arrow independence must be dictatorial, antidictatorial (which means always going against the strict preferences of the "antidictator"), or constant (i.e., independent of the profile of preferences). As a two-tier SOF cannot be dictatorial or anti-dictatorial, for the reasons explained earlier, it must be constant.[11] From this observation, one derives the following conclusion.

Theorem 4.4 *On the domain* $\mathcal{E}^*$, *there exists a unique two-tier SOF satisfying* Pareto efficiency, anonymity, *and* Arrow independence. *It selects all the allocations such that one agent consumes* Ω. *On the domain* $\mathcal{E}$, *no two-tier SOF satisfies* Pareto efficiency *and* Arrow independence.

Proof. The first result comes from the fact that the allocations in which one agent consumes Ω are the only allocations of $Z(E)$ that are efficient for all profiles R_N in $\mathcal{E}^*$. By anonymity, all of them must be selected.

The second result comes from the fact that no allocation of $Z(E)$ is efficient for all profiles R_N in $\mathcal{E}$. Let $z_N \in \max|_{\mathbf{R}(E)} Z(E)$ and $z'_N \notin \max|_{\mathbf{R}(E)} Z(E)$ such that for all $i \in N$, $z_i \ll z'_i$ or $z_i \gg z'_i$. Let $E' = (R'_N, \Omega)$ be such that $z_N \notin P(E')$. Then one can no longer have $z_N \, \mathbf{P}(E' \int) z'_N$. It is, however, required by Arrow independence because for all $i \in N$, R_i and R'_i agree on $\{z_N, z'_N\}$. Hence, there is a contradiction. ∎

This result shows that Arrow independence cannot be satisfied by a reasonable allocation rule, and that the fact that allocation rules correspond to two-tier SOFs is not a sufficient explanation for the success of the theory of fair allocation in terms of positive results. The key condition of social choice that must be weakened to obtain positive results for allocation rules is, as for any kind of SOF, Arrow independence.

There is, however, a grain of truth in the idea that allocation rules are easier to obtain than more fine-grained SOFs. They are indeed less informationally demanding thanks to the weakening of Pareto requirements into Pareto efficiency. Indeed, weakening the Pareto requirement in this fashion is sufficient to turn the negative results of the previous section into positive ones. Let us develop this point.

---

[10] See Figure 1.5, which displays two allocations, z_N and z'_N, in a two-agent economy; by Arrow independence, the fact that individual preferences about z_N and z'_N are the same in both profiles implies that social preferences should be identical for the two cases; but with the profile R_N, z_N is an equal-budget competitive equilibrium and z'_N is not, so $z_N \, \mathbf{P}_{SW}(E) z'_N$; the reverse occurs with the profile R'_N.

[11] Fleurbaey et al. (2005b) provide a simple direct proof of this fact.

First, on the domain $\mathcal{E}$, there exists a SOF satisfying *Pareto efficiency*, *anonymity*, and *unchanged-cone independence*. In fact, as far as fairness is concerned, much more than anonymity can be satisfied. The example that proves this claim is the egalitarian Walrasian allocation rule, viewed as a two-tier SOF. It satisfies Pareto efficiency because Walrasian equilibria are efficient. It is clearly anonymous. To check that it satisfies unchanged-cone independence, observe that when preferences change but the supporting cones at z_N remain the same, then whether z_N is an egalitarian Walrasian equilibrium cannot be changed. As this determines the position of z_N in the two-tier ranking defined by this SOF, unchanged-cone independence is satisfied.[12]

This positive fact, however, turns into an impossibility again if one adds to the list of axioms the requirement that the selection made by the SOF be essentially single-valued, that is, that the allocations selected by the SOF for any given economy be Pareto indifferent.[13]

Second, on the domain $\mathcal{E}$, there also exists a SOF satisfying *Pareto efficiency*, *anonymity*, and *unchanged-F-set independence* (and therefore *unchanged-subspace independence*). This is exemplified by the egalitarian-equivalent allocation rule, viewed as a two-tier SOF. Pareto efficiency and anonymity are again obvious. unchanged-F-set independence is satisfied for the following reason. If $F(z_N, z'_N) \supseteq \{q \in X \mid q \leq \Omega\}$, a change of preferences outside this set cannot change whether z_N or z'_N is efficient and egalitarian-equivalent and therefore cannot change their ranking by this SOF. If $F(z_N, z'_N) \not\supseteq \{q \in X \mid q \leq \Omega\}$ they are not in $P(E)$ and there is no change in preferences that can move them to $P(E)$ so they are deemed equivalent by this SOF independently of the preference profile R_N.

Observe that this second example generates an essentially single-valued selection, so the problem encountered in this respect with unchanged-cone independence does not occur with unchanged-F-set independence.

In conclusion, abandoning Arrow independence is indispensable to obtain possibility results in the theory of fair allocation just as in the theory of SOFs developed in this book. It is true, however, that allocation rules are informationally less demanding than fully Paretian SOFs, as they require only local information about preferences.

4.5   CONCLUSION

To avoid an Arrovian type of impossibility, our theory of SOFs must make room for a richer informational basis. When two allocations must be compared, one must know not just the population preferences over these two allocations,

---

[12] In a model with private endowments, Sakai (2009) shows that one can actually obtain a characterization of the Walrasian correspondence, viewed as a SOF, on the basis of Pareto efficiency and unchanged-cone independence, among other axioms.

[13] See Fleurbaey et al. (2005b).

but also some substantial parts of the agents' indifference sets at these two allocations.

This additional information is still only about ordinal noncomparable preferences, but it makes it possible to "compare" the agents' situations by comparing their indifference sets. If i's indifference set is above j's set everywhere, we can conclude that i is better off than j. When the indifference sets cross, who is better off depends on the relative position of the indifference sets in the relevant portion of the consumption set. It is therefore not surprising that we have found it impossible to obtain efficient and anonymous SOFs on the sole basis of strictly local information such as pairwise preferences or supporting cones at the bundles under consideration. By focusing on very limited information about indifference sets, the theory of social choice could not obtain positive results.

Moreover, we have also seen that if one wants the SOFs not only to be anonymous and egalitarian but also to satisfy fairness properties associated with the equal-split allocation, it is necessary to make the ranking of allocations depend on the available resources Ω. This is another important extension of the informational basis compared with social choice theory.

In contrast, the difference between the SOFs studied in this book and the allocation rules of the theory of fair allocation is less important than is often thought, because both objects provide complete orderings that rely on more information than allowed by Arrow independence. Allocation rules, however, provide only two-tier orderings and, because of this, cannot fully satisfy the standard Pareto axioms. This makes it possible to obtain fair allocation rules with local information about indifference sets, such as supporting cones. In other words, allocation rules are slightly less demanding, in terms of information about preferences, than fully Paretian SOFs. Nonetheless, this difference appears to be of second order compared with their basic similarity regarding the need to relax Arrow independence and the need to take account of Ω.

DISTRIBUTION

After Part I, which introduced the approach, its general features, and its relationship with the rest of welfare economics, we are now ready to start the real work – namely, constructing social criteria for the evaluation of allocations. Part II is about the same model that served as a workhorse for the generalities of Part I. Even though the division problem is not the most exciting when one is eager to say something about the pressing social problems of the real world, this model is very convenient to understand the basic concepts.

The two subapproaches that are highlighted in the next chapter appear to haunt all the models that have been examined so far, and they reflect the classic divide, in the theory of fair allocation, between egalitarian-equivalence and the Walrasian approach.[1] The former evaluates individual situations by looking at specific parts of indifference curves that are located in well-chosen parts of the consumption set, whereas the latter compares individuals in terms of budget sets that are either their actual budget sets or hypothetical budget sets that are suitably related to the general configuration of the allocation under consideration. These two ways of analyzing individual situations in the context of social evaluation are so basic and natural that one may suspect that any conceivable approach that similarly ignores utility information and focuses on indifference curves and resource bundles must in some way derive from one of them.

The two other chapters of this part explore how the approach developed in this book can be specialized to specific domains of preferences or specific goods, or extended to tackle broader issues than the main ones studied here. Specific domains sometimes yield surprising results. For instance, when non-convex preferences are allowed, the egalitarian-equivalence approach can be defended as the best extension of the Walrasian approach. When the smaller domain of homothetic preferences is considered, the Walrasian approach widens and certain criteria with moderate inequality aversion appear interesting. When

---

[1] This divide parallels the distinction between Deaton's distance function and Samuelson's money-metric utility. Whereas the former is in the spirit of egalitarian-equivalence, the latter is more in line with a Walrasian approach.

indivisible goods are considered, the egalitarian-equivalence and the Walrasian approaches seem to come closer, if not merge.

In this part we also illustrate the possibility of constructing libertarian social orderings that sanctify property rights, or, in another part of the ideological spectrum, social orderings that suggest an interesting solution to the indexing problem for the capabilities approach proposed by Sen. We also see how to go beyond the standard social choice exercise of ranking social alternatives for a given population with fixed preferences, and consider the problem of ranking social alternatives for populations with different preferences, which is quite relevant in the context of comparisons of living standards.

CHAPTER 5

Fair Distribution of Divisible Goods: Two Approaches

5.1 INTRODUCTION

This chapter and the next one pursue the analysis of the model that provided the framework of Part I. Our aim now is to obtain precise conclusions about how to rank allocations. We already know from Chapter 3 that a good deal of egalitarianism is necessarily part of the picture, but it remains to be determined how individual situations should be measured and compared with one another.

Among a variety of options, two main social orderings are highlighted here. One has already been introduced in Chapter 1 – namely, the Ω-equivalent leximin SOF. Another one also appears salient, and is more closely connected to the market mechanism. The choice between one or the other of these two different SOFs can be made easier, we hope, with the results of this chapter that show how they derive from different ethical principles.[1]

In the next section, a first series of results highlight the Ω-equivalent leximin SOF on the basis of axioms focusing on the equal split of the available resources. In Section 5.3, the alternative approach of a Walrasian kind of social preferences is introduced and motivated on the basis of axioms that relate to responsibility and neutrality (with respect to individual preferences) and to efficiency. Section 5.4 shows how these social ordering functions can be used for the selection of allocations in the second-best context in which the policymaker does not know individuals' characteristics but has information about the statistical distribution of characteristics. Section 5.5 concludes with comments on the differences between the two SOFs analyzed here.

5.2 FROM EQUAL SPLIT TO Ω-EQUIVALENCE

In Chapter 2 we saw that the Pareto principle is compatible with egalitarian axioms that can be restricted in two ways – namely, by restricting the region of the consumption set in which the transfer principle applies (e.g., proportional allocations), or by restricting the type of agents to which it applies (e.g., agents

---

[1] This chapter is inspired by Fleurbaey (2005b, 2007b) and Fleurbaey and Maniquet (2008a,b).

with identical preferences). The following result shows the typical consequences of combining the two kinds of egalitarian axioms, together with Pareto and independence axioms. Recall that $u_\Omega(z_i, R_i)$ denotes the Ω-equivalent utility.

Theorem 5.1 *On the domain* $\mathcal{E}$, *if a SOF satisfies* strong Pareto, transfer among equals, proportional-allocations transfer, *and* unchanged-contour independence, *then for all* $E = (R_N, \Omega) \in \mathcal{E}$ *and* $z_N, z'_N \in X^N$,

$$\min_{i \in N} u_\Omega(z_i, R_i) > \min_{i \in N} u_\Omega(z'_i, R_i) \Rightarrow z_N \, \mathbf{P}(E) \, z'_N. \tag{5.1}$$

In other words, the SOF then exhibits a maximin property with respect to Ω-equivalent utilities: if the smallest utility is greater in one allocation, this allocation is preferred. The Ω-equivalent leximin SOF satisfies this property, but is not the only one that does.

The proof makes use of Corollary 3.1, which says that the SOF must satisfy nested-contour priority, as a lemma.[2] Let us give an intuitive description of the argument (the full proof is in the appendix). This description is illustrated in Figure 5.1. Consider a two-agent economy with $N = \{j, k\}$ and two allocations z_N, z'_N such that

$$u_\Omega(z'_j, R_j), u_\Omega(z_j, R_j), u_\Omega(z_k, R_k) > u_\Omega(z'_k, R_k). \tag{5.2}$$

The ranking of the first three terms does not matter, but the case that is not immediate is when $u_\Omega(z'_j, R_j) > u_\Omega(z_j, R_j)$ – that is, the better-off loses while the worse-off gains when one moves from z'_N to z_N.

By strong Pareto, which implies Pareto indifference, it is not restrictive to assume that these allocations are proportional to Ω, as in the Figure 5.1.

The argument is a reductio ad absurdum. Suppose that, contrary to the claim, one has $z'_N \, \mathbf{R}(E) \, z_N$. The basic structure of the proof can be explained as follows. Let u_j, u'_j, u_k, u'_k be the numbers corresponding to the Ω-equivalent well-being levels of agents j and k at the relevant bundles – that is, $u_j = u_\Omega(z_j, R_j), u'_j = u_\Omega(z'_j, R_j), u_k = u_\Omega(z_k, R_k)$, and $u'_k = u_\Omega(z'_k, R_k)$. In the case illustrated in Figure 5.1, we have $u'_k < u_j < u'_j < u_k$. The objective is to construct an allocation (z''_j, z''_k), with associated Ω-equivalent well-being levels u''_j and u''_k such that

$$u'_k < u''_k \leq u''_j < u_j < u'_j < u_k.$$

Then, by an argument involving some priority view (that is, absolute priority to the worse-off), we will be able to conclude that the allocation leading to well-being levels (u''_j, u''_k) is preferable to the one leading to (u'_j, u'_k), whereas, by strong Pareto, the allocation leading to (u_j, u_k) is preferable to the one leading to (u''_j, u''_k), in contradiction to the premise of the argument, according to which (u'_j, u'_k) is preferable to (u_j, u_k).

---

[2] Theorem 3.1 involves Pareto indifference, which is why strong Pareto is invoked in Theorem 5.1. But the result is also true with weak Pareto, as explained in the appendix.

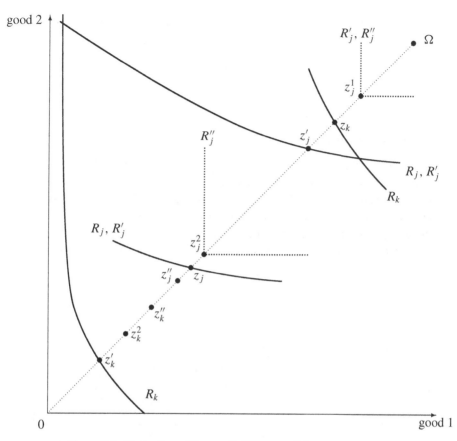

good 2

R'_j, R''_j

Ω

z^1_j

R''_j

z'_j

z_k

R_j, R'_j

R_k

R_j, R'_j

z^2_j

z''_j z_j

z''_k

z^2_k

z'_k

R_k

0

good 1

Figure 5.1. Illustration of the proof of Theorem 5.1

The difficulty lies in the fact that nested-contour priority is not sufficient to develop the required priority argument, because the agents' indifference curves through z'_k, z_j, z'_j and z_k may not be nested, as illustrated in the Figure 5.1. The argument cannot be made in economy E.

Nested-contour priority is not sufficient for two reasons. First, agent j's indifference curve through z'_j crosses agent k's indifference curve through z'_k. Second, agent j's indifference curve through z_j also crosses agent k's indifference curve through z'_k, and that turns out to be more problematic. Indeed, as z'_j belongs to the allocation that, according to the premise of the argument, is socially preferred, it is easy to modify agent j's preferences and solve the difficulty. That is done in step 1. On the other hand, z_j belongs to the allocation that is socially worse, with the consequence that, no matter how we modify agent j's preferences, agent j's indifference curve through z_j always crosses agent k's indifference curve through z'_k. This is why nested-contour priority needs to be complemented with proportional-allocations transfer. That is done in step 2.

Step 1. Let R_j'' be such that the corresponding indifference curves through z_j^1 and z_j^2 are as in the figure; that is,

$$U(z_j^1, R_j'') = \{x \in X \mid x \geq z_j^1\}$$
$$U(z_j^2, R_j'') = \{x \in X \mid x \geq z_j^1\}.$$

By nested-contour priority,

$$(z_j^2, z_k^2) \, P(R_j'', R_k, \Omega)(z_j^1, z_k'). \qquad (5.3)$$

It is impossible, however, to go directly from $E = (R_N, \Omega)$ to $E'' = (R_j'', R_k, \Omega)$, as agent j's indifference curve through z_j' at R_j crosses his or her indifference through z_j^2 at R_j''. An intermediary step is needed. It requires defining $E' = (R_j', R_k, \Omega)$ in which R_j' is such that j's indifference curve through z_j' remains the same as at R_j, whereas the one through z_j^1 is changed. By unchanged-contour independence,

$$z_N' \, \mathbf{R}(E) \, z_N \Rightarrow z_N' \, \mathbf{R}(E') \, z_N.$$

By strong Pareto,

$$z_N' \, \mathbf{R}(E') \, z_N \Rightarrow (z_j^1, z_k') \, \mathbf{P}(E') \, z_N.$$

By unchanged-contour independence again,

$$(z_j^1, z_k') \, \mathbf{P}(E') \, z_N \Rightarrow (z_j^1, z_k') \, \mathbf{P}(E'') \, z_N.$$

Using (5.3), by transitivity,

$$(z_j^2, z_k^2) \, P(E'') \, z_N. \qquad (5.4)$$

Step 2. Let (z_j'', z_k''), such that $z_j'' \geq z_k''$, satisfy the following two properties: First, it can be obtained from (z_j^2, z_k^2) by a transfer,

$$z_k'' - z_k^2 = z_j^2 - z_j'',$$

and, second, that transfer implies that j's bundle "jumps" over z_j,

$$z_j'' < z_j < z_j^2.$$

By proportional-allocations transfer,

$$(z_j'', z_k'') \, P(E'')(z_j^2, z_k^2),$$

which implies, by transitivity and using (5.4),

$$(z_j'', z_k'') \, P(E'') \, z_N,$$

in contradiction to strong Pareto.

This reasoning illustrates the basic argument that underlies many of our characterization results.

Besides, in this particular theorem, the direction of proportionality referred to in proportional-allocations transfer can be anything, so this kind of result can be adapted to support any SOF that involves a ray of reference not necessarily containing Ω. It is even possible to take one axis as the reference ray, if one restricts the domain to preferences such that all indifference sets intersect this axis. The meaning of proportional-allocations transfer in this case is that allocations in which only this particular good is distributed can be submitted to the transfer principle independent of the agents' preferences. However, we argued in Chapter 2 that the ray containing Ω is attractive when one takes the equal split allocation as a benchmark.

It is also worth noting that in the proof above, proportional-allocations transfer is not used in its full force. Let us observe that, even if $z_j'' > z_k''$ in the figure, we could perfectly well have defined $z_j'' = z_k''$. Consequently, the only consequence of proportional-allocations transfer that is really used is that an egalitarian allocation proportional to Ω is better than another proportional but nonegalitarian allocation using fewer total resources (z_N^2). This is essentially an equal-split requirement.

We now turn to another result that gives the prominent role to an equal-split axiom; indeed, the interesting feature of this result is that it does not involve transfer among equals. The only egalitarian axiom refers to equal-split.

Theorem 5.2 *On the domain $\mathcal{E}$, if a SOF satisfies* strong Pareto, equal-split transfer, separation, *and* replication, *then for all $E = (R_N, \Omega) \in \mathcal{E}$ and $z_N, z_N' \in X^N$,*

$$\min_{i \in N} u_\Omega(z_i, R_i) > \min_{i \in N} u_\Omega(z_i', R_i) \Rightarrow z_N \, \mathbf{P}(E) \, z_N'.$$

The appendix presents and proves a stronger result, which involves weak Pareto and a weakening of separation. Here we focus on the preceding statement, for which an intuitive argument is easier.

First, by Theorem 3.4 (involving Pareto indifference, equal-split transfer, separation, and replication), the SOF must satisfy equal-split priority. Second, by Lemma 4.1 (involving separation and replication), it is insensitive to multiplications of Ω by a rational number.

Consider the two-agent case $\{i_0, j\}$ and assume that

$$\min_{i \in N} u_\Omega(z_i, R_i) > \min_{i \in N} u_\Omega(z_i', R_i).$$

Invoking strong Pareto, we can focus on the special case when $z_N, z_N' \in \mathrm{Pr}(\Omega)$ and

$$z_j' \gg z_j \gg z_{i_0} \gg z_{i_0}'.$$

(As explained after Theorem 5.1, in the other cases one can always find z_N^1, z_N^2 satisfying these conditions and such that $z_N \, \mathbf{P}(E) \, z_N^2$ and $z_N^1 \, \mathbf{P}(E) \, z_N'$ by strong Pareto, so if one can prove that $z_N^2 \, \mathbf{R}(E) \, z_N^1$, then by transitivity, $z_N \, \mathbf{P}(E) \, z_N'$.)

Take $E' = (R_N, q\Omega)$, where q is a rational number such that

$$z_j' \gg z_j \gg q\Omega \gg z_{i_0} \gg z_{i_0}'.$$

By equal-split priority, one has $z_N \, \mathbf{R}(E') \, z'_N$. By separation and replication (by virtue of Lemma 4.1), this implies $z_N \, \mathbf{R}(E) \, z'_N$.

When there are more than two agents, one can similarly end up with a situation in which for all $j \neq i_0$,

$$z_j^1 \gg z_j^2 \gg q\Omega \gg z_{i_0}^2 \gg z_{i_0}^1,$$

and by strong Pareto, $z_N \, \mathbf{P}(E) \, z_N^2$ and $z_N^1 \, \mathbf{P}(E) \, z'_N$. A repeated application of equal-split priority yields $z_N^2 \, \mathbf{R}(E') \, z'_N$. Separation and replication imply $z_N^2 \, \mathbf{R}(E) \, z_N^1$ and the desired conclusion is obtained by transitivity.

These results (Theorems 5.1 and 5.2) strongly point in the direction of $\mathbf{R}^{\Omega\text{lex}}$. Nonetheless, they fail to uniquely characterize it, because there are other SOFs that satisfy the axioms of the theorems. The existence of reasonable axioms that would force us to have $\mathbf{R} = \mathbf{R}^{\Omega\text{lex}}$ seems doubtful. Consider the SOF $\mathbf{R}^{\Omega\Omega'\text{lex}}$, defined as follows. Take any arbitrary Ω' that is not proportional to Ω. Let $z_N \, \mathbf{R}^{\Omega\Omega'\text{lex}}(E) \, z'_N$ whenever either $z_N \, \mathbf{P}^{\Omega\text{lex}}(E) \, z'_N$, or $z_N \, \mathbf{I}^{\Omega\text{lex}}(E) \, z'_N$ and $z_N \, \mathbf{R}^{\Omega'\text{lex}}(E) \, z'_N$. This SOF satisfies all the axioms of the preceding theorems. It is also anonymous, in the sense that it does not give any biased consideration to any particular agent's situation (permuting the agents' preferences and their bundles does not alter the evaluation of the allocations).[3] In view of this fact, we leave open what kind of additional ethical principle, in this model, would single out the leximin SOF.

5.3 A WALRASIAN SOF

The previous section provided justifications for the egalitarian-equivalent approach to the definition of social orderings. As recalled from Chapter 1, however, this is not the only approach. In the theory of fair allocation, another important contender is the Walrasian approach, which relies on the idea that agents should be given fair endowments and left free to trade these endowments at competitive prices. The allocation rule $S^{EW}(E)$, defined in Section 1.2, selects the subset of egalitarian Walrasian allocations for E.

Certainly, by referring to such competitive allocations, the Walrasian approach sounds quite natural to those who live in market economies, but it remains to pin down the ethical justifications for this alternative view. The theory of fair allocation actually provides many arguments for it, most of which can be related to the idea that preferences should be respected in a neutral way.

Take, for instance, the heraldic no-envy condition (saying that the selected allocation z_N should be such that for all $i, j \in N, z_i \, R_i \, z_j$). It is satisfied when, for every $i \in N, z_i$ is the best bundle for R_i in some common set containing all the bundles. A situation in which agents are able to choose their own bundle in some common set of options may indeed be taken to reflect such neutrality about preferences. As is well known, an egalitarian Walrasian allocation (i.e., a

---

[3] Recall that anonymity is, in fact, implied by replication as we formulated it, as an economy in which preferences are permuted across agents is a 1-replica of the original economy.

competitive equilibrium with identical endowments) is always envy-free, and conversely, in large economies with sufficient diversity of preferences, envy-free efficient allocations are egalitarian Walrasian.[4]

In Chapter 2, we discussed how to make use of the no-envy concept in the definition of requirements for SOFs; nested-contour transfer, in particular, was connected to this idea. Here is another axiom that, in the most immediate fashion, translates the no-envy requirement, as it is usually defined for allocation rules that select a first-best allocation in the feasible set $Z(E)$, into a requirement for SOFs. It simply says that the first-best allocation in $Z(E)$, when it is selected by the SOF, should satisfy the no-envy condition.

Axiom 5.1 Envy-Free Selection
For all $E = (R_N, \Omega) \in \mathcal{D}$ and $z_N \in \max|_{\mathbf{R}(E)} Z(E)$, for all $i, j \in N$, $z_i\, R_i\, z_j$.

Another axiom that has been used for the justification of Walrasian allocations is the monotonicity requirement, saying that when an allocation is selected, it should remain so when the individual upper contour sets at this allocation shrink, meaning that the corresponding bundles go up in individual preferences relative to other bundles.[5] Here the idea is that the social decision should not be too sensitive to the agents' preferences; this can be motivated by responsibility and neutrality concerns (as well as incentive concerns). Indeed, if agents are responsible for their preferences, and if we do not want to give them a treatment that is biased in favor of particular types of preferences, the case in which the bundle they are already granted goes up in their preferences seems a natural case in which no redistribution of resources is needed.

Axiom 5.2 Selection Monotonicity
For all $E = (R_N, \Omega)$, $E' = (R'_N, \Omega) \in \mathcal{D}$, and $z_N \in \max|_{\mathbf{R}(E)} Z(E)$, if for all $i \in N$, $U(z_i, R'_i) \subseteq U(z_i, R_i)$, then $z_N \in \max|_{\mathbf{R}(E')} Z(E')$.

Selection monotonicity[6] entails envy-free selection when one considers a Paretian SOF that also satisfies transfer among equals. Under strong Pareto, it actually implies the egalitarian Walrasian way of obtaining envy-free allocations.

---

[4] For the former point, see Kolm (1972), and for the latter, Varian (1976) and Champsaur and Laroque (1981).

[5] See Gevers (1986). This is closely related to Maskin monotonicity (Maskin 1999).

[6] These axioms are formulated about the first-best selection in $Z(E)$ and not in terms of selection in any subset $A \subseteq X^{|N|}$. This seems indeed essentially impossible. For instance, an axiom saying that the selection in any subset A should be envy-free whenever A contains envy-free allocations is incompatible with Pareto requirements because it may be that all envy-free allocations are Pareto inefficient in A. Even the weaker condition that the selection in any subset A should be envy-free whenever A contains envy-free *efficient* allocations is incompatible with Pareto indifference because envy-free efficient allocations may be Pareto indifferent to allocations with envy. Similar concerns can be formulated about selection monotonicity, because it is somehow stronger than envy-free selection in an egalitarian context, as shown in the next theorem.

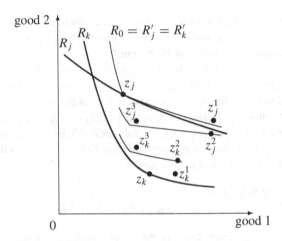

Figure 5.2. Proof of Theorem 5.3

Theorem 5.3 *On the domain* $\mathcal{E}$, *any SOF satisfying* weak Pareto, selection monotonicity, *and* transfer among equals *also satisfies* envy-free selection. *If it also satisfies* strong Pareto, *then for all* $E = (R_N, \Omega) \in \mathcal{E}$, $S^{EW}(E) \subseteq \max|_{\mathbf{R}(E)} Z(E)$.

Proof. **Part 1.** Let $E = (R_N, \Omega) \in \mathcal{E}$ and $z_N \in \max|_{\mathbf{R}(E)} Z(E)$. Suppose there exist $j, k \in N$ such that $z_j \, P_k \, z_k$. Then there exists R_0 such that $U(z_j, R_0) \subseteq U(z_j, R_j)$ and $U(z_k, R_0) = U(z_k, R_k)$, implying $z_j \, P_0 \, z_k$ (see Figure 5.2).

Let $E' = (R'_N, \Omega)$, with $R'_N \in \mathcal{R}$ being defined by $R'_j = R'_k = R_0$ and $R'_i = R_i$ for all $i \neq j, k$. By selection monotonicity, $z_N \in \max|_{\mathbf{R}(E')} Z(E')$. In addition, one can choose R_0 so there exist $z^1_N, z^2_N \in X^N$, $z^3_N \in Z(E')$, $\Delta \in \mathbb{R}^\ell_{++}$ such that for all $i \in N$, $z^1_i \, P'_i \, z_i$ and $z^3_i \, P'_i \, z^2_i$; $z^2_j = z^1_j - \Delta \gg z^1_k + \Delta = z^2_k$; and for all $i \neq j, k$, $z^2_i = z^1_i$ (see Figure 5.2).

By weak Pareto, $z^1_N \, \mathbf{P}(E') \, z_N$ and $z^3_N \, \mathbf{P}(E') \, z^2_N$. By transfer among equals, $z^2_N \, \mathbf{R}(E') \, z^1_N$. By transitivity, $z^3_N \, \mathbf{P}(E') \, z_N$. Because $z^3_N \in Z(E')$, this contradicts $z_N \in \max|_{\mathbf{R}(E')} Z(E')$.

Part 2. Consider $E = (R_N, \Omega) \in \mathcal{E}$, and $z_N \in S^{EW}(e)$. Let p be a price vector supporting[7] z_N, and R_p be defined by:

$$\forall x, x' \in X, \; x \, R_p \, x' \Leftrightarrow px \geq px'.$$

Let $E_p = \left((R_p)_{i \in N}, \Omega \right) \in \mathcal{E}$, and consider $z^*_N \in \max|_{\mathbf{R}(E_p)} Z(E_p)$. By part 1, one must have $z^*_i \, I_p \, z^*_j$ for all $i, j \in N$ (when preferences are identical, envy-freeness implies that agents have bundles on the same indifference curve). By strong Pareto, $z^*_N \in P(E_p)$, so $z^*_i \, I_p \, z_i$ for all $i \in N$, so strong Pareto implies $z^*_N \, \mathbf{R}(E) \, z_N$, so $z_N \in \max|_{\mathbf{R}(E_p)} Z(E_p)$. As a consequence, by selection monotonicity, $z_N \in \max|_{\mathbf{R}(E)} Z(E)$. ∎

---

[7] That is, for all $i \in N$, z_i is a best bundle for R_i in the set $\{x \in X \mid px \leq pz_i\}$.

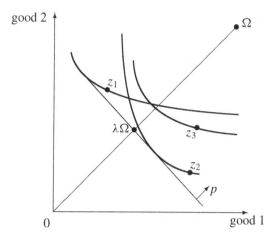

Figure 5.3. Evaluation of an allocation by $\mathbf{R}^{EW}$

Among the three SOFs introduced in Chapters 1 and 2 (namely, $\mathbf{R}^{RU}$, $\mathbf{R}^{\Omega\text{lex}}$, and $\mathbf{R}^{\Omega\text{Nash}}$), only $\mathbf{R}^{RU}$ satisfies selection monotonicity, and none of them satisfies envy-free selection. We now present a SOF that satisfies both axioms. It relies on the maximin criterion applied to money-metric utilities (defined in Section 1.8), but with the peculiar feature that the reference price that serves to measure such utilities is specific to every allocation, and is computed to obtain the most favorable maximin evaluation for the contemplated allocation.

Social ordering function 5.1 Egalitarian Walrasian ($\mathbf{R}^{EW}$)
For all $E = (R_N, \Omega) \in \mathcal{E}$, $z_N, z'_N \in X^N$,

$$z_N \, \mathbf{R}^{EW}(E) \, z'_N \Leftrightarrow \max_{p:p\Omega=1} \min_{i\in N} \min \{px \mid x \, R_i \, z_i\}$$

$$\geq \max_{p:p\Omega=1} \min_{i\in N} \min \left\{px \mid x \, R_i \, z'_i\right\}.$$

To make the discussion of money-metric utilities easier, let $u_p(z_i, R_i) = \min \{px \mid x \, R_i \, z_i\}$ and $\Pi_\Omega = \{p \mid p\Omega = 1\}$. When $p \in \Pi_\Omega$, $u_p(z_i, R_i) = \min \{px/p\Omega \mid x \, R_i \, z_i\}$.

The definition of $\mathbf{R}^{EW}$ may look complicated, but there is a simple geometric way of evaluating an allocation with it. It suffices to look for the smallest point on the ray of Ω that belongs to the convex hull of the union of the individual upper contour sets at the contemplated allocation. Figure 5.3 illustrates this. On the figure, the relevant point for evaluation is $\lambda\Omega$, and in this example one has, for the corresponding $p \in \Pi_\Omega$,

$$\lambda = u_p(z_1, R_1) = u_p(z_2, R_2) < u_p(z_3, R_3).$$

It is clear from the figure that for any other $p' \in \Pi_\Omega$, $\lambda > u_{p'}(z_1, R_1)$ or $\lambda > u_{p'}(z_2, R_2)$, so that

$$\lambda = \max_{p \in \Pi_\Omega} \min_{i \in \{1,2,3\}} u_p(z_i, R_i).$$

The name of this SOF comes from the observation that for all $E = (R_N, \Omega) \in \mathcal{E}$,

$$\max|_{\mathbf{R}^{EW}(E)} Z(E) = S^{EW}(E).$$

In other words, $\mathbf{R}^{EW}$ always selects, in $Z(E)$, each and every egalitarian Walrasian allocation, and no other allocation. This can be proved as follows. For any $z_N \in S^{EW}(E)$, with supporting price vector $p \in \Pi_\Omega$, one has

$$u_p(z_i, R_i) = p z_i = p \frac{\Omega}{|N|} = \frac{1}{|N|}.$$

Conversely, for any $z_N \in Z(E)$, any $p \in \Pi_\Omega$, if $u_p(z_i, R_i) \geq 1/|N|$ for all $i \in N$, this means that $p z_i \geq p \Omega / |N|$ for all $i \in N$, which, in view of the fact that $\sum_{i \in N} z_i \leq \Omega$, is possible only if $p z_i = p \Omega / |N|$ and $z_i \in \max|_{R_i} B(\Omega/|N|, p)$ for all $i \in N$. This, in turn, entails that $z_N \in S^{EW}(E)$, with supporting price vector p (and also that $u_p(z_i, R_i) = 1/|N|$ for all $i \in N$). As a consequence, one has $z_N \in S^{EW}(E)$ if and only if $\max_{p \in \Pi_\Omega} \min_{i \in N} u_p(z_i, R_i) = 1/|N|$ and for all $z_N \in Z(E) \setminus S^{EW}(E)$, $\max_{p \in \Pi_\Omega} \min_{i \in N} u_p(z_i, R_i) < 1/|N|$.

Observe that $\mathbf{R}^{EW}$ bears some similarity with $\mathbf{R}^{RU}$, as the latter evaluates allocations by computing the expression

$$\max_{p \in \Pi_\Omega} \sum_{i \in N} u_p(z_i, R_i),$$

in which, compared with $\mathbf{R}^{EW}$, the summation operator has replaced the minimum.

Let us now focus on $\mathbf{R}^{EW}$. In addition to the previous two axioms (selection monotonicity and envy-free selection), it also satisfies weak Pareto, Pareto indifference (but not strong Pareto – we come back on that issue at the end of this section), transfer among equals, nested-contour transfer, equal-split selection, unchanged-contour independence, and replication. Interestingly, as with $\mathbf{R}^{RU}$, it does not satisfy any of the separability axioms. More specifically, there is a strong incompatibility between separability axioms and selection monotonicity or envy-free selection, as can be seen from the following result.

Theorem 5.4 *On the domain* $\mathcal{E}$, *no SOF satisfies* strong Pareto, envy-free selection, *and* separability.

Proof. Let $\mathbf{R}$ satisfy the axioms. Let $N = \{1, 2, \ldots, n\}$ and let $E = (R_N, \Omega) \in \mathcal{E}$ be such that for all $i \in N \setminus \{1, 2\}$, $R_i = R_p$ (defined in the proof of Theorem 5.3). Figure 5.4 illustrates the proof.

We claim that $\left(z_1^*, z_2^*, \frac{\Omega}{n}, \ldots, \frac{\Omega}{n}\right) \in \max|_{\mathbf{R}(E)} Z(E)$. Let $z_N \in Z(E)$ be such that for all $i, j \in N$, $z_i R_i z_j$. By envy-free selection, it must be the

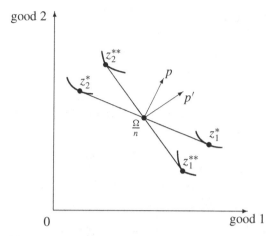

Figure 5.4. Proof of Theorem 5.4

case that for all $i, j \in N \setminus \{1, 2\}$, $z_i \, I_i \, z_j$. It is impossible to have $\frac{\Omega}{n} \, P_3 \, z_3$, as this would imply either $z_1 \, P_3 \, z_3$ or $z_2 \, P_3 \, z_3$, violating envy-free selection. It is impossible to have $z_3 \, P_3 \, \frac{\Omega}{n}$, as well. Indeed, this implies that for some bundle $z_3' \in X$ such that $z_3' \, I_3 \, z_3$, either $z_3' \, P_1 \, z_1$ or $z_3' \, P_2 \, z_2$, and, if n is sufficiently large, there is an allocation that is Pareto indifferent to z_N and is such that agent 3 receives z_3', in contradiction to envy-free selection. Therefore $z_i \, I_i \, \frac{\Omega}{n}$ for all $i \in N \setminus \{1, 2\}$. For the same reason, one cannot have $p z_1 \neq p \frac{\Omega}{n}$ or $p z_2 \neq p \frac{\Omega}{n}$.

Therefore, by strong Pareto, $\left(z_1^*, z_2^*, \frac{\Omega}{n}, \ldots, \frac{\Omega}{n} \right) \in \max|_{\mathbf{R}(E)} Z(E)$. In particular, we have

$$\left(z_1^*, z_2^*, \frac{\Omega}{n}, \ldots, \frac{\Omega}{n} \right) \mathbf{P}(E) \left(z_1^{**}, z_2^{**}, \frac{\Omega}{n}, \ldots, \frac{\Omega}{n} \right).$$

Let $E' = \left(R_N', \Omega \right) \in \mathcal{E}$ be such that $R_1 = R_1'$ and $R_2 = R_2'$ and for all $i \in N \setminus \{1, 2\}$, $R_i' = R_{p'}$. By a similar argument to the previous paragraph, we can prove that

$$\left(z_1^{**}, z_2^{**}, \frac{\Omega}{n}, \ldots, \frac{\Omega}{n} \right) \mathbf{P}(E') \left(z_1^*, z_2^*, \frac{\Omega}{n}, \ldots, \frac{\Omega}{n} \right),$$

violating separability. ∎

Nonetheless, $\mathbf{R}^{EW}$ does satisfy a separability axiom that takes account of the egalitarian context of the analysis. This axiom restricts the application of separation to agents who are not only unconcerned but are also obviously better off than others in the allocations under consideration, because each of them receives a better bundle in the two allocations than another agent with the same preferences. It is only in that case that the ranking of the two allocations is required not to be affected by their absence.

Axiom 5.3 Well-Off Separation
*For all $E = (R_N, \Omega) \in \mathcal{D}$ with $|N| \geq 2$, and $z_N, z_N' \in X^N$, if there are $i, j \in N$
such that $R_i = R_j$, $z_i \, P_i \, z_j$, $z_i' \, P_j \, z_j'$, $z_i = z_i'$, then*

$$z_N \, \mathbf{R}(E) \, z_N' \Leftrightarrow z_{N \setminus \{i\}} \, \mathbf{R}(R_{N \setminus \{i\}}, \Omega) \, z_{N \setminus \{i\}}'.$$

This axiom is also obviously satisfied by $\mathbf{R}^{\Omega \text{lex}}$ and $\mathbf{R}^{\Omega \text{Nash}}$, which already
satisfy separation.[8] We are now able to give an argument to the effect that $\mathbf{R}^{EW}$
is a key player in this game.

Theorem 5.5 *On the domain $\mathcal{E}$, if a SOF satisfies strong Pareto, transfer among
equals, selection monotonicity, unchanged-contour independence, well-off separation, and replication, then for all $E = (R_N, \Omega) \in \mathcal{E}$ and $z_N, z_N' \in X^N$,*

$$z_N \, \mathbf{P}^{EW}(E) \, z_N' \Rightarrow z_N \, \mathbf{P}(E) \, z_N'.$$

The main idea of the proof (provided in the appendix) is the follow-
ing. Assume that $z_N \, \mathbf{P}^{EW}(E) \, z_N'$ and that, contrary to the desired conclusion,
$z_N' \, \mathbf{R}(E) \, z_N$. One then constructs an economy $E' = (R_{N'}, m\Omega)$, in which the
population of agents is modified by well-off separation and replication, and allo-
cations $z_{N'}^1$ and $z_{N'}^2$, such that $z_{N'}^1 \, \mathbf{P}(E') \, z_{N'}^2$ as a consequence of $z_N' \, \mathbf{R}(E) \, z_N$,
strong Pareto, weak transfer among equals, and unchanged-contour indepen-
dence. However, these allocations are constructed to have $z_{N'}^2 \in S^{EW}(E')$ and
$z_{N'}^1 \in Z(E')$, which, by strong Pareto, weak transfer among equals, selection
monotonicity, and Theorem 5.3, implies $z_{N'}^2 \in \max|_{\mathbf{R}(E')} Z(E')$ and therefore
$z_{N'}^2 \, \mathbf{R}(E') \, z_{N'}^1$. This is a contradiction.[9]

The fact that $\mathbf{R}^{EW}$ bears some similarity with $\mathbf{R}^{RU}$ may suggest that it
reflects a greater concern for efficiency than the (Ω-equivalent) SOFs such as
$\mathbf{R}^{\Omega \text{lex}}$ and $\mathbf{R}^{\Omega \text{Nash}}$. This impression is vindicated by the next result. It relies on
a weak variant of proportional-allocations transfer that gives a preference to
efficient allocations over wasteful allocations. More precisely, it says that if a
proportional allocation z_N is efficient in the economy with total endowment
equal to its total consumption $\sum_{i \in N} z_i$, whereas z_N' is comparatively wasteful
in the sense that its average consumption $\frac{1}{|N|} \sum_{i \in N} z_i'$ is below z_i for all $i \in N$,
then z_N is at least as good as z_N'.

Axiom 5.4 Proportional-Efficient Dominance
*For all $E = (R_N, \Omega) \in \mathcal{D}$, and $z_N \in Pr(E)$, $z_N' \in X^N$, if $z_N \in
P(R_N, \sum_{i \in N} z_i)$ and for all $i \in N$*

$$z_i \gg \frac{1}{|N|} \sum_{i \in N} z_i',$$

then $z_N \, \mathbf{R}(E) \, z_N'$.

---

[8] It is also satisfied by $\mathbf{R}^{\Omega \text{min}}$, the maximin variant of $\mathbf{R}^{\Omega \text{lex}}$ defined before the statement of Theorem
A.1 in the appendix. It is not satisfied by $\mathbf{R}^{RU}$, which appears to be strongly nonseparable.

[9] The full force of strong Pareto is not used in the proof of Theorem 5.5 (and the proof of Theorem
5.3). Only weak Pareto and Pareto indifference are used, and we suspect that Pareto indifference
is not necessary for Theorem 5.5 to hold (the second part of Theorem 5.3, however, is not true in
absence of Pareto indifference).

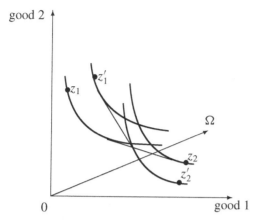

Figure 5.5. $z_N \, \mathbf{P}^{EW}(E) \, z'_N$

In this axiom, the premise that for all $i \in N$, z_i is above the average bundle of z'_N implies that when z_N is less egalitarian (i.e., there are low z_i), it remains better than z'_N only if the latter is sufficiently wasteful (i.e., its mean is below the lowest z_i). In this way, this axiom does not give an absolute priority to efficiency concerns and reckons with some trade-off between efficiency and equality. When there is more inequality in z_N, the waste in z'_N has to be greater to vindicate the requirement that z_N is (weakly) better.

In a one-dimensional setting ($\ell = 1$), when this configuration occurs – that is, when a distribution has its entire support above the mean of another – necessarily there is generalized Lorenz dominance, a very strong argument in favor of the former distribution.[10] Therefore the preceding axiom is quite weak in terms of egalitarianism.

Theorem 5.6 *On the domain $\mathcal{E}$, if a SOF satisfies* weak Pareto, transfer among equals, proportional-efficient dominance, unchanged-contour independence, *and* replication, *then for all $E = (R_N, \Omega) \in \mathcal{E}$ and $z_N, z'_N \in X^N$,*

$$z_N \, \mathbf{P}^{EW}(E) \, z'_N \Rightarrow z_N \, \mathbf{P}(E) \, z'_N.$$

The argument in the proof is not very different, in its basic structure, from the proof of Theorem 5.1, but it is worth explaining how proportional efficient dominance and replication play their part here. Consider allocations z_N, z'_N in Figure 5.5. Imagine that, contrary to the desired result, one has $z'_N \, \mathbf{R}(E) \, z_N$.

---

[10] Generalized Lorenz dominance of $(x_1, \ldots, x_n)$ over $(y_1, \ldots, y_n)$ means that, for all $k = 1, \ldots, n$, $\sum_{i=1}^{k} x_{(i)} \geq \sum_{i=1}^{k} y_{(i)}$, where $x_{(i)}$ is the component of $(x_1, \ldots, x_n)$ which is at the ith rank by increasing order: $x_{(1)} \leq \ldots \leq x_{(n)}$. By a variant of the Hardy-Littlewood-Polya (1952) theorem, it is equivalent to having $W(x_1, \ldots, x_n) \geq W(y_1, \ldots, y_n)$ for all increasing and quasiconcave functions W. If for all $i = 1, \ldots, n$, $x_i > \frac{1}{n} \sum_{i=1}^{n} y_i$, necessarily one has generalized Lorenz dominance of $(x_1, \ldots, x_n)$ over $(y_1, \ldots, y_n)$ because one then has, for all $k = 1, \ldots, n$,

$$\sum_{i=1}^{k} x_{(i)} > \frac{k}{n} \sum_{i=1}^{n} y_i \geq \sum_{i=1}^{k} y_{(i)}.$$

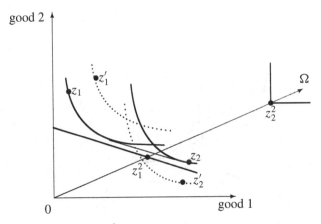

Figure 5.6. $z_N \, \mathbf{P}(E) \, z_N^2$

Recall that by unchanged-contour independence, other indifference curves could be anything. Therefore, by a combined use of weak Pareto, transfer among equals, unchanged-contour independence, and Lemma A.1 (see footnote 6 in Section 3.2), one can show that allocation z_N^2, as shown in Figure 5.6, is worse than z_N. By transitivity, $z_N' \, \mathbf{R}(E) \, z_N^2$.

By replication, every agent can be given an arbitrarily large (but equal) number $m - 1$ of clones without altering the comparison, so in the replicated economy $E' = (R_{N'}, m\Omega)$, $z_{N'}' \, \mathbf{R}(E') \, z_{N'}^2$. Let $z_{N'}^1$ be an allocation such that one agent of each sort is just better off than in $z_{N'}'$, whereas all this agant's $m - 1$ clones are given z_2^2. By weak Pareto, $z_{N'}^1 \, \mathbf{R}(E') \, z_{N'}'$. By transitivity, $z_{N'}^1 \, \mathbf{R}(E') \, z_{N'}^2$.

Because indifference curves are nested, one can refer to unchanged-contour independence and notice that every clone who receives z_2^2 in $z_{N'}^1$ could have the same preferences as any of the initial agents. Therefore, by Lemma A.1, the clones at z_2^2 in $z_{N'}^1$ can be brought back near the indifference curves at z_1^1 or z_2^1 (dotted curves in the figure) in arbitrary proportions. This yields a new allocation $z_{N'}^3$ which is just above the indifference curves at $z_{N'}'$. Then, by transitivity, one has $z_{N'}^3$ preferred to $z_{N'}^2$.

However, if the bundles in $z_{N'}^3$ are well located, and if the reallocation of clones among initial agents is well apportioned, one can obtain

$$\frac{1}{m \, |N|} \sum_{i \in N'} z_i^3 \ll z_1^2.$$

In addition, $z_{N'}^2$ is efficient in the economy with endowment equal to its total consumption. By proportional-efficient dominance, then, one should have $z_{N'}^2$ weakly better than $z_{N'}^3$; this yields a contradiction. The detailed proof is in the appendix.

This last result suggests that $\mathbf{R}^{EW}$ is more sensitive than $\mathbf{R}^{\Omega\text{lex}}$ to the efficiency, or lack of efficiency, of allocations (in particular, proportional allocations). Obviously, though, this does not make $\mathbf{R}^{EW}$ satisfy strong Pareto, and one may wonder how to refine $\mathbf{R}^{EW}$ to remedy this deficiency. A natural option is to use the leximin criterion applied to $\left(u_p(z_i, R_i)\right)_{i\in N}$, for $p \in \arg\text{lex}_{p\in\Pi_\Omega} \min_{i\in N} u_p(z_i, R_i)$ (meaning that p is chosen also with the leximin criterion). Let us call it $\mathbf{R}^{EW\text{lex}}$ for further reference.

One drawback of $\mathbf{R}^{EW\text{lex}}$ is that it satisfies well-off separation only on the subdomain of differentiable preferences, because when indifference curves of badly-off agents have cusps, a well-off agent may influence the computation of p, no matter how great that agent's share is. A lexicographic combination of $\mathbf{R}^{EW}$ and $\mathbf{R}^{\Omega\text{lex}}$ (i.e., $z_N \mathbf{R}(E) z_N'$ iff either $z_N \mathbf{P}^{EW}(E) z_N'$, or $z_N \mathbf{I}^{EW}(E) z_N'$ and $z_N \mathbf{R}^{\Omega\text{lex}}(E) z_N'$) is better in this respect.

$\mathbf{R}^{EW}$ has been called the egalitarian Walrasian SOF in reference to the fact that it selects $S^{EW}(E)$ for all $E \in \mathcal{E}$. Actually, a whole family of SOFs, with an arbitrarily low degree of inequality aversion, have this feature. Let W be any social welfare function (defined over vectors $x_N \in \mathbb{R}_+^N$) which is minimally Paretian and inequality averse in the following sense: *The maximum of $W(x_N)$ under the constraint $\sum_{i\in N} x_i \leq c$ is attained only by the egalitarian vector x_N such that $x_i = c/|N|$ for all i.* A typical example of such a function is $W(x_N) = \sum_{i\in N} \varphi(x_i)$, with a strictly concave φ, but the family of functions W satisfying the preceding property is much larger. We have the following simple result.

Theorem 5.7 *Let $\mathbf{R}$ be defined on the domain $\mathcal{E}$ by: for all $E = (R_N, \Omega) \in \mathcal{E}$ and $z_N, z_N' \in X^N$,*

$$z_N \mathbf{R}(E) z_N' \Leftrightarrow \max_{p\in\Pi_\Omega} W\left((u_p(z_i, R_i))_{i\in N}\right) \geq \max_{p\in\Pi_\Omega} W\left((u_p(z_i', R_i))_{i\in N}\right).$$

Then, for all $E \in \mathcal{E}$,

$$\max|_{\mathbf{R}(E)} Z(E) = S^{EW}(E).$$

Proof. Let $E = (R_N, \Omega) \in \mathcal{E}$, $z_N \in S^{EW}(E)$, with supporting price vector $p^* \in \Pi_\Omega$, and $z_N' \in Z(E)$. Let $p' \in \Pi_\Omega$ maximize $W\left((u_p(z_i', R_i))_{i\in N}\right)$. For all $i \in N$, $u_{p'}(z_i', R_i) \leq p'z_i'$. Therefore one has

$$\sum_{i\in N} u_{p'}(z_i', R_i) \leq \sum_{i\in N} p'z_i' \leq \sum_{i\in N} p^*z_i = 1,$$

and moreover $p^*z_i = u_{p^*}(z_i, R_i) = 1/|N|$ for all $i \in N$. By the property of W,

$$W\left((u_{p'}(z_i', R_i))_{i\in N}\right) \leq W\left((u_{p^*}(z_i, R_i))_{i\in N}\right).$$

Because

$$W\left((u_{p'}(z_i', R_i))_{i\in N}\right) = \max_{p\in\Pi_\Omega} W\left((u_p(z_i', R_i))_{i\in N}\right)$$

and

$$W\left(\left(u_{p^*}(z_i, R_i)\right)_{i \in N}\right) \leq \max_{p \in \Pi_\Omega} W\left(\left(u_p(z_i, R_i)\right)_{i \in N}\right),$$

one obtains

$$\max_{p \in \Pi_\Omega} W\left(\left(u_p(z'_i, R_i)\right)_{i \in N}\right) \leq \max_{p \in \Pi_\Omega} W\left(\left(u_p(z_i, R_i)\right)_{i \in N}\right).$$

with a strict inequality if $z'_N \notin S^{EW}(E)$ because in that case either $(u_{p'}(z'_i, R_i))_{i \in N}$ is unequal or $\sum_{i \in N} u_{p'}(z_i, R_i) < 1$, implying

$$W\left(\left(u_{p'}(z'_i, R_i)\right)_{i \in N}\right) < W\left(\left(u_{p^*}(z_i, R_i)\right)_{i \in N}\right). \qquad \blacksquare$$

Among the whole family depicted in Theorem 5.7, however, only one of them satisfies transfer among equals, namely $\mathbf{R}^{EW}$.

5.4 SECOND-BEST APPLICATIONS

In public economics, the problem of distributing unproduced commodities is less prominent than contexts involving production, because if wealth is observable, it appears easy to redistribute it by lump-sum transfers. When such transfers are not possible, however, as in Ramsey's (1927) approach, substantial analysis is required to figure out what the optimal allocation looks like. Ramsey considered a single individual, which made the impossibility of a lump-sum tax quite artificial. When there are several individuals,[11] lump-sum transfers are not possible if wealth is not observable, or if preferences are not observable and are important for measuring well-being. Then one faces an interesting problem.

Our simple model is useful to illustrate how our specific SOFs can be relied on in the evaluation of allocations under incentive constraints. The informational context on which we focus is the standard setting for taxation theory.[12] The policymaker knows the statistical distribution of the agents' characteristics, without knowing the exact profile. For instance, in a two-agent economy, the policymaker knows that the profile is either $R_N = (R, R')$ or the permuted $R_N^\pi = (R', R)$, but no more. Let $E = (R_N, \Omega)$ and $E^\pi = (R_N^\pi, \Omega)$. This lack of information is not too bad if the social ordering is itself anonymous, because the policymaker can then propose a menu of bundles $\{z, z'\}$ to the agents, knowing in advance that the agent with R will choose z and the agent with R' will choose z'. If the social ordering is anonymous, it does not matter at all whether $z_N = (z, z')$ is obtained in E or $z_N^\pi = (z', z)$ is obtained in E^π, because if z_N is the best allocation in some subset for $\mathbf{R}(E)$, then z_N^π is also the best in the corresponding permuted subset for $\mathbf{R}(E^\pi)$. (With a nonanonymous social

---

[11] Ramsey's analysis has been extended to several individuals by Diamond and Mirrlees (1971) and Diamond (1975).

[12] Unlike most of the literature on commodity taxation, we examine the set of incentive-compatible allocations rather than the smaller set of allocations obtainable by linear excise taxes.

ordering, things are more difficult for the policymaker if, to favor an agent i over another agent j, it is important to know what i's and j's true preferences are.)

Nonetheless, as is well documented in taxation theory, the lack of precise knowledge of the profile reduces the set of feasible allocations, because it makes it impossible to give precise agents with particular (unobservable) characteristics a menu that is less favorable than others'. Because the purpose of this section is only to provide a simple illustration of the general method, we focus on the two-agent case. The two-agent case is often used as a heuristic device in optimal taxation theory (e.g., Stiglitz 1982). The analysis of incentive compatibility in terms of self-selection constraints does not correspond to dominant strategy implementation unless there is a continuum of agents (see, e.g., Hammond 1979). The two-agent case is actually equivalent to a continuum population with two homogeneous groups of agents of equal size. The following exercise, therefore, can be interpreted in either way. Moreover, it allows us to use the Edgeworth box for graphical representations. Let $E = (R_N, \omega_N)$ with $N = \{1, 2\}$. Agents have private endowments, but we suppose that these endowments are not particularly legitimate, so the only morally relevant information about resources is the total amount $\Omega = \sum_{i \in N} \omega_i$ and the relevant SOF is either $\mathbf{R}^{\Omega \text{lex}}$ or $\mathbf{R}^{EW}$.

We suppose that the policymaker does not observe endowments ω_i, preferences R_i, or final consumption z_i, but only the agents' net trades $z_i - \omega_i$. By anonymity, it is undesirable to give some agents with a particular name (which is observable) a less favorable menu than to others', and incentive compatibility, as explained previously makes it also impossible to discriminate among agents with different unobservable characteristics. As a consequence, the relevant set of allocations among which the policymaker can choose is the set $\widehat{Z}(E)$ defined by:

$$\widehat{Z}(E) = \left\{ z_N \in Z(E) \mid \forall i, j \in N, \ z_i \ R_i \ \omega_i + z_j - \omega_j \text{ or } \omega_i + z_j - \omega_j \notin X \right\}.$$

The condition $\omega_i + z_j - \omega_j \notin X$ corresponds to the simple situation in which i cannot envy j's trade because it is impossible for i (it would entail negative consumption for some goods). The first part of the incentive constraint defining this set can also be written

$$\omega_i + (z_i - \omega_i) \ R_i \ \omega_i + \left(z_j - \omega_j \right),$$

which makes it more transparent that no agent should envy another's net trade. This condition is satisfied in a given allocation z_N if and only if it can be obtained by letting agents choose from a menu of net trades that contains at least $(z_i - \omega_i)_{i \in N}$.

The restriction to two agents is helpful to simplify the incentive constraint. If $z_1 + z_2 \leq \omega_1 + \omega_2$, then for $i \neq j$, $z_j - \omega_j \leq -(z_i - \omega_i)$, so

$$\omega_i + z_j - \omega_j \leq \omega_i - (z_i - \omega_i) = 2\omega_i - z_i.$$

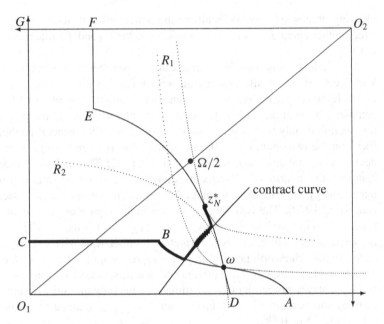

Figure 5.7. Incentive compatibility in the Edgeworth box

Therefore, if for all $i \in \{1, 2\}$,

$$z_i \, R_i \, 2\omega_i - z_i, \qquad (5.5)$$

then necessarily $z_i \, R_i \, \omega_i + z_j - \omega_j$ for all $i, j \in \{1, 2\}$. Conversely, if an allocation is balanced (i.e., $z_1 + z_2 = \omega_1 + \omega_2$), then $\omega_i + z_j - \omega_j = 2\omega_i - z_i$, and if it is incentive-compatible, then it satisfies (5.5). Incidentally, it can be shown that wasting resources would not help in any way to achieve a better allocation, for a SOF satisfying weak or strong Pareto, so we can focus on balanced allocations.

The relevant incentive constraint is then (5.5) in the two-agent case. This constraint can be given a simple geometric representation in terms of an adaptation of the Kolm curve (Kolm 1972 defines it for $\omega_i = \Omega/|N|$):

$$K(\omega_i, R_i) = \{x \in X \mid x \, I_i \, 2\omega_i - x\}.$$

This set contains ω_i and is symmetric with respect to it, because

$$x \in K(\omega_i, R_i) \Leftrightarrow 2\omega_i - x \in K(\omega_i, R_i),$$

and this combined with $x \, I_i \, 2\omega_i - x$ also implies that the marginal rates of substitution for this set at ω_i are the same as for agent i's indifference set $I(\omega_i, R_i)$. The incentive constraint then boils down to z_i being in $K(\omega_i, R_i)$ or above it.

Figure 5.7 illustrates how this produces a simple graphical representation in the Edgeworth box. The dotted curves are some of the agents' indifference curves. The set $K(\omega_1, R_1)$ is represented in the figure by the curve AB, and $K(\omega_2, R_2)$ is depicted by DE. The line segments BC and EF are the rest of the frontier of the set of incentive-compatible allocations; they correspond to the case in which $\omega_i + z_j - \omega_j \notin X$, which forms part of the definition of $\widehat{Z}(E)$. This set, in the figure, is therefore represented by the area $CB\omega EFG$. Notice that the line segments BC and EF themselves do not belong to the set of incentive-compatible allocations, which therefore turns out not to be closed in this example.

The thick curve in the figure represents the subset of allocations that are Pareto efficient in $\widehat{Z}(E)$, or second-best efficient allocations, for short. As in the figure, this subset typically contains part of the contract curve and part of the two Kolm curves.[13] It never contains allocations in the interior of $\widehat{Z}(E)$ that are not part of the contract curve, because for every such allocation one finds other allocations in $\widehat{Z}(E)$ that are better for both agents. The endpoints are the allocations that are the best for one agent under the incentive constraint of the other. Rigorously speaking, BC does not belong to this set, but is thickened because it contains allocations that are Pareto efficient in the closure of $\widehat{Z}(E)$. Such allocations are almost incentive-compatible, as there are incentive-compatible allocations arbitrarily close to any of them.

An additional constraint that may be added to the analysis is the individual rationality constraint:

$$\forall i \in N, \ x \, R_i \, \omega_i. \tag{5.6}$$

In this model there is no deep reason to impose it, but the political context may make it relevant (e.g., a poll tax may seem unacceptable). In the particular context of the two-agent economy, it turns out that (5.6) implies (5.5). Indeed, convexity of preferences entails that if $2\omega_i - x \, P_i \, x$, then $(x + 2\omega_i - x)/2 = \omega_i \, P_i \, x$. Therefore, in this special case, individual rationality trumps incentive constraints. The extra-thick part of the contract curve illustrates this in the figure.

The best policy, in this context, consists of choosing the point in the thick (or extra-thick) curve that is the best for the social ordering $\mathbf{R}(E)$. When $\mathbf{R}(E) = \mathbf{R}^{\Omega \text{lex}}(E)$, in the example of Figure 5.7, the best incentive-compatible allocation is z_N^* because the corresponding indifference curve for agent 1 cuts the ray of Ω just above $\Omega/2$, whereas agent 2's indifference curve intersects the ray below the DE curve and, therefore, farther away from $\Omega/2$. Notice that z_N^* is not first-best Pareto efficient in $Z(E)$. To improve agent 1's situation, agent 2 is induced by public policy to trade more than would be efficient. The best incentive-compatible and individually rational allocation is the highest point on the extra-thick curve.

Determining the best point for $\mathbf{R}^{EW}(E)$ seems less easy graphically. We conclude this section with a few observations. First, moving from one point to

---

[13] The subset of a particular Kolm curve that contains second-best efficient allocations is not necessarily connected, because the agents' Kolm curves can cross several times.

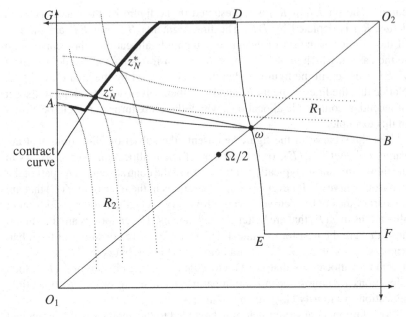

Figure 5.8. The richer is worse off

the other on the thick curve always makes one agent better off and the other worse off. This is obvious on the contract curve but it is also true on the relevant parts of the Kolm curves, because, as can be seen from the construction of the Kolm curve, for any agent i, the farther from ω_i a point is on $K(\omega_i, R_i)$, the worse for R_i.

Second, it may be that the best point on the thick curve belongs to a line segment such as BC, so this point is not incentive-compatible. This implies that, in such a case, there is no best incentive-compatible allocation for $\mathbf{R}(E)$, but at the same time that it is possible to find an incentive-compatible allocation arbitrarily close to this point. The nonexistence of a best incentive-compatible allocation, in this configuration, is therefore not really problematic in practice.

A third, more exotic, observation is that the second-best allocation for $\mathbf{R}^{\Omega\text{lex}}(E)$ or $\mathbf{R}^{EW}(E)$ may turn out to be better than the competitive equilibrium for the agent who has the greater endowment, and worse than the competitive equilibrium for the agent with the smaller endowment. In other words, the best policy may consist in taxing the poor at the benefit of the rich. Figure 5.8 illustrates this possibility for $\mathbf{R}^{\Omega\text{lex}}(E)$. The Kolm curve for agent 1 is AB; for agent 2, it is DE (extended by EF in order to take account of the second part of the incentive constraint). The set of incentive-compatible allocations is $A\omega DG$, the set of Pareto efficient allocations among incentive-compatible allocations is the thick curve.

In this example, agent 1 is better endowed than agent 2, but at the competitive equilibrium z_N^c, agent 1's indifference curve cuts the ray of Ω closer to $\Omega/2$ than

Table 5.1. *Properties of two SOFs*

	$\mathbf{R}^{\Omega\text{lex}}$	$\mathbf{R}^{EW}$
Strong Pareto	+	−
Nested-contour priority	+	+
Equal-split priority	+	−
Proportional-allocations transfer	+	−
Equal-split selection	+	+
Separation	+	−
Well-off separation	+	+
Envy-free selection	−	+
Selection monotonicity	−	+
Proportional-efficient dominance	−	+

agent 2's indifference curve. Therefore, the optimal second-best allocation for $\mathbf{R}^{\Omega\text{lex}}(E)$, z_N^*, is better for agent 1 and worse for agent 2. In this example, it is also the optimal first-best allocation. For $\mathbf{R}^{EW}(E)$ a similar paradox may occur simply because, as is well known from the "transfer paradox," starting from the egalitarian Walrasian allocation, it may happen that a transfer of endowment from an agent to the other produces a new equilibrium that is better than the egalitarian Walrasian allocation for the donor and worse for the recipient.

5.5 CONCLUSION

The Ω-equivalent leximin SOF $\mathbf{R}^{\Omega\text{lex}}$ on one side and the egalitarian Walrasian SOF $\mathbf{R}^{EW}$ on the other provide two different ways of evaluating individual situations and allocations. The latter gives more attention to efficiency (proportional efficient dominance), responsibility, and neutrality with respect to preferences (envy-free selection, selection monotonicity), whereas the former is more favorable to equal-split allocations (proportional-allocations transfer, equal-split transfer) and satisfies more separability properties (separation and weaker axioms). Table 5.1 recalls the various properties satisfied by these two SOFs. When several properties are logically related, we retain only the strongest that is satisfied in similar fashion to the others.

The fact that the Ω-equivalent SOFs focus more on equal split has an interesting consequence. They cater more to the preferences of agents who particularly like bundles proportional to Ω. This "bias" can be seen in the following thought experiment. Suppose that agent i's preferences change from R_i to R_i', such that for all $\lambda > 0$, $U(\lambda\Omega, R_i') \subseteq U(\lambda\Omega, R_i)$, which means that bundles proportional to Ω go up in i's ranking. Then, in any allocation z_N, necessarily $u_\Omega(z_i, R_i') \leq u_\Omega(z_i, R_i)$, implying that agent i's degree of priority in the egalitarian social evaluation can only go up if it changes. See Figure 5.9 for an illustration.

In the figure, agent i at z_i gets a lower Ω-equivalent utility with preferences that exhibit a stronger complementarity between goods, with an optimal

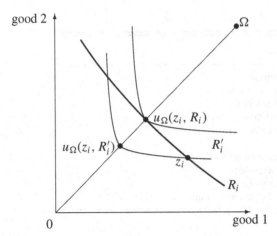

Figure 5.9. Preference changes and $\mathbf{R}^{\Omega\text{lex}}$

proportion corresponding to the direction of the social endowment Ω. If a change of allocation is considered, the interests of agents with such preferences are therefore given priority, by $\mathbf{R}^{\Omega\text{lex}}$, over those of agents with more substitutability in their preferences. This slight bias must not, however, be interpreted as a perfectionist view trying to impose "good" preferences on the population. The $\mathbf{R}^{\Omega\text{lex}}$ satisfies strong Pareto and therefore never goes against the agents' actual preferences.

Let us compare this with the egalitarian Walrasian SOF $\mathbf{R}^{EW}$. It actually also favors some preferences. With this SOF, however, there is no *absolute* kind of preferences that are likely to put an agent in higher priority; rather, it is a matter of *relative* situation in the population profile. Roughly speaking, being more eccentric – that is, having preferences more different from those of the rest of the population – is more likely to put an agent in the category of the worst-off. For instance, in Figure 5.3, one may consider agent 1 as eccentric compared with the others; one sees that this agent is indeed considered to be one of the worst-off in this example. The fact that $\mathbf{R}^{EW}$ satisfies properties reflecting ideas of responsibility and neutrality with respect to preferences – in particular, envy-free selection and selection monotonicity – is therefore in agreement with this observation that there is no special type of preferences, defined absolutely, that it particularly favors.[14]

To complete this chapter, let us consider yet another way of looking at the difference between $\mathbf{R}^{\Omega\text{lex}}$ and $\mathbf{R}^{EW}$. In Figure 5.10, allocation (z_1, z_2) is preferred to (z'_1, z'_2), according to $\mathbf{R}^{EW}$ as $\lambda > \lambda'$. If we take those λ and λ' as measure of the well-being levels of the worst-off agents in both allocations, we conclude that the well-being of the worst-off has improved, whereas agent 1,

---

[14] Fleurbaey (1996) studies relative and absolute reward patterns of allocation rules. We simply adapt the discussion to SOFs.

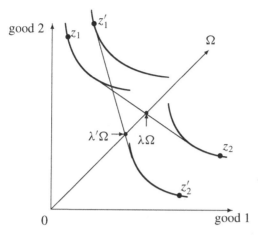

Figure 5.10. A decrease in the well-being of the worst-off agent does not necessarily decrease social welfare for $\mathbf{R}^{EW}$.

one of the worst-off, is worse off. The social judgment goes against the welfare of the worst off. That would be impossible with $\mathbf{R}^{\Omega\text{lex}}$. Why is this so?

The reason why the well-being index of agent 1 has increased in spite of her lower welfare level is that the former also depends on the bundle and preferences of agent 2. That follows from the failure of $\mathbf{R}^{EW}$ to satisfy separability. Moreover, one sees from the picture that the bundle assigned to agent 2 is larger in (z_1, z_2) than in (z_1', z_2'). Consequently, if one views the lambdas as a measure of the average quantity of resources contained in the bundles of the poor agents, then it has increased, in spite of a decrease in the bundle of agent 1. That, in turn, illustrates that $\mathbf{R}^{EW}$ is more sensitive to the amount of resources used than $\mathbf{R}^{\Omega\text{lex}}$, even if that means taking some average of the bundles of the poor agents. That is properly captured by proportional-efficient dominance.

The two ethical approaches presented in this chapter illustrate our claim in the introduction to the book that this study is about clarifying value judgments and their implications rather than proposing a unique kind of social criteria. We have just identified a first ethical divide. It separates social preferences focusing on special kinds of allocations (equal split, here) and therefore favoring agents whose preferences are oriented toward such allocations, from social preferences displaying a greater concern for responsibility and neutrality and a greater preference for efficient allocations. Other important divides will appear in the next chapters, for different contexts, but this one is essential in the sense that it appears in almost all contexts.

CHAPTER 6

Specific Domains

6.1 INTRODUCTION

The results of the previous chapter suggest that $\mathbf{R}^{\Omega\text{lex}}$ and $\mathbf{R}^{EW}$ are salient social ordering functions for the problem of distribution of unproduced commodities. The characterization results have highlighted the ethical underpinnings of such criteria. The analysis of the previous chapter focused on the canonical framework and the basic concepts; we now turn to a series of extensions of the analysis to different frameworks or different concepts.

First, we focus on different domains of preference profiles. Section 6.2 is about a particular domain restriction, namely, that which occurs when preferences correspond to expected utility maximization and the various goods are contingent amounts of money in different states of nature. In Section 6.3 we examine what happens when the domain of profiles of individual preferences is enlarged to admit nonconvex preferences. This is more than a technical issue because nonconvexities in preferences are very likely to occur in many contexts. In this larger domain, the results single out $\mathbf{R}^{\Omega\text{lex}}$ as the outstanding solution. Section 6.4 is devoted to the special case of homothetic preferences. In this smaller domain, the $\mathbf{R}^{\Omega\text{Nash}}$ SOF, introduced in Section 2.3 and based on the product of Ω-equivalent utilities, becomes interesting for the Walrasian perspective. Section 6.5 is devoted to the distribution of indivisible goods in the presence of an additional divisible good such as money. Indivisibilities affect the description of allocations, the domain of preferences, many of the axioms, and the definition of solutions.

6.2 EXPECTED UTILITY

In this section, we examine a specific domain restriction, which corresponds to the case of individual preferences based on expected utility maximization.

Suppose that the ℓ goods are, in fact, contingent goods corresponding to the consumption of a single physical good in ℓ distinct states of nature, so $z_{is} \in \mathbb{R}_+$ is agent i's consumption in state s. Agent i's preferences R_i are now *ex ante* preferences over contingent bundles $z_i \in \mathbb{R}_+^\ell$. To avoid any ethical problem linked to the fact that the agents' preferences in such a setting may reflect imperfect beliefs and irrational behavior, we restrict attention to the case in which agents are expected utility maximizers (with state-independent utilities) and the probabilities of the various states of nature are objective (or at least the subjective probabilities of the agents are identical). Agent i's expected utility is written

$$EU_i(z_i) = \sum_{s=1}^{\ell} \pi_s U_i(z_{is}),$$

where π is the vector of ℓ probabilities and $U_i : \mathbb{R}_+ \to \mathbb{R}$ is i's Bernoulli utility function. Let $\mathcal{E}^R$ denote this restricted domain of economies.

In Section 4.2, the Ω_0-equivalent leximin SOF $\mathbf{R}^{\Omega_0 \text{lex}}$, which relies on a fixed reference bundle Ω_0 and therefore satisfies independence of the feasible set, has been criticized for failing to satisfy equal-split selection. There are, however, cases in which a fixed reference Ω_0 offers itself as a natural benchmark; in such cases, a condition such as equal-split selection may appear less compelling. This seems to occur here. In the current setting, indeed, certainty bundles provide a natural reference. As a consequence, equal-split selection loses its appeal because even when $\Omega / |N|$ is efficient, it may happen that agents suffer from the risk in $\Omega / |N|$ differently. Checking efficiency of equal split may not be enough, then, if one wants to evaluate individual situations accurately. The only case in which the evaluation may disregard individual risk aversions, or so it seems, is obtained with "riskless" allocations (i.e., allocations containing only bundles z_i such that $z_{is} = z_{is'}$ for all $s, s' \in \{1, \ldots, \ell\}$).

All bundles in such allocations are proportional to one another, so this corresponds to a case of proportional allocations. Moreover, the marginal rate of substitution at a certainty bundle is equal to the ratio of probabilities for all preferences based on expected utility. This implies that every certainty allocation is, in this restricted domain, Pareto efficient with respect to all possible redistributions (including risky ones) of the total quantity consumed in this allocation. Therefore, it appears that applying the transfer principle to such allocations, independently of individual preferences, is quite sensible. For further reference, let X_c denote the subset of certainty bundles.

This suggests that in this particular framework, the relevant ray of reference is not the ray to Ω but the certainty ray (i.e., the ray of certainty bundles). Let $\mathbf{1}_\ell = (1, \ldots, 1) \in \mathbb{R}_+^\ell$. Let $c(z_i, R_i)$ denote the "certainty-equivalent utility" – that is, the real number such that $z_i\, I_i\, c(z_i, R_i)\mathbf{1}_\ell$. The $\mathbf{R}^{1_\ell \text{lex}}$ SOF assesses individual situations by the certainty-equivalent utilities and applies the leximin criterion.

The restriction of the domain of preferences, however, makes it doubtful that leximin is the only acceptable aggregator of certainty-equivalent utility levels. Recall that all the theorems proving that the combination of efficiency, transfer, and robustness axioms leads to priority axioms have been derived under the assumption of a full domain of preferences. The same kind of proofs cannot be developed here. In particular, unchanged-contour independence loses some (but not all) power on this domain, because knowing two indifference curves of an agent leaves a limited leeway about the rest of the indifference map when an agent is an expected utility maximizer.[1] However, the following variant of Theorem 5.1 suggests that $\mathbf{R}^{1_\ell \text{lex}}$ is justified. This result relies on an adaptation of proportional-allocations transfer that focuses on certainty allocations:

Axiom 6.1 Certainty Transfer
For all $E = (R_N, \Omega) \in \mathcal{D}$, and $z_N, z'_N \in X_c^N$, if there exist $j, k \in N$, and $\Delta \in \mathbb{R}_{++}^\ell$ such that

$$z_j - \Delta = z'_j \gg z'_k = z_k + \Delta$$

and for all $i \neq j, k$, $z_i = z'_i$, then $z'_N \, \mathbf{R}(E) \, z_N$.

Theorem 6.1 *On the domain $\mathcal{E}^R$, if a SOF satisfies weak Pareto, nested-contour transfer, certainty transfer, and separation, then for all $E = (R_N, \Omega) \in \mathcal{E}^R$ and $z_N, z'_N \in X^N$,*

$$\min_{i \in N} c(z_i, R_i) > \min_{i \in N} c(z'_i, R_i) \Rightarrow z_N \, \mathbf{P}(E) \, z'_N.$$

Here is an intuition for the proof. Starting from z'_N, introduce one clone for every $j \neq i_0$ (where, as usual, i_0 has the smallest $c(z'_i, R_i)$), such that the clone of every j has the same preferences as j, and is given a risk-free bundle lying strictly between $c(z'_{i_0}, R_{i_0})\mathbf{1}_\ell$ and $(\min_{i \in N} c(z_i, R_i))\mathbf{1}_\ell$. By a variant of Theorem 3.2 (recall that this theorem derives nested-contour priority from nested-contour transfer, Pareto indifference, and separability), one can move the clones up by a small amount while the corresponding agents $j \neq i_0$ are moved down below $(\min_{i \in N} c(z_i, R_i)) \mathbf{1}_\ell$. Then, by certainty transfer, the clones are moved back to their original positions and i_0, who remained below them, is moved up a little. Removing the clones by separation, one obtains an allocation that is worse than z_N for every agent. One then applies weak Pareto. (See the appendix for details).

Expected utility provides an interesting domain restriction, but the analysis of this section is valid only when individual well-being can be evaluated exclusively from the *ex ante* standpoint. When individuals care not so much about their chances but above all about their final situation, it appears more respectful of their own concerns to conclude that the analysis must focus on final situations. In particular, when risk is idiosyncratic and there is no macroeconomic risk, the distribution of final situations is known *ex ante* and the evaluation can examine the distribution of final situations directly as if there was no risk. The theory of SOFs that is being developed in the rest of this book is therefore directly applicable to risky contexts, provided there is no macroeconomic risk.

---

[1] Whether Theorem 5.1 itself still holds, for instance, is doubtful, but is quite hard to ascertain. We leave this for future research.

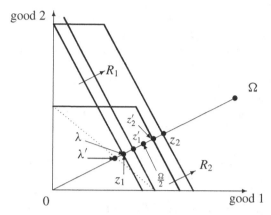

Figure 6.1. Allocation (z_1, z_2) is first-best for $\mathbf{R}^{EW}$, with $\lambda = \max_{p \in \Pi_\Omega}$ $\min_{i \in \{1,2\}} u_p(z_i, R_i)$. Allocation (z_1', z_2') is feasible, too, but $\lambda' = \max_{p \in \Pi_\Omega}$ $\min_{i \in \{1,2\}} u_p(z_i', R_i) < \lambda$.

When there is macroeconomic risk, specific criteria must be devised; this is an interesting topic of ongoing research.[2]

6.3   NONCONVEX PREFERENCES

It is well known that the competitive mechanism may break down in nonconvex economies. This difficulty has echoes in the theory of fairness – for instance, in the possible nonexistence of envy-free and efficient allocations, or even of efficient allocations in which no individual bundle strictly dominates another.[3]

The egalitarian Walrasian SOF $\mathbf{R}^{EW}$ partly remedies this difficulty. It selects Walrasian allocations with equal budgets whenever they exist, even in nonconvex economies, and is well defined in all economies, including the nonconvex. One could then imagine that in nonconvex economies it provides, by its first-best selection, an interesting generalization of the concept of Walrasian equilibrium. Unfortunately, the fact that $\mathbf{R}^{EW}$ is able to select an allocation in nonconvex economies does not mean that it always selects a satisfactory allocation, or, more generally, that it still yields appealing social preferences in this context. In particular, it does no longer satisfy equal-split selection (saying that whenever the equal-split allocation is efficient, it should be ranked among the best of the feasible allocations) in this context.

The following example illustrates the problem. Figure 6.1 displays an economy with two agents, in which the first-best optimal allocation for $\mathbf{R}^{EW}$ may

---

[2] See Fleurbaey (2010) for a proposal about how to deal with a combination of macro and micro risks.

[3] See, e.g., Varian (1974) and Maniquet (1999).

be, for some preferences,[4] as in the figure. It is quite unequal; this seems rather unjustified when one looks at the agents' indifference curves. In particular, the indifference curve of agent 2 strongly dominates that of agent 1. In contrast, $\mathbf{R}^{\Omega\text{lex}}$ always avoids such gross inequalities and, at the minimum, always guarantees that, at the first-best optimal allocation, all agents are at least as well off as at the equal-split allocation.

The next result examines what happens to social preferences when, in the wider domain allowing for nonconvex preferences, one requires the SOF to satisfy equal-split selection. Recall that, in the convex domain $\mathcal{E}$, both $\mathbf{R}^{\Omega\text{lex}}$ and $\mathbf{R}^{EW}$ satisfy this axiom. Let $\mathcal{E}^{**}$ denote the domain of economies $E = (R_N, \Omega)$ such that for all $i \in N$, R_i is a continuous, monotonic, but not necessarily convex, ordering. Although $\mathbf{R}^{EW}$ no longer satisfies equal-split selection in $\mathcal{E}^{**}$, one may hope to define a variant of $\mathbf{R}^{EW}$ for nonconvex economies that satisfies this condition. The following theorem dashes such hope, and proves that, paradoxically enough, $\mathbf{R}^{\Omega\text{lex}}$ is singled out on this larger domain by axioms that are also satisfied by $\mathbf{R}^{EW}$ when preferences are restricted to be convex.[5] In the list that follows, equal-split selection is the only axiom that is not satisfied by $\mathbf{R}^{EW}$ on $\mathcal{E}^{**}$.

Theorem 6.2 *On the domain $\mathcal{E}^{**}$, if a SOF satisfies* weak Pareto, transfer among equals, equal-split selection, unchanged-contour independence, *and* independence of proportional expansion, *then for all* $E = (R_N, \Omega) \in \mathcal{E}^{**}$ *and* $z_N, z'_N \in X^N$,

$$\min_{i \in N} u_\Omega(z_i, R_i) > \min_{i \in N} u_\Omega(z'_i, R_i) \Rightarrow z_N \, \mathbf{P}(E) \, z'_N.$$

To see how this is obtained, recall the proof of Theorem 5.1 as intuitively explained in Section 5.2. Let us reproduce the relevant part of the corresponding figure. (Figure 5.1), but with indifference curves, to be able to address the efficiency issue (see Figure 6.2; for clarity, agent j's indifference curves are thick and i_0's are thin). By the same reasoning as in Section 5.2, one arrives at allocations z_N^2, z_N^3 such that $z_N^3 \, \mathbf{P}(E'') \, z_N^2$ in economy E'' with preferences $R_N'' = (R_{i_0}, R_j'')$. The end of the proof, however, is different. The argument goes by worsening on z_N^2 to arrive at an allocation that is egalitarian like z_N^2 but is, moreover, efficient (after some suitable expansion or reduction of Ω), and uses still more resources than z_N^3 (so z_N^3 is not efficient). This produces a contradiction with equal-split selection.

In more detail, this last step proceeds as follows. First, let z_N^4 be such that

$$z_{i_0}^2 \gg z_{i_0}^4 \gg z_j^4 \gg \frac{1}{2}\left(z_{i_0}^3 + z_j^3\right),$$

---

[4] There are some conditions about the other indifference curves for this statement to be true. The details are omitted here.

[5] Fleurbaey and Maniquet (1996b), in the context of production economies, have obtained similar results with allocation rules: an egalitarian-equivalent rule may be, on a nonconvex domain, the only one that satisfies weak versions of axioms satisfied by a Walrasian rule on a convex domain.

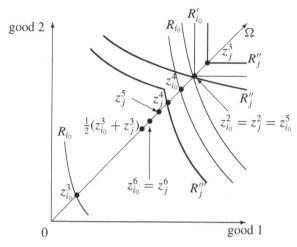

good 2

R'_{i_0}

R_{i_0}

Ω

z^3_j

R''_j

$z^4_{i_0}$

R''_j

z^5_j

z^4_j

$\frac{1}{2}(z^3_{i_0} + z^3_j)$

$z^2_{i_0} = z^2_j = z^5_{i_0}$

R_{i_0}

$z^6_{i_0} = z^6_j$

R'''_j

$z^3_{i_0}$

0

good 1

Figure 6.2. Proof of Theorem 6.2

and let R'''_j be such that $I(z^2_j, R'''_j) = I(z^2_j, R''_j)$, $I(z^3_j, R'''_j) = I(z^3_j, R''_j)$ and

$$U(z^4_{i_0}, R_{i_0}) \cap L(z^4_j, R'''_j) = \emptyset;$$

that is, the indifference curves at $z^4_{i_0}$ and z^4_j do not meet or cross. The existence of such R'''_j is guaranteed to be possible only if the domain admits nonconvex preferences. In Figure 6.2, in particular, $U(z^4_j, R'''_j)$ is not convex.

By unchanged-contour independence, $z^3_N \, \mathbf{P}(E''') \, z^2_N$ for $E''' = ((R_{i_0}, R'''_j), \Omega)$. By weak pareto, $z^2_N \, \mathbf{P}(E''') \, z^4_N$ so, by transitivity, $z^3_N \, \mathbf{P}(E''') \, z^4_N$. Let R'_{i_0} be such that $I(z^3_{i_0}, R'_{i_0}) = I(z^3_{i_0}, R_{i_0})$, $I(z^4_{i_0}, R'_{i_0}) = I(z^4_{i_0}, R_{i_0})$ and

$$U(z^2_{i_0}, R'_{i_0}) = \left\{ x \in X \mid x \geq z^2_{i_0} \right\}.$$

By unchanged-contour independence, $z^3_N \, \mathbf{P}(E^0) \, z^4_N$ for $E^0 = ((R'_{i_0}, R'''_j), \Omega)$. Let $z^5_{i_0} = z^2_{i_0}$ and

$$z^4_j \gg z^5_j \gg \frac{1}{2} \left(z^3_{i_0} + z^3_j \right).$$

(See Figure 6.2.) Because

$$z^2_{i_0} \gg z^4_{i_0} \gg z^4_j \gg z^5_j,$$

then by Theorem 3.1 – or, more precisely, by its variant Lemma A.1[6] (which remains valid on the wider domain $\mathcal{E}^{**}$) – $z^4_N \, \mathbf{P}(E^0) \, z^5_N$. By transitivity, $z^3_N \, \mathbf{P}(E^0) \, z^5_N$.

---

[6] This lemma is mentioned in Footnote 6 of Section 3.2.

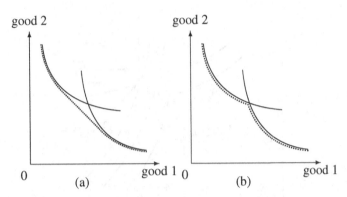

Figure 6.3. A hypothetical worst-off agent

Finally, let z_N^6 be such that

$$z_j^5 \gg z_{i_0}^6 = z_j^6 \gg \frac{1}{2}\left(z_{i_0}^3 + z_j^3\right)$$

and let R_{i_0}'' be such that $I(z_{i_0}^3, R_{i_0}'') = I(z_{i_0}^3, R_{i_0}')$, $I(z_{i_0}^5, R_{i_0}'') = I(z_{i_0}^5, R_{i_0}')$ and

$$U(z_{i_0}^6, R_{i_0}') = \left\{ x \in X \mid x \geq z_{i_0}^6 \right\}.$$

By unchanged-contour independence, $z_N^3 \, \mathbf{P}(E^{00}) \, z_N^5$ for $E^{00} = ((R_{i_0}'', R_j'''), \Omega)$ and by weak Pareto, $z_N^5 \, \mathbf{P}(E^{00}) \, z_N^6$, so by transitivity, $z_N^3 \, \mathbf{P}(E^{00}) \, z_N^6$. This raises a contradiction with equal-split selection, because z_N^6 (after expansion or reduction of Ω and invoking independence of proportional expansion) is an efficient equal-split allocation and z_N^3 is not efficient (as it wastes quantities).

This argument illustrates how much more constraining the combination of weak pareto, transfer among equals, and unchanged-contour independence is in the wider domain $\mathcal{E}^{**}$ admitting nonconvex preferences.

The result of this section can be related to the following simple observation, illustrated in Figure 6.3. Take a given allocation z_N and imagine adding a hypothetical agent who would be unambigously worse off than every agent of the actual population, in the sense that this agent's indifference curve would lie below the indifference curve of everyone else. In more rigorous terms, this agent's upper contour set would contain all the agents' upper contour sets.

Now look for the smallest contour set (with respect to inclusion) having this property (this amounts to seeking the most favorable situation for the hypothetical worst-off agent). If one looks for such a contour set among convex preferences, then one obtains a contour set that coincides with the convex hull of the union of all agents' upper contour sets (Figure 6.3(a)). This is the object that serves to evaluate an allocation with $\mathbf{R}^{EW}$. If, in contrast, one looks for such a contour set among convex and nonconvex preferences, then one simply obtains a contour set that coincides with the union of all agents' upper contour sets

(Figure 6.3(b)). This can serve to evaluate an allocation with $\mathbf{R}^{\Omega\text{lex}}$ or, rather, its maximin variant, which evaluates allocations computing $\min_{i \in N} u_\Omega(z_i, R_i)$:

Social ordering function 6.1 Ω-Equivalent Maximin ($\mathbf{R}^{\Omega min}$)
For all $E = (R_N, \Omega) \in \mathcal{E}$, $z_N, z'_N \in X^N$,

$$z_N \, \mathbf{R}^{\Omega min}(E) \, z'_N \Leftrightarrow \min_{i \in N} u_\Omega(z_i, R_i) \geq_{lex} \min_{i \in N} u_\Omega(z'_i, R_i).$$

In other words, the same operation that leads to computing $\mathbf{R}^{EW}(E)$ in a convex domain produces $\mathbf{R}^{\Omega min}(E)$ in the wider domain.

6.4 HOMOTHETIC PREFERENCES

The subdomain of profiles in which all individual preferences are homothetic offers a different outlook for some of the issues dealt with in the previous chapters. Let $\mathcal{E}^H \subseteq \mathcal{E}$ denote the subset of economies $E = (R_N, \Omega)$ such that for all $i \in N$, $z_i, z'_i \in X$, $\alpha \in \mathbb{R}_{++}$,

$$z_i \, R_i \, z'_i \Leftrightarrow \alpha z_i \, R_i \, \alpha z'_i.$$

Homotheticity entails two interesting properties for Ω-equivalent utilities and money-metric utilities. First, for all $z_i, z'_i \in X$, $R_i \in \mathcal{R}$, $\Omega, \Omega' \in \mathbb{R}_{++}^\ell$,

$$\frac{u_\Omega(z_i, R_i)}{u_\Omega(z'_i, R_i)} = \frac{u_{\Omega'}(z_i, R_i)}{u_{\Omega'}(z'_i, R_i)}.$$

Second, for all $z_i, z'_i \in X$, $R_i \in \mathcal{R}$, $\Omega, p \in \mathbb{R}_{++}^\ell$,

$$\frac{u_\Omega(z'_i, R_i)}{u_\Omega(z_i, R_i)} = \frac{u_p(z'_i, R_i)}{u_p(z_i, R_i)}.$$

On this restricted domain, $\mathbf{R}^{\Omega\text{Nash}}$ satisfies a larger set of properties than on $\mathcal{E}$. Recall that this SOF is defined as follows:

$$z_N \, \mathbf{R}^{\Omega\text{Nash}}(E) \, z'_N \Leftrightarrow \prod_{i \in N} u_\Omega(z_i, R_i) \geq \prod_{i \in N} u_\Omega(z'_i, R_i).$$

Most remarkable is the fact[7] that for all $E \in \mathcal{E}^H$ one has

$$\max|_{\mathbf{R}^{\Omega\text{Nash}}(E)} Z(E) = S^{EW}(E).$$

In other words, on this subdomain, $\mathbf{R}^{\Omega\text{Nash}}$ selects the egalitarian Walrasian allocations, such as $\mathbf{R}^{EW}$ or related SOFs highlighted in Theorem 5.7.

---

[7] This observation is from Eisenberg (1961).

Here is a simple proof of this fact.[8] Let $E = (R_N, \Omega) \in \mathcal{E}^H$, $z_N \in S^{EW}(E)$, with supporting price vector $p \in \Pi_\Omega$, and $z'_N \in Z(E)$. Because $z'_N \in Z(E)$, one has

$$\sum_{i \in N} u_p(z'_i, R_i) \le \sum_{i \in N} u_p(z_i, R_i) = 1.$$

The geometric mean is below the arithmetic mean except in case of equality. Note that $u_p(z_i, R_i) = 1/|N|$ for all $i \in N$. Therefore,

$$\left[\prod_{i \in N} u_p(z'_i, R_i) \right]^{\frac{1}{|N|}} \le \frac{1}{|N|} \sum_{i \in N} u_p(z'_i, R_i) \le \frac{1}{|N|} = \left[\prod_{i \in N} u_p(z_i, R_i) \right]^{\frac{1}{|N|}},$$

(6.1)

which implies

$$\prod_{i \in N} \frac{u_p(z'_i, R_i)}{u_p(z_i, R_i)} \le 1.$$

By homotheticity of preferences, for all $i \in N$,

$$\frac{u_\Omega(z'_i, R_i)}{u_\Omega(z_i, R_i)} = \frac{u_p(z'_i, R_i)}{u_p(z_i, R_i)},$$

so

$$\prod_{i \in N} u_\Omega(z'_i, R_i) = \prod_{i \in N} u_\Omega(z_i, R_i) \frac{u_p(z'_i, R_i)}{u_p(z_i, R_i)}$$

$$= \left[\prod_{i \in N} u_\Omega(z_i, R_i) \right] \left[\prod_{i \in N} \frac{u_p(z'_i, R_i)}{u_p(z_i, R_i)} \right] \le \prod_{i \in N} u_\Omega(z_i, R_i);$$

that is, $z_N \, \mathbf{R}^{\Omega\mathrm{Nash}}(E') \, z'_N$. If $z'_N \notin S^{EW}(E)$, then the first inequality in (6.1) is strict and $z_N \, \mathbf{P}^{\Omega\mathrm{Nash}}(E') \, z'_N$. This completes the proof.

The fact that $\mathbf{R}^{\Omega\mathrm{Nash}}$ selects egalitarian Walrasian allocations implies that it satisfies selection monotonicity on $\mathcal{E}^H$. Another interesting property that $\mathbf{R}^{\Omega\mathrm{Nash}}$ satisfies on $\mathcal{E}^H$ (but not on $\mathcal{E}$) is independence of the feasible set. This is somewhat surprising as Ω appears in the definition of this SOF.

This fact is shown as follows. Consider $E = (R_N, \Omega)$, $E' = (R_N, \Omega') \in \mathcal{E}^H$, $z_N, z'_N \in X^N$ such that $z_N \, \mathbf{R}^{\Omega\mathrm{Nash}}(E) \, z'_N$. If $\prod_{i \in N} u_\Omega(z_i, R_i)$ or $\prod_{i \in N} u_\Omega(z'_i, R_i)$ equals zero, the same holds for $\prod_{i \in N} u_{\Omega'}(z_i, R_i)$ or $\prod_{i \in N} u_{\Omega'}(z'_i, R_i)$, respectively; therefore, $z_N \, \mathbf{R}^{\Omega\mathrm{Nash}}(E') \, z'_N$ as well. We now focus on the case in which both products are positive.

---

[8] This is a simplified version of Eisenberg's proof, which proves a more general statement. Milleron (1970) gives a simple analytical proof for the case of differentiable preferences.

The fact that $z_N \, \mathbf{R}^{\Omega\text{Nash}}(E) \, z'_N$ means that

$$\prod_{i \in N} u_{\Omega}(z_i, R_i) \geq \prod_{i \in N} u_{\Omega}(z'_i, R_i)$$

and is equivalent to

$$\prod_{i \in N} \frac{u_{\Omega}(z_i, R_i)}{u_{\Omega}(z'_i, R_i)} \geq 1.$$

By homotheticity of preferences, for all $i \in N$,

$$\frac{u_{\Omega}(z_i, R_i)}{u_{\Omega}(z'_i, R_i)} = \frac{u_{\Omega'}(z_i, R_i)}{u_{\Omega'}(z'_i, R_i)}.$$

Therefore

$$\prod_{i \in N} \frac{u_{\Omega}(z_i, R_i)}{u_{\Omega}(z'_i, R_i)} \geq 1 \Leftrightarrow \prod_{i \in N} \frac{u_{\Omega'}(z_i, R_i)}{u_{\Omega'}(z'_i, R_i)} \geq 1,$$

the latter meaning that $z_N \, \mathbf{R}^{\Omega\text{Nash}}(E') \, z'_N$, as was to be proved.

Another feature that gives some advantage to $\mathbf{R}^{\Omega\text{Nash}}$ over $\mathbf{R}^{EW}$ is that it satisfies separation (on the whole domain) for allocations z_N in which every $z_i \, P_i \, 0$ for all $i \in N$. This indicates that the conflict between the Walrasian approach and separability almost vanishes in the homothetic domain. Let us denote this restricted version of separation as restricted separation.

In summary, the $\mathbf{R}^{\Omega\text{Nash}}$ SOF, on the $\mathcal{E}^H$ domain, selects $S^{EW}(E)$ for all E, satisfies independence of the feasible set, and is separable for most allocations. Are there other interesting SOFs satisfying these properties? The following result gives a negative answer and therefore singles out $\mathbf{R}^{\Omega\text{Nash}}$ as outstanding in this context.

Theorem 6.3 *On the domain $\mathcal{E}^H$, if a SOF $\mathbf{R}$ satisfies Pareto indifference, independence of the feasible set, restricted separation, and continuity, and if $\max|_{\mathbf{R}(E)} Z(E) = S^{EW}(E)$ for all E, then $\mathbf{R}$ coincides with $\mathbf{R}^{\Omega\text{Nash}}$.*

The intuition for this result is the following. The requirements imply that $\mathbf{R}(E)$ is representable by

$$W((u_i(z_i))_{i \in N}) = \sum_{i \in N} \varphi_i (u_i (z_i)),$$

where u_i is equal to $u_{\Omega}(\cdot, R_i)$ and is homogeneous when R_i is homothetic. Assuming differentiability (for the purpose of this intuitive explanation), the first-order condition for maximization of W over $Z(E)$ implies that for all $k = 1, \dots, \ell$,

$$\varphi'_i (u_i (z_i)) \frac{\partial u_i}{\partial z_{ik}} (z_i) = \lambda_k (\Omega),$$

where $\lambda (\Omega)$ is the vector of Lagrange multipliers for the resource constraint $\sum_{i \in N} z_i \leq \Omega$. Because the maximizer z_N belongs to $S^{EW}(E)$, one has $\lambda(\Omega) z_i = \lambda(\Omega) \Omega / |N|$ for all $i \in N$. Besides, u_i being homogeneous implies

$$\lambda(\Omega) z_i = \sum_{k=1}^{\ell} \varphi_i'(u_i(z_i)) \frac{\partial u_i}{\partial z_{ik}}(z_i) z_{ik} = \varphi_i'(u_i(z_i)) u_i(z_i).$$

Summarizing, one has, for all $\Omega \in \mathbb{R}_{++}^{\ell}$, all $z_N \in S^{EW}(R_N, \Omega)$, all $i \in N$,

$$\varphi_i'(u_i(z_i)) u_i(z_i) = \lambda(\Omega) \Omega / |N|.$$

Considering the possibility that preferences may be different for some agents then allows one to conclude that $\varphi_i'(u_i) u_i$ is actually constant (see the appendix for the precise argument). By integration, one obtains that φ_i is logarithmic.

One should not conclude from this section, however, that $\mathbf{R}^{\Omega \text{Nash}}$ is unquestionably the best SOF in the subdomain of homothetic preferences. It remains true on this subdomain that, contrary to $\mathbf{R}^{\Omega \text{lex}}$ and $\mathbf{R}^{EW}$, $\mathbf{R}^{\Omega \text{Nash}}$ does not satisfy transfer among equals and that, contrary to $\mathbf{R}^{\Omega \text{lex}}$, it does not satisfy equal-split transfer. Actually, these two properties are violated by every member of the class of SOFs defined by: for all $z_N, z_N' \in X^N$, $z_N \mathbf{R}^{\Omega \alpha}(E) z_N'$ if and only if

$$\frac{1}{1-\alpha} \sum_{i \in N} (u_\Omega(z_i, R_i))^{1-\alpha} \geq \frac{1}{1-\alpha} \sum_{i \in N} (u_\Omega(z_i', R_i))^{1-\alpha},$$

where $\alpha \geq 0$, $\alpha \neq 1$ is a given parameter. By taking the limit when $\alpha \to 1$, $\mathbf{R}^{\Omega \text{Nash}}$ can be considered a member of this class. The violation of transfer among equals and equal-split transfer can be shown easily in a two-good, two-agent economy by considering Leontief preferences R^L represented by $\min \{z_{i1}, z_{i2}\}$. For $\Omega = (3, 3)$, one obtains, for $\varepsilon \in [0, 1)$,

$$u_\Omega((1, 1), R^L) = 1/3,$$

$$u_\Omega((1 + \varepsilon, 2), R^L) = (1 + \varepsilon)/3,$$

$$u_\Omega((5 - \varepsilon, 4), R^L) = 4/3,$$

$$u_\Omega((5, 5), R^L) = 5/3.$$

One has $(5, 5) - (5 - \varepsilon, 4) = (1 + \varepsilon, 2) - (1, 1)$, $u_\Omega((5, 5), R^L) - u_\Omega$ $((5 - \varepsilon, 4), R^L) = 1/3$, and $u_\Omega((1 + \varepsilon, 2), R^L) - u_\Omega((1, 1), R^L) = \varepsilon/3$. For every α there is ε small enough that $((1, 1), (5, 5)) \mathbf{P}^{\Omega \alpha}(E)$ $((1 + \varepsilon, 2), (5 - \varepsilon, 4))$, in contradiction to both transfer axioms. In other words, an absolute priority to the worst-off remains attractive in this subdomain. Interestingly, this is obtained in spite of the results of Chapter 3 no longer being true (in particular, unchanged-contour independence becomes vacuous in this domain).

6.5 INDIVISIBLES

Many division problems of interest involve goods, or objects, that are not perfectly divisible. This section studies how SOFs can be defined and axiomatized in economies with indivisibilities.[9] Contrary to the previous sections of this chapter, this is not about a specific domain of preferences, but rather about a different technology of resource sharing.

A great variety of models with indivisibles can be studied. Here we concentrate on the allocation of desirable objects having the property that each agent may consume at most one of these objects. Think of apartments in a housing complex, seats at a concert, parking lots, tasks in a board of directors, and so on. Again, preferences may differ among agents. We assume that monetary compensations are allowed for those who do not receive any objects or who receive an object they would be willing to exchange for another object. The question we have to address is: What could be an equitable way of assigning objects among those agents, and how should the compensations be computed?

Let us begin by defining the model formally. There is an infinite set $\mathcal{A}$ of objects. In specific economies, an agent may be assigned either an available object from $\mathcal{A}$ or no object at all. In the latter case, we say that this agent receives the "null object," which is denoted ν. Let $\mathcal{A}^* \equiv \mathcal{A} \cup \{\nu\}$. The resources available in an economy are described by a finite set of objects $A \subseteq \mathcal{A}$. We assume that there are at least two agents and that there is at least one object to assign but never more objects than agents; that is, $|N| \geq 2$ and $1 \leq |A| \leq |N|$. Preferences are defined over bundles $z_i = (a_i, m_i) \in \mathcal{A}^* \times \mathbb{R}$, where a_i is the object received by i, and m_i is a money transfer, which is positive if i receives money and negative if i has to pay. For simplicity, we assume that there is no bound on how much an agent may have to pay (no liquidity constraint). We assume that preferences are continuous and strictly monotonic with respect to money. We also assume that all objects are desirable and their value is always finite; that is, for all $(a_i, m_i) \in \mathcal{A} \times \mathbb{R}$, $(a_i, m_i) \, P_i \, (\nu, m_i)$, and there exists $m_i' \in \mathbb{R}$ such that $(a_i, m_i) \, I_i \, (\nu, m_i')$. Let $\mathcal{R}^{ind}$ and $\mathcal{E}^{ind}$, respectively, denote the set of all such preferences and the set of all such economies.

In the preceding chapters and sections, SOFs were required to be able to rank feasible and infeasible allocations. The basic reason for that requirement was that infeasible allocations may become feasible after operations that are associated with axioms, notably the removal of agents implied by separation.

It is not immediate to determine the set of allocations that a SOF should be required to rank in the current model. By assumption, each object comes in exactly one unit and will never be consumed by more than one agent. On the other hand, the total amount of money associated to an allocation may be strictly positive; thus, this allocation is not feasible as long as money does not come from outside the economy, but the arrival of new agents is likely to make this allocation feasible. Nevertheless, given the simple structure of the model,

---

[9] This section is largely inspired by Maniquet (2008).

we can restrict ourselves to allocations that do not require money from outside. This assumption makes some reasoning longer but does not change the nature of the results. It simply shows that in this context, no proof requires consideration of infeasible allocations. Consequently, we require SOFs to rank allocations z_N for an economy $E = (R_N, A) \in \mathcal{E}^{ind}$ such that all objects assigned in z_N come from A, no two agents are assigned the same "real" object (there is no limit on the set of agents who receive the null object), and no money is required from outside ($\sum_{i \in N} m_i \leq 0$). Let $Z(E)$ denote this set of allocations.

Let us begin our study by adapting the two major SOFs encountered in Chapter 5 and in the previous sections of this chapter to the current setting. There is no immediate way of defining bundles that are "proportional" to the available set of objects. On the other hand, given that there is only one divisible good – money – it seems natural to measure well-being in money. One possible solution consists in applying the leximin criterion to indices $u_m(z_i, R_i)$ defined as the amount of money that leaves the agent indifferent between his or her assigned bundle and receiving that amount of money and no object; that is,

$$u_m(z_i, R_i) = m \Leftrightarrow z_i \, I_i \, (v, m).$$

This yields the following SOF:

Social ordering function 6.2 m-Equivalent Leximin ($\mathbf{R}^{mlex}$)
For all $E = (R_N, A) \in \mathcal{E}^{ind}$, $z_N, z'_N \in Z(E)$,

$$z_N \, \mathbf{R}^{mlex} \, (E) \, z'_N \Leftrightarrow (u_m(z_i, R_i))_{i \in N} \geq_{lex} \left(u_m(z'_i, R_i) \right)_{i \in N}.$$

The egalitarian Walrasian SOF is easier to adapt to this model than the egalitarian-equivalent SOF. The price of the divisible good can be fixed at 1, so we focus on price vectors $p \in \mathbb{R}^A_+$, and, abusing notation, we let the money value of a bundle $z_i = (a_i, m_i)$ be defined as

$$pz_i = p_{a_i} + m_i \text{ if } a_i \in A, \text{ and}$$

$$pz_i = m_i \text{ if } a_i = v.$$

Thus, the SOF $\mathbf{R}^{EW}$ is defined as follows.

Social ordering function 6.3 Egalitarian Walrasian ($\mathbf{R}^{EW}$)
For all $E = (R_N, A) \in \mathcal{E}^{ind}$, $z_N, z'_N \in Z(E)$,

$$z_N \, \mathbf{R}^{EW} \, (E) \, z'_N \Leftrightarrow \max_{p \in \mathbb{R}^A_+} \min_{i \in N} \min \left\{ px \mid x \, R_i \, z_i \right\}$$

$$\geq \max_{p \in \mathbb{R}^A_+} \min_{i \in N} \min \left\{ px \mid x \, R_i \, z'_i \right\}.$$

In this model, for any fixed $p \in \mathbb{R}^A_+$, the money-metric utility associated with a pair (z_i, R_i) is the quantity of money that, given price vector p, enables this agent to buy an object (perhaps the "null" object) and reach the same satisfaction level as at z_i. So, clearly, $\min \{px \mid x \, R_i \, z_i\} \leq u_m(z_i, R_i)$, because $(v, u_m(z_i, R_i)) \, R_i \, z_i$ and the value of the bundle $(v, u_m(z_i, R_i))$ is $u_m(z_i, R_i)$.

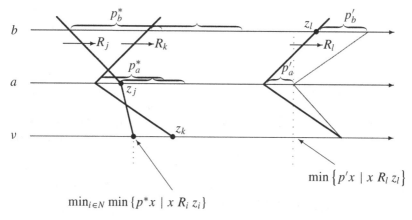

$$\min_{i \in N} \min \{ p^* x \mid x \, R_i \, z_i \}$$

Figure 6.4. Equivalence between the $\mathbf{R}^{EW}$ and $\mathbf{R}^{mlex}$ SOFs

Moreover, when the price of the real objects is high enough, the agent indeed chooses not to buy any of them and reaches a well-being level of $u_m(z_i, R_i)$; that is,

$$\max_{p \in \mathbb{R}_+^A} \min \{ px \mid x \, R_i \, z_i \} = u_m(z_i, R_i).$$

This reasoning extends to groups of agents. For a fixed p, one has

$$\min_{i \in N} \min \{ px \mid x \, R_i \, z_i \} \leq \min_{i \in N} u_m(z_i, R_i),$$

and for sufficiently high prices of the real objects, the two terms are equal, so

$$\max_{p \in \mathbb{R}_+^A} \min_{i \in N} \min \{ px \mid x \, R_i \, z_i \} = \min_{i \in N} u_m(z_i, R_i).$$

This fact is illustrated in Figure 6.4. The economy is composed of the set $N = \{j, k, l\}$ of agents, and the set $A = \{a, b\}$ of objects. The horizontal axes measure the quantity of money, and each axis corresponds to a specific object (the lower axis corresponds to the null object). On the right part of the figure, the money-metric utility of bundle z_l is computed, given the price vector $p' = (p'_a, p'_b)$ and preferences R_ℓ. The thin curve depicts the monetary value of each of the three bundles that are on the same indifference curve as z_l. For instance, if agent l is endowed with the amount of money corresponding to the right end of the bracket on the upper axis and then pays p'_b, the agent ends up with z_l. If the agent starts with the amount of money corresponding to the right end of the bracket on the middle axis and then pays p'_a, the agent ends up with a bundle comprising object a that he or she considers just as good as z_l. We can deduce that the minimum quantity of money that is necessary to help agent l reach the same well-being as at z_l corresponds to the agent's buying good a. This defines $\min \{ p'x \mid x \, R_l \, z_l \}$. In the left part of the figure, the price vector is now endogenous, and it is computed to maximize the money-metric utility of agent j, as agent j appears to be the poorest one. The large brackets on the upper axis correspond to p_b^*, and the smaller brackets on the middle axis correspond to p_a^*. The thin curves joining the right ends of the brackets are not drawn, but one can easily see that the right ends of the brackets are all on the right of $u_m(z_j, R_j)$, which is then equal to $\min_{i \in N} \min\{p^*x \mid x \, R_i \, z_i\}$. It is obviously impossible to raise $\min_{i \in N} \min\{px \mid x \, R_i \, z_i\}$ more by changing the price, because the point representing $\min_{i \in N} u_m(z_i, R_i)$ on the lower axis cannot be moved. This proves that the price vector $p^* = (p_a^*, p_b^*)$ is therefore an example of a maximizing price vector, and that $\min_{i \in N} u_m(z_i, R_i)$ is necessarily equal to $\max_{p \in \mathbb{R}_+^A} \min_{i \in N} \min\{px \mid x \, R_i \, z_i\}$.

To sum up, the preceding discussion has shown that the two SOFs defined so far are actually almost identical in the current model, as $\mathbf{R}^{mlex}$ is a refinement of $\mathbf{R}^{EW}$. More formally, we have proved the following lemma.

Lemma 6.1 *For all* $E = (R_N, A) \in \mathcal{E}^{ind}$, $z_N, z'_N \in Z(E)$,

$$z_N \, \mathbf{P}^{EW} \, z'_N \Rightarrow z_N \, \mathbf{P}^{mlex} \, z'_N.$$

We can therefore expect $\mathbf{R}^{mlex}$ to satisfy a long list of axioms. It is easily seen that it satisfies strong Pareto, unchanged-contour independence, separation, and independence of the feasible set. Let us add two axioms to this list. First, this SOF is independent of changes in preferences over infeasible bundles. Indeed, if only objects a and b are currently available but preferences over object c change, then the ranking of the allocations we must rank does not change, as an agent's money-metric utility of the feasible bundles remains unaffected. In the division model of Chapter 5 (with divisible commodities), $\mathbf{R}^{\Omega lex}$ shares this property with $\mathbf{R}^{mlex}$, whereas $\mathbf{R}^{EW}$ does not.

Axiom 6.2 Independence of Preferences over Infeasible Bundles
For all $E = (R_N, A)$, $E' = (R'_N, A) \in \mathcal{D}$, and $z_N, z'_N \in X^N$, if for all $a, b \in A \cup \{v\}$ and $m, m' \in \mathbb{R}$,

$$\forall i \in N : (a, m) \, R_i \, (b, m') \Leftrightarrow (a, m) \, R'_i \, (b, m'),$$

then $z_N \, \mathbf{R}(E) \, z'_N \Leftrightarrow z_N \, \mathbf{R}(E') \, z'_N$.

The second additional axiom that turns out to be satisfied by $\mathbf{R}^{mlex}$ is the following consistency axiom. It belongs to the family of axioms such as separability and separation. It requires that the ranking of two allocations be unaffected by the withdrawal from society of an agent consuming the same bundle in the two allocations, providing that this agent withdraws from society by bringing the bundle with him or her, with the consequence that the set of available objects shrinks.[10] Formally, the axiom is presented as follows.

---

[10] Unlike separability or separation, consistency parallels the consistency axiom studied in the fair allocation literature. See Bevia (1996) and Tadenuma and Thomson (1991).

Axiom 6.3 Consistency

For all $E = (R_N, A) \in \mathcal{D}$ with $|N| \geq 3$, and $z_N, z'_N \in X^N$, if there is $i \in N$ such that $z_i = z'_i = (a_i, m_i)$, then

$$z_N \, \mathbf{R}(E) \, z'_N \Rightarrow z_{N\setminus\{i\}} \, \mathbf{R}(R_{N\setminus\{i\}}, A \setminus \{a_i\}) \, z'_{N\setminus\{i\}},$$

and

$$z_N \, \mathbf{P}(E) \, z'_N \Rightarrow z_{N\setminus\{i\}} \, \mathbf{P}(R_{N\setminus\{i\}}, A \setminus \{a_i\}) \, z'_{N\setminus\{i\}}.$$

Not many SOFs defined up to now satisfy this axiom. On the one hand, in the division problem of an amount Ω of divisible goods, our two main SOFs fail to satisfy consistency, and, in both cases, this comes from the fact that the withdrawal of an agent typically changes the aggregate endowment, and both $\mathbf{R}^{\Omega\text{lex}}$ and $\mathbf{R}^{EW}$ are sensitive to such changes.

On the other hand, some SOFs that do not depend on the aggregate endowment do satisfy this axiom, such as $\mathbf{R}^{\Omega_0\text{lex}}$ (which consists of applying the leximin criterion to indices that are built by reference to the fraction of some fixed amount of resources Ω_0 that leaves the agent indifferent to his or her current bundle), defined in Section 4.2, and $\mathbf{R}^{1_\ell\text{lex}}$, the certainty equivalent leximin SOF, defined in Section 6.2 (which consists of applying the leximin aggregator to indices that are built by reference to the certain amount of money leaving the agent indifferent with his or her current, possibly uncertain, bundle).

The combination of strong pareto, independence of preferences over infeasible bundles, and consistency force us to focus our attention on SOFs that aggregate individual utility levels measured according to the u_m representation of preferences. Indeed, only preferences over feasible bundles matter, but consistency, and the withdrawal of agents consuming the current available objects, force us to focus on the bundles that would remain feasible after some agents leave the economy. These bundles are the ones involving the "null" object. As the set of bundles involving the "null" object can be used to build one and only one numerical representation of the preferences, it is not surprising that this representation becomes the one that ends up being used. If we add the fairness requirements of transfer among equals and anonymity among equals, then only $\mathbf{R}^{m\text{lex}}$ satisfies the axioms.

Theorem 6.4 *On the domain $\mathcal{E}^{ind}$, a SOF $\mathbf{R}$ satisfies strong Pareto, independence of preferences over infeasible bundles, consistency, transfer among equals, and anonymity among equals if and only if it coincides with $\mathbf{R}^{m\text{lex}}$.*

We could replace independence of preferences over infeasible bundles and consistency by independence of the feasible set and separation. Let us insist that $\mathbf{R}^{m\text{lex}}$ is the only SOF that satisfies the listed axioms, whereas we typically failed in the previous chapters and sections to single out the leximin from a set of SOFs giving absolute priority to the worst off. That is, of course, related to the simple structure of the current model, and the fact that the set of bundles that are feasible in each and every economy (the set of bundles composed of money and the null objects) is one-dimensional.

There are many other models involving indivisible goods in which fairness questions arise: models in which agents can consume more than one object, models in which objects are not desirable, matching models, and so forth. This section suggests that it could be a fruitful exercise to study SOFs in these other models as well.

6.6 CONCLUSION

Although Chapter 2 gave warnings about the necessary caution in the formulation of principles of equality of resources, the subsequent chapters have provided positive results and highlighted two broad approaches.

The first, "equivalent," approach refers to simple benchmark allocations (equal-split) and evaluates other allocations by considering benchmark allocations to which every agent is indifferent. The second, Walrasian, approach refers to similar benchmark allocations but considers them as defining potential endowments used for market trades.

These two approaches remain prominent in the extensions studied in this chapter, although some advantage seems to be given to the former (equivalence) when preferences may be nonconvex, when one is looking for an evaluation that is independent of the vector of total resources (as becomes possible with homothetic preferences), or when a particular region of the consumption set offers itself as a natural anchor for the evaluation of bundles, as in the context of risk.

This advantage, depending on the context, may or may not compensate for another difference that was described at the end of Chapter 5 and that one may consider as a slight disadvantage, namely the fact that the egalitarian-equivalent SOFs are less neutral with respect to individual preferences. The fact that the two approaches converge in the model of indivisibles studied in the last section is a useful reminder that in some simple contexts, certain ethical dilemmas simply vanish.

CHAPTER 7

Extensions

7.1 INTRODUCTION

This chapter considers extensions of the analysis in three directions. In Section 7.2, we study how the analysis can be extended to deal with the evaluation of allocations in different economies. The practice of social evaluation is indeed seldom limited to the comparison of alternative allocations for a given population; economists are often asked to compare allocations of resources involving different populations, such as international comparisons of standards of living or assessment of national growth, inequalities, and social welfare over long periods. We show how such problems require extending the standard social choice approach, and how the social ordering functions introduced here can be refined for this purpose.

In Section 7.3 we explore the possibility of incorporating dimensions of well-being that are not consumptions of resources but correspond to various "functionings," such as health or education. Such functionings may be the direct objects of individual preferences, along with material consumption, although they do not fit the current framework because they cannot be transferred across individuals, or because it seems meaningless to add them up to compute total or average amounts. This section shows that the introduction of such additional dimensions of well-being in our approach is possible, and once again illustrates the usefulness of the equivalence methodology epitomized by $\mathbf{R}^{\Omega\text{lex}}$.

In Section 7.4 we examine the case in which, contrary to an implicit basic ethical assumption made so far, the agents have private endowments of resources that are considered legitimate. In other words, suppose that the total resources Ω have already been distributed in some fair way, although there may remain some opportunities for mutually beneficial trades among agents. How should one evaluate reallocations of resources following such trades? This section, in particular, shows how the egalitarian social ordering function $\mathbf{R}^{EW}$ can be generalized to rationalize any Walrasian equilibrium, not just the egalitarian equilibrium.

In Section 7.5, we study how to proceed if one starts with a given allocation rule and would like to extend it into a reasonable ranking of all allocations – that is, a social ordering function that satisfies, at least, Pareto indifference and weak Pareto. Specifically, we introduce two methods for building a SOF that is devoted to rationalizing the selections made by any given allocation rule. Which of the two exhibits the most interesting properties depends on which allocation rule is rationalized.

7.2 CROSS-PROFILE SOFS

The SOFs that are the focus of this book rank all allocations for any given profile of preferences. They provide useful guidelines for the evaluation of public policies for any given population. They cannot, however, serve for the comparisons of allocations across time and space, such as comparisons of the situations in a country at different periods, or comparisons of situations in different countries. Both kinds of comparisons are commonly performed by policymakers who analyze growth statistics, gross domestic product (GDP), and human development rankings, and they arouse great interest in public debates. The SOFs analyzed so far are not relevant for such comparisons because the populations involved in these comparisons are not the same, and, in particular, their preferences are typically different. It would be useful to be able to define social preferences over allocations that are given to different populations; this requires an extension of the above analysis.

Another motivation for such an extension has to do with the evaluation of allocation procedures. Suppose we want to compare two different institutions that organize the distribution of resources in different ways. Such institutions may be games (such as divide-and-choose mechanisms), competitive equilibria, or second-best policies in which the policymaker makes use of some information about the statistical distribution of characteristics in the population. The comparison of different procedures is made difficult by the fact that a given procedure may perform well for certain profiles and badly for other profiles. Just to record this, one must be able to compare allocations across profiles. Otherwise, one cannot even say whether the situation produced by the procedure is more or less satisfactory in various profiles.

Whatever the motivation, it should be clear by now that cross-profile comparisons of allocations would be a valuable tool for policy analysis. We do not devote much space to this issue but show in this section that the required extension is not out of reach.

Let us first extend the notion of SOF into the notion of a *cross-profile social ordering function* (CPSOF), which deals with different preference profiles. The extension to different population sizes and different resources is considered later. An economy $\bar{E}$ is now defined simply as a population $N \subseteq \mathbb{Z}_{++}$ such that $|N| < \infty$ and a vector of resources $\Omega \in \mathbb{R}_{++}^{\ell} : \bar{E} = (N, \Omega)$. Let $\bar{\mathcal{E}}$ denote this domain of economies. A CPSOF $\bar{\mathbf{R}}$ maps any $\bar{E}$ of its domain $\bar{\mathcal{D}}$ into a complete ordering $\bar{\mathbf{R}}(\bar{E})$ over "allocations profiles" $(z_N, R_N) \in X^N \times \mathcal{R}^N$. That is, we now write $(z_N, R_N) \bar{\mathbf{R}}(z'_N, R'_N)$ to denote that the society composed of population N having preferences R_N and consuming bundles z_N is at least as desirable as the society composed of the same population but having preferences R'_N and consuming bundles z'_N. At the end of this section, we show how to extend the comparison to different populations.

The axioms defined up to now can be directly applied to this new setting, observing that they express requirements about comparisons only over pairs $(z_N, R_N), (z'_N, R_N)$ with a same profile R_N. The axiomatic analysis of the previous chapters, therefore, remains valid in this new setting and yields results about how to rank pairs (z_N, R_N), (z'_N, R_N) with the same preference profile. It remains to be seen how to obtain conclusions about how to rank pairs (z_N, R_N), (z'_N, R'_N) with different preference profiles.

To do this, the only axiom that we will extend into a requirement over changes of preferences is unchanged-contour independence. In its extended version, it will say that the ranking of two allocations profiles should only depend on indifference curves at each of these allocations profiles. This is a very natural extension of unchanged-contour independence in this context, because the motivation is the same as for the original condition – namely, the idea that the evaluation of an allocation in a given profile should depend only on the agents' indifference curves at this allocation.

Axiom 7.1 Cross-Profile Independence
For all $\bar{E} = (N, \Omega) \in \overline{\mathcal{D}}$, $z_N, z'_N \in X^N$, $R_N, R'_N, \hat{R}_N, \hat{R}'_N \in \mathcal{R}^N$, if for all $i \in N$,

$$I(\hat{R}_i, z_i) = I(R_i, z_i) \text{ and } I(\hat{R}'_i, z'_i) = I(R'_i, z'_i),$$

then $(z_N, R_N)\, \bar{\mathbf{R}}(\bar{E})\, (z'_N, R'_N) \Leftrightarrow (z_N, \hat{R}_N)\, \bar{\mathbf{R}}(\bar{E})\, (z'_N, \hat{R}'_N)$.

It is not difficult to imagine how to extend the definition of the SOFs studied in the previous chapter into CPSOFs. Because these SOFs evaluate an allocation in terms of fraction(s) of Ω (the smallest Ω-equivalent utilities, lexicographically, for $\mathbf{R}^{\Omega\text{lex}}$, the smallest $p\Omega$-equivalent utility for $\mathbf{R}^{EW}$), one can simply proceed similarly with the comparison of such fractions of Ω for different allocations, independent of changes of preferences. This yields the following CPSOFs.

Cross-Profile SOF 7.1 Ω-Equivalent Leximin ($\bar{\mathbf{R}}^{\Omega\text{lex}}$)
For all $\bar{E} = (N, \Omega) \in \overline{\mathcal{E}}$, all $z_N, z'_N \in X^N$, $R_N, R'_N \in \mathcal{R}^N$,

$$(z_N, R_N)\, \bar{\mathbf{R}}^{\Omega\text{lex}}(\bar{E})\, \left(z'_N, R'_N\right) \Leftrightarrow (u_\Omega(z_i, R_i))_{i \in N} \geq_{lex} \left(u_\Omega(z'_i, R'_i)\right)_{i \in N}.$$

Cross-Profile SOF 7.2 Egalitarian Walrasian ($\bar{\mathbf{R}}^{EW}$)
For all $\bar{E} = (N, \Omega) \in \overline{\mathcal{E}}$, all $z_N, z'_N \in X^N$, $R_N, R'_N \in \mathcal{R}^N$,

$$(z_N, R_N)\, \bar{\mathbf{R}}^{EW}(\bar{E})\, \left(z'_N, R'_N\right) \Leftrightarrow \max_{p \in \Pi_\Omega} \min_{i \in N} u_p(z_i, R_i) \geq \max_{p \in \Pi_\Omega} \min_{i \in N} u_p(z'_i, R'_i).$$

One must, of course, wonder whether there are other reasonable extensions of $\mathbf{R}^{\Omega\text{lex}}$ and $\mathbf{R}^{EW}$ in this context. The answer is negative, as stated in the following result.

Theorem 7.1 *If a CPSOF $\bar{\mathbf{R}}$ coincides with $\mathbf{R}^{\Omega lex}$ (respectively, $\mathbf{R}^{EW}$) on single-profile rankings and satisfies cross-profile independence, then $\bar{\mathbf{R}} = \bar{\mathbf{R}}^{\Omega lex}$ except possibly over pairs (z_N, R_N), (z'_N, R'_N) such that for all $i, j \in N$, $u_\Omega(z_i, R_i) = u_\Omega(z_j, R_j) = u_\Omega(z'_i, R_i) = u_\Omega(z'_j, R_j)$ (respectively, $\bar{\mathbf{R}} = \bar{\mathbf{R}}^{EW}$).*

In other words, the only new condition that is needed to extend SOFs into CPSOFs is cross-profile independence, and in this result it is the only require-ment involving comparisons of allocations profiles for different preferences. To understand how this axiom operates in this extension, it is important to see that it is equivalent to the property that $(z_N, R_N) \bar{\mathbf{I}}(\bar{E})(z_N, R'_N)$ whenever $I(z_i, R_i) = I(z_i, R'_i)$ for all $i \in N$. It is obvious that this property implies cross-profile independence. To prove the converse, it suffices to apply the definition of cross-profile independence to the particular case $z'_N = z_N$, $\hat{R}_N = R'_N$ and $\hat{R}'_N = R_N$. The axiom then concludes

$$(z_N, R_N) \bar{\mathbf{R}}(\bar{E})(z_N, R'_N) \Leftrightarrow (z_N, R'_N) \bar{\mathbf{R}}(\bar{E})(z_N, R_N),$$

which is equivalent to $(z_N, R_N) \bar{\mathbf{I}}(\bar{E}) (z_N, R'_N)$.

As an illustration of how the extension from a SOF to a CPSOF is made with cross-profile independence, consider a two-agent economy $\{i, j\}$ in which

$$u_\Omega(z'_i, R'_i) = u_\Omega(z_j, R_j) < u_\Omega(z_i, R_i) = u_\Omega(z'_j, R'_j).$$

One must show that, if the CPSOF $\bar{\mathbf{R}}$ coincides with $\mathbf{R}^{\Omega lex}$ on single-profile rankings, then one must have $(z_N, R_N) \bar{\mathbf{I}}(\bar{E}) (z'_N, R'_N)$. Let $z_0 = u_\Omega(z_j, R_j)\Omega$, $z_1 = u_\Omega(z_i, R_i)\Omega$. The reasoning is illustrated in Figure 7.1.

Let R^a_j be such that $I(z_j, R^a_j) = I(z_j, R_j)$ and

$$U(z_1, R^a_j) = \{x \in X \mid x \geq z_1\}.$$

By cross-profile independence, $(z_N, R_N) \bar{\mathbf{I}}(\bar{E})(z_N, (R_i, R^a_j))$. By applica-tion of $\mathbf{R}^{\Omega lex}$,

$$\left(z_N, \left(R_i, R^a_j\right)\right) \bar{\mathbf{I}}(\bar{E}) \left((z_0, z_1), \left(R_i, R^a_j\right)\right).$$

Let R^a_i be such that $I(z_0, R^a_i) = I(z_0, R_i)$ and

$$U(z_1, R^a_i) = \{x \in X \mid x \geq z_1\}.$$

By cross-profile independence,

$$\left((z_0, z_1), \left(R_i, R^a_j\right)\right) \bar{\mathbf{I}}(\bar{E}) \left((z_0, z_1), \left(R^a_i, R^a_j\right)\right).$$

By application of $\mathbf{R}^{\Omega lex}$,

$$\left((z_0, z_1), \left(R^a_i, R^a_j\right)\right) \bar{\mathbf{I}}(\bar{E}) \left((z_1, z_0), \left(R^a_i, R^a_j\right)\right).$$

Let R^b_i be such that $I(z_1, R^b_i) = I(z_1, R^a_i)$ and $I(z_0, R^b_i) = I(z_0, R'_i)$. By cross-profile independence,

$$\left((z_1, z_0), \left(R^a_i, R^a_j\right)\right) \bar{\mathbf{I}}(\bar{E}) \left((z_1, z_0), \left(R^b_i, R^a_j\right)\right).$$

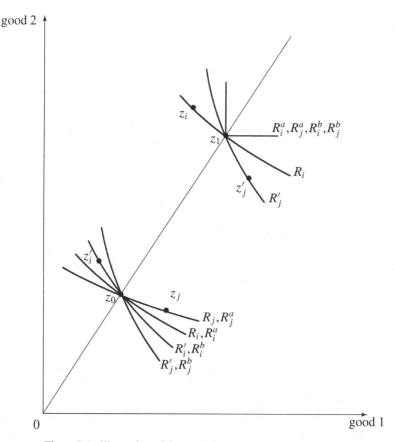

Figure 7.1. Illustration of the extension argument

By application of $\mathbf{R}^{\Omega\text{lex}}$,

$$\left((z_1, z_0), \left(R_i^b, R_j^a\right)\right) \, \bar{\mathbf{I}}(\bar{E}) \, \left((z_0, z_1), \left(R_i^b, R_j^a\right)\right).$$

Let R_j^b be such that $I(z_1, R_j^b) = I(z_1, R_j^a)$ and $I(z_0, R_j^b) = I(z_0, R_j')$. Observe that

$$I(z_1, R_i^b) = I(z_1, R_j^b) = I(z_1, R_i^a) = I(z_1, R_j^a).$$

By cross-profile independence,

$$\left((z_0, z_1), \left(R_i^b, R_j^a\right)\right) \, \bar{\mathbf{I}}(\bar{E}) \, \left((z_0, z_1), \left(R_i', R_j^b\right)\right).$$

By application of $\mathbf{R}^{\Omega\text{lex}}$,

$$\left((z_0, z_1), \left(R_i', R_j^b\right)\right) \, \bar{\mathbf{I}}(\bar{E}) \, \left((z_1, z_0), \left(R_i', R_j^b\right)\right).$$

By cross-profile independence,

$$\left((z_1, z_0), \left(R_i', R_j^b\right)\right) \, \bar{\mathbf{I}}(\bar{E}) \, \left((z_1, z_0), \left(R_i', R_j'\right)\right).$$

By application of $\mathbf{R}^{\Omega lex}$,

$$\left((z_1, z_0), \left(R_i', R_j'\right)\right) \bar{\mathbf{I}}(\bar{E}) \left(z_N', R_N'\right).$$

One can now apply transitivity over this chain of allocations profiles and conclude that $(z_N, R_N) \bar{\mathbf{I}}(\bar{E}) \left(z_N', R_N'\right)$.

We complete this section with the observation that further extension of the concepts is possible. So far we have extended the notion of SOF only to cover the possibility of having different preferences in a given population N for a given amount of resources Ω. This is appropriate for the examination of procedures, in terms of how well they perform depending on the profile of preferences. Nevertheless, in the perspective of international or intertemporal comparisons of allocations, which typically involve different populations and different resources, one would actually like to produce *a complete ordering* $\overline{\overline{\mathbf{R}}}$ over "allocations economies" (z_N, R_N, Ω).

Extending the analysis to different populations N raises the difficult issue of the optimal size of the population.[1] There are, however, some contexts in which one simply wants to be neutral about size. For instance, in a comparison between countries, it makes sense to seek such neutrality and to be interested in the distribution of well-being independent of the size of the population. When this is the case, the extension of the previous concepts is quite easy. For instance, the definition of $\mathbf{R}^{\Omega lex}$ can be extended as follows:

$$(z_N, R_N, \Omega) \overline{\overline{\mathbf{R}}}^{\Omega lex} \left(z_{N'}', R_{N'}', \Omega\right) \Leftrightarrow (u_\Omega(z_i, R_i))_{i \in N} \geq_{lex} \left(u_\Omega(z_i', R_i')\right)_{i \in N'},$$

where the leximin for vectors of different dimensions is defined as the application of the standard leximin to replicas of the vectors that have the same dimension. For instance, the vector (2,5,7) can be compared with the vector (2,5) by comparing their replicas (2,2,5,5,7,7) and (2,2,2,5,5,5). This extension can be justified by relying, in particular, on a new axiom requiring the ranking to be indifferent to replications (i.e., $(z_N, R_N, \Omega) \overline{\overline{\mathbf{I}}} (z_{N'}, R_{N'}, \Omega')$ whenever $(R_{N'}, \Omega')$ is a replica of (R_N, Ω) and $z_{N'}$ is a replica of z_N).

Extending the analysis to resources of different size is also easy, provided that the vectors of available resources are proportional to one another. It is a simple matter of applying independence of proportional expansion to single-profile rankings. The extended definition of $\mathbf{R}^{\Omega lex}$, for instance, would then become:

$$(z_N, R_N, \Omega) \overline{\overline{\mathbf{R}}}^{\Omega lex} \left(z_{N'}', R_{N'}', \Omega'\right) \Leftrightarrow (u_\Omega(z_i, R_i))_{i \in N} \geq_{lex} \left(u_\Omega(z_i', R_i')\right)_{i \in N'}$$

$$\Leftrightarrow (u_{\Omega'}(z_i, R_i))_{i \in N} \geq_{lex} \left(u_{\Omega'}(z_i', R_i')\right)_{i \in N'}.$$

Extending the analysis to vectors of resources that are *not* proportional to each other, by contrast, is much more problematic, because SOFs such as $\mathbf{R}^{\Omega lex}$ and $\mathbf{R}^{EW}$ do not satisfy independence of the feasible set. This problem has

---

[1] On this topic, see Broome (2004) and Blackorby et al. (2005).

already been addressed in Section 4.2 and there is little to add here. Nonetheless, it is worth emphasizing that the extension into an ordering $\overline{\overline{R}}$ is quite simple for a SOF that does satisfy independence of the feasible set. The analysis of this section applies just as well, for instance, to the extension of Ω_0-equivalent SOFs that refer to a fixed bundle Ω_0. One can then define the ordering $\overline{\overline{R}}^{=\Omega_0 \mathrm{lex}}$ as follows:

$$(z_N, R_N, \Omega) \, \overline{\overline{R}}^{=\Omega_0 \mathrm{lex}} \, \left(z'_{N'}, R'_{N'}, \Omega'\right) \Leftrightarrow \left(u_{\Omega_0}(z_i, R_i)\right)_{i \in N} \geq_{lex} \left(u_{\Omega_0}(z'_i, R'_i)\right)_{i \in N'}.$$

7.3 FUNCTIONINGS

In most of this book we focus on allocations of resources. In Part III, leisure comes to the front of the stage. This is a rather special kind of resource, as it is not perfectly transferable across individuals. In this section, more broadly, we want to examine the possibility of extending the SOF approach to settings in which, beyond material consumption of goods and services, there are various "functionings" that matter to individuals, such as health, education, safety, social status, and so on. Some of these functionings may be purely personal, whereas others may involve interactions between individuals. The notion of functionings has been popularized by A.K. Sen[2] and, in the most general sense, covers all "doings and beings" that pertain to an individual life.

The central part of the SOF approach is to find ways to compare indifference sets across individuals. The $\mathbf{R}^{\Omega \mathrm{lex}}$ SOF compares individual situations in terms of Ω-equivalent utilities, whereas the $\mathbf{R}^{EW}$ evaluates them in terms of money-metric utilities – in both cases, indifference sets are the relevant informational basis of interpersonal comparisons. In this light, there is no particular difficulty in extending the analysis to nonmaterial functionings, provided that individual preferences are well-defined over these functionings alongside material consumption.

Suppose that for each $i \in N$, R_i bears on pairs (z_i, f_i), where $z_i \in X \subseteq \mathbb{R}^\ell_+$ is, as previously, a vector of consumptions and $f_i \in F \subseteq \mathbb{R}^m$ is a vector of functionings. Preferences are assumed to be continuous in (z_i, f_i) and monotonic and convex in z_i. For simplicity, let us assume that feasible functioning vectors in any given economy depend only on the available resources Ω. An important observation is that, even if some functionings may reflect social interactions, it remains sensible to evaluate individual situations in terms of what happens to the individual, rather than in holistic terms. Taking account of social interactions does not require abandoning the basic principle that individuals are the primary units of evaluation.

In this enlarged framework, there is no particular difficulty in formulating axioms like the various Pareto requirements, unchanged-contour independence, separability, and so on. The transfer axioms are less obvious to adapt because

---

[2] See, e.g., Sen (1985, 1992).

transfers of functionings across individuals may appear less natural than transfers of resources. Fortunately, important parts of our analysis and results remain valid even if one restricts transfers to resources only. For instance, the axiom of transfer among equals can be rewritten as follows. The idea is to restrict the transfer axiom not only to cases of equal preferences, but also to cases in which the two individuals have the same functioning vectors.

Axiom 7.2 Transfer among Equals
For all $E = (R_N, \Omega) \in \mathcal{D}$, and $(z_N, f_N), (z'_N, f'_N) \in X^N \times F^N$, if there exist $j, k \in N$ such that $R_j = R_k$ and $\Delta \in \mathbb{R}^\ell_{++}$ such that

$$z_j - \Delta = z'_j \gg z'_k = z_k + \Delta,$$

$$f_j = f'_j = f'_k = f_k,$$

and for all $i \neq j, k$, $(z_i, f_i) = (z'_i, f'_i)$, then $z'_N \mathbf{R}(E) z_N$.

It is then an easy exercise to adapt Theorem 3.1 and show that priority among equals follows from transfer among equals, combined with Pareto indifference and unchanged-contour independence. As a matter of fact, by Pareto indifference, the restriction $f_j = f'_j = f'_k = f_k$ does not have much bite and one can therefore show that $z'_N \mathbf{R}(E) z_N$ when the two individuals affected by the change, j and k, are such that $R_j = R_k$ and

$$(z_j, f_j) \ P_j \ (z'_j, f'_j) \ P_j \ (z'_k, f_k) \ P_k \ (z_k, f_k).$$

In other words, absolute priority is given to the individual whose indifference set is the lower.

The reference to equal split, which plays a central role in the fair distribution model as it underlies the definition of $\mathbf{R}^{\Omega\text{lex}}$ and $\mathbf{R}^{EW}$, now becomes more problematic. If some individuals are affected by inequalities in functionings, seeking to equalize their material consumption may run against the most basic sense of fairness. However, suppose that the ideal of equality of resources remains sensible when all individuals enjoy the same level of functionings, at least at a particular reference level f^*. Then the analysis is easily adapted because by Pareto indifference, every allocation (z_N, f_N) in a certain subset is Pareto equivalent to an allocation (z^*_N, f^*_N) in which $f^*_i = f^*$ for all $i \in N$. For such allocations (z_N, f_N), one can then deduce a reasonable ranking from the application of $\mathbf{R}^{\Omega\text{lex}}$ or $\mathbf{R}^{EW}$ to the "equivalent" allocations of goods z^*_N.

More precisely, this means extending $\mathbf{R}^{\Omega\text{lex}}$ into a $\mathbf{R}^{\Omega f^*\text{lex}}$ SOF that compares individuals in terms of Ωf^*-equivalent utilities $u_{\Omega f^*}((z_i, f_i), R_i)$ defined by:

$$u_{\Omega f^*}((z_i, f_i), R_i) = \lambda \Leftrightarrow (z_i, f_i) \ I_i \ (\lambda\Omega, f^*).$$

Similarly, one extends $\mathbf{R}^{EW}$ into a $\mathbf{R}^{f^*EW}$ SOF that relies on the computation of

$$\max_{p \in \Pi_\Omega} \min_{i \in N} \left\{ px \mid (x, f^*) \ R_i \ (z_i, f_i) \right\}.$$

It is a consequence of the basic tension between transfer principles and the Pareto principle identified in Theorem 2.1 that this extension must rely on a single reference vector f^* and cannot involve a greater number of vectors f^*. For instance, imagine that two references f^* and f^{**} were considered. Changing the allocation might then reduce inequalities in the distribution of $\left(u_{\Omega f^*}((z_i, f_i), R_i)\right)_{i \in N}$ and increase inequalities in $\left(u_{\Omega f^{**}}((z_i, f_i), R_i)\right)_{i \in N}$.

This raises a new ethical problem – namely, the choice of the vector f^*. This problem is not totally new, however, because the Ω-equivalent utilities underlying $\mathbf{R}^{\Omega \mathrm{lex}}$ also rely on a reference bundle Ω. What triggers the choice of this particular bundle in our analysis? It derives from axioms such as equal-split transfer or proportional-allocations transfer, which say that a certain type of equality of resources is desirable even between individuals with different preferences. The same kind of considerations apply here. The choice of f^* must be dictated by the fact that it is when all individuals enjoy $f_i = f^*$ that the ideal of equality of material consumption is sensible.

As an example, consider health. When all individuals have the same level of health, is it desirable to equalize their levels of consumption? Not necessarily. In case of bad health, some of them may need a greater compensation if health is more important according to their preferences than according to others' preferences. If all enjoy good health, it seems sensible to seek to equalize their material consumption, and it would sound somewhat incongruous to consider that those who care less about health should consume more than the others. Such a view imposes good health as the proper reference level for health because it is only when everyone enjoys good health that individual preferences over health-consumption trade-offs can be disregarded. Not all dimensions of functionings provide such an obvious reference, but at least it should be clear that the need for a particular f^* is not an insurmountable obstacle for the application of this approach.[3]

7.4 LEGITIMATE ENDOWMENTS

Throughout this book we generally assume that agents' endowments are not a legitimate source of inequality, adopting a "pure" view of fairness and equality. In this section, however, we show that the approach is flexible enough to accommodate quite different perspectives. Suppose that the agents have personal initial endowments of resources and that, for some reason, such endowments are considered legitimate, so much so that the purpose of social policy is no longer to redistribute toward more equality, but simply to achieve a proper sharing of the advantage obtained by agents over and above their legitimate initial position.

---

[3] On health, see Fleurbaey (2005a). Fleurbaey and Gaulier (2009) apply this approach to make international comparisons of living standards that take account of leisure, life expectancy, household size, and the risk of losing one's job.

Let $\omega_i \in X$ denote agent i's endowment, assuming that

$$\sum_{i \in N} \omega_i = \Omega.$$

The framework is now slightly different, with an economy being defined as $E = (R_N, \omega_N)$. The domain is now denoted $\mathcal{E}^E$ and contains economies $E = (R_N, \omega_N)$ such that $R_N \in \mathcal{R}^N$ and for all $i \in N$, $\omega_i \in \mathbb{R}^{\ell}_{++}$. A positive endowment of every good is required, to avoid situations in which an agent considers his or her endowment to be so bad that any multiple of thus endowment would still be worse than the agent's current consumption z_i.

The adaptation of the SOFs studied earlier to this different setting is actually quite simple. Recall that the central concepts are the Ω-equivalent utility function $u_\Omega(z_i, R_i)$ defined by

$$z_i \, I_i \, u_\Omega(z_i, R_i)\Omega$$

and the money-metric utility function $u_p(z_i, R_i)$ computed at prices p such that $p\Omega = 1$:

$$u_p(z_i, R_i) = \min\{px \mid x \, R_i \, z_i\} = \min\{px/p\Omega \mid x \, R_i \, z_i\}.$$

The reference to Ω in these formulas may in fact be interpreted as pointing to the premise that the appropriate endowment of agents in the fairness ideal should be the equal split $\Omega/|N|$. If the *current* endowment ω_i is actually the legitimate one, then one simply must replace Ω in the formula by ω_i, to obtain new functions:

$$u_{\omega_i}(z_i, R_i) \text{ such that } z_i \, I_i \, u_{\omega_i}(z_i, R_i)\omega_i,$$

$$u_p(z_i, R_i)/p\omega_i = \min\{px/p\omega_i \mid x \, R_i \, z_i\}.$$

(Replacing Ω by ω_i instead of $|N| \omega_i$ involves a change of scale that has no consequence – priority is given here to simplicity of the formulas.) Applying the same definitions of SOFs as earlier to these new functions yields the following two SOFs in particular.

Social ordering function 7.1 ω-Equivalent Leximin ($\mathbf{R}^{\omega lex}$)
For all $E = (R_N, \omega_N) \in \mathcal{E}^E$, $z_N, z'_N \in X^N$,

$$z_N \, \mathbf{R}^{\omega lex}(E) \, z'_N \Leftrightarrow \left(u_{\omega_i}(z_i, R_i)\right)_{i \in N} \geq_{lex} \left(u_{\omega_i}(z'_i, R_i)\right)_{i \in N}.$$

Let $\Delta_\ell = \left\{ p \in \mathbb{R}^{\ell}_+ \mid \sum_{k=1}^{\ell} p_k = 1 \right\}$.

Social ordering function 7.2 Walrasian ($\mathbf{R}^W$)
For all $E = (R_N, \omega_N) \in \mathcal{E}^E$, $z_N, z'_N \in X^N$,

$$z_N \, \mathbf{R}^W(E) \, z'_N \Leftrightarrow \max_{p \in \Delta_\ell} \min_{i \in N} u_p(z_i, R_i)/p\omega_i \geq \max_{p \in \Delta_\ell} \min_{i \in N} u_p(z'_i, R_i)/p\omega_i.$$

Again, one can interpret the first SOF as being more focused on securing that for every $i \in N$, $z_i \, R_i \, \omega_i$, and hence tends to favor the agents whose preferences are oriented toward the combination of goods featured in their endowment. In contrast, the second one, which selects the subset of Walrasian allocations in $Z(E)$, is more sensitive to the degree of efficiency of allocations and is more neutral regarding individual preferences.

The fact that, for all $E \in \mathcal{E}^E$, $\max|_{\mathbf{R}^W(E)} Z(E)$ coincides with the set of Walrasian equilibria deserves to be fully understood. Let z_N^* be a Walrasian equilibrium; that is, $\sum_{i \in N} z_i^* = \Omega$ and for some $p^* \in \Delta_\ell$, for all $i \in N$, $z_i^* \in \max|_{R_i} B(\omega_i, p^*)$. This implies that for all $i \in N$,

$$u_{p^*}(z_i^*, R_i) = p^* \omega_i.$$

Take any vector $p \in \Delta_\ell$ and any allocation $z_N \in Z(E)$. Necessarily,[4] $\Omega \in \sum_{i \in N} U(z_i, R_i)$ and

$$\sum_{i \in N} u_p(z_i, R_i) = \min \left\{ pq \mid q \in \sum_{i \in N} U(z_i, R_i) \right\},$$

so

$$\sum_{i \in N} u_p(z_i, R_i) \le p\Omega.$$

Recalling that $\Omega = \sum_{i \in N} \omega_i$, this implies that for some $i \in N$, $u_p(z_i, R_i) \le p\omega_i$ and that it is impossible to have $u_p(z_i, R_i) \ge p\omega_i$ for all $i \in N$ with a strict inequality for some i. As a consequence,

$$\max_{p \in \Delta_\ell} \min_{i \in N} u_p(z_i^*, R_i)/p\omega_i = 1 \ge \max_{p \in \Delta_\ell} \min_{i \in N} u_{p,\omega_i}(z_i, R_i)/p\omega_i,$$

or, equivalently, $z_N^* \mathbf{R}^W(E) z_N$. Suppose that for all $i \in N$,

$$u_p(z_i, R_i)/p\omega_i = 1.$$

This implies that

$$\sum_{i \in N} u_p(z_i, R_i) = p\Omega,$$

and therefore that z_N is Pareto efficient, with supporting price vector p. One then has $z_i \in \max|_{R_i} B(\omega_i, p)$ for all $i \in N$; that is, z_N is a Walrasian equilibrium associated with the price vector p.

It is worth emphasizing that $\mathbf{R}^W$ does not require any redistribution and rationalizes the competitive equilibrium even though it is based on the maximin criterion. This illustrates our claim of Section 3.5 that even a libertarian policy can be accommodated in our approach. It all depends on how individual situations are measured and compared. The money-metric utilities $u_p(z_i, R_i)/p\omega_i$ take

---

[4] Recall from the introduction that the sum of sets used in the expression is defined as follows:

$$\sum_{i \in N} U(z_i, R_i) = \left\{ x \in X \mid \exists x_N \in \prod_{i \in N} U(z_i, R_i), \ x = \sum_{i \in N} x_i \right\}.$$

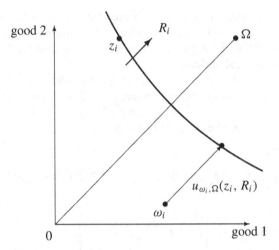

Figure 7.2. Construction of $u_{\omega_i,\Omega}(z_i, R_i)$

account of legitimate endowments and compute the fraction of one's endowment that would, with possibility of trade, yield the current level of satisfaction. Putting priority on the agents for whom this fraction is the smallest is a natural way to rationalize the competitive approach.

The two SOFs introduced in this section share the unappealing feature that an agent with a greater endowment is mechanically granted a greater claim on resources, because utilities are measured in proportion to endowments. Let us introduce a variant of $\mathbf{R}^{\omega\mathrm{lex}}$ that alleviates this problem. Consider the function

$$u_{\omega_i,\Omega}(z_i, R_i), \text{ such that } z_i \, I_i \, \omega_i + u_{\omega_i,\Omega}(z_i, R_i)\Omega.$$

The construction of $u_{\omega_i,\Omega}(z_i, R_i)$ is illustrated in Figure 7.2.

Applying the leximin criterion to such utilities amounts to comparing individual situations in terms of fractions of Ω that are added to or subtracted from individual endowments. When legitimate endowments are the equal-split bundle $\Omega/|N|$, this SOF coincides with $\mathbf{R}^{\Omega\mathrm{lex}}$, just like $\mathbf{R}^{\omega\mathrm{lex}}$.

An additive variant of the Walrasian SOF can also be conceived. In the definition, one could replace the expression $u_p(z_i, R_i)/p\omega_i$ by the expression

$$u_p(z_i, R_i) - p\omega_i,$$

which computes the difference between minimal expenditure and the value of the endowment at price p. Like $\mathbf{R}^W$, the new SOF obtained in this way also selects Walrasian allocations.

One drawback of this variant is that, for the ranking of suboptimal allocations, it is not independent on the choice of price normalization (i.e., $p \in \Delta_\ell$ or otherwise) used in the computation of $\max_p \min_{i \in N} \left[u_p(z_i, R_i) - p\omega_i \right]$. Its attractiveness, however, lies in the fact that it appears very natural to compute the difference between the "equivalent value" of z_i – that is, $u_p(z_i, R_i)$ – and the value of ω_i. This measures how much the agent gains or loses with respect to an ordinary Walrasian situation (at hypothetical prices p). This can easily be connected to standard notions of cost–benefit analysis, as explained in Section 1.7.

We do not explore the axiomatic analysis of SOFs for this framework, as our purpose here is simply to hint at the possibility of dealing with legitimate endowments. A detailed study of this setting would require more than one section.

7.5 RATIONALIZING ALLOCATION RULES

In this section, we study how SOFs can be constructed when desirable allocation rules have been identified and one would like to extend them into fine-grained social orderings. In other words, given an allocation rule S defined on a domain $\mathcal{D}$, we look for a SOF $\mathbf{R}$ that rationalizes it in the sense that the allocations in $S(E)$ must always be top-ranked by the social ordering $\mathbf{R}(E)$. More precisely, let us say that $\mathbf{R}$ rationalizes S if for all $E \in \mathcal{D}$, $S(E) = \max|_{\mathbf{R}(E)} Z(E)$. One can consider $S(E) \subseteq \max|_{\mathbf{R}(E)} Z(E)$ and $S(E) \supseteq \max|_{\mathbf{R}(E)} Z(E)$ as forms of partial rationalization.[5]

As explained in Section 4.4, an allocation rule can always be rationalized by a two-tier SOF in which selected allocations are socially indifferent to one another and form the first class, and nonselected allocations are also socially indifferent to one another and form the second class. However, the resulting social orderings typically fail to satisfy basic properties such as weak Pareto.

Let us introduce two general methods of constructing SOFs from allocation rules. They are both based on a real-valued function computing what could be called the value of an allocation depending on the parameters of the economy and on the allocation rule S to be rationalized. The corresponding SOF is then derived from the principle that an allocation is socially preferred if its value is greater.

According to the first method, the value of an allocation z_N for an economy $E = (R_N, \Omega)$ is given by the highest real number λ satisfying the property that an S-optimal allocation z'_N that is Pareto inferior to z_N exists in the economy $(R_N, \lambda\Omega)$. Formally, this amounts to computing, for all $E = (R_N, \Omega) \in \mathcal{D}$,

$$V_S^*(z_N, E) = \sup\{\lambda \in \mathbb{R}_+ \mid \exists z'_N \in S(R_N, \lambda\Omega) \text{ s.t. } \forall i \in N, \ z_i \, R_i \, z'_i\}.$$

One then derives the corresponding SOF $\mathbf{R}_S^*$ as follows:

$$z_N \, \mathbf{R}_S^*(e) \, z'_N \Leftrightarrow V^*(z_N, E) \geq V^*(z'_N, E).$$

---

[5] The limitations of partial rationalization are similar to the limitations of partial implementation (on which, see Thomson 1996). It is easy to satisfy $S(E) \subseteq \max_{\mathbf{R}(E)} Z(E)$ when $\mathbf{R}$ is widely indifferent. And $S(E) \supseteq \max_{\mathbf{R}(E)} Z(E)$ is compatible with the correspondence $E \mapsto \max_{\mathbf{R}(E)} Z(E)$, failing to satisfy important properties of S (such as anonymity).

The second value function is similar to the first one, except that the supremum is defined no longer with respect to economies $(R_N, \lambda\Omega)$ but to economies $(R'_N, \lambda\Omega)$, in which the choice of R'_N is simply restricted by the condition that agent i's indifference sets at z_i be the same at R_i as at R'_i:

$$V_S^{**}(z_N, E) = \sup\{\lambda \in \mathbb{R}_+ \mid \exists R'_N \in \mathcal{R}^N, \exists z'_N \in S(R'_N, \lambda\Omega)$$
$$\text{s.t. } \forall i \in N, \ z_i \, R_i \, z'_i \text{ and } I(z_i, R_i) = I(z_i, R'_i)\}.$$

The corresponding SOF is denoted $\mathbf{R}_S^{**}$.[6] Obviously, one always has $V_S^{**}(z_N, E) \geq V_S^*(z_N, E)$. The main motivation for introducing V_S^{**} and $\mathbf{R}_S^{**}$ is that $\mathbf{R}_S^{**}$ always satisfies unchanged-contour independence because $V_S^{**}(z_N, E)$ depends only on the indifference sets at z_N. We will, however, see that $\mathbf{R}_S^*$ also sometimes satisfies unchanged-contour independence.

The value of $V_S^*(z_N, E)$ and $V_S^{**}(z_N, E)$ is finite when S is such that for λ great enough, no allocation in $S(R_N, \lambda\Omega)$ is Pareto inferior to z_N. This is always true for instance when S satisfies Pareto efficiency. The following result examines the Pareto and rationalization properties of $\mathbf{R}_S^*$ and $\mathbf{R}_S^{**}$.

Theorem 7.2 *The following statements hold:*

(1a) For all $E \in \mathcal{D}$, all $z_N, z'_N \in X^N$, if for all $i \in N$, $z_i \, R_i \, z'_i$, then $z_N \, \mathbf{R}_S^*(E) \, z'_N$ and $z_N \, \mathbf{R}_S^{**}(E) \, z'_N$.

(1b) If S is continuous[7] with respect to Ω and for all $E \in \mathcal{D}$, $V_S^*(z_N, E) < +\infty$ for all $z_N \in X^N$, then $\mathbf{R}_S^*$ satisfies weak Pareto.

(2a) If S satisfies Pareto efficiency, then for all $E \in \mathcal{D}$,

$$S(E) \subseteq \max|_{\mathbf{R}_S^*(E)} Z(E) \cap \max|_{\mathbf{R}_S^{**}(E)} Z(E).$$

(2b) Assume that S is upper-hemicontinuous with respect to Ω and satisfies Pareto efficiency and the following property: For all $E \in \mathcal{D}$, all $z_N \in S(E)$, $z'_N \in Z(E)$, if for all $i \in N$, $z'_i \, I_i \, z_i$, then $z'_N \in S(E)$. Then $\mathbf{R}_S^*$ rationalizes S.

An immediate consequence of (1a) is that $\mathbf{R}_S^*$ and $\mathbf{R}_S^{**}$ satisfy Pareto indifference. Some parts of this theorem are direct consequences of the definitions. For instance, when for all $i \in N$, $z_i \, R_i \, z'_i$, necessarily

$$\{\lambda \in \mathbb{R}_+ \mid \exists q_N \in S(R_N, \lambda\Omega) \text{ s.t. } z'_i \, R_i \, q_i, \forall i \in N\}$$
$$\subseteq \{\lambda \in \mathbb{R}_+ \mid \exists q_N \in S(R_N, \lambda\Omega) \text{ s.t. } z_i \, R_i \, q_i, \forall i \in N\},$$

---

[6] It is important to define V_S^{**} in terms of sup rather than max because the maximum is often not defined. This problem, however, vanishes with the alternative, equivalent definition:

$$V_S^{**}(z_N, E) = \sup\{\lambda \in \mathbb{R}_+ \mid \exists R'_N \in \mathcal{R}^N, \exists z'_N \in S(R'_N, \lambda\Omega)$$
$$\text{s.t. } \forall i \in N, \ U(z_i, R_i) \subseteq U(z'_i, R'_i)\}.$$

[7] A correspondence f is continuous if it is upper- and lower-hemicontinuous. It is upper-hemicontinuous if $x_n \to x$, $y_n \to y$, and $y_n \in f(x_n)$ for all n implies $y \in f(x)$. It is lower-hemicontinuous if for all x, all $x_n \to x$, all $y \in f(x)$, there is $y_n \to y$ such that $y_n \in f(x_n)$ for all n.

which implies $V_S^*(z_N, E) \geq V_S^*(z_N', E)$ and therefore $z_N \, \mathbf{R}_S^*(E) \, z_N'$. A similar observation applies to $\mathbf{R}_S^{**}(E)$.

It is also easy to see why, when S is Pareto efficient, one has $V_S^*(z_N, E) \leq 1$ for all $z_N \in Z(E)$. Indeed, if one had $V_S^*(z_N, E) > 1$, by definition there would exist $\lambda > 1$ and $z_N' \in S(R_N, \lambda\Omega)$ such that $z_i \, R_i \, z_i'$ for all $i \in N$. This is impossible because $z_N \in Z(E)$, whereas, as S is Pareto efficient, one would then have $z_N' \in P(R_N, \lambda\Omega)$. Now, for all $z_N \in S(E)$, necessarily $V_S^*(z_N, E) \geq 1$, which implies that $V_S^*(z_N, E) = 1$ by the previous fact. Therefore, one must always have $z_N \, \mathbf{R}_S^*(E) \, z_N'$ when $z_N \in S(E)$ and $z_N' \in Z(E)$.

The theorem is more precise about $\mathbf{R}_S^*$ than about $\mathbf{R}_S^{**}$. Although $\mathbf{R}_S^{**}$ typically satisfies weak Pareto as well, this involves some continuity condition with respect to the preference profile and will not be studied in detail here.

The value functions $V_S^*(z_N, E)$ and $V_S^{**}(z_N, E)$, which refer to fractions of Ω, generalize Debreu's coefficient of resource utilization. Actually, Debreu's coefficient corresponds to the value computed by either method for the Pareto rule $P(E)$. That is, when $S = P$, $\mathbf{R}_S^* = \mathbf{R}_S^{**} = \mathbf{R}^{RU}$. When $S = S^{EE}$, one observes that for all $E \in \mathcal{E}$, all $z_N, z_N' \in X^N$, $z_N \, \mathbf{R}_S^*(E) \, z_N'$ if and only if

$$\min_{i \in N} u_\Omega \, (z_i, R_i) \geq \min_{i \in N} u_\Omega \, (z_i', R_i),$$

which, incidentally, shows that $\mathbf{R}_S^*$ may satisfy unchanged-contour independence even when $V_S^*(z_N, E)$ does not depend only on the indifference sets at z_N. When $S = S^{EW}$, $z_N \, \mathbf{R}_S^{**}(E) \, z_N'$ if and only if $z_N \, \mathbf{R}^{EW}(E) \, z_N'$. As a consequence, $\mathbf{R}_{S^{EE}}^*$ rationalizes S^{EE} and $\mathbf{R}_{S^{EW}}^{**}$ rationalizes S^{EW}.

When $S = S^{EE}$, one has $V_S^{**}(z_N, E) = 1$ for all $z_N \in S^{EW}(E)$. This is because, for any allocation $z_N \in S^{EW}(E)$, one can construct indifference curves that are just below $I(z_i, R_i)$ and cross at a bundle proportional to Ω (think of linear indifference curves that have a slope equal to the relative prices of the supporting price vector at z_N). Therefore, unlike $\mathbf{R}_{S^{EE}}^*$, $\mathbf{R}_{S^{EE}}^{**}$ is an eclectic SOF that includes the S^{EE}-optimal and the S^{EW}-optimal allocations in its top rank: for all $E \in \mathcal{D}$,

$$S^{EE}(E) \cup S^{EW}(E) \subseteq \max|_{\mathbf{R}_{S^{EE}}^{**}(E)} Z(E).$$

Let us now illustrate further the two methods by considering other allocation rules. Consider the allocation rule that selects all Pareto efficient allocations such that every individual is at least as well off as at the equal-split allocation.

Allocation rule 7.1 Equal-Split Efficient S^{ESE}
For all $E = (R_N, \Omega) \in \mathcal{E}$,

$$S^{ESE}(E) = \{z_N \in P(E) \mid \forall i \in N, \; z_i \, R_i \, \Omega / |N|\}.$$

Let $E = (R_N, \Omega)$ and take any allocation $z_N \in Z(E)$. Let λ be such that there is $z_N' \in P(R_N, \lambda\Omega)$ Pareto indifferent to z_N. If for all $i \in N$, $z_i \, R_i \, \lambda\Omega / |N|$, then $z_N' \in S^{ESE}(R_N, \lambda\Omega)$ and therefore $V_{S^{ESE}}^*(z_N) = V_{S^{ESE}}^{**}(z_N) = \lambda$. Therefore, the corresponding SOF coincides with $\mathbf{R}^{RU}$ for allocations that are sufficiently egalitarian or inefficient.

In contrast, if there is $i \in N$ such that $\lambda \Omega / |N| \, P_i \, z_i$, then both $\mathbf{R}^*_{S^{ESE}}$ and $\mathbf{R}^{**}_{S^{ESE}}$ correspond to the Ω-equivalent maximin SOF $\mathbf{R}^{\Omega \min}$. Indeed, $V^*_{S^{ESE}}(z_N) = V^{**}_{S^{ESE}}(z_N) = |N| \min_{i \in N} u_{\Omega} (z_i, R_i)$. This is proved as follows. Let R'_N and z'_N be such that for some $\alpha \geq 0$, $z'_N \in P(R'_N, \alpha\Omega)$ and for all $i \in N$, $U(z_i, R_i) \subseteq U(z'_i, R'_i)$. If for all $i \in N$, $u_{\Omega}(z'_i, R'_i) = \min_{j \in N} u_{\Omega}(z_j, R_j)$, then $\alpha / |N| \leq \min_{i \in N} u_{\Omega}(z_i, R_i)$. If for all $i \in N$, $U(z'_i, R'_i) = U(z_i, R_i)$, then $\alpha = \lambda$ and therefore $\alpha / |N| > \min_{i \in N} u_{\Omega}(z_i, R_i)$. By continuity, there is α such that $z'_N \in P(R'_N, \alpha\Omega)$, for all $i \in N$, $U(z_i, R_i) \subseteq U(z'_i, R'_i)$, and $\alpha / |N| = \min_{i \in N} u_{\Omega}(z_i, R_i)$. One then has $z'_N \in S^{ESE}(R'_N, \alpha\Omega)$, which implies that $V^{**}_{S^{ESE}}(z_N) \geq |N| \min_{i \in N} u_{\Omega}(z_i, R_i)$. Imposing $R'_N = R_N$ does not alter this reasoning; therefore, $V^*_{S^{ESE}}(z_N) \geq |N| \min_{i \in N} u_{\Omega}(z_i, R_i)$. As one obviously has $V^*_{S^{ESE}}(z_N)$, $V^{**}_{S^{ESE}}(z_N) \leq |N| \min_{i \in N} u_{\Omega}(z_i, R_i)$, equality is obtained. In other words, the corresponding SOF coincides with $\mathbf{R}^{\Omega \min}$ for allocations that are sufficiently *in*egalitarian and efficient.

In conclusion, one has $\mathbf{R}^*_{S^{ESE}} = \mathbf{R}^{**}_{S^{ESE}}$; this SOF coincides with $\mathbf{R}^{RU}$ and with $\mathbf{R}^{\Omega \min}$ on two different subsets that partition the set $Z(E)$. Let us now turn to another allocation rule – namely, the allocation rule that selects the efficient and envy-free allocations.

Allocation rule 7.2 Envy-Free Efficient S^{EFE}
For all $E = (R_N, \Omega) \in \mathcal{E}$,

$$S^{EFE}(E) = \left\{ z_N \in P(E) \mid \forall i, j \in N, \ z_i \, R_i \, z_j \right\}.$$

Let $E = (R_N, \Omega)$ and $z_N \in Z(E)$. If there is $z'_N \in S^{EFE}(E)$ that is Pareto indifferent to z_N, then $V^*_{S^{EFE}}(z_N) = V^{**}_{S^{EFE}}(z_N) = 1$. If z_N is not efficient and for some $\lambda < 1$ there is $z'_N \in P(R_N, \lambda\Omega)$ that is Pareto indifferent to z_N, then $V^*_{S^{EFE}}(z_N)$, $V^{**}_{S^{EFE}}(z_N) \leq \lambda$. If z_N is efficient but there is no $z'_N \in S^{EFE}(E)$ that is Pareto indifferent to z_N, then necessarily $V^*_{S^{EFE}}(z_N) < 1$. However, in this case it is possible to have $V^{**}_{S^{EFE}}(z_N) = 1$, as illustrated in Figure 7.3. In the figure, by expanding the upper contour set of agent i, one renders z_N Pareto indifferent to an allocation z'_N that is then envy-free and efficient. In conclusion, $\mathbf{R}^*_{S^{EFE}}$ rationalizes the allocation rule that contains S^{EFE} and the allocations that are Pareto indifferent to the allocations of S^{EFE}. This is the smallest allocation rule, with respect to inclusion, that contains S^{EFE} and always treats any pair of Pareto indifferent allocations in the same way, either selecting both or rejecting both.[8] In contrast, $\mathbf{R}^{**}_{S^{EFE}}$ rationalizes a larger allocation rule.

These examples have shown that the rationalization of allocation rules is a complex exercise for which there is no unique recipe. The SOFs $\mathbf{R}^*_S$ and $\mathbf{R}^{**}_S$ appear to be prominent candidates, but the choice between them may depend on the particular allocation rule under consideration.

---

[8] It is easy to refine $\mathbf{R}^*_{S^{EFE}}$ to rationalize S^{EFE} exactly. It suffices to say that z_N is strictly better than z'_N if $z_N \, \mathbf{I}^*_{S^{EFE}}(E) \, z'_N$ and z_N is envy-free, whereas z'_N is not. The resulting SOF violates Pareto indifference.

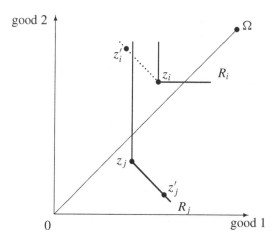

Figure 7.3. $V^{**}_{SEFE}(z_N) = 1$ even if z_N is not Pareto indifferent to an allocation of $S^{EFE}(E)$.

7.6 CONCLUSION

Our study of the distribution of unproduced goods is now coming to a close. In this chapter, we have hinted at more radical generalizations of the approach, which are relevant beyond the distribution problem and have been discussed here for convenience. The notion of cross-profile SOFs is essential for the comparison of social welfare across countries or over periods of time and should become an important object of study for social choice theory in addition to the traditional SOF. The idea of taking account of legitimate endowments is one example of the possibility of varying the set of personal characteristics for which the agents are held responsible and that are therefore not subject to redistribution or compensation by other goods. Delineating this sphere of responsibility is an important ethical problem that has far-reaching consequences over redistributive policies. The importance of this issue will appear again in the next part of this book.

We have stressed in the introduction that each particular context requires a specific analysis because fairness principles are typically special to the form of redistribution, the kind of resources and dimensions of well-being, and the way in which resources are produced. The next part of the book will tackle the specific questions pertaining to production, which are essential for applications to income taxation.

We have devoted many chapters to the distribution of unproduced goods because this setting provides the basic elements in which key concepts can be introduced without undue complication. In particular, the last section of this chapter has shown that extensions to nonmaterial aspects of well-being are easy to conceive in principle (if not in practice) because the basis of the SOF approach is the possibility of comparing individual situations in terms of indifference sets. Precise ways of making interpersonal comparisons of indifference sets may depend a great deal on concrete aspects of the context (as shown by the example of health), but the key assumption that individuals have well-defined preferences over the relevant dimensions of their own well-being is all that is needed at the most basic level.

PART III

PRODUCTION

How does the study of the fair division problem carried out in Part II generalize to problems involving production? This is the topic of this part of the book. More precisely, we consider that the economy is endowed with a stock of private goods that can be used to produce other commodities, which can be public or private goods. In Chapter 8 and the beginning of Chapter 9, the initial stock of private goods is legitimately owned by the agents themselves, and the problem boils down to identifying fair ways of jointly using the production technology. In Chapter 8, the commodity that can be produced is a public good, whereas in Chapter 9 it is a private one.

The general picture that will emerge from these chapters is, first, that the specific features of the problems involving production allow us to define several specific fairness conditions, which, in turn, yield specific social ordering functions. We take it as an illustration that the approach we propose is quite flexible and takes advantage of the richness of a model to offer richer possible definitions of what is fair. Second, the developments in these chapters also confirm some key conclusions of the previous chapters, and, in particular, confirm that our axiomatic analysis ends up justifying social ordering functions that give absolute priority to the worst-off.

In the last section of Chapter 9, we drop the assumption that agents are the legitimate owners of some stock of private goods, and we replace it with the assumption that all agents have an identical claim on the resources of the economy. Dropping any restriction on the number and the nature (public versus private) of the commodities, we axiomatize a social ordering function inspired by what we axiomatized in the previous chapters. The lesson of this last exercise is that the approach presented in this book can be used to compute general indices of well-being.

In Chapter 10, we retain the assumption that agents are not the legitimate owners of the inputs of the economy, but we formalize it in a completely different way. The story that best fits that model is that inputs are quantities of labor, the individuals have unequal productivities, and it is considered that they should not bear the consequences of their unequal endowments in productive skills. This chapter is a central one in the development of our approach, as it shows that our objective of resource equality can be adapted to situations involving internal resources (here, productive skills). We then try to define our social objective by considering that external resources should be allocated unequally to compensate the agents suffering from a poor endowment in internal resources. The resulting model is richer than the ones studied before, and the richest one in the whole book. Consequently, a long list of plausible fairness properties appear, and a large part of the work consists of identifying the trade-offs between fairness axioms.

All the second-best applications associated with that model are gathered in Chapter 11, the last chapter of this part. Indeed, given that the model is a canonical one to study the taxation of earnings, we devote an entire chapter to studying the consequences of our social preferences on the shape of the tax function. This is also a good opportunity to illustrate the difference between our second-best applications and the typical public economics approach to second-best allocation in terms of utilitarian social objectives. In particular, some taxation policies receive a strong support from our analysis, whereas they are hard to justify from a classical utilitarian viewpoint. That will conclude Part III.

CHAPTER 8

Public Goods

8.1 INTRODUCTION

Assume agents share a technology. The technology can be used to transform quantities of a private good that is currently owned by the agents into a public good (that is, the consumption of the good is nonrival: think of a software jointly developed by several firms, a public facility produced by members of a community, transportation infrastructures, and the like). How much should each agent be asked to contribute to the production, and how much should be produced? Also, assuming it is possible to exclude some agents from the consumption of the public good (think of hours of TV programs, or access to a public facility), should that possibility be used, and if so, how much of the public good should each agent be allowed to consume? These are the questions we raise in this chapter.[1]

Even if the model we study here remains simple (there is one private good and one public good), the new ingredient we introduce – that is, the production technology – will turn out to sufficiently enrich the model to enable us to study new fairness properties.

Two axioms are introduced. The first one is based on the comparison of what an agent gets and what the agent would get if he or she were alone in the economy, and could use the production technology by himself or herself. When the good to produce is a public good, being alone in the economy is a bad situation – actually, the worst situation one can think of. The stand-alone situation sets an intuitive (lower) benchmark. An obviously inequitable situation would be one in which one agent is worse off than at the benchmark, whereas one other agent is better off. We study the condition saying that in such situations, a transfer of resource from the latter agent to the former agent should be a social improvement. We call this condition *stand-alone transfer*.

The second equity condition we introduce is based on the idea that each agent should contribute to covering the production cost, or, at least, so should each

[1] This chapter is largely inspired by Maniquet and Sprumont (2004, 2005), and the second-best application draws from Maniquet (2007).

agent who consumes the produced good. Consequently, if two agents consume the same quantity of the produced good, but one of them contributes negatively (namely, he or she receives some amount of the input from the others) whereas the other one contributes positively, then a transfer from the former to the latter should be a social improvement. We call this condition *free-lunch transfer*.

We complement these two equity conditions with a third one reminiscent of the equal-split transfer condition introduced in Chapter 2. It turns out that stand-alone transfer and equal-split transfer are easy to combine, whereas either one is incompatible with free-lunch transfer.

These three equity conditions force us to focus our attention on two social ordering functions. Unsurprisingly, they both give absolute priority to the worst-off. This confirms one of the main lessons that could be drawn from Parts I and II: only an infinite inequality aversion is compatible with weak equity conditions and robustness conditions.

One of the social ordering functions that ends up being characterized is quite similar to the Ω-equivalent leximin of Part II, with the social endowment Ω replaced by the cost function: the individual well-being levels are now calibrated with respect to the satisfaction an agent would reach if he or she were given free access to "fractions" of the cost function.

The second social ordering function uses another way of calibrating individual well-being levels – that is, one now must look at the quantity of the produced good, which, when consumed free (that is, with a zero contribution) leaves an agent indifferent to his or her assigned bundle. Again, the ordering of allocations works by maximizing the minimal calibrated level of well-being.

After having presented the model (Section 8.2), the equity axioms (Section 8.3), and the two prominent social ordering functions (Section 8.4), we show in Section 8.5 how the results extend to the case in which the produced commodity is a pure public good. Then, in Section 8.6 we develop simple second-best applications in which we compare the optimal choice associated with our two social ordering functions when exclusion is possible and when it is not.

8.2   THE MODEL

The new ingredient in this chapter is that one desirable public good is not initially available, but can be produced from one private good. The *cost function* $C : \mathbb{R}_+ \to \mathbb{R}_+$ is strictly increasing, strictly convex, $C(0) = 0$, and $\lim_{g \to \infty} C(g)/g = \infty$.[2] The set of all cost functions satisfying these conditions is denoted by $\mathcal{C}$. All agents are assumed to be endowed with some quantity of the private good. Moreover, we consider that the quantity they will eventually be asked to contribute is small compared with their endowment. Consequently,

---

[2] The last assumption guarantees that, independent of the number and preferences of the agents, the set of feasible allocations that Pareto dominate the no-activity allocation (that is, the allocation in which all agents consume their endowment and no public good is produced) is compact.

we do not need to specify the quantity of private good they begin with, and we only measure their contribution without imposing an upper bound on it. The implicit assumption is that the distribution of wealth before production is fair. This assumption allows us to disentangle two issues: redistributing wealth and sharing production costs. This chapter is concerned only with the latter.

Bundles are pairs $z_i = (t_i, g_i) \in \mathbb{R} \times \mathbb{R}_+$, where t_i denotes agent i's contribution to the production cost, and g_i agent i's consumption of the public good. Individual preferences are assumed to be continuous, strictly decreasing in the private good contribution level t_i, strictly increasing in the produced good consumption level g_i, and convex. Let $\mathcal{R}$ denote the set of preferences satisfying these conditions.

An economy is now a list $E = (R_N, C)$, where N is a nonempty finite subset of the set of integers, $R_N \in \mathcal{R}^N$, and $C \in \mathcal{C}$. Let $\mathcal{E}$ denote the set of such economies, and $\mathcal{D}$ the domain of definition of the SOF to be constructed. As far as the allocations to be ranked by the SOF are concerned, we will restrict our attention to allocations, which we call admissible for that economy, in which no agent obviously contributes too little or too much – that is, for each $i \in N$, there exists a production level $\overline{g}_i$ such that

$$(0, \overline{g}_i) \; R_i \; z_i \; R_i \; (0, 0).$$

The first part of the admissibility condition says that no agent prefers his or her bundle to the opportunity of consuming an arbitrarily large quantity of the produced good free. The second part means that everyone agrees to participate (not participating would mean not contributing, but not consuming the produced good either); that is, everyone gets a nonnegative share of the surplus generated by the production. We denote the set of admissible allocations by $A(R_N)$, and the set of admissible bundles for agent $i \in N$ by $A_i(R_i)$.

An allocation z_N is feasible for an economy $E = (R_N, C)$ if and only if

$$\sum_{i \in N} t_i \geq C \left(\max\{g_i\}_{i \in N} \right).$$

Let $Z(E)$ denote the set of feasible allocations. This definition of feasibility assumes that different agents may consume different levels of the public good and, therefore, that exclusion is possible.

An allocation with exclusion can never be Pareto optimal when preferences are strictly monotonic with respect to the public good because, starting from an allocation with exclusion, it costs nothing to let every agent consume the full quantity of the public good. On the other hand, it has been proved that exclusion may alleviate the free-rider problem – that is, when one takes incentive compatibility constraints into account, threatening to exclude an agent from consuming fractions of the available quantity of the public good may help design the incentives properly (see Moulin 1994). Consequently, the set of allocations among which the policymaker will likely have to choose may contain allocations with exclusion. We come back to this issue in our second-best applications of Section 8.6.

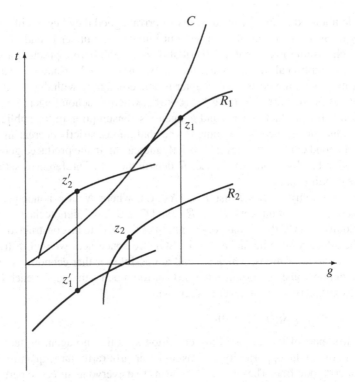

Figure 8.1. A two-agent public-good economy, and two allocations

We now study the construction of SOFs over admissible allocations in economies satisfying the preceding definitions. This is illustrated in Figure 8.1, in which two allocations are described in a two-agent economy. Allocation (z_1, z_2) is such that agent 1 consumes strictly more of the public good than agent 2, who is, therefore, partially excluded. Allocation (z'_1, z'_2) has no exclusion, but agent 1 contributes negatively – that is, agent 1 receives a strictly positive amount of the private good (in addition to the amount this agent owns at the beginning). How does one rank these two allocations? That is the question we answer in this chapter.

Several axioms introduced in Part I are easily adapted to the current setting. The Pareto axioms do not need to be rewritten, nor do the axioms of unchanged-contour independence or separability, as they do not involve any reference to the social resources. Even some fairness axioms, such as transfer among equals or nested transfer, are readily adapted. On the other hand, equal-split transfer or proportional allocations transfer were specific to the fair division problem. Perhaps they could yield similar axioms in the current model; this needs a careful discussion, however, which we develop in the next section.

The only robustness condition that involves changes in the resources is replication. When an economy is replicated, it must hold that an allocation is feasible in the initial economy if and only if the replicated allocation is feasible in the replicated economy. This requirement yields the following definition of the replica of a cost function. The production cost of a given amount of the public good is r times more expensive in the r-replica of the economy: C_r is an r-replica of C if for all $g \in \mathbb{R}_+$, $C_r(g) = rC(g)$. Consequently, $E' = (R_{N'}, C_r)$ is an r-replica of $E = (R_N, C)$ if C_r is an r-replica of C, and, as before, there exists a mapping $\gamma : N' \rightarrow N$ such that for all $i \in N$, $|\gamma^{-1}(i)| = r$ and for all $j \in \gamma^{-1}(i)$, $R_j = R_i$.

8.3 THREE AXIOMS

Should agents consuming the same level of the public good contribute the same amount of the private good? One may think of it as an evident fairness property: resource equalization requires that we ask each agent to contribute identically. That would give us the following axiom: a transfer of private goods between two agents is a weak social improvement if they both have the same quantity of the public good and the beneficiary of the transfer contributes strictly more than the other, before and after the transfer.

Axiom 8.1 Transfer
For all $E = (R_N, C) \in \mathcal{D}$, $z_N, z_N' \in A(R_N)$, $\Delta \in \mathbb{R}_{++}$, and $j, k \in N$ such that $g_j = g_j' = g_k = g_k'$, if

$$t_k - \Delta = t_k' > t_j' = t_j + \Delta$$

and for all $i \neq j, k$, $z_i' = z_i$, then z_N' $\mathbf{R}(E)$ z_N.

As we know from Chapter 2, for any sufficiently rich domain $\mathcal{D}$ such an axiom conflicts with Pareto axioms. Does that mean that we have to forgo the general ideal of resource equality? As a matter of fact, the public good case offers a nice illustration of why an axiom such as transfer is not compelling.

Indeed, assume agent k, in the comparison of the two allocations contemplated in the axiom, has a high willingness to pay for the public good, whereas j has a low willingness to pay; assume further that the production level of the public good is large, in better harmony with k's demand than with j's demand. Given that they both consume the same quantity of the public good, which, for Pareto efficiency reasons, should be good news, it seems natural to request a greater contribution from k than from j. Conversely, if k has a lower willingness to pay but the produced quantity is small, closer to k's aspiration, again it may be fair to ask k to pay more, and compensate j for the fact that j's consumption of the public good is low. For these reasons, equalizing resources physically is not the most appropriate fairness objective. That is why we have to define axioms that are logically weaker than transfer, and that embody a more compelling notion of fairness.

The first two fairness axioms we introduce in this section follow the idea that individual resource distribution should be given some bounds, or, more precisely, that the value agents give to resources, as a function of their preferences, should be given some bounds. Imposing lower and upper bounds is consistent with the idea that, on the one hand, all agents should be provided with a "safety net" and, on other hand, no one should reach an excessive well-being level at the expense of others.[3]

Define the stand-alone welfare level of an agent as the level this agent would enjoy at an efficient allocation if he or she were the only agent in the economy. In the nonrival environment we are considering, being alone is not desirable because the cost of producing the public good cannot be shared with others. The stand-alone welfare level should be an agent's lower welfare bound – this fairness principle was introduced by Moulin (1987).

Somehow similarly, we may define the unanimity welfare level of an agent as the level the agent would enjoy at an efficient allocation if the others had the same preferences as his or hers and everyone were treated equally. In public good environments, disagreeing constitutes a social burden. Indeed, if all agents actually have identical preferences, they are all able to enjoy their unanimity welfare level. As soon as preferences differ, however, no feasible allocation provides their unanimity welfare level to all agents. The unanimity welfare level should be an agent's upper welfare bound – this fairness principle was introduced by Moulin (1990) and further applied by Sprumont (1998).

We apply these bounds in our context as follows. Suppose that an agent enjoys an "insufficient" welfare level, – that is, the agent is strictly worse off than at his or her stand-alone level. Then a private good transfer to this agent from an agent strictly better off than his or her own stand-alone level should be viewed as a social improvement. This is the stand-alone transfer axiom. Likewise, suppose that an agent enjoys an "excessive" welfare level – that is, the agent is strictly better off than at his or her unanimity level. Then a private good transfer from this agent to an agent who is strictly worse off than at his or her own unanimity level is a social improvement. That is the equal-split transfer axiom. Both axioms express a form of well-being inequality aversion, but, again, a rather limited one.

Both axioms can be related to the equal-split transfer condition of Chapters 2 and 5. Indeed, in the fair division model of Part I, equal split can be justified from two different viewpoints: on one hand, it is a natural safety net, and, on the other hand, it corresponds to the bundle an agent would consume if all other agents had the same preferences as those of this agent. When a decision about how much of a public good to produce must be taken, those two ideas give different axioms, but two axioms that, as is proved below, turn out to be compatible with each other.

[3] The introduction of welfare lower and upper bounds in the literature on fairness is largely the work of Moulin. See, in particular, Moulin (1991, 1992).

Formally, if $R_i \in \mathcal{R}$ and $C \in \mathcal{C}$, by a slight abuse of notation, we let $\max|_{R_i} C$ denote the unique[4] bundle $z_i = (t_i, g_i)$ in $\max|_{R_i} \{(t, g)|t \geq C(g)\}$. Our axioms read as follows – note that a transfer of private good corresponds to a "transfer" of contribution in the opposite direction; that is, if we transfer some private good from j to k, the contribution of k decreases, that of j increases.

Axiom 8.2 Stand-Alone Transfer
For all $E = (R_N, C) \in \mathcal{D}$, $z_N, z'_N \in A(R_N)$, $\Delta \in \mathbb{R}_{++}$, and $j, k \in N$ such that $g_j = g'_j$, $g_k = g'_k$, if

$$\max|_{R_k} C \; P_k \, z'_k = (t_k - \Delta, g_k) \; P_k \, z_k$$

and

$$z_j \, P_j \, z'_j = (t_j + \Delta, g_j) \; P_j \, \max|_{R_j} C$$

and for all $i \neq j, k$, $z'_i = z_i$, then $z'_N \, \mathbf{R}(E) \, z_N$.

Axiom 8.3 Equal-Split Transfer
For all $E = (R_N, C) \in \mathcal{D}$, $z_N, z'_N \in A(R_N)$, $\Delta \in \mathbb{R}_{++}$, and $j, k \in N$ such that $g'_j = g_j$, $g'_k = g_k$, if

$$\max|_{R_k} (C/|N|) \; P_k \, z'_k = (t_k - \Delta, g_k) \; P_k \, z_k$$

and

$$z_j \, P_j \, z'_j = (t_j + \Delta, g_j) \; P_j \, \max|_{R_j} (C/|N|)$$

and for all $i \neq j, k$, $z'_i = z_i$, then $z'_N \, \mathbf{R}(E) \, z_N$.

Actually, the close relationship between the two ideas is confirmed formally by Lemma 8.1, which requires a technical step that we develop now. As we know from Lemma 4.1, combining separation and replication leads to some independence of the feasible set in the sense that multiplying or reducing the available resources should not affect social rankings. In the current context, any SOF satisfying separation and replication ranks allocations in the same way if the cost function is C or if it is qC, for any rational number $q > 0$. These irrelevant multiplication operations allow us to change the premises of stand-alone transfer into the premises of equal-split transfer, so the two axioms become equivalent.

Lemma 8.1 *On the domain $\mathcal{E}$, if a SOF satisfies* separation *and* replication, *then it satisfies* stand-alone transfer *if and only if it satisfies* equal-split transfer.

The proof mimics that of Lemma 4.1 and is therefore omitted. Because of the possibility of multiplying the cost function by any positive rational number, implied by the combination of separation and replication, one can also deduce the following lemma.

---

[4] Uniqueness follows from strict convexity of C. The abuse of notation comes from the fact that our $\max|_{R_i}$ terminology typically stands for a set of bundles, and not the bundles themselves.

Lemma 8.2 *On the domain* $\mathcal{E}$, *if a SOF satisfies* separation, replication, *and either* stand-alone transfer *or* equal-split transfer, *then it satisfies* nested-contour transfer *(and, consequently,* transfer among equals*)*.

Proof. Let $E = (R_N, C) \in \mathcal{E}$, $z_N, z'_N \in A(R_N)$ be such that for $\Delta \in \mathbb{R}_{++}$, *and* $j, k \in N$ such that $g'_j = g_j$, $g'_k = g_k$,

$$t'_j = t_j + \Delta, \quad t'_k = t_k - \Delta,$$

$$U(z'_j, R_j) \cap L(z'_k, R_k) = \emptyset$$

and for all $i \neq j, k$, $z_i = z'_i$.

As $U(z'_j, R_j) \cap L(z'_k, R_k) = \emptyset$, there is $q \in \mathbb{Q}_{++}$ such that $\max|_{R_k} qC \, P_k \, z'_k$ and $z'_j \, P_j \, \max|_{R_j} qC$. Therefore, by stand-alone transfer, $z'_N \, \mathbf{R}(R_N, qC) \, z_N$. As the ranking of allocations is unchanged when the cost function is rescaled in this way, one obtains $z'_N \, \mathbf{R}(E) \, z_N$. This proves nested-contour transfer. Transfer among equals is implied by nested-contour transfer (it corresponds to nested-contour transfer restricted to the case in which $R_j = R_k$). ∎

Finally, we turn to our third axiom, free-lunch transfer. Consider a profile R_N and an allocation at which two agents, j and k, consume the same quantity of the public good. Suppose that k's private good contribution is positive but j's contribution is negative. We claim that in this case agent j is unambiguously enjoying a higher well-being level than agent k. Indeed, if differences in preferences may justify that two agents consuming the same quantity of the public good contribute unevenly to its production, they do not justify that one agent contributes while the other agent receives some private good subsidy. Because j enjoys a "free lunch," a transfer of private good from j to k that does not reverse the signs of their contributions should be deemed to increase social welfare. The axiom reads as follows: a transfer of private good between two agents is a weak social improvement if they both have the same quantity of the public good and the beneficiary has a strictly positive contribution, whereas the donor has a strictly negative contribution, before and after the transfer.

Axiom 8.4 Free-Lunch Transfer
For all $E = (R_N, C) \in \mathcal{D}$, $z_N, z'_N \in A(R_N)$, $\Delta \in \mathbb{R}_+$, *and* $j, k \in N$ *such that* $g'_j = g_j = g'_k = g_k$, *if*

$$t_k + \Delta = t'_k > 0 > t'_j = t_j - \Delta$$

and for all $i \neq j, k$, $z'_i = z_i$, *then* $z'_N \, \mathbf{R}(E) \, z_N$.

As might be expected by now, no SOF satisfies weak Pareto, free-lunch transfer, and either stand-alone transfer or equal-split transfer. Figure 8.2 shows an economy $E = (R_N, C)$, $N = \{1, 2\}$, and four allocations $z_N, z'_N, z''_N, z'''_N \in A(R_N)$, such that

- $g_1 = g'_1 = g'_2 = g_2$, $g''_1 = g'''_1 = g'''_2 = g''_2$,
- $t_1 + t_2 = t'_1 + t'_2$, $t''_1 + t''_2 = t'''_1 + t'''_2$,

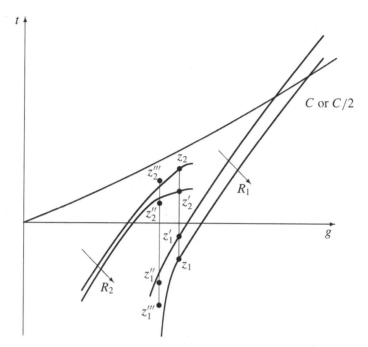

Figure 8.2. Free-lunch transfer versus stand-alone (or equal-split) transfer

- $t_1 < t_1' \leq 0 \leq t_2' < t_2$, $t_1''' < t_1'' \leq 0 \leq t_2'' < t_2'''$,
- $z_1\ P_1\ z_1'''\ P_1\ z_1''\ P_1\ z_1'$ and $z_2''\ P_2\ z_2'\ P_2\ z_2\ P_2\ z_2'''$,
- $\max|_{R_1}\ C\ P_1\ z_1'''$ and $z_2'''\ P_2\ \max|_{R_2}\ C$.

By free-lunch transfer, $z_N'\ \mathbf{R}(E)\ z_N$, and by stand-alone transfer, $z_N'''\ \mathbf{R}(E)$ z_N''. By weak Pareto, $z_N''\ \mathbf{P}(E)\ z_N'$ and $z_N\ \mathbf{P}(E)\ z_N'''$, which creates a cycle. If the graph of C is reinterpreted as that of $C/2$, then Figure 8.2 illustrates the incompatibility between free-lunch transfer and equal-split transfer.

8.4   TWO SOLUTIONS

The axioms introduced in the previous section force us to focus on two specific SOFs. Both SOFs give absolute priority to the worst-off, according to specific well-being indices. The first index, a utility representation of the preferences, works as follows. The cost function is divided by the real number that would leave the agent indifferent between his or her actual bundle and the best bundle the agent could get if he or she were alone in the economy and had free access to that rescaled cost function. The associated well-being level is this number. Formally, for each $R_i \in \mathcal{R}$, $z_i \in A_i(R_i)$, and $C \in \mathcal{C}$,

$$u_C(z_i, R_i) = a \Leftrightarrow z_i\ I_i\ \max|_{R_i}\ C/a$$

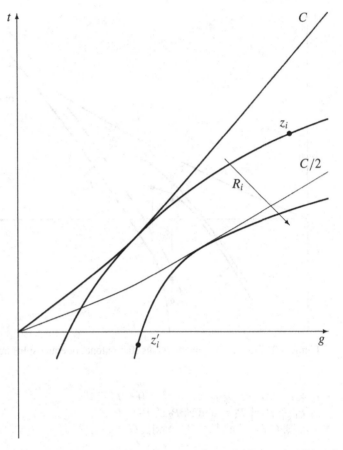

Figure 8.3. Cost-equivalent representation of R_i: $u_C(z_i, R_i) = 1$ and $u_C(z'_i, R_i) = 2$

if such an a exists, and 0 otherwise.[5] We call the numerical representation $u_C(\cdot, R_i)$ agent i's *cost-equivalent utility function*. By definition of this representation, agent i is indifferent between receiving bundle z_i or maximizing R_i subject to the cost function $C/u_C(z_i, R_i)$. This is illustrated on Figure 8.3.

The C-equivalent leximin SOF $\mathbf{R}^{Clex}$ works by applying the leximin criterion to the cost-equivalent utility levels of the agents at the allocations we compare.

Social ordering function 8.1 C-Equivalent Leximin ($\mathbf{R}^{Clex}$)
For all $E = (R_N, \Omega) \in \mathcal{E}$, z_N, $z'_N \in A(R_N)$,

$$z_N \, \mathbf{R}^{Clex}(E) \, z'_N \Leftrightarrow (u_C(z_i, R_i))_{i \in N} \geq_{lex} \left(u_C(z'_i, R_i)\right)_{i \in N}.$$

---

[5] The latter case occurs only if $z_i \, I_i \, (0, 0)$ and the agent's marginal rate of substitution in the (g, t) space is infinite at $(0, 0)$.

Table 8.1. *Properties of the Two SOFs*

	$\mathbf{R}^{Clex}$	$\mathbf{R}^{glex}$
Strong Pareto	+	+
Transfer among equals	+	+
Nested-contour transfer	+	+
Stand-alone transfer	+	−
Equal-split transfer	+	−
Free-lunch transfer	−	+
Unchanged-contour independence	+	+
Separation	+	+
Replication	+	+
Independence of the feasible set	−	+

We now turn to the second SOF. The associated utility representation of the preferences is the quantity of public good that, if received free, would leave the agent indifferent between what he or she actually consumes and that quantity. Formally, for each $R_i \in \mathcal{R}$ and $z_i \in A_i(R_i)$, there is a unique level of the public good, $g_i^0 \in \mathbb{R}_+$, such that $z_i \, I_i \, (0, g_i^0)$. We may therefore define the numerical well-being representation function $u_g(., R_i) : A_i(R_i) \to \mathbb{R}_+$ by letting

$$u_g(z_i, R_i) = g_i^0 \Leftrightarrow z_i \, I_i \, (0, g_i^0).$$

We call the numerical representation $u_g(\cdot, R_i)$ agent i's *output-equivalent utility function*. By definition of this representation, agent i is indifferent between receiving the bundle z_i or consuming $u_g(z_i, R_i)$ of the public good free.

The g-equivalent leximin SOF $\mathbf{R}^{glex}$ applies the leximin criterion to the output-equivalent utility levels of the agents at the allocations to be compared.

Social ordering function 8.2 g-Equivalent Leximin ($\mathbf{R}^{glex}$)
For $E = (R_N, \Omega) \in \mathcal{E}$, $z_N, z'_N \in A(R_N)$,

$$z_N \, \mathbf{R}^{glex}(E) \, z'_N \Leftrightarrow \left(u_g(z_i, R_i) \right)_{i \in N} \geq_{lex} \left(u_g(z'_i, R_i) \right)_{i \in N}.$$

Table 8.1 summarizes the relative merits of both solutions.

As suggested by the table, there is a trade-off between independence of the feasible set (in the current model, this axiom requires the ranking to be independent of changes in the cost function) and the fairness axioms of stand-alone transfer and equal-split transfer, under Pareto requirements. This trade-off is illustrated in Figure 8.4. If the cost function is C (respectively, $C/2$), then agent 1 (respectively, agent 2) is enjoying an insufficient (respectively, excessive) well-being level according to stand-alone transfer (respectively, equal-split transfer) and $z'_N \, \mathbf{R}(R_N, C) \, z_N$. If the cost function is C', the situation of the two agents appears reversed and one obtains $z'''_N \, \mathbf{R}\left(R_N, C'\right) z''_N$. Independence of the feasible set then implies $z'''_N \, \mathbf{R}(R_N, C) \, z''_N$. As weak Pareto imposes that $z''_N \, \mathbf{P}(R_N, C) \, z'_N$ and $z_N \, \mathbf{P}(R_N, C) \, z'''_N$, this creates a cycle.

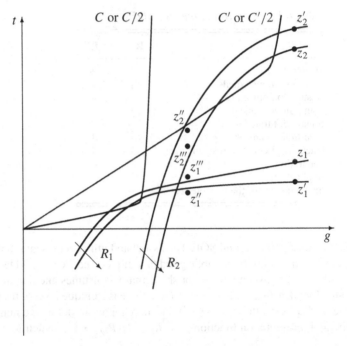

Figure 8.4. Incompatibility between independence of the feasible set and either stand-alone transfer or equal-split transfer

These two SOFs give absolute priority to the worst-off. The reason that the combination of robustness conditions and either stand-alone transfer or equal-split transfer yields a C-equivalent leximin function is quite similar to what we obtained with the Ω-equivalent leximin in Chapter 5. Indeed, as for equal-split transfer in Part I, the axioms of stand-alone transfer or equal-split transfer can be strengthened into "priority" axioms when the social rankings are required to be independent of changes in preferences or of changes in the number of agents.

Let us define two axioms of stand-alone priority and equal-split priority that convey an infinite aversion to inequality. Stand-alone priority is similar to stand-alone transfer, except that the beneficiary of the transfer can get an arbitrarily small quantity of the private good, and the donor may remove an arbitrarily large amount of the private good.

Axiom 8.5 Stand-Alone Priority
For $E = (R_N, C) \in \mathcal{D}$, $z_N, z'_N \in A(R_N)$, and $j, k \in N$ such that $g_j = g'_j, g_k = g'_k$, if

$$\max|_{R_k} C \; P_k \; z'_k \, P_k \, z_k \; and \; z_j \, P_j \, z'_j \, P_j \, \max|_{R_j} C$$

and for all $i \neq j, k$, $z'_i = z_i$, then $z'_N \, \mathbf{R}(E) \, z_N$.

As for equal-split priority, it is similar to equal-split transfer, except that now the beneficiary of the transfer can get an arbitrarily small quantity of the private good, and the donor may lose an arbitrarily large amount of the private good.

Axiom 8.6 Equal-Split Priority
For $E = (R_N, C) \in \mathcal{D}$, $z_N, z'_N \in A(R_N)$, and $j, k \in N$ such that $g'_j = g_j, g'_k = g_k$, if

$$\max|_{R_k} (C / |N|) \, P_k \, z'_k \, P_k \, z_k \text{ and } z_j \, P_j \, z'_j \, P_j \, \max|_{R_j} (C / |N|)$$

and for all $i \neq j, k$, $z'_i = z_i$, then $z'_N \, \mathbf{R}(E) \, z_N$.

We then have the following.

Lemma 8.3 *(a) On $\mathcal{E}$, if a SOF $\mathbf{R}$ satisfies Pareto indifference, separation, replication, and stand-alone transfer (or equal-split transfer), then it satisfies stand-alone priority and equal-split priority.*
(b) On $\mathcal{E}$, if a SOF $\mathbf{R}$ satisfies Pareto indifference, unchanged-contour independence, and stand-alone transfer (respectively, equal-split transfer), then it satisfies stand-alone priority (respectively, equal-split priority).

Proof. (a) Let $E = (R_N, C) \in \mathcal{E}$, $z_N = (t_N, g_N), z'_N = (t'_N, g'_N) \in A(R_N)$, and $j, k \in N$ be such that $g_j = g'_j, g_k = g'_k$,

$$\max|_{R_k} C \, P_k \, z'_k \, P_k \, z_k \text{ and } z_j \, P_j \, z'_j \, P_j \, \max|_{R_j} C,$$

and for all $i \neq j, k$, $z'_i = z_i$. We want to show that $z'_N \, \mathbf{R}(E) \, z_N$. Let R_0, $z_0^a, z_0^b, z_0^c, z_0^d$ be such that

$$z_0^b \, I_0 \, z_0^c \, P_0 \, \max|_{R_0} C,$$

$$z'_j \, P_0 \, z_0^a \, I_0 \, z_0^d,$$

$$U(z_0^a, R_0) = U(z_0^a, R_j),$$

$$g_0^a = g_0^b,$$

$$g_0^c = g_0^d,$$

$$\frac{(t'_j - t_j)}{(t_0^c - t_0^d)} = \frac{(t_k - t'_k)}{(t_0^b - t_0^a)} \in \mathbb{N}.$$

Let $E' = ((R_j, R_k, R_0), C)$ and $E'' = ((R_j, R_k, R_0), qC)$ where $q \in \mathbb{Q}_{++}$ is chosen so that $\max|_{R_0} qC \, P_0 \, z_0^a$ and $z'_j \, P_j \, \max|_{R_j} qC$. Let $\Delta_1 = t_0^b - t_0^a$ and $\Delta_2 = t_0^c - t_0^d$. This configuration is illustrated in Figure 8.5, which is similar to Figure 3.4.

By stand-alone transfer,

$$\left(z_j, z_k - (\Delta_1, 0), z_0^b\right) \, \mathbf{R}(E') \, \left(z_j, z_k, z_0^a\right).$$

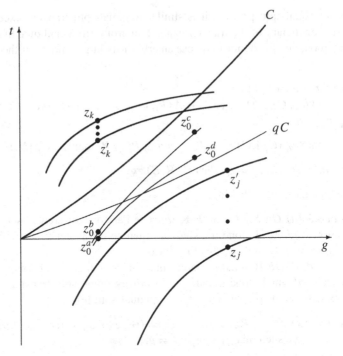

Figure 8.5. From stand-alone (or equal-split) transfer to stand-alone (and equal-split) priority

By Pareto indifference,

$$\left(z_j, z_k - (\Delta_1, 0), z_0^c\right) \mathbf{I}(E') \left(z_j, z_k - (\Delta_1, 0), z_0^b\right).$$

By stand-alone transfer,

$$\left(z_j + (\Delta_2, 0), z_k - (\Delta_1, 0), z_0^d\right) \mathbf{R}(E'') \left(z_j, z_k - (\Delta_1, 0), z_0^c\right).$$

By Pareto indifference,

$$\left(z_j + (\Delta_2, 0), z_k - (\Delta_1, 0), z_0^a\right) \mathbf{I}(E'') \left(z_j + (\Delta_2, 0), z_k - (\Delta_1, 0), z_0^d\right).$$

By separation and replication, one has $\mathbf{R}(E'') = \mathbf{R}(E')$. Therefore, wrapping up the previous lines, one obtains, by transitivity:

$$\left(z_j + (\Delta_2, 0), z_k - (\Delta_1, 0), z_0^a\right) \mathbf{R}(E') \left(z_j, z_k, z_0^a\right).$$

Repeating the argument $(t_j' - t_j)/(t_0^c - t_0^d)$ times (Figure 8.5 illustrates the case in which three steps are needed), one eventually obtains

$$\left(z_j', z_k', z_0^a\right) \mathbf{R}(E') \left(z_j, z_k, z_0^a\right).$$

By separation, this is equivalent to $z_N' \mathbf{R}(E) z_N$. It is an immediate extension of Lemma 8.1 that, under separation and replication, stand-alone priority and equal-split priority are equivalent.

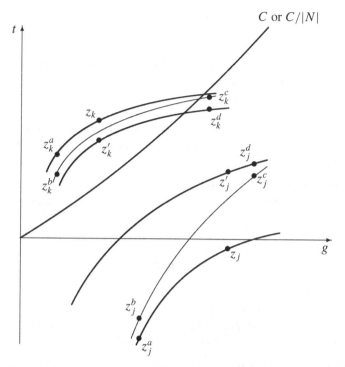

Figure 8.6. From stand-alone (or equal-split) transfer to stand-alone (and equal-split) priority

(b) The proof is essentially identical to that of Theorem 3.1; its basic line is illustrated in Figure 8.6.

By unchanged-contour independence, one has z'_N $\mathbf{R}(E)$ z_N if and only if z'_N $\mathbf{R}(E')$ z_N, where $E' = (R'_N, C)$ is such that the indifference curves for j, k are as in the figure. By Pareto indifference,

$$\left(z^a_j, z^a_k, z_{N\setminus\{j,k\}}\right) \mathbf{I}(E') \left(z_j, z_k, z_{N\setminus\{j,k\}}\right).$$

By stand-alone transfer,

$$\left(z^b_j, z^b_k, z_{N\setminus\{j,k\}}\right) \mathbf{R}(E') \left(z^a_j, z^a_k, z_{N\setminus\{j,k\}}\right).$$

By Pareto indifference,

$$\left(z^c_j, z^c_k, z_{N\setminus\{j,k\}}\right) \mathbf{I}(E') \left(z^b_j, z^b_k, z_{N\setminus\{j,k\}}\right).$$

By stand-alone transfer,

$$\left(z^d_j, z^d_k, z_{N\setminus\{j,k\}}\right) \mathbf{R}(E') \left(z^c_j, z^c_k, z_{N\setminus\{j,k\}}\right).$$

By Pareto indifference,

$$\left(z'_j, z'_k, z_{N\setminus\{j,k\}}\right) \mathbf{I}(E') \left(z^d_j, z^d_k, z_{N\setminus\{j,k\}}\right).$$

By transitivity, and taking account of the fact that $z'_{N\setminus\{j,k\}} = z_{N\setminus\{j,k\}}$, one obtains z'_N $\mathbf{R}(E')$ z_N. ∎

Regarding free-lunch transfer, similar results are obtained. Separability (which is weaker than separation) is sufficient to yield absolute priority to the worst-off on the subdomain $\mathcal{E}^3 \subseteq \mathcal{E}$ of economies with $|N| \geq 3$. First, we define free-lunch priority. It is identical to free-lunch transfer, except that the beneficiary of the transfer can get an arbitrarily small quantity of the private good, and the donor may give away an arbitrarily large amount of the private good.

Axiom 8.7 Free-Lunch Priority
For all $E = (R_N, C) \in \mathcal{D}$, $z_N, z'_N \in A(R_N)$, *and* $j, k \in N$ *such that* $g'_j = g_j = g'_k = g_k$, *if*

$$t_j < t'_j < 0 < t'_i < t_i$$

and for all $i \neq j, k$, $z'_i = z_i$, *then* z'_N $\mathbf{R}(E)$ z_N.

Lemma 8.4 *(a) On* $\mathcal{E}^3$, *if a SOF* $\mathbf{R}$ *satisfies* Pareto indifference, free-lunch transfer, *and* separability, *then it satisfies* free-lunch priority.
(b) On $\mathcal{E}$, *if a SOF* $\mathbf{R}$ *satisfies* strong Pareto, free-lunch transfer, *and* unchanged-contour independence, *then it satisfies* free-lunch priority.

Proof. (a) The proof is very similar to that of Lemma 8.3 (a). We provide only the illustration in Figure 8.7. The thin indifference curves belong to a third agent l.

(b) The logic of the proof is basically the same as for Lemma 8.3 (b), but the constraint to have equal quantities of the public good makes it impossible, in some cases, to construct a figure like Figure 8.6. Figure 8.8 illustrates the additional steps.

We want to prove that z'_N $\mathbf{R}(E)$ z_N. Suppose not – that is, z_N $\mathbf{P}(E)$ z'_N.

By unchanged-contour independence, one then has z_N $\mathbf{P}(E')$ z'_N, where $E' = (R'_N, C)$ is such that $R'_{N\setminus\{j\}} = R_{N\setminus\{j\}}$, $I(z_j, R'_j) = I(z_j, R_j)$, $I(z'_j, R'_j) = I(z'_j, R_j)$, and $I(z^*_j, R'_j)$ is the thin curve of Figure 8.8 that contains z^*_j.

By strong Pareto, $(z^*_j, z_{N\setminus\{j\}})$ $\mathbf{P}(E')$ z'_N. By unchanged-contour independence, one then has $(z^*_j, z_{N\setminus\{j\}})$ $\mathbf{P}(E'')$ z'_N, where $E'' = (R''_N, C)$ is such that $R''_{N\setminus\{j\}} = R_{N\setminus\{j\}}$, $I(z^*_j, R''_j) = I(z^*_j, R'_j)$, $I(z'_j, R''_j) = I(z'_j, R_j)$, and $I(z_j, R''_j)$ is the thin curve of Figure 8.8 that contains z_j. It is then obvious how to complete the proof, following the steps of Lemma 8.3 (b).

One can see on Figure 8.8 that it was impossible to construct suitable intermediate indifference curves between $I(z_j, R_j)$ and $I(z'_j, R_j)$, because agent k's indifference curves make it impossible to make a transfer backed by free-lunch transfer on the extreme left side of the graph. This problem would vanish, however, if nonconvex preferences were allowed. ∎

We are now ready to state the main results of this section.

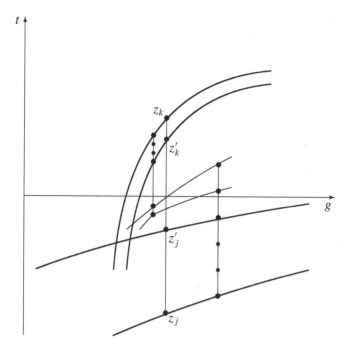

Figure 8.7. Proof (a) from free-lunch transfer to free-lunch priority

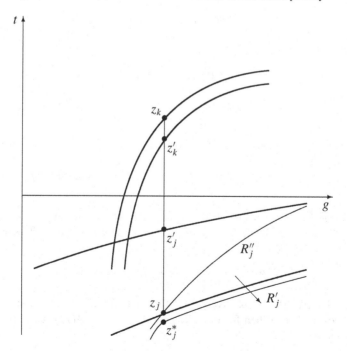

Figure 8.8. Proof (b) from free-lunch transfer to free-lunch priority

Theorem 8.1 *On $\mathcal{E}$, if a SOF* **R** *satisfies* strong Pareto, separation, replication, *and either* stand-alone transfer *or* equal-split transfer, *then for all* $E = (R_N, C)$ *and all* $z_N, z'_N \in A(R_N)$,

$$\min_{i \in N} u_C(z_i, R_i) > \min_{i \in N} u_C(z'_i, R_i) \Rightarrow z_N \, \mathbf{P}(E) \, z'_N.$$

Proof. Let $E = (R_N, C)$ and $z_N, z'_N \in A(R_N)$ be such that $\min_{i \in N} u_C(z_i, R_i) > \min_{i \in N} u_C(z'_i, R_i)$.

As in the proofs of Chapter 5, one first finds $\hat{z}_N, \hat{z}'_N \in A(R_N)$ such that by strong Pareto, $z_N \, \mathbf{P}(E) \, \hat{z}_N, \hat{z}'_N \, \mathbf{P}(E) \, z'_N$, and such that there is $i_0 \in N$ for which for all $j \neq i_0$,

$$u_C(\hat{z}'_j, R_j) > u_C(\hat{z}_j, R_j) > u_C(\hat{z}_{i_0}, R_{i_0}) > u_C(\hat{z}'_{i_0}, R_{i_0}).$$

There is $q \in \mathbb{Q}_{++}$ such that $1/q \in \left(u_C(\hat{z}_{i_0}, R_{i_0}), \min_{j \neq i_0} u_C(\hat{z}_j, R_j) \right)$. One therefore has $\max|_{R_{i_0}} qC \, P_{i_0} \, \hat{z}_{i_0}$ and for all $j \neq i_0$, $\hat{z}_j \, P_j \, \max|_{R_j} qC$. Let $\hat{z}_{i_0}^1, \ldots, \hat{z}_{i_0}^{n-2}$ be such that

$$u_C(\hat{z}_{i_0}, R_{i_0}) > u_C(\hat{z}_{i_0}^{n-2}, R_{i_0}) > \cdots > u_C(\hat{z}_{i_0}^1, R_{i_0}) > u_C(\hat{z}'_{i_0}, R_{i_0}).$$

Let the $n - 1$ agents other than i_0 be numbered $1, \ldots, n - 1$. By $n - 1$ applications of stand-alone priority (permitted by Lemma 8.3), one obtains

$$\left(\hat{z}_1, \hat{z}'_2, \ldots, \hat{z}'_{n-1}, \hat{z}_{i_0}^1 \right) \mathbf{R}(R_N, qC) \hat{z}'_N,$$

$$\left(\hat{z}_1, \hat{z}_2, \hat{z}'_3, \ldots, \hat{z}'_{n-1}, \hat{z}_{i_0}^2 \right) \mathbf{R}(R_N, qC) \left(\hat{z}_1, \hat{z}'_2, \ldots, \hat{z}'_{n-1}, \hat{z}_{i_0}^1 \right),$$

$$\vdots$$

$$\left(\hat{z}_1, \hat{z}_2, \ldots, \hat{z}_{n-2}, \hat{z}'_{n-1}, \hat{z}_{i_0}^{n-2} \right) \mathbf{R}(R_N, qC) \left(\hat{z}_1, \hat{z}_2, \ldots, \hat{z}'_{n-3}, \hat{z}'_{n-2}, \hat{z}'_{n-1}, \hat{z}_{i_0}^{n-3} \right),$$

$$\left(\hat{z}_1, \ldots, \hat{z}_{n-1}, \hat{z}_{i_0} \right) \mathbf{R}(R_N, qC) \left(\hat{z}_1, \hat{z}_2, \ldots, \hat{z}_{n-2}, \hat{z}'_{n-1}, \hat{z}_{i_0}^{n-2} \right),$$

implying by transitivity that $\hat{z}_N \, \mathbf{R}(R_N, qC) \hat{z}'_N$.

By separation and replication, this implies $\hat{z}_N \, \mathbf{R}(R_N, C) \, \hat{z}'_N$. By transitivity, $z_N \, \mathbf{P}(E) \, z'_N$.

By Lemma 8.1, stand-alone transfer can be replaced by equal-split transfer. ∎

Theorem 8.2 *On $\mathcal{E}$ (respectively, $\mathcal{E}^3$), if a SOF* **R** *satisfies* strong Pareto, free-lunch transfer, *and* unchanged-contour independence *(respectively, separability), then for all* $E = (R_N, C)$ *and all* $z_N, z'_N \in A(R_N)$,

$$\min_{i \in N} u_g(z_i, R_i) > \min_{i \in N} u_g(z'_i, R_i) \Rightarrow z_N \, \mathbf{P}(R) \, z'_N.$$

Proof. By part (b) (respectively, part (a)) of Lemma 8.4, free-lunch priority must be satisfied. When for two allocations $z_N, z'_N \in A(R_N)$ and two agents j, k, one has

$$u_g(z'_j, R_j) > u_g(z_j, R_j) > u_g(z_k, R_k) > u_g(z'_k, R_k),$$

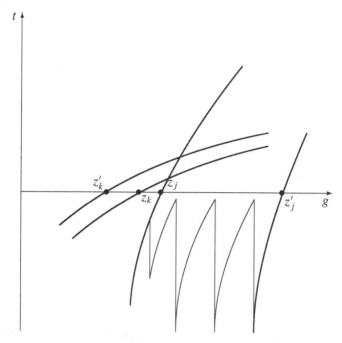

Figure 8.9. Application of free-lunch priority in the presence of vertical asymptotic lines

while $z_i' = z_i$ for all $i \neq j, k$, then Pareto indifference and free-lunch priority imply that z_N $\mathbf{R}(E)$ z_N'. This is not immediate because $I(z_j', R_j)$ may have a vertical asymptotic line above $u_g(z_j, R_j)$, which makes it impossible to apply free-lunch priority in one blow, and requires the intervention of Pareto indifference. Figure 8.9 illustrates the problem and its solution. As preferences are continuous and *strictly* monotonic, it is always possible to follow a *finite* sequence of vertical line segments and indifference curves, as in the figure. This corresponds to a sequence of applications of free-lunch priority, along the vertical line segments, and Pareto indifference, along the indifference curves.

We can now prove the theorem. Let $E = (R_N, C) \in \mathcal{E}$ (respectively, $\mathcal{E}^3$) and z_N, $z_N' \in A(R_N)$ be such that $\min_{i \in N} u_g(z_i, R_i) > \min_{i \in N} u_g(z_i', R_i)$. Let $\hat{z}_N$, $\hat{z}_N' \in A(R_N)$ be such that by strong Pareto, z_N $\mathbf{P}(E)$ $\hat{z}_N$, $\hat{z}_N'$ $\mathbf{P}(E)$ z_N', and such that there is $i_0 \in N$ for which for all $j \neq i_0$,

$$u_g(\hat{z}_j', R_j) > u_g(\hat{z}_j, R_j) > u_g(\hat{z}_{i_0}, R_{i_0}) > u_g(\hat{z}_{i_0}', R_{i_0}).$$

By $n - 1$ applications of free-lunch priority, as justified previously, one obtains that $\hat{z}_N$ $\mathbf{R}(E)$ $\hat{z}_N'$. By transitivity, z_N $\mathbf{P}(E)$ z_N'. ∎

The latter theorem is somehow surprising, as very few axioms lead to sharp consequences. Indeed, the axioms complement each other quite efficiently, as, even if strong pareto, separability, and unchanged-contour independence are reasonably weak axioms (at least in the sense that the large majority of SOFs we study in this book satisfy these axioms), combining them with free-lunch transfer forces us to focus on output-equivalent utility levels, and to aggregate them using a criterion, such as the leximin, that respects the strict-preference part of the maximin criterion.

8.5 PURE PUBLIC GOODS

The SOFs characterized above rank allocations in which agents may consume different quantities of the public good. We argued in Section 8.3 that this is useful for making second-best social decisions. However, exclusion may be altogether impossible (or exceedingly costly), as the nonrival good may be a pure public good. In this case, the set of admissible allocations should be redefined, as mentioned earlier (see Section 8.2), to incorporate the constraint that all agents consume the same quantity of the good.

The axioms are rewritten without any further correction. Separability and separation become much weaker, as they apply only when comparing allocations z_N, z'_N that both involve the same level of public good. Consequently, Pareto indifference plays a new and crucial role. Indeed, the comparison between two allocations that are associated with two different public good levels is always Pareto equivalent to the comparison of two allocations associated with the same produced level of public good. Therefore, all arguments involving separability or separation can be recovered by combining either axiom with Pareto indifference. All the results presented in Section 8.4, therefore, generalize to the pure public good case, with a slight complication for part (b) of Lemma 8.3, in which strong Pareto must replace Pareto indifference, for the same reason as it already does in part (b) of Lemma 8.4 in which, by definition of free-lunch transfer, the quantities of public good consumed by the two agents must be identical.

That both characterization results hold true is good news, of course, but one may object that the model is no longer appropriate for the case of the pure public good. Indeed, we have assumed that contributions can be negative. This is legitimate if we think that a transfer could compensate an excluded agent, but when exclusion is altogether impossible, we may simply restrict our attention to allocations in which contributions are all nonnegative. As a consequence, free-lunch transfer is no longer applicable to the model. On the other hand, a small variant of it – requiring that, if one agent contributes a strictly positive amount while another agent does not contribute at all, there should exist some transfer from the latter to the former that improves social welfare – can be formulated, and results in a characterization of a g-equivalent maximin function.[6]

On the other hand, all our results regarding stand-alone transfer and equal-split transfer remain valid, as none of our arguments uses allocations involving

---

[6] See Fleurbaey and Sprumont (2009) for details.

negative contributions. Consequently, the C-equivalent leximin function is justified in exactly the same way as before.

This discussion leads us naturally toward a solution that, surprisingly, is
completely absent from the discussion so far: the Lindahl correspondence. The
egalitarian Lindahl allocation rule is defined as follows. It selects the set of
efficient allocations that can be decentralized through individualized prices for
the public good and the equal sharing of the profit of the production sector.

Allocation rule 8.1 Egalitarian Lindahl S^{EL}
*For all $E = (R_N, C) \in \mathcal{E}$, $S^{EL}(E)$ is the set of allocations $z_N \in Z(E)$ such
that for some $p \in \mathbb{R}_+^{|N|}$,*

(a) g maximizes $g \sum_{i \in N} p_i - C(g)$;
(b) for all $i \in N$, $z_i \in \max|_{R_i} \left\{ (t, g') \mid g' p_i = t + \left(g \sum_{i \in N} p_i - C(g) \right) / |N| \right\}$.

What is its relationship with the SOFs and the axioms discussed so far?
The preceding discussion has implicitly made clear that it is hard to justify
the Lindahl approach to public goods in the framework of SOFs. There are
three reasons for that, all of which are illustrated in Figure 8.10. Allocation
$z^L = (z_1^L, z_2^L)$ is an egalitarian Lindahl allocation (π denotes the profit of the
firm producing the public good, and p_i, for $i = 1, 2$, denotes the individualized
price paid by agent i). Any SOF consistent with Lindahlian ethics would
recommend this allocation as the socially preferred one among the feasible
ones.

The first problem comes from the fact that $z_1^L \neq z_2^L$, whereas agents 1 and
2 are identical. Consequently, any such SOF would violate transfer among
equals. The second problem comes from the fact that $u_C(z_2^L, R_2) < 1$; that
is, agent 2 ends up worse off than if he or she were alone in the economy:
stand-alone transfer must be violated as well. The third problem is that agent
1 enjoys a free lunch and is strictly better off than if both agents had the same
bundle. Consequently, any Lindahl SOF would violate free-lunch transfer and
equal-split transfer.

For all those reasons, we must conclude that no desirable SOF would recommend us to single out the Lindahl allocations as the best ones. This shows
the limits of the Lindahl correspondence, and it also sheds doubts on the common wisdom that the Walrasian correspondence is "extended" into the Lindahl
correspondence when there are public goods.

The Lindahl correspondence has inspired the definition of other interesting
allocation rules in the public good model. An example is the ratio equilibrium
allocation rule, introduced by Kaneko (1977). Surprisingly, it is possible to
define a SOF that satisfies several desirable properties and that singles out the
ratio equilibrium allocations as the best ones.

Let us begin by defining that rule. First, it selects efficient allocations. That
implies that all agents consume the same quantity of the public good, but
possibly contribute different shares to the production cost. Second, the precise
bundle that an agent consumes is exactly the one that the agent would choose
had he or she be given free access to the share of the technology corresponding

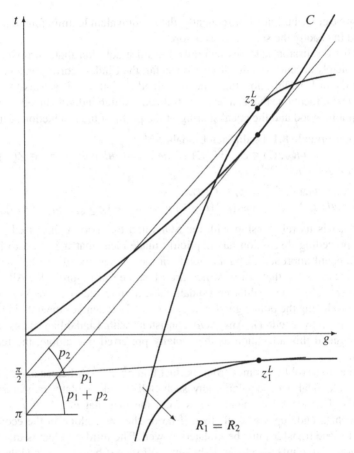

Figure 8.10. Any SOF consistent with the egalitarian Lindahl correspondence violates transfer among equals, stand-alone transfer, equal-split transfer, and free-lunch transfer.

to the fraction of the cost he or she pays. Another way of presenting that rule is to say that it is a Lindahlian correspondence selecting the allocations in which one agent's share in the profit of the firm is proportional to the agent's contribution.

Allocation rule 8.2 Ratio Equilibrium S^R

For all $E = (R_N, C) \in \mathcal{E}$, $S^R(E)$ is the set of allocations $z_N \in Z(E)$ such that for some $p \in \mathbb{R}_+^{|N|}$,

(a) g maximizes $g \sum_{i \in N} p_i - C(g)$;

(b) for all $i \in N$, $z_i \in \max|_{R_i} \left\{ (t, g') \mid g' p_i = t + \left(g \sum_{i \in N} p_i - C(g) \right) \frac{t_i}{\sum_{j \in N} t_j} \right\}$.

That rule is illustrated in Figure 8.11. Allocation (z_1^R, z_2^R) is a ratio equilibrium allocation. Agent 1 contributes two-thirds of the production cost, and z_1

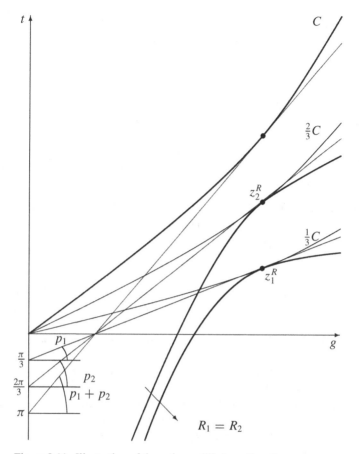

Figure 8.11. Illustration of the ratio-equilibrium allocations

is precisely the bundle agent 1 would choose if he or she had free access to the
cost function defined as two-thirds of the cost function C. There is a connection
between this property and the definition of the C-equivalent well-being index.
Indeed, $u_C(z_1^R, R_1) = 3$. In the same way, we can compute $u_C(z_2^R, R_2) = \frac{3}{2}$.
Using that terminology, we can express the Samuelson condition associated
with that allocation as

$$\frac{1}{u_C(z_1^R, R_1)} + \frac{1}{u_C(z_2^R, R_2)} = 1.$$

This is a general property: at a ratio equilibrium allocation, the sum of the
inverse of the C-equivalent well-being levels of the agents is equal to 1. Let us
prove that fact and then build on it to construct a SOF rationalizing the ratio
equilibrium rule S^R.

The key observation is the following property of the C-equivalent numerical representation of preferences. For all $E = (R_N, C) \in \mathcal{E}$, all $i \in N$, all $g \geq 0$,

$$u_C((\alpha C(g), g), R_i) \leq 1/\alpha.$$

The equality is obtained whenever $(\alpha C(g), g)$ is agent i's precise choice when agent i is given free access to a share α of the cost function. Otherwise, the inequality is strict.

The conclusion of that discussion is that the following SOF (which is utilitarian in a numerical representation of the preferences that is the opposite of the inverse of the C-equivalent representation) singles out the ratio equilibrium allocations as the best ones among the feasible allocations.

Social ordering function 8.3 Ratio-Equivalent Utilitarian ($\mathbf{R}^{Rutil}$)
For $E = (R_N, \Omega) \in \mathcal{E}$, $z_N, z'_N \in A(R_N)$,

$$z_N \, \mathbf{R}^{Rutil}(E) \, z'_N \Leftrightarrow \sum_{i \in N} \frac{-1}{u_C(z_i, R_i)} \geq \sum_{i \in N} \frac{-1}{u_C(z'_i, R_i)}.$$

The ratio-equivalent utilitarian SOF satisfies strong Pareto, separation, replication, and unchanged-contour independence. The allocations it selects among the feasible ones – that is, the ratio-equilibrium allocations – guarantee to each agent a well-being level at least equal to the agent's stand-alone well-being level.

On the other hand, as could be expected, this SOF performs badly as soon as key fairness properties are concerned: it does not even satisfy transfer among equals. Even if the ratio-equilibrium allocation rule is easier to adapt to the SOF approach than the egalitarian Lindahl rule, it is still far from being compatible with our basic fairness requirements.

8.6   SECOND-BEST APPLICATIONS

In this section, we illustrate how the SOFs axiomatized in the previous sections can be used to identify second-best allocations. We distinguish two cases, depending on whether the public good is excludable. In the case of a pure (nonexcludable) public good, the set of feasible and incentive-compatible allocations is particularly simple. That allows us to characterize the second-best optimal allocations associated with our two SOFs. In the case of an excludable public good, the set of feasible and incentive-compatible allocations is much harder to characterize. We are then able to identify only a few properties of the second-best allocations.

Before that, and to evaluate the second-best allocations, let us begin by illustrating the first-best allocations in a two-agent economy.

In Figure 8.12, allocation (z_1^C, z_2^C) (respectively, (z_1^g, z_2^g)) represents the optimal feasible allocation for the C-equivalent leximin SOF $\mathbf{R}^{Clex}$ (respectively, the g-equivalent leximin SOF $\mathbf{R}^{glex}$). They are associated in the graph with the same production level of the public good, but there is nothing essential in that

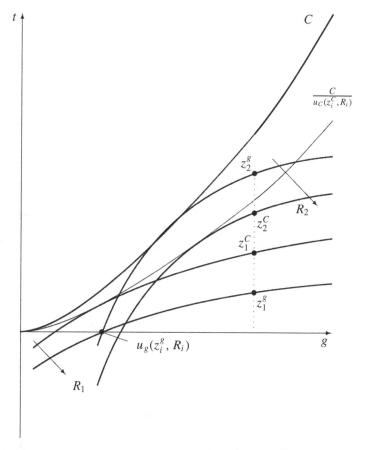

Figure 8.12. Optimal feasible allocations for $\mathbf{R}^{glex}$ and $\mathbf{R}^{Clex}$ in a two-agent economy

(it only allows us to simplify the figure). They both are Pareto efficient, which can be guessed from the graph, as the Samuelson conditions are satisfied (the marginal rate of transformation along the cost function is equal to the sum of the marginal rates of substitution along the indifference curves). What is essential is that agent 1, the agent with low willingness to pay, strictly prefers z_1^g over z_1^C, and the opposite preference holds for agent 2. At a first-best allocation, $\mathbf{R}^{glex}$ favors the agent with lower willingness to pay, whereas $\mathbf{R}^{Clex}$ favors the agent with greater willingness to pay.

Let us now move toward second-best applications, by concentrating first on the case of a pure public good. In this case, given that all agents will consume the same quantity of the produced good, the incentive constraint (that is, the no-envy constraint) boils down to requiring that all contributions are also equal. It is easy to check that if one type of agents must pay less, all agents have a strict incentive to pretend that they are of that particular type, and the allocation is not incentive-compatible. Therefore, the set of allocations among which the policymaker can choose is the set $\widehat{Z}(E)$, which has the following simple structure: for all $E = (R_N, C) \in \mathcal{E}$,

$$\widehat{Z}(E) = \left\{ z_N \in A(R_N) \mid \forall i, j \in N, \ z_i = z_j \right\}.$$

Assume that we have a finite number of (types of) agents, and assume further that the agents' preferences satisfy the Spence–Mirrlees single-crossing property – that is, an indifference curve of an agent crosses an indifference curve of another agent once, at most. More precisely, we assume that for any pair of agents, either they have identical preferences or the intersection of two of their indifference curves (one for each agent) contains at most one point. A consequence of this property is that agents can be ordered according to their preferences over the public good. Indeed, if there exists a cost function such that an agent's optimal bundle involves a lower production level than another agent's optimal bundle, then, by this single-crossing property, it is also the case for any other cost function. Therefore, we do not lose any generality by assuming that $N = \{1, 2, \ldots, n\}$; that agent 1 has the lowest preference for the public good, agent 2 the second lowest, and so on; agent n has the largest preference for the public good.

For all $i \in N$, let $g_i^* \in \mathbb{R}_+$ be the demand in the public good of agent i under the proviso that the production cost is divided equally; that is,

$$\max\!\mid_{R_i} (C/n) = \left(\frac{C\left(g_i^*\right)}{n}, g_i^* \right).$$

The Spence–Mirrlees single-crossing property implies that $g_1^* \leq g_2^* \leq \cdots \leq g_n^*$.

Let z_N^g and z_N^C be the second-best optimal allocations obtained when the policymaker maximizes the g-equivalent leximin SOF and the C-equivalent leximin SOF, respectively. Let $g^{g\mathrm{lex}}$ and $g^{C\mathrm{lex}}$ be the corresponding levels of the public good; that is, for all $i \in N$,

$$z_i^g = \left(\frac{C(g^{C\mathrm{lex}})}{n}, g^{C\mathrm{lex}} \right), \quad \text{and}$$

$$z_i^C = \left(\frac{C(g^{C\mathrm{lex}})}{n}, g^{C\mathrm{lex}} \right).$$

We have the following result: under the g-equivalent leximin SOF, the optimal quantity of the public good is the one that is preferred by the agent with the lowest willingness to pay:

$$g^{g\mathrm{lex}} = g_1^*,$$

whereas, under the C-equivalent leximin SOF, the optimal quantity of the public good is larger than that of the agent with the lowest willingness to pay and lower than that of the agent with the highest willingness to pay (with strict

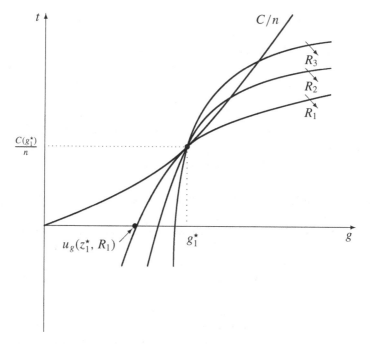

Figure 8.13. Second-best provision of a pure public good

inequalities as soon as the preferences of these agents differ), the C-equivalent well-being levels of the agents with the lowest and the highest willingness to pay are equalized, and all the other agents' well-being levels are strictly larger:

$$g_1^* \leq g^{Clex} \leq g_n^*$$
$$g_1^* < g^{Clex} < g_n^* \text{ if } R_1 \neq R_n$$
$$u_C(z_1^C, R_1) = u_C(z_n^C, R_n) \leq u_C(z_j^C, R_j) \forall j \neq 1, n.$$

This can be proved using Figure 8.13. Let us begin by noting that if all agents consume some bundle (t, g) such that $t \geq 0$, then the agent having the lowest output-equivalent utility level is agent 1. Indeed, as agent 1 has the lowest preference for the good, he or she also has the lowest willingness to pay for the consumption of the quantity g, so the quantity of the public good that leaves agent 1 indifferent to (t, g) is the lowest.

When all agents consume $(\frac{C(g_1^*)}{n}, g_1^*)$, one sees in Figure 8.13 that agent 1, the agent with the lowest output-equivalent utility level, is precisely the agent maximizing at that bundle. Now, given that agent 1's preferred bundle in $\widehat{Z}(E)$ is that bundle, changing the level of production of the public good will necessarily decrease agent 1's welfare (under the constraint that the cost must be divided equally). Consequently, the allocation in which all agents consume that bundle is the second-best optimal for the g-equivalent leximin function.[7]

It is also clear that the cost-equivalent utility level of agent 1 is equal to $\frac{1}{|N|}$ at that bundle, whereas the utility level of all other agents is lower (strictly lower if they have different preferences, as in Figure 8.13). As a consequence, whenever one agent has a strictly higher preference for the public good than agent 1, increasing the level of production above g_1^* necessarily increases the well-being of the agent with the lowest cost-equivalent utility level. More generally, if the quantity of the public good is g and $g_i^* < g_j^* < g$ or $g_i^* > g_j^* > g$, then $u_C(z_i^C, R_i) < u_C(z_j^C, R_j)$. Consequently, by continuity of C, there exists a level $g^{C\text{lex}}$ such that $u_C(z_1^C, R_1) = u_C(z_n^C, R_n)$. By the preceding property, all agents between 1 and n have a larger C-equivalent well-being level.

Assume that exclusion is possible: some agents may be prevented from consuming the whole available quantity of the public good, and, therefore, may be asked to pay a lower contribution. Is this good news, and if so, for whom? The answers to these questions depend on the SOF we use.

If the policymaker wishes to maximize the g-equivalent leximin SOF $\mathbf{R}^{g\text{lex}}$, then the possibility of exclusion is never bad news for the low-demand agent, in the sense that this agent may never be worse off at the second-best optimal allocation under exclusion than without exclusion. On the other hand, in some cases it may be bad news for the high-demand agents. Figure 8.14 illustrates these two facts.

Allocation (z_1^*, z_1^*) is the optimal second-best allocation for $\mathbf{R}^{g\text{lex}}$ in the absence of exclusion. As we showed earlier, the g-equivalent well-being level of agent 1 is lower than that of agent 2. Therefore, if some new welfare opportunities appear, agent 1 should benefit from it; this proves the first point. Now, observe that this allocation is also first-best Pareto optimal (we can deduce from the fact that both agents maximize on $\frac{C}{2}$ that the Samuelson conditions are satisfied). Any other first-best or second-best allocation that assigns a strictly higher well-being level to agent 1 must assign a strictly lower well-being level to agent 2. In other words, the possibility of exclusion benefits the agent who ends up being excluded.

One such allocation is illustrated in Figure 8.14. Allocation (z_1', z_2'), which assigns to agent 1 a strictly larger welfare level than at z^*, is incentive-compatible. Consequently, whether or not (z_1', z_2') is second-best optimal, agent 1 will strictly prefer the second-best bundle he or she is assigned when exclusion is possible to the one he or she is assigned in the absence of exclusion. Thus, in this case, exclusion strictly benefits the agent with a low willingness to pay, at the expense of the agent with a higher willingness to pay.

---

[7] This reasoning gives a justification to the allocation rule that associates each economy with its corresponding y_1^* and shares the cost equally. This rule has received a different axiomatic justification by Moulin (1994) on the basis of dominant strategy implementation (strategy-proofness) and voluntary participation (all agents should prefer to participate in the mechanism over staying out of it [and not consuming the public good]).

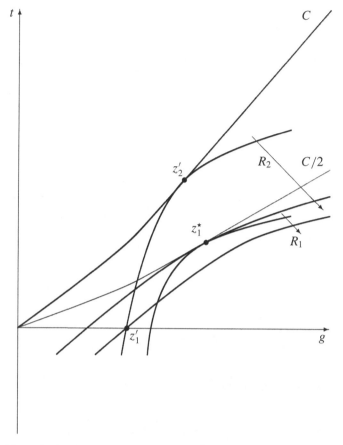

Figure 8.14. If the planner maximizes $\mathbf{R}^{glex}$, then an agent with a high willingness to pay can be worse off at the second-best optimum when exclusion is possible than when it is not possible, whereas an agent with a low willingness to pay is always better off if exclusion is possible.

If the policymaker wishes to maximize the C-equivalent leximin SOF $\mathbf{R}^{Clex}$, then, with two agents, the possibility of exclusion always leads to a Pareto improvement. This comes from the fact that if an allocation is optimal for $\mathbf{R}^{Clex}$, then the C-equivalent well-being levels are equalized between the two agents. Indeed, agents have continuous single-peaked preferences over bundles in $\widehat{Z}(E)$, and the peak corresponds to a well-being level of $\frac{1}{2}$. There necessarily exists an allocation in $\widehat{Z}(E)$ that equalizes the C-equivalent well-being levels, as illustrated in Figure 8.15. It is the second-best allocation recommended by $\mathbf{R}^{Clex}$ if exclusion is not possible.

If exclusion is possible, however, so some new welfare opportunities appear, then the minimal well-being level cannot decrease, which means that the new

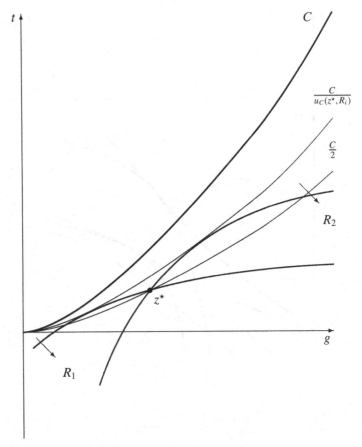

Figure 8.15. Optimal second-best allocation for $\mathbf{R}^{Clex}$

optimal allocation must Pareto dominate the one without exclusion: exclusion benefits both agents.[8]

In conclusion, there is a huge difference between the case of a pure public good and the case of an excludable public good. In the former, the set of feasible and incentive-compatible allocations is easy to determine, with the consequence that we have been able to identify the second-best allocations according to our two SOFs. In the latter case, we did not determine that set, and consequently, we have not been able to derive more than a few properties of the second-best allocations.

8.7 CONCLUSION

The first lesson that should be drawn from this chapter is that models involving production confirm the main ideas developed in exchange models: fairness

---

[8] If there are more than two agents, then the agents with the highest and the highest willingness to pay will gain, but it may be the case that other agents lose.

axioms need to be defined carefully to avoid incompatibilities with efficiency axioms; fairness axioms of the transfer type lead to infinite inequality aversion axioms when the SOF is also required to obey Pareto efficiency and cross-economy robustness axioms.

We have also observed that the specificity of the production model – that is, the fact that the goods involved do not have the same status (one is a private good contribution and the other is a public good that no one owns in strictly positive quantity before production takes place) – allows us to define new axioms and axiomatize new solutions. Indeed, free-lunch transfer is technically grounded on the fact that contributions can be negative, whereas consuming a negative quantity of the produced good does not make much sense. It is somehow comparable with what we observed in Section 6.2, in the allocation problem of uncertain quantities, in which the set of certainty bundles ended up playing a specific role. In that case, as in this chapter, one advantage is that the resulting SOF satisfies independence of the feasible set.

Another lesson is that it is hard to justify SOFs that would rationalize the Lindahl correspondence. This first-best solution has received so many justifications parallel to the ones received by the Walrasian correspondence that one might have conjectured that it would have received some justification in the SOF framework. Other well-known solutions to the public good first-best problem also did not receive proper justification in our approach (such as the ratio equilibrium from Kaneko and its generalization by Mas-Colell 1980). The public good case seems to be one in which only SOFs inspired by the general idea of egalitarian equivalence can be axiomatically justified. We will see later that if all goods are private, then, even in the presence of production, Walrasian allocations can also receive a strong justification.

CHAPTER 9

Private Goods

9.1 INTRODUCTION

In this chapter, we continue our analysis of production economies, under the assumption that the produced good is a private good. In the first sections of the chapter, we stick to the assumption that agents own some endowments of the input privately. The most natural interpretation is that the inputs are agents' labor contributions and the output is their income. The resulting model is not much different from the model of the previous chapter. Consequently, we could replicate the axiomatic study we carried out in Chapter 8, but in this chapter we put the emphasis on other issues.

As the model under study is a pure private good model, we can expect to see the (equal income) Walrasian allocations play a role again. We do see them back in the picture, but we focus here on a different justification. In Chapter 5, we showed how a Walrasian social ordering function could be derived axiomatically. The existence of a production technology does not prevent us at all from deriving a similar social ordering function in the current model. The adaptation of the axiomatic analysis of Chapter 5 will not be examined here, however, as it is rather straightforward.

We propose, instead, a derivation of the Walrasian allocations from an implementation point of view. That is, our focus is on a specific social ordering function, the P-equivalent leximin social ordering function (P denotes the production set), that is reminiscent in the current model of the Ω-equivalent leximin social ordering function of Part II and the C-equivalent leximin social ordering function of the previous chapter. We discuss its axiomatic merits in Section 9.2. In Section 9.3, we present a first application of that social ordering function to the assessment of reforms. We derive our main result in Section 9.4. We assume that the policymaker is restricted to using linear consumption functions – that is, individual consumptions need to be a linear function of their corresponding labor time. We prove that, if the policymaker wishes to maximize the P-equivalent leximin social ordering function under incentive-compatibility constraints, he or she must choose the Walrasian allocations.

In Section 9.5, we drop the assumption that some endowments are privately owned by the agents. Moreover, we do not impose any restriction on the (finite) number of goods, or on the nature (private or public) of the goods that are produced. We show that the generalization of the Ω-equivalent leximin social ordering function to that model is immediate. This proves that the approach developed in this book is not confined to simple models, and can be used to build indices of well-being in more general contexts. From a technical point of view, it is good news that our approach is not confined to simple models. From the point of view of possible applications, though, we think that our approach is less suited to general statements on the development level reached by a society than to evaluating reforms of specific social policies.

9.2 A SIMPLE MODEL WITH PRIVATE RIGHTS ON THE INPUT

Let us first define the model. There are two goods in the economy: labor, denoted ℓ, and a private consumption good, denoted c. There is a set N of agents, and each agent $i \in N$ has continuous and convex preferences R_i over (ℓ_i, c_i) bundles, which are decreasing in ℓ_i (working is painful) and increasing in c_i (the consumption good is always desirable). The consumption set is $X = \mathbb{R}_+^2$.

There is a production set $P \subset \mathbb{R}_+^2$ that describes what consumption level can be produced with any given labor contribution; that is, $(\ell, c) \in P$ means that a total labor contribution of ℓ is sufficient to produce the level c of consumption. Let ∂P denote the upper boundary of P. The set P is assumed to be closed, strictly convex, and such that $(0, 0) \in \partial P$. An economy is now a list $E = (R_N, P)$; we denote by $\mathcal{E}$ the set of all economies satisfying the above restrictions.

The assumption of a strictly convex production set (decreasing marginal returns) is essential to the model. By using the technology – that is, with a strictly positive labor time – an agent affects the labor productivity of others. If there were no such externality, then fairness would be reached by simply letting agents freely choose their labor time (laissez-faire). Given that marginal returns are decreasing, and given that the technology is commonly owned, fairness requires that the returns to one's labor time be computed by taking the agent's influence on others' productivity into account. The typical interpretation of the model is that the agents are members of a cooperative firm, or that P is an open-access technology (the typical tragedy of the commons).

An allocation $z_N = (\ell_N, c_N) \in X^N$ is feasible for $E = (R_N, P)$ if the sum of labor contributions is sufficient, given the technology, to produce the sum of the consumptions:

$$\left(\sum_{i \in N} \ell_i, \sum_{i \in N} c_i \right) \in P.$$

Let $Z(E)$ denote the set of feasible allocations for E.

In this section, we present a SOF and we discuss its axiomatic merits. In the next two sections, we propose two applications of that SOF. It is similar, in this private-good context, to the C-equivalent leximin SOF defined in the previous chapter. By analogy, we call the new SOF the *P-equivalent leximin SOF*. It consists of applying the leximin to vectors of utility representations that are constructed in this way: the utility level that is associated to one bundle is equal to the parameter by which the production set needs to be rescaled so the agent is indifferent between that bundle and being alone and free to use the rescaled production set.

In spite of this analogy, there is a slight difference between the private-good model of this chapter and the public-good model of the previous one. When goods are private, the unanimity well-being level cannot be defined with respect to a simple reduction of the cost function: both the cost and the production need to be rescaled. Formally, for a production set P and a positive real number a, the production set aP is defined by:

$$(\ell, c) \in aP \Leftrightarrow \left(\frac{\ell}{a}, \frac{c}{a} \right) \in P.$$

For each $i \in N$, $R_i \in \mathcal{R}$, let $A_i(R_i)$ denote the set of bundles for which the utility representation we now construct is well-defined. For each $E = (R_N, P) \in \mathcal{E}$,

$$u_P(z_i, R_i) = a \Leftrightarrow z_i \, I_i \, \max|_{R_i} aP.$$

Sets $A_i(R_i)$ are precisely those for which such a number a exists. The set $A(E)$ of admissible allocations is the set of allocations composed of admissible bundles. If P satisfies the conditions:

(a) for each $(\ell, c) \in P$, there exists a sufficiently large positive a such that $(a\ell, ac) \notin P$, and

(b) for each $(\ell, c) \notin P$, there exists a sufficiently small positive a such that $(a\ell, ac) \in P$,

then $A_i(R_i) = \{(\ell_i, c_i) \in X | (\ell_i, c_i) R_i (0, 0)\}$. We call the numerical representation $u_P(\cdot, R_i)$ agent i's *P-equivalent utility function*. We require from the SOFs we study here only that they rank allocations in $A(E)$.

The P-equivalent leximin SOF $\mathbf{R}^{Plex}$ works by applying the leximin criterion to the P-equivalent utility levels of the agents at the allocations we compare.

Social ordering function 9.1 P-Equivalent Leximin ($\mathbf{R}^{Plex}$)
For $E = (R_N, P) \in \mathcal{E}$, $z_N, z'_N \in A(R_N)$,

$$z_N \, \mathbf{R}^{Plex}(E) \, z'_N \Leftrightarrow (u_P(z_i, R_i))_{i \in N} \geq_{lex} \left(u_P\left(z'_i, R_i \right) \right)_{i \in N}.$$

As is clear from the definition of this SOF, it fails to satisfy independence of the feasible set (in the same way as the Ω-leximin and the C-leximin SOFs of Chapters 5 and 8 also do). Otherwise, it satisfies strong Pareto, transfer among equals, nested transfer, unchanged-contour independence, and separation. It also satisfies the axioms we could define in the current model by analogy to equal-split transfer and replication. A characterization result in the same vein as Theorem 8.1 can be proved, but we do not enter into the details here.

We want to insist here on a dilemma between two fairness axioms and on a justification of the P-equivalent leximin SOF based on that dilemma. We first need to introduce a new axiom, which is reminiscent of the stand-alone transfer axiom from the previous chapter. In the current production model with decreasing marginal returns, being alone to use the technology is the best situation one agent could think of. We define one agent's stand-alone well-being level as the level associated with the bundle[1] $\max|_{R_i} P$ that the agent would consume if he or she were indeed alone in the economy. We use that well-being level as a threshold: if one agent is strictly above his or her stand-alone level, whereas another agent is strictly below it, we view the former agent as strictly richer than the latter, and a transfer between the two cannot decrease social welfare. Our axiom reads as follows: a transfer of consumption good between two agents is a weak social improvement if the beneficiary has bundles yielding well-being levels below his or her stand-alone level, and the donor has bundles yielding well-being levels above his or her stand-alone level, before and after the transfer.

Axiom 9.1 Stand-Alone Transfer

For all $E = (R_N, P) \in \mathcal{D}$, $z_N = (\ell_N, c_N)$, $z'_N = (\ell'_N, c'_N) \in A(R_N)$, $\Delta \in \mathbb{R}_+$, and $j, k \in N$, if

$$\max|_{R_k} P \; P_k \, z'_k = (\ell_k, c_k + \Delta) \; P_k \, z_k \; and \, z_j \; P_j \, z'_j = \left(\ell_j, c_j - \Delta\right) \; P_j \, \max|_{R_j} P$$

and for all $i \neq j, k : z'_i = z_i$, then $z'_N \; \mathbf{R}(E) \, z_N$.

If z_N is feasible, then so is z'_N.

Here begins the axiomatic discussion of this section: the P-equivalent leximin SOF $\mathbf{R}^{Plex}$ satisfies stand-alone transfer, whereas no SOF rationalizing the egalitarian Walrasian allocations does. Let us prove this.

Allocation z_N^{EW} is an egalitarian Walrasian allocation if there exist π^{EW} and ω^{EW} such that each agent maximizes his or her preferences over the budget set defined by profit π^{EW} and wage ω^{EW}, and the resulting production plan is feasible and maximizes the total profit of the firm:

$$\forall i \in N, \quad z_i^{EW} \in \max|_{R_i} \{(\ell, c) \in X \mid c \leq \pi^{EW} + \omega^{EW}\ell\},$$

$$\left(\sum_{i \in N} \ell_i, \sum_{i \in N} c_i \right) \in P,$$

$$\forall (\ell', c') \in P, \quad c' \leq n\pi^{EW} + \omega^{EW}\ell'.$$

---

[1] Uniqueness follows from strict convexity of P.

The last property is equivalent to

$$\forall (\ell', c') \in \frac{1}{n} P, \quad c' \leq \pi^{EW} + \omega^{EW} \ell'.$$

This property will be used in the graphical representation that follows.

An egalitarian Walrasian allocation can be such that one agent enjoys a strictly higher well-being level than his or her stand-alone level. This occurs when this agent has an extreme aversion to work and consumes his or her share of the profit of the production sector. When such an agent is better off than at his or her stand-alone level, another agent is necessarily strictly worse off.

This is illustrated in Figure 9.2 Agent 1 is strictly better off at z_1^{EW} than if he or she were alone in the economy, and both agents 2 and 3 are strictly worse off. A transfer between agent 1 and either agent 2 or 3 would be a weak social improvement, according to stand-alone transfer, whereas for a SOF rationalizing the egalitarian Walrasian allocation rule, the egalitarian Walrasian allocations should be socially preferred to any other feasible allocation. Therefore, any SOF rationalizing the egalitarian Walrasian allocation rule must violate stand-alone transfer. This is actually true even if we weaken our requirement that Walrasian allocations be selected to the requirement that envy-free allocations be selected. This amounts to the envy-free selection axiom that was introduced in Section 5.3. Its definition is immediately adapted to the current setting and we omit it. This incompatibility shows the deep conflict between Walrasian ethics and stand-alone transfer. On the other hand, the P-equivalent leximin SOF satisfies envy-free selection in economies with no more than two agents. We view these results as a strong case in favor of the P-equivalent leximin SOF (and against Walrasian ethics) in this model.

The following theorem summarizes the above discussion. Let $\mathcal{E}^2$ denote the domain of two-agent economies.

Theorem 9.1 *No SOF satisfies* strong Pareto, envy-free selection, *and* stand-alone transfer *over the full domain* $\mathcal{E}$. *The P-equivalent leximin SOF satisfies* strong Pareto *and* stand-alone transfer *over* $\mathcal{E}$, *and* envy-free selection *over* $\mathcal{E}^2$.

Proof. We sketch the proof of only the first statement, which bears on known properties of the egalitarian Walrasian allocation rule. By strong Pareto and envy-free selection, the best allocations are envy-free and efficient allocations. For an economy with a large but finite number of agents having sufficiently diverse preferences, the envy-free and efficient allocations are close to the egalitarian Walrasian allocations. If all Egalitarian Walrasian allocations have an agent above his or her stand-alone level, and if the envy-free and efficient allocations are sufficiently close to the egalitarian Walrasian allocations, one obtains the desired contradiction. Figure 9.2 represents an Egalitarian Walrasian allocation with one agent, agent 1, above his or her stand-alone well-being level. ∎

In the next two sections, we study the P-equivalent leximin SOF as the major one in this model, and we apply it in two different contexts. The surprising result we reach in Section 9.4 is that, in spite of the difficulty of axiomatically justifying the egalitarian Walrasian allocations in this model, these allocations will appear as the outcome of the maximization process of the P-equivalent leximin SOF in a specific context.

9.3 ASSESSING REFORMS

We now propose two applications of the P-equivalent leximin SOF. In this section, we show how to use it to assess reforms under information asymmetry. By reform, we mean a slight change from a status quo. Assume that the set of agents is fixed, $N = \{1, \dots, n\}$, and assume that the economy $E = (R_N, P) \in \mathcal{E}$ is such that the policymaker knows the distribution of preferences but does not know which agent has which preferences; that is, the policymaker knows R_N up to a permutation.

As in the previous chapters, the policymaker must restrict his or her attention to incentive-compatible allocations $z_N \in A(R_N)$ – that is, to allocations satisfying the no-envy, or self-selection, condition: for all $i, j \in N$, $z_i R_i z_j$. If this condition is satisfied, then it cannot be the case that one agent has a lower labor contribution and a higher consumption level than another agent. Consequently, there exists a nondecreasing consumption function $\phi : \mathbb{R}_+ \to \mathbb{R}_+$ such that for all $i \in N : c_i = \phi(\ell_i)$ and for all (ℓ'_i, c'_i) such that $c'_i = \phi(\ell'_i)$, $(\ell_i, c_i) R_i (\ell'_i, c'_i)$.

We raise the following question: assume a society is applying some ϕ function. If the policymaker is interested in reforming this consumption function, how should he or she modify it – that is, which agent should be paid more and which agent should be paid less? We show how to answer this question graphically.

The key step consists in identifying which agent has the lowest P-equivalent well-being level. The only information that is needed to evaluate the well-being level of an agent is the agent's indifference curve through the bundle he or she chooses. Given that the chosen bundles are observable, and given that, when the incentive compatibility constraints are satisfied, the agents reveal their preferences, the policymaker, who knows the list of preferences in the economy, is able to compute the well-being levels of the agents with different types of preferences.

Let us illustrate this reasoning in Figure 9.1. To make it simple, it represents a two-agent economy. Given consumption function ϕ, agent 1 chooses z_1 and agent 2 z_2. Then, the policymaker is able to identify that the agent having chosen z_1 has a higher utility level than the other agent according to the P-equivalent measure. A reform of ϕ should then increase the consumption level around z_2 and decrease the one around z_1. Indeed, given that the SOF in which we are interested gives absolute priority to the worst-off, identifying the worst-off agent according to the constructed well-being measure is all that is needed to identify the direction of a strict social improvement. As a result, assessing

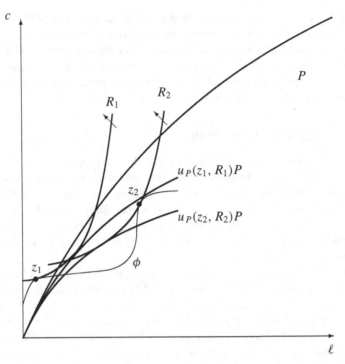

Figure 9.1. How to assess a reform by using the P-equivalent leximin SOF: given a consumption function ϕ, one computes utility indices $u_P(z_1, R_1)$ and $u_P(z_2, R_2)$.

reforms is much easier than if the aggregator is, for example, utilitarian, which would force us to measure the impact of the reform on the well-being measure of all agents.

9.4 A THIRD-BEST ANALYSIS

Our second application restricts the set of feasible consumption functions even further. Assume, indeed, that only linear consumption functions can be used; that is, there should exist some $\pi \in \mathbb{R}$ and $\omega \in \mathbb{R}_+$ such that for all $i \in N$: $\phi(\ell_i) = \pi + \omega \ell_i$.

In such a framework, we try to identify the values of π and ω that maximize the P-equivalent leximin SOF. Some possible consumption functions are the egalitarian Walrasian ones – that is, the ones in which ω is a competitive wage of that economy, whereas π is the per capita competitive profit of the firm operating the technology at that wage. Formally, ϕ^{EW} is an egalitarian Walrasian consumption function if $\pi = \pi^{EW}$ and $\omega = \omega^{EW}$.

We know that the allocation emerging from this consumption function is Pareto efficient in the set of allocations emerging from linear consumption functions (as it is Pareto efficient within the set of all allocations), but there are other linear consumption functions that yield allocations that are Pareto undominated. Moreover, in view of Theorem 9.1, there is no clear connection between the P-equivalent leximin SOF and the egalitarian Walrasian allocations.

We can show, however, that the optimal linear consumption functions are the Walrasian ones in economies satisfying the following richness property about preferences. At any feasible allocation emerging from linear consumption function, there should exist at least one agent consuming a bundle that is average in the sense that it would be feasible that all agents consume that precise bundle. Formally, the domain $\mathcal{D}^A \subset \mathcal{E}$ gathers all economies such that for all $z_N \in Z(E)$, if there exist $\pi \in \mathbb{R}$ and $\omega \in \mathbb{R}_+$ such that for all $i \in N$:

$$z_i \in \max|_{R_i} \{(\ell, c) \in X | c \leq \pi + \omega \ell\},$$

then there exists one agent $j \in N$ such that $nz_j \in P$.

This is a very demanding condition. In particular, it requires that, at all egalitarian Walrasian allocations, there be one agent whose bundle is exactly the average of all other bundles. In large economies, it is consistent with the French proverb that "all tastes are in nature," so any kind of preferences is represented by at least one agent. Of course, the condition can also hold in finite economies (think, for instance, of economies in which preferences are such that labor supplies do not depend on wages and one agent's labor supply is equal to the average of all labor supplies).

We are then able to derive the following result.

Theorem 9.2 *Let $E = (R_N, P) \in \mathcal{D}^A$. If a policymaker maximizes the P-equivalent leximin function $\mathbf{R}^{Plex}$ and only linear consumption functions can be used, then she can choose the egalitarian Walrasian consumption functions.*

Again, the proof can be graphical. In Figure 9.2, a Walrasian allocation in a three-agent economy is drawn, z_N^{EW}. The corresponding wage is ω^{EW} and the equal profit is π^{EW}. One easily checks that each agent maximizes his or her welfare given π^{EW} and ω^{EW}. Let us observe that agent 2 is an average agent in the sense defined previously: This agent's labor contribution is precisely one-third of the total labor supply.[2] Let us assume that the economy belongs to the $\mathcal{D}^A$ domain. The key argument is that the two properties of this allocation (it being egalitarian Walrasian and agent 2 being an average agent) imply that bundle z_2^{EW} is precisely agent 2's best bundle over the production set that one obtains by dividing P by 3, as illustrated in the figure. That means that agent 2's

---

[2] Labor supplies do not appear on the graph, for the sake of clarity, but this property of agent 2's labor supply is illustrated by the fact that $z_2^{EW} = \frac{z_1^{EW} + z_3^{EW}}{2}$.

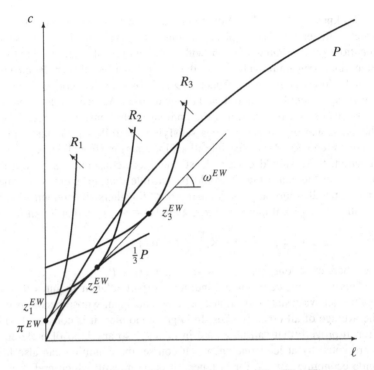

Figure 9.2. The egalitarian Walrasian allocation $(z_1^{EW}, z_2^{EW}, z_3^{EW})$ is optimal for the P-equivalent leximin SOF among linear consumption functions.

P-equivalent well-being level is precisely $\frac{1}{3}$, and that agent 2 is the worst-off agent in terms of P-equivalent well-being levels at z_N^{EW}.

By the definition of $\mathcal{D}^A$, for any other allocation that emerges from a linear consumption function, there is one agent choosing a bundle that lies in the set $\frac{1}{3}P$, so the reduction of P to which this agent's indifference curve is tangent is smaller than $\frac{1}{3}P$. Consequently, the P-equivalent well-being level of that agent is below $\frac{1}{3}$, proving that z_N^{EW} is optimal.[3]

The reason that the egalitarian Walrasian allocations turn out to be justified by a maximizing exercise of the P-equivalent SOF under the constraints we impose can be explained as follows. First, the egalitarian Walrasian allocations have attractive incentive properties, as they are envy-free. Second, they have a simple structure (they are linear) and we have, by assumption, restricted our attention to those kinds of allocations. Third, the egalitarian Walrasian

---

[3] If, moreover, preferences are continuously differentiable, then the well-being level of that agent is strictly below $\frac{1}{3}$ at any non-egalitarian Walrasian allocation. In that case, the planner must choose an egalitarian Walrasian allocation.

allocations turn out to be reasonably fair, even if fairness is evaluated by using the P-leximin SOF, which is the surprising feature of the preceding result.

9.5 A GENERAL MODEL OF PRODUCTION AND ALLOCATION

This section contains the most general model that is studied in this book. There is a finite but arbitrarily large number of private goods that can be used as inputs or outputs, and an arbitrarily large number of public goods that can be produced by using the private goods.

The axiomatic analysis that we propose is grounded on generalizations of axioms introduced previously; the main result of the section is an axiomatic characterization of a SOF that generalizes the Ω-equivalent, the C-equivalent, and the P-equivalent leximin SOFs. The lesson from this section is mainly technical, which is why we do not devote too much space to it. It shows that the approach presented in this book can be used to construct indices of social welfare in a general context.

We assume that there is a set L of private goods and a set M of public goods. An agent's consumption set is $X = \mathbb{R}_+^{L \cup M}$ and a typical consumption bundle is denoted $z_i = (c_i, g_i)$. An economy is now defined as a quadruple $E = (R_N, \Omega, V, Q)$, where $N \subset \mathbb{N}$ stands for the finite set of agents, $R_N \in \mathcal{R}^N$ stands for the preferences of these agents, $\Omega \in \mathbb{R}_+^L$ is the social endowment in private goods, $V \subset \mathbb{R}^L$ is the private good production set, and $Q \subset \mathbb{R}^L \times \mathbb{R}_+^M$ is the public good production set. For vectors belonging to V or Q, negative components stand for inputs.

Contrary to what we assumed in Chapter 8 and in the previous sections of this chapter, agents are not assumed to own any endowment privately. The assumption we imposed there, that private endowments were fair, is no longer imposed here. Consequently, the numerical representation of preferences is slightly different from the C-equivalent and the P-equivalent representations.

We assume that (1) for all $N \subset \mathbb{N}$, all $i \in N$, all $R_i \in \mathcal{R}$, R_i is continuous, convex, and monotonic in each (private and public) good, (2) V is closed, strictly convex, comprehensive (if $v \in V$, then $v' \in V$ for all $v' \leq v$), and such that $0 \in \partial V$, where $0 \in \mathbb{R}^L$ is the null vector and ∂V denotes the upper boundary of V, and (3) Q is closed, strictly convex, comprehensive, and such that $0 \in \partial Q$. Let $\mathcal{E}$ denote the set of economies satisfying those assumptions.

Let $E = (R_N, \Omega, V, Q) \in \mathcal{E}$. An allocation is a list $z_N \in X^N$. An allocation $z_N = \big((c_i, g_i)_{i \in N} \big) \in X^N$ is feasible for E if there exists $v \in V$ and $q \in Q$ such that

$$\sum_{i \in N} c_i \leq \Omega + v + q_L,$$

$$\max_{i \in N} g_{ik} \leq q_k, \forall k \in M.$$

Let $Z(E)$ denote the set of feasible allocations for E.

Let $r \in \mathbb{R}_+$. If production possibilities are multiplied by r, we obtain the production sets rV and rQ, defined by:

$$rV = \left\{ v \in \mathbb{R}^L \mid \frac{1}{r}v \in V \right\},$$

$$rQ = \left\{ q = (q_L, q_M) \in \mathbb{R}^L \times \mathbb{R}_+^M \mid \left(\frac{1}{r}q_L, q_M \right) \in Q \right\}.$$

The difference between the two multiplications comes from the different nature of the goods. For $r > 1$, rV is bigger than V, thanks to the convexity of V, whereas rQ is smaller than Q. This definition of rQ is motivated by the use of the replication axiom in the analysis that follows. Indeed, an allocation is feasible with n agents and resources Ω, V, Q if and only if it is feasible with kn agents and resources $k\Omega$, kV, kQ. In particular, the kn agents will consume the same quantity of public goods q_M as the initial n agents with k times as much inputs q_L. This is the natural adaptation to this context of the replication operations defined in the previous chapters. Figure 9.3 illustrates the possibilities obtained with (Ω, V, Q) and with $(2\Omega, 2V, 2Q)$ in the case of a three-good economy such that $L = \{1, 2\}$, $M = \{3\}$, Ω is a quantity of good 1 (which can, therefore, serve as an input in either the production of good 2 or good 3, and only good 1 can serve as an input in the production of good 3 (this is why the figure represents Q as a subset of $\mathbb{R}^2$ instead of $\mathbb{R}^3$.

Finally, we denote by $\max|_{R_i} (\Omega, V, Q)$ the best bundle, according to R_i, among all bundles that can be produced and consumed given resources Ω, V, Q.

We are now equipped to construct the numerical representation of the preferences that will be used in the SOF we will axiomatize. Let $E = (R_N, \Omega, V, Q) \in \mathcal{E}$. Each R_i admits a unique numerical representation $u_{\Omega V Q} (\cdot, R_i)$ defined over a set of "admissible bundles" $A_{VQ}(R_i)$, which is formally defined below, such that $u_{\Omega V Q}(0^{L \cup M}, R_i) = 0$ and for all $r \in \mathbb{R}_{++}$,

$$u_{\Omega V Q} (z_i, R_i) = r \Leftrightarrow z_i \ I_i \ \max|_{R_i} (r\Omega, rV, rQ).$$

We call $u_{\Omega V Q} (z_i, R_i)$ agent i's *resource-equivalent well-being level* at bundle z_i. The set $A_{VQ}(R_i)$ is the set of admissible bundles for agent i – that is, the subset of X where $u_{\Omega V Q}$ is well-defined. That $A_{VQ}(R_i)$ is a strict subset of X follows from the fact that even if the set of bundles obtainable with resources $r\Omega, rV, rQ$ grows as r grows unboundedly, the well-being level of one agent freely maximizing over these resources may be bounded. This is the case, for instance, if agent i is interested only in the public goods, because with $r\Omega, rV, rQ$ the production of public goods is bounded for all r at the level that is producible with Ω, V, Q. Let $A_{VQ}(R_N)$ denote the set of admissible allocations (i.e., allocations such that $z_i \in A_{VQ}(R_i)$ for all $i \in N$).

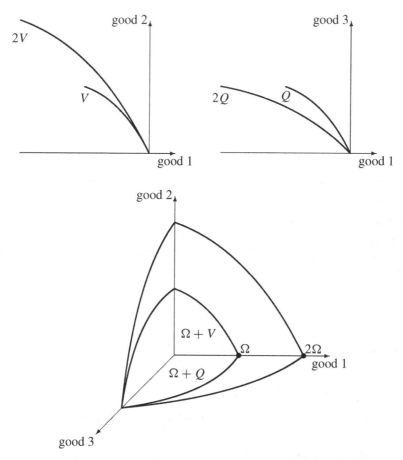

Figure 9.3. Illustration of the production and consumption possibilities with (Ω, V, Q) and $(2\Omega, 2V, 2Q)$

What remains to be done is the rewriting of the axioms and the statement of the result.

Axiom 9.2 Stand-Alone Transfer
For all $E = (R_N, \Omega, V, Q) \in \mathcal{E}$, $z_N = (c_N, g_N), z'_N = (c'_N, g'_N) \in X^N$, $\Delta \in \mathbb{R}^L_+$, and $j, k \in N$, if

$$\max|_{R_k} (\Omega, V, Q) \; P_k \, z'_k = (c_k + \Delta, g_k) \; P_k \, z_k \quad and$$

$$z_j \, P_j \, z'_j = (c_j - \Delta, g_j) \; P_j \; \max|_{R_j} (\Omega, V, Q),$$

and for all $i \neq j, k$, $z'_i = z_i$, then $z'_N \; \mathbf{R}(E) z_N$.

Axiom 9.3 Equal-Split Transfer

For all $E = (R_N, \Omega, V, Q) \in \mathcal{E}$, $z_N = (c_N, g_N), z'_N = (c'_N, g'_N) \in X^N$, $\Delta \in \mathbb{R}^L_+$, and $j, k \in N$, if

$$\max|_{R_k} \left(\frac{1}{|N|}\Omega, \frac{1}{|N|}V, \frac{1}{|N|}Q \right) \, P_k \, z'_k = (c_k + \Delta, g_k) \, P_k \, z_k \quad and$$

$$z_j \, P_j \, z'_j = (c_j - \Delta, g_j) \, P_j \, \max|_{R_j} \left(\frac{1}{|N|}\Omega, \frac{1}{|N|}V, \frac{1}{|N|}Q \right),$$

and for all $i \neq j, k$, $z'_i = z_i$, then $z'_N \, \mathbf{R}(E) \, z_N$.

Separation is defined exactly as in the previous models. Replicas of profiles of preferences or allocations are also defined as defined earlier.

Axiom 9.4 Replication

For all $E = (R_N, \Omega, V, Q) \in \mathcal{E}$, $z_N, z'_N \in X^N$, and $r \in \mathbb{Z}_{++}$, if $E' = (R_{N'}, \Omega, V, Q) \in \mathcal{E}$ is such that $R_{N'}$ is an r-replica of R_N, $z_{N'}, z'_{N'}$ are the corresponding r-replicas of z_N and z'_N respectively, $\Omega' = r\Omega$, $V' = rV$ and $Q' = rQ$, then

$$z_N \, \mathbf{R}(E) \, z'_N \Leftrightarrow z_{N'} \, \mathbf{R}(E') \, z'_{N'}.$$

Theorem 9.3 *On the domain $\mathcal{E}$, if a SOF $\mathbf{R}$ satisfies strong Pareto, separation, replication, and either stand-alone transfer or equal-split transfer, then for all $E = (R_N, \Omega, V, Q) \in \mathcal{E}$ and all $z_N, z'_N \in A_{VQ}(R_N)$,*

$$\min_{i \in N} u_{\Omega VQ}(z_i, R_i) > \min_{i \in N} u_{\Omega VQ}(z'_i, R_i) \Rightarrow z_N \, \mathbf{P}(E) \, z'_N.$$

The proof is an immediate adaptation of the proof of Theorem 8.1.

9.6 CONCLUSION

Let us sum up the contents of this chapter. First, on the axiomatic side, we briefly examined how to extend the previous results to models of production of private goods. In Section 9.5, we showed how to axiomatize a SOF in a general model of production and allocation of private and public goods. Second, on the application side, we have illustrated two different uses of SOFs. First, we saw how to use $\mathbf{R}^{Plex}$ to assess reforms. Starting with an arbitrary incentive-compatible allocation, it is sufficient to identify the bundle chosen by the agent having the lowest P-equivalent well-being level and to increase the assigned consumption level in the neighborhood of that bundle. We also observed how the remarkable simplicity of the egalitarian Walrasian allocations makes it possible to single them out as the linear allocations that maximize the $\mathbf{R}^{Plex}$ SOF.

The objective of the SOF approach presented in this book is to build indices of social welfare based on fairness considerations and to apply these indices in the design of social institutions. Fairness has been interpreted here as equality of resources; the first two chapters of this part of the book have shown that equality of resources can receive precise axiomatic definitions independent of whether goods are public or private, and whether goods are available or must be produced.

One key assumption that was imposed in this chapter, as well as in all previous chapters of this book, is that the only relevant information about agents are their preferences. In the next chapters, we introduce the possibility that agents differ in terms of some internal resources, and those resources are assumed to be nontransferable. Resource equality, therefore, requires distributing external resources in an unequal way to compensate the agents with lower internal resources. That will be the final topic of this book.

CHAPTER 10

Unequal Skills

10.1 INTRODUCTION

In this chapter, we present and study a new model, which is a variant of the private good production model of the previous chapter. Compared with that model, we assume that the production set is linear and that the agents may have different production skills. Consequently, the agents are characterized by two parameters: their preferences and their skills. The natural interpretation of the model, which was introduced in the literature a long time ago, from different viewpoints, by Mirrlees (1971) and Pazner and Schmeidler (1974), is that input is the labor time of the agents and their skill is the wage rate at which they are able to find a job. This is the canonical setting in which labor income taxation issues can be addressed. In the next chapter, we show how some of the social ordering functions we derive here can be used to design optimal income tax schemes.

Productive skills are assumed to be fixed and independent of the labor time. This amounts to assuming that agents use a linear technology. In view of such linearity, the laissez-faire allocations – that is, the allocations at which agents choose their labor time and consume the share of the production that corresponds to their share in the contribution – are natural candidates to qualify as equitable allocations. Indeed, each agent freely chooses his or her preferred bundle and there is no externality among agents.

One can argue, however, that these allocations are inequitable, in particular if differences in skills come (at least partly) from inherited features that cannot be attributed to the agents' responsibility, or if agents could be more productive but are constrained by the unavailability of jobs with higher wage rates.[1] In this chapter, we endorse the viewpoint that, in the presence of unequal skills, laissez-faire is unfair, and we study the fairness objectives of (1) neutralizing the consequences of differential skills and (2) being neutral with respect to the preferences – that is, not correcting for different choices of labor time.

---

[1] It may be, however, that agents' skills are also partly the outcome of previous personal choices about investment in human capital. Symmetrically, one may argue that agents are only partly responsible for their preferences over consumption and leisure.

We believe that these two objectives capture some basic ingredients of the classical debate about labor income taxation. Some people argue that differences in productive skills call for redistribution, whereas others claim that hardworking agents should benefit from their hard work. The social ordering functions we propose in this chapter show possible ways out of the dilemma, and the study of income tax in the next chapter shows how tax schemes can be related to particular ways of finding a compromise between the two major fairness objectives defined in the previous paragraph.

Let us consider these two objectives more closely. To capture the idea that differential skills should not entail unequal individual outcomes, let us consider allocating resources between two agents who have the same preferences. As they differ only with respect to their skills, society should help them reach the same outcome, in terms of well-being. We call it the *objective of compensation*.

To capture the idea that the various preferences displayed in the population should not be treated differently – that is, that the agents should not receive any differential amount of resources on the pure basis that they have "good" or "bad" preferences – let us consider allocating resources between two agents who have the same skill. As they differ only with respect to their preferences, it is natural to consider that society should submit them to the same treatment in terms of redistribution. This implies that, ideally, agents with identical skills should be submitted to the same lump-sum transfer that does not depend on their preferences and their choice of labor. In such a situation, two agents with identical skills have the same linear budget set with a slope equal to their skill. If that is achieved, when an agent changes preferences, one additional labor time unit results in an increased consumption by exactly the corresponding additional amount of production and society is not concerned with the agent's change in preferences. We call it the *objective of responsibility*.[2]

The main lesson of this chapter, from the point of view of fairness, is that there exists a deep conflict between these two objectives. One cannot simultaneously say that well-being should not depend on skills when agents have identical preferences, and that transfers should not depend on preferences when agents have identical skills. Given the richness of the model, we are able to propose different axioms of either compensation or responsibility, and check for their mutual compatibility problems. The results of our study are the characterizations of families of social ordering functions that offer reasonable compromises between the two objectives, that is, that satisfy combinations of appropriate weakenings of our basic requirements.

Many fair allocation problems involve agents having different needs, talents, handicaps, and so forth – that is, untransferable attributes that determine how successful they may be in transforming external resources into personal outcomes. A widespread ethical view on those matters is that external resources

---

[2] This is called "liberal reward" by Fleurbaey (2008), who states that two different conceptions of the implications of responsibility for reward schemes are distinguished, the "liberal" and the "utilitarian." We focus here on the former.

must be allocated or reallocated among these agents in a differentiated way to counterbalance such differences in personal attributes.[3] We conceived this chapter and the following one to illustrate how to address these questions with the help of social ordering functions.

10.2 THE MODEL

The model of this chapter (and the next one) is a variant of the model we studied in Sections 9.2 through 9.4. Individual bundles are composed of a quantity of labor time (ℓ) and a level of consumption (c). We further add the restriction that labor time is bounded above by a "full time" level ($\ell \leq 1$). The new and key ingredient of the current analysis is the agent's *production skill* $s_i \geq 0$, enabling the agent to produce the quantity $s_i \ell_i$ of consumption good with labor time ℓ_i. We further assume that $s_i \in S = [s_{min}, s_{max}]$, where s_{min} denotes the lowest possible production skill in society, or, in some applications, the lowest wage rate at which agents can find jobs, and s_{max} is symmetrically the greatest possible s_i.[4] Compared with the previous chapter, this amounts to assuming that the production function is fixed and linear, and it can be normalized as $f(\ell) = \ell$ for all $\ell \geq 0$, so we can forget about f in the definition of economies. An economy is now a list $E = (s_N, R_N)$, and the domain of all such economies is $\mathcal{E}$.

An allocation $z_N = (z_i)_{i \in N} \in X^N$ is feasible in economy $E = (s_N, R_N) \in \mathcal{E}$ if

$$\sum_{i \in N} c_i \leq \sum_{i \in N} s_i \ell_i.$$

Let $Z(E)$ denote the set of feasible allocations for E.

The following terminology will prove useful. For $s_i \in \mathbb{R}_+$ and $z_i = (\ell_i, c_i) \in X$, let $B(s_i, z_i) \subset X$ denote the *budget set* obtained with skill s_i and such that z_i is on the budget frontier:

$$B(s_i, z_i) = \{(\ell_i', c_i') \in X \mid c_i' - s_i \ell_i' \leq c_i - s_i \ell_i\}.$$

In the special case in which $s_i = 0$ and $c_i = 0$, we adopt the convention that

$$B(s_i, z_i) = \{(\ell_i', c_i') \in X \mid c_i' = 0, \ell_i' \geq \ell_i\}.$$

For $s_i \in \mathbb{R}_+$, $R_i \in \mathcal{R}$ and $z_i = (\ell_i, c_i) \in X$, let $B^*(s_i, R_i, z_i) \subset X$ denote the *implicit budget* at bundle z_i for any agent with characteristics (s_i, R_i) – that is, the budget set with slope s_i having the property that z_i is indifferent for R_i to the preferred bundle in that budget set:

$$B^*(s_i, R_i, z_i) = B(s_i, z_i') \text{ for any } z_i' \text{ such that } z_i' \, I_i \, z_i \text{ and } z_i' \in \max|_{R_i} B(s_i, z_i').$$

---

[3] This broader class of compensation problems is the subject of Fleurbaey (2008).
[4] Unvoluntary unemployment can be modeled by fixing $s_{min} = 0$.

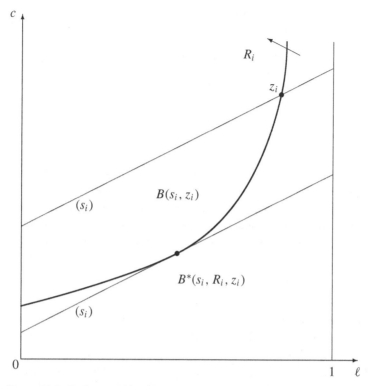

Figure 10.1. Budgets and implicit budgets

By strict monotonicity of preferences, this definition is unambiguous. Notice that bundle z_i need not belong to the implicit budget. Figure 10.1 illustrates these definitions. In the figures of this chapter, we adopt the convention that the slopes of budget lines are in parentheses below the line.

This new model does not require much rewriting of the axioms studied in the previous chapters. For instance, agents are now equals if they have the same preferences and skills. Also, independence of the feasible set amounts to requiring independence of the vector of skills.

10.3 COMPENSATION VERSUS RESPONSIBILITY: ETHICAL DILEMMAS

Let us now introduce the basic axioms capturing the two ethical objectives discussed in the previous section. Recall that, according to the objective of compensation, differential skills should not entail unequal individual outcomes. Consider two agents who have the same preferences but different skills. If one agent has a larger consumption, whereas they have the same labor time, one can argue that the preceding ethical goal is not fully satisfied and that, other things being equal, it would be a social improvement (or at least not a worsening) to transfer an amount of the consumption good from the richer to the poorer agent. The resulting axiom is logically stronger than transfer among equals.

Axiom 10.1 Equal-Preferences Transfer
For all $E = (s_N, R_N) \in \mathcal{D}$, *and* $z_N = (\ell_N, c_N)$, $z'_N = (\ell'_N, c'_N) \in X^N$, *if there exist* $j, k \in N$ *such that* $R_j = R_k$, *and* $\Delta \in \mathbb{R}_{++}$ *such that* $\ell_j = \ell_k = \ell'_j = \ell'_k$,

$$c_j - \Delta = c'_j > c'_k = c_k + \Delta,$$

and for all $i \neq j, k$, $z_i = z'_i$, *then* $z'_N \mathbf{R}(E) z_N$.

Let us now turn to the ethical objective of responsibility. It implies that the various preferences displayed in the population should not be treated differently; that is, the agents should not receive any differential amount of resources on the pure basis that they have "good" or "bad" preferences. Therefore, agents with identical skills should ideally receive equal lump-sum transfers and then be left free to choose their preferred bundles in the same budget set with a slope equal to their skill. Therefore, the next axiom requires that a transfer of resources between two agents having the same skill and having received unequal lump-sum transfers should be a weak social improvement.

Before stating the axiom, we need to make the following formal point. Let us assume that agent j receives a lump-sum transfer and therefore maximizes his or her preferences over a budget with a slope equal to his or her skill, s_j. If $z_j = (\ell_j, c_j)$ is agent j's chosen bundle, then $c_j - s_j \ell_j$, which may be negative, is equal to the lump-sum transfer this agent received and is a simple measure of the value of his or her budget. This measure allows us to introduce the notion of a "budget transfer" (corresponding to a transfer in lump-sum grants). If we move from an allocation where $z_j = (\ell_j, c_j)$ and $z_k = (\ell_k, c_k)$ to another allocation where $z'_j = (\ell'_j, c'_j)$ and $z'_k = (\ell'_k, c'_k)$, and if both agents maximize their welfare over budgets of slopes $s_j = s_k$, then we say that there has been a transfer of budget from j to k if $(c_j - s_j \ell_j) - (c'_j - s'_j \ell'_j) = (c'_k - s'_k \ell'_k) - (c_k - s_k \ell_k)$. Our main responsibility requirement can be phrased as follows: a budget transfer from an agent having a larger budget to another agent having the same skill should be viewed as a (weak) social improvement.

Axiom 10.2 Equal-Skill Transfer
For all $E = (s_N, R_N) \in \mathcal{D}$, $z_N = (\ell_N, c_N)$, $z'_N = (\ell'_N, c'_N) \in X^N$, $\Delta \in \mathbb{R}_{++}$, *if there exist* $j, k \in N$ *such that* $s_j = s_k$, $(c_j - s_j \ell_j) - \Delta = (c'_j - s'_j \ell'_j) > (c'_k - s'_k \ell'_k) = (c_k - s_k \ell_k) + \Delta$,

$$z_j \in \max|_{R_j} B(s_j, z_j), \quad z'_j \in \max|_{R_j} B(s_j, z'_j),$$

$$z_k \in \max|_{R_k} B(s_k, z_k), \quad z'_k \in \max|_{R_k} B(s_k, z'_k),$$

and for all $i \in N, i \neq j, k$, $z_i = z'_i$, *then* $z'_N \mathbf{R}(E) z_N$.

The first basic result of this chapter states that equal-preferences transfer and equal-skill transfer are incompatible with each other: it is impossible to guarantee at the same time that agents having identical preferences will be

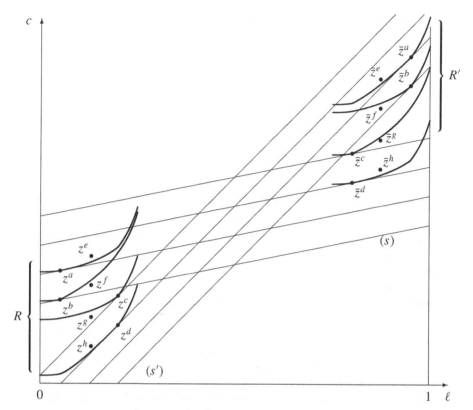

Figure 10.2. No SOF satisfies weak Pareto, equal-preferences transfer, and equal-skill transfer.

treated independently of their skills, whereas agents with identical skills will be treated, in terms of budgets, independently of their preferences.[5]

Theorem 10.1 *On the domain $\mathcal{E}$, no SOF satisfies* weak Pareto, equal-preferences transfer, *and* equal-skill transfer.

Proof. The proof is illustrated in Figure 10.2. Several budgets are depicted, associated to either skill s or s', with $s < s'$, and several indifference curves are drawn, representing preferences R and R'.

Let us consider the four-agent economy $E = ((s, s, s', s'), (R, R', R, R'))$. Applying equal-skill transfer twice, first to the pair of agents (s, R) and (s, R'), and then to the pair (s', R) and (s', R'), we reach the conclusion that

$$(z^a, \bar{z}^d, z^d, \bar{z}^a) \, \mathbf{R}(E) \, (z^b, \bar{z}^c, z^c, \bar{z}^b).$$

---

[5] This result, and much of this chapter, draws from Fleurbaey and Maniquet (2005). There has been a long literature on the compensation responsibility dilemma, surveyed in Fleurbaey and Maniquet (2010) and Fleurbaey (2008).

Applying equal-preferences transfer twice, first to the pair of agents (s, R) and (s', R), and then to the pair (s, R') and (s', R'), we reach the conclusion that

$$(z^f, \bar{z}^g, z^g, \bar{z}^f) \, \mathbf{R}(E) \, (z^e, \bar{z}^h, z^h, \bar{z}^e).$$

Now, by weak Pareto, we get

$$(z^b, \bar{z}^c, z^c, \bar{z}^b) \, \mathbf{P}(E) \, (z^f, \bar{z}^g, z^g, \bar{z}^f)$$

and

$$(z^e, \bar{z}^h, z^h, \bar{z}^e) \, \mathbf{P}(E) \, (z^a, \bar{z}^d, z^d, \bar{z}^a)$$

which forms a cycle of strict social preference, a contradiction. ■

This simple illustration clearly demonstrates the tension between the two ethical objectives. Agent (s, R), for instance, when consuming z_a, is considered relatively well-off when compared with agent (s', R) (who has the same preferences), according to the objective of compensation, but agent (s, R) is considered relatively disadvantaged when compared with agent (s, R') (who has the same skill), according to the objective of responsibility. This turns out to be the case for each of the four agents of that economy, with the consequence that the successive application of the axioms leads to a cycle.

The conflict between the two objectives is serious. We even find it impossible to combine them when we remove the egalitarian objective embedded in our two axioms, and when we replace them with anonymity axioms. Equal-preferences anonymity requires that permuting the bundles of two agents having the same preferences should not affect social welfare. Note that this axiom is not logically related to equal-preferences transfer.

Axiom 10.3 Equal-Preferences Anonymity
For all $E = (s_N, R_N) \in \mathcal{D}$, $z_N, z'_N \in X^N$, $j, k \in N$, *if* $R_j = R_k$, $z_j = z'_k$ *and* $z_k = z'_j$, *and for all* $i \in N$ *such that* $i \neq j, k$, $z_i = z'_i$, *then* $z'_N \, \mathbf{I}(E) \, z_N$.

Equal-skill anonymity requires that permuting the budgets (lump-sum grants) of two agents having the same skill, when they are precisely consuming their best bundles in their respective budgets, before and after the permutation, should not affect social welfare.

Axiom 10.4 Equal-Skill Anonymity
For all $E = (s_N, R_N) \in \mathcal{D}$, $z_N, z'_N \in X^N$, $j, k \in N$, *if* $s_j = s_k$, $B(s_j, z_j) = B(s_k, z'_k)$, $B(s_j, z'_j) = B(s_k, z_k)$, *and*

$$z_j \in \max|_{R_j} B(s_j, z_j), \quad z'_j \in \max|_{R_j} B(s_j, z'_j),$$

$$z_k \in \max|_{R_k} B(s_k, z_k), \quad z'_k \in \max|_{R_k} B(s_k, z'_k),$$

and for all $i \in N, i \neq j, k$, $z_i = z'_i$, *then* $z'_N \, \mathbf{I}(E) \, z_N$.

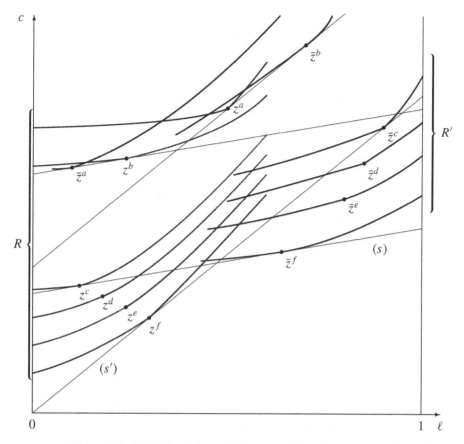

Figure 10.3. No SOF satisfies weak Pareto, equal-preferences anonymity, and equal-skill anonymity.

The second result of this chapter, unfortunately, confirms the difficulty, revealed by Theorem 10.1, of combining the objectives of compensation and responsibility.

Theorem 10.2 *On the domain* $\mathcal{E}$, *no SOF satisfies* weak Pareto, equal-preferences anonymity, *and* equal-skill anonymity.

Again, the proof can be graphical, involving an economy with two skill levels and two preferences $E = ((s, s, s', s'), (R, R', R, R'))$. We construct a cycle of allocations in Figure 10.3. Let us start with allocation $(z^b, \bar{z}^f, z^e, \bar{z}^d)$. By weak Pareto, $(z^a, \bar{z}^e, z^d, \bar{z}^c)$ is a strictly preferred allocation. By equal-preferences anonymity, it is indifferent to $(z^d, \bar{z}^e, z^a, \bar{z}^c)$, which, by equal-skill anonymity, is indifferent to $(z^d, \bar{z}^e, z^f, \bar{z}^b)$, itself indifferent to $(z^d, \bar{z}^b, z^f, \bar{z}^e)$, by equal-preferences anonymity. By weak Pareto, $(z^c, \bar{z}^a, z^e, \bar{z}^d)$ is strictly preferred, but it turns out to be indifferent to the allocation we started with, $(z^b, \bar{z}^f, z^e, \bar{z}^d)$, by application of equal-skill anonymity.

10.4   WEAKENING THE BASIC AXIOMS

One possible way out of the preceding negative results consists of weakening the axioms. In this section, we study examples of such weakened axioms.

The first weakenings follow the idea that, in some economies, we know perfectly well what the optimal allocations should look like. Let us first apply this idea to the compensation objective. In an economy in which all agents have the same preferences, the only optimal allocations should be the Pareto efficient ones at which all agents are assigned bundles they deem equivalent. Indeed, no agent finds his or her bundle worse than that of any other agent, so that final outcomes can be claimed to have been equalized.

If we apply the same idea to the responsibility objective, we look at economies in which all agents have the same skill. In those economies, inequalities are justified, provided they come only from different choices. Consequently, letting agents maximize in the same budget set is optimal, and this is what laissez-faire prescribes. This leads us to the following two axioms.

Axiom 10.5 Equal-Welfare Selection
For all $E = (s_N, R_N) \in \mathcal{D}$, $z_N \in \max|_{\mathbf{R}(E)} Z(E)$, if for all $i, j \in N$, $R_i = R_j$, then for all $i, j \in N$, $z_i \, I_i \, z_j$.

Axiom 10.6 Laissez-Faire Selection
For all $E = (s_N, R_N) \in \mathcal{D}$, $z_N \in \max|_{\mathbf{R}(E)} Z(E)$, if for all $i, j \in N$, $s_i = s_j$, then for all $i \in N$, $z_i \in \max|_{R_i} B(s_i, (0, 0))$.

Equal-welfare selection is logically weaker than equal-preferences transfer,[6] whereas laissez-faire selection is logically weaker than equal-skill transfer. Surprisingly, the duality between skills and preferences stops here. More precisely, we will show that, although it is easy to combine laissez-faire selection with equal-preferences transfer, the dual result does not hold (more precisely, combining weak pareto, equal-welfare selection, equal-skill transfer, and separability is impossible). We begin by exploring the former possibility. First, we define the skill-equivalent utility. It is the skill level that leaves the agent indifferent between his or her current bundle and being free to choose his or her labor time at that skill level. Formally, for $z_i \in X$, and $R_i \in R$,

$$u_s(z_i, R_i) = u \Leftrightarrow z_i \, I_i \, \max|_{R_i} B(u, (0, 0)).$$

---

[6] More precisely, it is logically implied by equal-preferences transfer under Pareto indifference and Hansson independence.

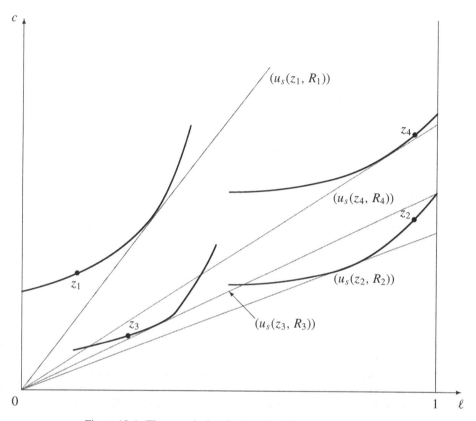

Figure 10.4. The s-equivalent leximin function

This well-being index is well defined only over bundles $z_i \in X$ such that $z_i \, R_i \, (0, 0)$. For $E = (s_N, R_N) \in \mathcal{E}$, let the set of admissible allocations $A(E)$ be defined as

$$A(E) = \{z_N \in Z(E) \mid z_i \, R_i \, (0, 0) \, \forall \, i \in N\}.$$

The following SOF is defined only over those allocations.

Social ordering function 10.1 s-Equivalent Leximin ($\mathbf{R}^{slex}$)
For all $E = (s_N, R_N) \in \mathcal{E}$, $z_N, z_N' \in A(E)$,

$$z_N \, \mathbf{R}^{slex}(E) \, z_N' \Leftrightarrow (u_s(z_i, R_i))_{i \in N} \geq_{lex} \left(u_s(z_i', R_i)\right)_{i \in N}.$$

This SOF is illustrated in Figure 10.4, representing a similar economy to the one used in the proof of the impossibility theorems 10.1 and 10.2. There are two skill levels, s and s', and two preferences, R and R'; the four agents have all the possible combinations of skill levels and preferences, so that $s_1 = s_2 = s < s_3 = s_4 = s'$, $R_1 = R_3 = R$ and $R_2 = R_4 = R'$. In allocation (z_1, z_2, z_3, z_4), agent 1, the low-skilled agent with low willingness to work, enjoys a larger satisfaction level than agent 3, who has the same preferences but a higher skill. On the other hand, among the agents with high willingness to work, the high-skilled one, agent 4, is assigned a better bundle than agent 2. According to the u_s well-being index, agent 2 is the worst-off agent, and agent 1 the best-off. At that allocation, R^{slex} would recommend redistribution from 1 and 4 to 2 and 3.

The preferred allocations for this SOF, among feasible allocations, are such that all the agents' skill-equivalent utilities are equal. This corresponds to the equal-wage equivalent allocation rule studied by Fleurbaey and Maniquet (1999).

Theorem 10.3 *On the domain $\mathcal{E}$, the s-equivalent leximin function $\mathbf{R}^{slex}$ satisfies strong Pareto, equal-preferences transfer, equal-preferences anonymity, laissez-faire selection, unchanged-contour independence, separation, replication, and independence of the feasible set. Conversely, if a SOF $\mathbf{R}$ satisfies strong Pareto, equal-preferences transfer, laissez-faire selection, unchanged-contour independence, and separation, then for all $E = (s_N, R_N) \in \mathcal{E}$, all $z_N, z_N' \in X^N$,*

$$\min_{i \in N} u_s(z_i, R_i) > \min_{i \in N} u_s(z_i', R_i) \Rightarrow z_N \, \mathbf{P}(E) \, z_N'.$$

The proof makes use of the fact that strong Pareto, equal-preferences transfer, and unchanged-contour independence imply an absolute priority for the worse off (in the form of equal-preferences priority), as explained in Section 10.6. The other key element of the proof is to justify a preference for z_N over z_N' when, for some $j, k \in N$,

$$u_s(z_j', R_j) > u_s(z_j, R_j) > u_s(z_k, R_k) > u_s(z_k', R_k),$$

while for $i \neq j, k, z_i' = z_i$.

This is done in the following way. First, introduce two agents a and b (by separation) with the same skill s_0 between $u_s(z_k, R_k)$ and $u_s(z_j, R_j)$, and such that $R_a = R_j$, $R_b = R_k$. Let z_a, z_b be the bundles these two agents choose from the laissez-faire budget set $B(s_0, (0, 0))$. Observe that $z_j \, P_j \, z_a$ and $z_b \, P_k \, z_k$. By unchanged-contour independence and equal-preferences priority, agent a's satisfaction can be raised a little while j is pulled down from z_j' to z_j, and agent b's satisfaction can be lowered a little while k is moved from z_k' to a better bundle z_k'' below z_k. By separation, one can focus on changes affecting a and b separately from the rest, and conclude that by laissez-faire selection, it would be at least as good to bring a and b back to their laissez-faire bundles. By separation again, one can remove a and b from the economy and conclude that moving j and k from z_j', z_k' to z_j, z_k'' is a weak improvement. By strong Pareto, moving them to z_j, z_k is a strict improvement. After this argument is made, it is easy to reach the conclusion of the theorem, in a similar fashion as has been done in the characterizations of Chapter 5.

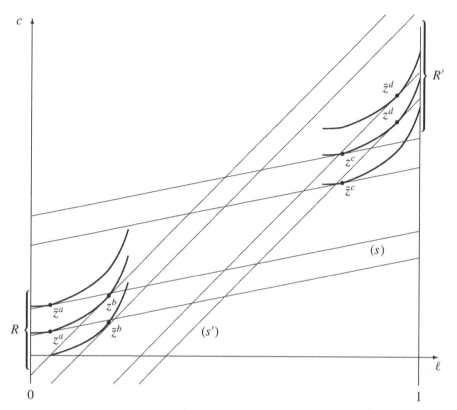

Figure 10.5. No SOF satisfies weak Pareto, equal-skill transfer, equal-welfare selection, and separability.

On the other hand, if we try to combine equal-welfare selection with equal-skill transfer, which is the dual to the combination of laissez-faire selection and equal-preferences transfer, we face the following difficulty.

Theorem 10.4 *On the domain $\mathcal{E}$, no SOF satisfies* weak Pareto, equal-skill transfer, equal-welfare selection, *and* separability.

Proof. The economy is $E = ((s, s', s, s'), (R, R, R', R'))$ but we will also consider the variants $E' = ((s, s', s, s'), (R, R, R, R))$ and $E'' = ((s, s', s, s'), (R', R', R', R'))$. The proof is illustrated in Figure 10.5.

By weak Pareto and equal-welfare selection, the unique best allocation in $Z(E')$ for $\mathbf{R}(E')$ is (z^a, z^b, z^a, z^b). Therefore,

$$\left(z^a, z^b, z^a, z^b\right) \mathbf{P}(E') \left(\bar{z}^a, \bar{z}^b, z^a, z^b\right).$$

By separability, this is equivalent to

$$\left(z^a, z^b, z^c, z^d\right) \mathbf{P}(E) \left(\bar{z}^a, \bar{z}^b, z^c, z^d\right).$$

By similar reasoning, as the unique best allocation in $Z(E'')$ for $\mathbf{R}(E'')$ is $\left(z^c, z^d, z^c, z^d\right)$, one deduces that

$$\left(\bar{z}^a, \bar{z}^b, z^c, z^d\right) \mathbf{P}(E) \left(\bar{z}^a, \bar{z}^b, \bar{z}^c, \bar{z}^d\right).$$

By transitivity,

$$\left(z^a, z^b, z^c, z^d\right) \mathbf{P}(E) \left(\bar{z}^a, \bar{z}^b, \bar{z}^c, \bar{z}^d\right).$$

By equal-skill transfer,

$$\left(\bar{z}^a, z^b, \bar{z}^c, z^d\right) \mathbf{R}(E) \left(z^a, z^b, z^c, z^d\right)$$

and

$$\left(\bar{z}^a, \bar{z}^b, \bar{z}^c, \bar{z}^d\right) \mathbf{R}(E) \left(\bar{z}^a, z^b, \bar{z}^c, z^d\right),$$

implying by transitivity:

$$\left(\bar{z}^a, \bar{z}^b, \bar{z}^c, \bar{z}^d\right) \mathbf{R}(E) \left(z^a, z^b, z^c, z^d\right).$$

One therefore has a contradiction. ∎

A similar impossibility would be reached if equal-skill transfer were replaced with equal-skill anonymity. The impossibility involves separability and vanishes in absence of this axiom. The axioms of strong Pareto, equal-skill transfer, and equal-welfare selection are satisfied by any SOF that applies the leximin criterion to indices of well-being defined as

$$\max \left\{ u_{R_N}(z) \mid z \in B^*(s_i, R_i, z_i) \right\},$$

where u_{R_N} is an increasing continuous utility function that depends on the profile R_N and satisfies the property that when there is R_0 such that for all $i \in N$, $R_i = R_0$, then u_{R_N} is a representation of R_0 (for instance, u_{R_N} can be the utility representation of an "average" of agents' preferences).

We now study another possible weakening of equal-skill transfer, proposed by Valletta (2009a) in a slightly different context. Let us define the following partial order on the set $\mathcal{R}$ of preferences. For R_i, $R_i' \in \mathcal{R}$, we say that R_i is at least as industrious as R_i', denoted $R_i \gtrsim^{\mathrm{MI}} R_i'$, if and only if for every possible budget set, the best bundle of R_i involves at least as much labor (and, therefore, at least as much consumption) as that of R_i'. Formally,

$$R_i \gtrsim^{\mathrm{MI}} R_i' \Leftrightarrow \forall s \in S, x \in X, \ \max|_{R_i} B(s, x) \geq \max|_{R_i'} B(s, x).$$

The "at least as industrious as" relationship is, of course, not complete.

The next axiom requires applying equal-skill transfer to pairs of agents such that the relatively richer agent is also more industrious. That axiom is consistent with the idea that consumption inequality, between two agents having the same skill, should be bounded above by what the difference in labor time justifies; that is, if $s_j = s_k$, $R_j \gtrsim^{\mathrm{MI}} R_k$, and $c_j - c_k > s_j(\ell_j - \ell_k)$, then j has a relatively too-large consumption level, and a budget transfer from j to k is desirable. What the axiom does not require, contrary to equal-skill transfer, is that the optimal difference in consumption be exactly the one related to the difference in labor time: $c_j - c_k = s_j(\ell_j - \ell_k)$. Consequently, the axiom also has a small compensation flavor, and that is why it is compatible with equal-preferences transfer.

Axiom 10.7 $\succsim^{MI}$-Equal-Skill Transfer
For all $E = (s_N, R_N) \in \mathcal{D}$, $z_N = (\ell_N, c_N)$, $z'_N = (\ell'_N, c'_N) \in X^N$, $\Delta \in \mathbb{R}_{++}$, if there exist $j, k \in N$ such that $s_j = s_k$, $R_j \succsim^{MI} R_k$, $(c_j - s_j\ell_j) - \Delta = (c'_j - s'_j\ell'_j) > (c'_k - s'_k\ell'_k) = (c_k - s_k\ell_k) + \Delta$,

$$z_j \in \max|_{R_j} B(s_j, z_j), \quad z'_j \in \max|_{R_j} B(s_j, z'_j),$$

$$z_k \in \max|_{R_k} B(s_k, z_k), \quad z'_k \in \max|_{R_k} B(s_k, z'_k),$$

and for all $i \in N$, $i \neq j, k$, $z_i = z'_i$, then $z'_N \mathbf{R}(E) z_N$.

The following SOF satisfies equal-preferences transfer and $\succsim^{MI}$-equal-skill transfer. It works by applying the leximin to the following $s_{\min}$-equivalent utility. It equals the lump-sum transfer that leaves the agent indifferent between his or her current bundle and being free to choose his or her labor time in a budget set defined by this lump-sum transfer and the minimal skill level. Formally, for $z_i \in X$, and $R_i \in \mathcal{R}$,

$$u_{s_{\min}}(z_i, R_i) = u \Leftrightarrow z_i \, I_i \, \max|_{R_i} B(s_{\min}, (0, u)).$$

Social ordering function 10.2 $s_{\min}$-Equivalent Leximin ($\mathbf{R}^{s_{\min}lex}$)
For all $E = (s_N, R_N) \in \mathcal{E}$, $z_N, z'_N \in X^N$,

$$z_N \mathbf{R}^{s_{\min}lex}(E) z'_N \Leftrightarrow \left(u_{s_{\min}}(z_i, R_i)\right)_{i \in N} \geq_{lex} \left(u_{s_{\min}}(z'_i, R_i)\right)_{i \in N}.$$

This SOF is illustrated in Figure 10.6, using the same economy and the same allocation as in Figure 10.4. As with $\mathbf{R}^{slex}$, agent 1 is considered better-off than agent 3, and agent 4 better-off than agent 2, but any SOF satisfying equal-preferences transfer would consider this. The interesting observation is that agent 1 is now considered worse-off than agent 4 and agent 3 worse-off than agent 2. A social-welfare–improving reform would now ask agent 4 to contribute more and agent 1 less than in the previous case. Compared with $\mathbf{R}^{slex}$, $\mathbf{R}^{s_{\min}lex}$ is less favorable to the hardworking agents.

We have the following axiomatization result, the proof of which is in the appendix.

Theorem 10.5 *On the domain $\mathcal{E}$, the $s_{\min}$-equivalent leximin function $\mathbf{R}^{slex}$ satisfies strong Pareto, equal-preferences transfer, equal-preferences anonymity, $\succsim^{MI}$-equal-skill transfer, unchanged-contour independence, separation, replication and independence of the feasible set. Conversely, if a SOF $\mathbf{R}$ satisfies strong Pareto, equal-preferences transfer, $\succsim^{MI}$-equal-skill transfer, unchanged-contour independence, and separation, then for all $E = (s_N, R_N) \in \mathcal{E}$, all $z_N, z'_N \in X^N$,*

$$\min_{i \in N} u_{s_{\min}}(z_i, R_i) > \min_{i \in N} u_{s_{\min}}(z'_i, R_i) \Rightarrow z_N \mathbf{P}(E) z'_N.$$

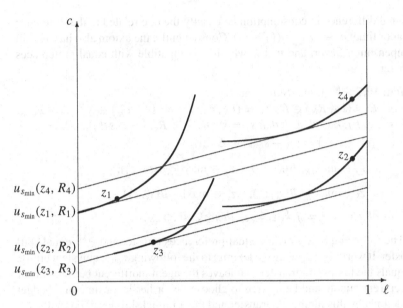

Figure 10.6. The $s_{\min}$-equivalent leximin function

The proof is similar to that of Theorem 10.3 and again relies on the fact that equal-preferences priority follows from strong Pareto, equal-preferences transfer, and unchanged-contour independence (see Section 10.6). One also proves that there must be a preference for z_N over z'_N when for some $j, k \in N$,

$$u_{s_{\min}}(z'_j, R_j) > u_{s_{\min}}(z_j, R_j) > u_{s_{\min}}(z_k, R_k) > u_{s_{\min}}(z'_k, R_k),$$

whereas for $i \neq j, k$, $z'_i = z_i$.

This is done in the following way. First, introduce two agents a and b (by separation) with skill equal to $s_{\min}$, and with $s_{\min}$-equivalent utilities between $u_{s_{\min}}(z_j, R_j)$ and $u_{s_{\min}}(z'_k, R_k)$. Their preferences are constructed so that the indifference curve of a (respectively, b) does not cross $I(z_j, R_j)$ (respectively, $I(z_k, R_k)$). Therefore, by unchanged-contour independence and equal-preferences priority, agent a's satisfaction can be raised a little while j is pulled down from z'_j to z_j, and agent b's satisfaction can be lowered a little while k is moved from z'_k to a better bundle z''_k below z_k. Moreover, their preferences must be such that for any budget with slope $s_{\min}$ or more, a chooses to work full time (this is obtained if a has linear preferences with a slope of indifference curves slightly less than $s_{\min}$). Therefore his preferences dominate those of b for $\succsim^{MI}$, making it possible to invoke $\succsim^{MI}$-equal-skill transfer and bring a and b back to their initial bundles. By separation, they can then be removed from the economy. In conclusion, one obtains that moving j and k from z'_j, z'_k to z_j, z''_k is acceptable. By strong Pareto, moving them to z_j, z_k is then a strict improvement.

10.5 COMPROMISE AXIOMS

Another way of avoiding the negative result of Section 10.3 is by defining axioms that combine the objectives of compensation for low skill and responsibility for preferences. We give an example of such an axiom in this section.[7] This axiom is consistent with Kolm's idea that members of a society should decide on a fraction $\tilde{\ell}$ of individual labor time such that incomes should be equalized among individuals working $\tilde{\ell}$ (see, e.g., Kolm 1996, 2004). More precisely, it requires that if two agents freely choose a labor time of $\tilde{\ell}$ but do not enjoy the same consumption level, then a transfer of consumption between them is a strict social improvement, provided they still end up freely choosing a labor time of $\tilde{\ell}$ after the transfer.

The compensation content of this axiom comes from the fact that the two agents may have different skills, so the larger consumption may originate in one agent having a higher skill. The axiom prevents the high-skilled agent from reaching a larger consumption level than the low-skilled one. The responsibility content of the axiom comes from the fact that it restricts its attention to agents having some particular preferences. Among such agents – that is, among agents choosing a labor time of $\tilde{\ell}$ – the objective of the axiom is to equalize consumption, so if the two agents have the same skill, a budget transfer between them is a social improvement.

Axiom 10.8 $\tilde{\ell}$-Labor Transfer
For all $E = (s_N, R_N) \in \mathcal{D}$, and $z_N = (\ell_N, c_N)$, $z'_N = (\ell'_N, c'_N) \in X^N$, if there exist $j, k \in N$ and $\Delta \in \mathbb{R}_{++}$ such that $\ell_j = \ell_k = \ell'_j = \ell'_k = \tilde{\ell}$,

$$c_j - \Delta = c'_j > c'_k = c_k + \Delta,$$

and

$$z_j \in \max|_{R_j} B(s_j, z_j), \quad z'_j \in \max|_{R_j} B(s_j, z'_j),$$

$$z_k \in \max|_{R_k} B(s_k, z_k), \quad z'_k \in \max|_{R_k} B(s_k, z'_k),$$

and for all $i \neq j, k$, $z_i = z'_i$, then $z'_N \mathbf{R}(E) z_N$.

We do not have a theory about how to determine the value of $\tilde{\ell}$ (see Kolm 2004, part IV, for a detailed discussion of how societies may choose $\tilde{\ell}$). We can simply state that the larger the $\tilde{\ell}$, the more redistributive social preferences will be.

The key observation of this section is that there are SOFs that satisfy $\tilde{\ell}$-labor transfer and equal-preferences transfer or $\tilde{\ell}$-labor transfer and equal-skill transfer. The SOFs that satisfy $\tilde{\ell}$-labor transfer and equal-preferences transfer are of the egalitarian-equivalent kind, and are somehow similar to the SOFs already defined in this chapter. A prominent example is the leximin SOF that measures individual well-being by the intersection of an agent's indifference curve with the vertical line of equation $\ell = \tilde{\ell}$.

---

[7] This section is drawn from Fleurbaey and Maniquet (2011).

We concentrate in this section on the SOFs that satisfy $\tilde{\ell}$-labor transfer and equal-skill transfer. They are of the Walrasian kind, but similar to egalitarian-equivalent SOFs, they also work by applying the leximin criterion to some index of well-being. Let us define this index. The novelty is that it depends on the skill of the agent. The level of well-being associated with a bundle is defined with respect to the budget that leaves the agent indifferent between this bundle and freely choosing in that budget the slope of which is now the real skill of the agent. when this budget has been identified, the value of the well-being index is the level of consumption that corresponds to a labor time of $\tilde{\ell}$ for that budget.

Formally, for $z_i \in X$, and $R_i \in R$,

$$u_{\tilde{\ell}}(z_i, s_i, R_i) = u \Leftrightarrow z_i \, I_i \, \max|_{R_i} B(s_i, (\tilde{\ell}, u)).$$

This well-being index is nonnegative only over bundles $z_i \in X$ such that $z_i \, R_i \, \max|_{R_i} B(s_i, (\tilde{\ell}, 0))$. For $E = (s_N, R_N) \in \mathcal{E}$, let the set of admissible allocations $A^{\tilde{\ell}}(E)$ be defined as

$$A^{\tilde{\ell}}(E) = \{z_N \in Z(E) \mid \forall i \in N, \; z_i \, R_i \, \max|_{R_i} B(s_i, (\tilde{\ell}, 0))\}.$$

The following SOF is defined only over those allocations.[8]

Social ordering function 10.3 $\tilde{\ell}$-Egalitarian Walrasian Leximin ($\mathbf{R}^{\tilde{\ell}EW}$)
For all $E = (s_N, R_N) \in \mathcal{E}$, $z_N, z'_N \in A^{\tilde{\ell}}(E)$,

$$z_N \, \mathbf{R}^{\tilde{\ell}EW}(E) \, z'_N \Leftrightarrow \left(u_{\tilde{\ell}}(z_i, s_i, R_i)\right)_{i \in N} \geq_{lex} \left(u_{\tilde{\ell}}(z'_i, s_i, R_i)\right)_{i \in N}.$$

This SOF is illustrated in Figure 10.7, using the same economy and the same allocation as before. The well-being index is now computed by drawing implicit budgets having the same slope as the real skill of the agents. The different values of the index are read on the vertical axis corresponding to a labor time of $\tilde{\ell}$, which is chosen in the graph to be equal to 0.6.

We can see that the social evaluation of the agents' positions is drastically different from the previous ones. Agent 4 is now considered the worst off: the income agent 4 would earn by choosing a labor time of $\tilde{\ell}$ in his or her implicit budget is too low. A social welfare improving reform would benefit this agent. The other striking feature of the figure is that agent 1 is now considered worse off than agent 3. This shows that $\mathbf{R}^{\tilde{\ell}EW}$ benefits the hardworking high-skilled agents and the lazy low-skilled ones. This conclusion depends on the value of $\tilde{\ell}$ and is valid only for intermediate values. For $\tilde{\ell}$ sufficiently low, the worse-off agents would become 3 and 4, the two high-skilled agents, whereas for large values of $\tilde{\ell}$, the worse-off would become 1 and 2, the two low-skilled agents.[9]

---

[8] Allowing for negative values of the index, it is easy to extend this SOF over all X^N. We do not do it here because the characterization of this SOF that is proposed in Section 10.6 works only for the admissible allocations.

[9] The allocation rules that select the best allocations for $\mathbf{R}^{\tilde{\ell}EW}$, for given values of $\tilde{\ell}$, were introduced by Kolm (1996) and axiomatized by Fleurbaey and Maniquet (1996a) and Maniquet (1998). The

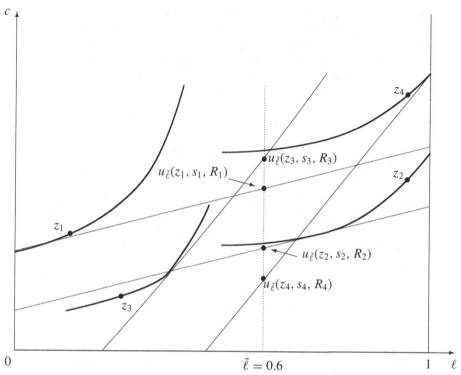

Figure 10.7. The $\tilde{\ell}$-egalitarian Walrasian leximin

The $\mathbf{R}^{\tilde{\ell}\mathrm{EW}}$ SOF satisfies strong Pareto, equal-skill transfer, equal-skill anonymity, $\tilde{\ell}$-labor transfer, unchanged-contour independence, separation, and replication. On the other hand, it does not satisfy independence of the feasible set, as the well-being index that it uses depends on the skills of the agents, so that changing the skill profile affects the social ranking. Importantly, many other SOFs satisfy the same list of axioms, and they do not all give absolute priority to the worst-off. We develop this issue in the next section.

10.6 FROM TRANSFER TO PRIORITY AXIOMS

All the SOFs that we have studied in this chapter up to now are leximin SOFs in a particular index of well-being. This is not a surprise, of course, given all the previous results, and given, especially, the discussion of Chapter 3. In this section, nonetheless, we look carefully at the results about infinite inequality aversion, as they are not all derived from the same combinations of axioms.

---

extreme cases in which $\tilde{\ell}$ are either 0 or 1 were discussed by Varian (1974) and Pazner and Schmeidler (1978a), respectively.

Combining equal-preferences transfer with Pareto axioms and either unchanged-contour independence or separation unsurprisingly leads to an axiom of equal-preferences priority. In contrast, a similar statement does not hold with equal-skill transfer. There are SOFs, indeed, that do satisfy strong Pareto, equal-skill transfer, and strong robustness requirements, and are not of the leximin type. Here is an example. Let $\alpha \leq 1$, $\alpha \neq 0$. The SOF **R** defined by:

for all $E \in \mathcal{E}$, $z_N, z'_N \in A^{\tilde{\ell}}(E)$,

$$ z_N \, \mathbf{R}(E) \, z'_N \Leftrightarrow \frac{1}{\alpha} \sum_{i \in N} (u_{\tilde{\ell}}(z_i, R_i))^\alpha \geq \frac{1}{\alpha} \sum_{i \in N} (u_{\tilde{\ell}}(z'_i, R_i))^\alpha, $$

satisfies strong Pareto, equal-skill transfer, equal-skill anonymity, unchanged-contour independence, separability, and replication.

Would it be promising to study non-leximin SOFs such as this one? This is doubtful. Indeed, for all values of α, the SOF just defined violates the simple transfer among equals axiom (recall that agents are equals in this model if they have both the same preferences and the same skill), and so would do any SOF satisfying Pareto indifference, equal-skill transfer, and unchanged-contour independence, as long as they do not satisfy equal-skill priority. This is what we prove now.

Axiom 10.9 Transfer among Equals
For all $E = (s_N, R_N) \in \mathcal{D}$, and $z_N = (\ell_N, c_N)$, $z'_N = (\ell'_N, c'_N) \in X^{|N|}$, $j, k \in N$, $\Delta \in \mathbb{R}_{++}$, if $s_j = s_k$ and $R_j = R_k$, $\ell_j = \ell_k = \ell'_j = \ell'_k$, and

$$ c_j - \Delta = c'_j > c'_k = c_k + \Delta, $$

and for all $i \neq j, k$, $z_i = z'_i$, then $z'_N \, \mathbf{R}(E) \, z_N$.

Axiom 10.10 Equal-Skill Priority
For all $E = (s_N, R_N) \in \mathcal{D}$, $z_N = (\ell_N, c_N)$, $z'_N = (\ell'_N, c'_N) \in X^N$, if there exist $j, k \in N$ such that $s_j = s_k$, $(c_j - s_j \ell_j) > (c'_j - s'_j \ell'_j) > (c'_k - s'_k \ell'_k) > (c_k - s_k \ell_k)$,

$$ z_j \in \max|_{R_j} B(s_j, z_j), \quad z'_j \in \max|_{R_j} B(s_j, z'_j), $$

$$ z_k \in \max|_{R_k} B(s_k, z_k), \quad z'_k \in \max|_{R_k} B(s_k, z'_k), $$

and for all $i \neq j, k$, $z_i = z'_i$, then $z'_N \, \mathbf{R}(E) \, z_N$.

Lemma 10.1 *On the domain $\mathcal{E}$, if a SOF **R** satisfies Pareto indifference, transfer among equals, equal-skill transfer, unchanged-contour independence, and separation, then it satisfies equal-skill priority.*[10]

---

[10] Separation can be weakened into separability in this lemma if there are at least four agents in the economy. Also, unchanged-contour independence can be dropped altogether if transfer among equals is strengthened into nested-contour transfer.

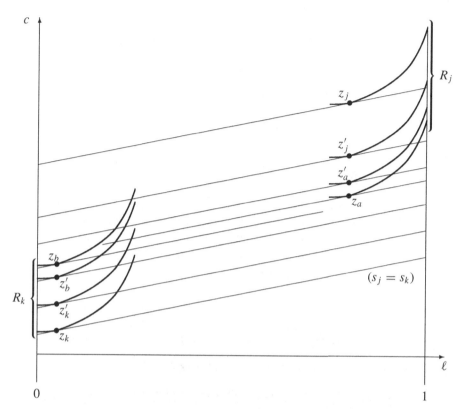

Figure 10.8. Pareto indifference, transfer among equals, equal-skill transfer, unchanged-contour independence, and separation imply equal-skill priority.

Proof. The proof, which bears some similarity with the proof of Theorem 10.5, is illustrated in Figure 10.8 which features four agents: j, k such that $s_j = s_k$, and a, b such that $(s_a, R_a) = (s_j, R_j)$ and $(s_b, R_b) = (s_k, R_k)$.

First, with the same reasoning as for Theorem 3.1, one sees that Pareto indifference, transfer among equals, and unchanged-contour independence imply priority among equals.

Axiom 10.11 Priority among Equals
For all $E = (s_N, R_N) \in \mathcal{D}$, and $z_N = (\ell_N, c_N), z'_N = (\ell'_N, c'_N) \in X^{|N|}$, $j, k \in N, \Delta \in \mathbb{R}_{++}$, if $s_j = s_k$ and $R_j = R_k$, $\ell_j = \ell_k = \ell'_j = \ell'_k$, and

$$c_j > c'_j > c'_k > c_k,$$

and for all $i \neq j, k$, $z_i = z'_i$, then $z'_N \mathbf{R}(E) z_N$.

Then, one can apply prority among equals between j and a and between k and b (see Figure 10.8) to derive that

$$\left(z'_j, z'_k, z'_a, z'_b\right) \mathbf{R}((s_j, s_k, s_j, s_k), (R_j, R_k, R_j, R_k)) \left(z_j, z_k, z_a, z_b\right).$$

By equal-skill transfer applied to a and b,

$$\left(z'_j, z'_k, z_a, z_b\right) \mathbf{R}((s_j, s_k, s_j, s_k), (R_j, R_k, R_j, R_k)) \left(z'_j, z'_k, z'_a, z'_b\right).$$

By transitivity,

$$\left(z'_j, z'_k, z_a, z_b\right) \mathbf{R}((s_j, s_k, s_j, s_k), (R_j, R_k, R_j, R_k)) \left(z_j, z_k, z_a, z_b\right).$$

By separation,

$$\left(z'_j, z'_k\right) \mathbf{R}((s_j, s_k), (R_j, R_k)) \left(z_j, z_k\right).$$

By separation again, reintroducing the other agents $i \neq j, k$ for whom $z'_i = z_i$, one obtains $z'_N \mathbf{R}(E) z_N$. ∎

Equal-skill transfer seemed to be compatible with a noninfinite rate of inequality aversion, but the addition of the basic requirement of transfer among equals forces us to reintroduce an infinite inequality aversion. Lemma 10.1 confirms that only leximin types of SOFs are left when one tries to combine axioms of efficiency, fairness, and robustness. Indeed, we get the following result.

Theorem 10.6 *On the domain* $\mathcal{E}$, *if a SOF* $\mathbf{R}$ *satisfies* strong Pareto, transfer among equals, equal-skill transfer, $\tilde{\ell}$-labor transfer, unchanged-contour independence, *and* separation, *then for all* $E = (s_N, R_N) \in \mathcal{E}$, *all* $z_N, z'_N \in X^N$,

$$\min_{i \in N} u_{\tilde{\ell}}(z_i, s_i, R_i) > \min_{i \in N} u_{\tilde{\ell}}(z'_i, s_i, R_i) \Rightarrow z_N \mathbf{P}(E) z'_N.$$

We simply illustrate the key part of the easy proof in Figure 10.9. It consists of showing that if for two agents $j, k \in N$,

$$u_{\tilde{\ell}}(z'_j, s_j, R_j) > u_{\tilde{\ell}}(z_j, s_j, R_j) > u_{\tilde{\ell}}(z_k, s_k, R_k) > u_{\tilde{\ell}}(z'_k, s_k, R_k),$$

whereas for $i \neq j, k$, $z'_i = z_i$, the allocation z_N is better than z'_N.

Introduce agents a, b such that $s_a = s_j$ and $s_b = s_k$. By Lemma 10.1, we know that we can apply equal-skill priority. Doing so between j and a, as well as between k and b, one sees that

$$\left(z_j, z''_k, z_a, z_b\right) \mathbf{R}((s_j, s_k, s_j, s_k), (R_j, R_k, R_a, R_b)) \left(z'_j, z'_k, z'_a, z'_b\right).$$

By $\tilde{\ell}$-labor transfer applied to a and b,

$$\left(z_j, z''_k, z'_a, z'_b\right) \mathbf{R}((s_j, s_k, s_j, s_k), (R_j, R_k, R_a, R_b)) \left(z_j, z''_k, z_a, z_b\right).$$

By transitivity,

$$\left(z_j, z''_k, z'_a, z'_b\right) \mathbf{R}((s_j, s_k, s_j, s_k), (R_j, R_k, R_a, R_b)) \left(z'_j, z'_k, z'_a, z'_b\right).$$

By separation,

$$\left(z_j, z''_k\right) \mathbf{R}((s_j, s_k), (R_j, R_k)) \left(z'_j, z'_k\right).$$

By strong Pareto,

$$\left(z_j, z_k\right) \mathbf{P}((s_j, s_k), (R_j, R_k)) \left(z'_j, z''_k\right),$$

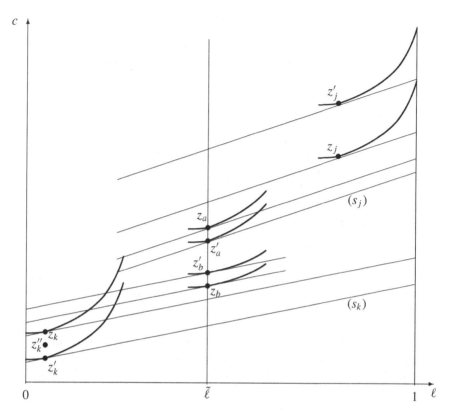

Figure 10.9. Illustration of the proof of Theorem 10.6

so

$$\left(z_j, z_k\right) \mathbf{P}(\left(s_j, s_k\right), \left(R_j, R_k\right)) \left(z'_j, z'_k\right).$$

By separation again, reintroducing the other agents (with unchanged bundles in z_N and z'_N), one obtains $z_N \mathbf{P}(E) z'_N$.

10.7 CONCLUSION

Several families of SOFs end up being characterized in this chapter. Table 10.1 summarizes the relative merits of each of them.

Again, this chapter has illustrated what can be expected from the SOF approach: identify the possible trade-offs between fairness axioms, capturing ethical views on the resource allocation problem at hand; and deduce the SOF that satisfies some relevant set of fairness properties, together with efficiency and robustness axioms. The main ethical conflict in the model we have studied here is the one between compensation for low skills and responsibility for individual preferences. We saw that those conflicting axioms end up justifying

Table 10.1. *Properties of the SOFs*

	$\mathbf{R}^{s\,\mathrm{lex}}$	$\mathbf{R}^{s_{\min}\mathrm{lex}}$	$\mathbf{R}^{\tilde{\ell}\mathrm{EW}}$
Strong Pareto	+	+	+
Transfer among equals	+	+	+
Equal-preferences transfer	+	+	−
Equal-preferences selection	+	+	−
Equal-skill transfer	−	−	+
Laissez-faire selection	+	−	+
$\gtrsim^{\mathrm{MI}}$-Equal-skill transfer	−	+	+
$\tilde{\ell}$-Labor transfer	−	−	+
Unchanged-contour independence	+	+	+
Separation	+	+	+
Replication	+	+	+
Independence of the feasible set	+	+	−

quite different SOFs. The $\mathbf{R}^{s\,\mathrm{lex}}$ SOF favors hardworking agents, the $\mathbf{R}^{s_{\min}\mathrm{lex}}$ SOF favors lazy agents, and they both favor low-skilled agents. The $\mathbf{R}^{\tilde{\ell}\mathrm{EW}}$ SOF, for intermediate values of $\tilde{\ell}$, favors hardworking high-skilled or lazy low-skilled agents.

Given that the current model is the canonical model in which labor income taxation is discussed, we now investigate it further to identify which income tax scheme may be compatible with the maximization process of the SOFs defined here.

CHAPTER 11

Income Taxation

11.1 INTRODUCTION

The ultimate objective of any approach to welfare economics is to provide criteria for the evaluation of social policies. In this chapter, we show how the social ordering functions axiomatized in the previous chapter engender such criteria.

After a policymaker has chosen the social ordering function that captures the policymaker's her ethical preferences, he or she typically faces information constraints that prevent him or her from being able to implement the allocations that are optimal according to the chosen social ordering function. The information constraints may be of different sorts, and we show here how the social ordering functions we have defined adjust to these different informational structures.

We study two informational structures. In some applications, we assume that labor time and earnings are observable, but skills are not. Agents may then choose to work at a lower wage rate than their skill warrants, if it is in their interest to do so. In other applications, we assume that labor time is no longer observable, and only earnings are. Under either set of assumptions, the policymaker must identify the optimal allocation among the ones that are compatible with the agents' incentives to hide their private information.

Our social ordering function approach turns out to accommodate these different structures easily. This comes from two central properties, on which we have already insisted. The first property is that the social ordering functions that satisfy the axioms we impose are of the leximin type. Consequently, social welfare is appropriately measured by the well-being index of the worst-off agents. It turns out to be measured easily. The second property is the informational simplicity of the well-being indices we use. They rely on ordinal information about individual preferences, so agents' choices reveal the information that is needed to compute these indices.

As is well known, restricting one's attention to incentive-compatible allocations is equivalent to studying income tax schemes. The applications we present here will turn into identifying properties that optimal tax schemes should satisfy. Here is a preview of the main results of the chapter.

First, we prove that social ordering functions satisfying equal-preferences transfer, the most demanding compensation axiom, call for more redistribution than the social ordering functions satisfying equal-skill transfer, the most demanding responsibility axiom. Second, we prove that all the social ordering functions highlighted here call for nonpositive marginal rates of taxation on low incomes. That is the most important result of the chapter. Both $\mathbf{R}^{s_{\min}\text{lex}}$ and $\mathbf{R}^{\tilde{\ell}EW}$, in spite of the considerable differences in the axioms that justify them, call for a zero marginal rate of taxation, whereas $\mathbf{R}^{s\text{lex}}$ calls for nonpositive marginal tax rates. The third conclusion is that $\mathbf{R}^{\tilde{\ell}EW}$, in spite of its egalitarian flavor, may call for low redistribution.

In Section 11.2, we define the model and study the incentive compatibility constraints. In Section 11.3, we derive the simple criteria that can be used to evaluate current income tax schemes and identify who should benefit in priority from a reform. In Section 11.4, we study some characteristics of the optimal tax schemes in simple economies composed of four types of agents. In Section 11.5, we turn to the characteristics of optimal tax schemes in general economies.

11.2 THE MODEL

We keep the same model as in the previous chapter. An economy is a list $E = (s_N, R_N) \in \mathcal{E}$ where for all $i \in N$, $s_i \in S = [s_{\min}, s_{\max}]$ denotes i's production skill and R_i i's preferences over labor time-consumption bundles $z_i = (\ell_i, c_i) \in X = [0, 1] \times \mathbb{R}_+$. There is no constraint on the value of $s_{\min}$, but the case $s_{\min} > 0$ is the most interesting. We come back to that issue in the conclusion of the chapter.

The policymaker has social preferences represented by a SOF $\mathbf{R}$ defined over all allocations. If information were complete, the policymaker could simply maximize $\mathbf{R}$ over the set of feasible allocations. We assume in this chapter that information is not complete. Skills and preferences are private information of the agents. The policymaker knows the different elements of s_N and R_N, but does not know who is who. To state it differently, the policymaker knows only the statistical distribution of types in the economy. Consequently, he or she must restrict attention to incentive-compatible allocations. The contents of the set of incentive-compatible allocations depend on what the policymaker is able to observe. We consider two different informational contexts in turn.

In the first context, the policymaker observes labor time and pretax income for each agent. Given that the policymaker does not observe the agent's skill, the agent can choose to work at a wage rate that is lower than his or her skill, if it is in the agent's interest. We denote by $w_i \leq s_i$ the wage rate at which agent $i \in N$ actually works; that is, w_i corresponds to the gross earnings/labor time ratio of agent i. By convention, we assume that the actual wage rate of an agent who does not work is $s_{\min}$.

An allocation $z_N \in X^N$ is *incentive compatible* if and only if there exists a list of individual wage rates $w_N \in S^N$ at which agents work such that no agent envies the bundle of any other agent working at a wage rate she could earn: for all $i, j \in N$,

$$s_i \geq w_j \Rightarrow (\ell_i, c_i) \, R_i \, (\ell_j, c_j). \tag{11.1}$$

We denote by $\widehat{Z}(E)$ the set of feasible incentive-compatible allocations for economy E when the policymaker observes labor times and earnings. Allocations that are Pareto undominated in $\widehat{Z}(E)$ are called *second-best efficient* for E when labor is observable.

There is a very convenient way of describing $\widehat{Z}(E)$. As the policymaker observes ℓ_i and $w_i \ell_i$, he or she can infer w_i. As a result, the policymaker can offer a tax function on labor time, $\tau_w : [0, 1] \to \mathbb{R}$, that is specific to each value of w. Agent $i \in N$ will then choose w_i and (ℓ_i, c_i), maximizing the agent's satisfaction subject to the constraint that

$$w_i \leq s_i$$
$$c_i \leq w_i \ell_i - \tau_{w_i}(\ell_i).$$

When $c_i = w_i \ell_i - \tau_{w_i}(\ell_i)$ for all $i \in N$, the allocation is feasible if and only if

$$\sum_{i \in N} \tau_{w_i}(\ell_i) \geq 0.$$

If the inequality is strict, we say that the allocation generates a budget surplus.

Every incentive-compatible allocation can be obtained by such a menu of tax functions. Moreover, as stated in the Lemma 11.1, every incentive-compatible allocation can be obtained in such a way that every $i \in N$ works at $w_i = s_i$ and is therefore submitted to the tax function τ_{s_i}. Intuitively, this is explained as follows. If an allocation is incentive-compatible, there exists, for each class of agents with a given skill s, an opportunity set in the (ℓ, c) space that contains the best bundle of all agents having an equal skill or a lower skill than theirs and that lies everywhere below their indifference curves.[1] The upper frontier of such sets can be used to construct suitable tax functions τ_s.

Lemma 11.1 *Let $E = (s_N, R_N) \in \mathcal{E}$. A feasible allocation $z_N = (\ell_N, c_N)$ for E is incentive-compatible when the policymaker observes labor time and earnings – that is, satisfies (11.1) – if and only if for all $w \in S$ there exists a tax function $\tau_w : [0, w] \to \mathbb{R}$ such that, for all $i \in N$:*

(a) $c_i = \ell_i s_i - \tau_{s_i}(\ell_i)$,
(b) for all $w \leq s_i, \ell \in [0, 1] : (\ell_i, c_i) \, R_i \, (\ell, \ell w - \tau_w(\ell))$.

Proof. Only if: Let $E = (s_N, R_N) \in \mathcal{E}$. Let $z_N = (\ell_N, c_N) \in \widehat{Z}(E)$. We need to construct a menu of τ_w satisfying the conditions of the lemma. Let $N_w = \{i \in$

---

[1] This equivalence between the no-envy property and the existence of a common opportunity set has been mentioned in the early literature on fairness.

$N \mid s_i \geq w\}$. For $w \in S$, let τ_w be such that the graph of $f_w(\ell) = w\ell - \tau_w(\ell)$ in the (ℓ, c) space is the lower envelope of the indifference curves of all individuals $j \in N$ such that $s_j \geq w$; that is,

$$\tau_w(\ell) = \sup\{t \in \mathbb{R} \mid \exists i \in N_w, \ (\ell, w\ell - t)\, R_i\, (\ell_i, c_i)\}.$$

To prove condition (a), we need to prove that for all $i \in N$, $\tau_{s_i}(\ell_i) = s_i \ell_i - c_i$. When $t = s_i \ell_i - c_i$, one has $(\ell_i, s_i \ell_i - t) = (\ell_i, c_i)$, implying $(\ell_i, s_i \ell_i - t)\, R_i\, (\ell_i, c_i)$ and therefore

$$s_i \ell_i - c_i \in \{t \in \mathbb{R} \mid \exists j \in N_{s_i}, \ (\ell_i, s_i \ell_i - t)\, R_j\, (\ell_j, c_j)\},$$

so necessarily, $\tau_{s_i}(\ell_i) \geq s_i \ell_i - c_i$. Suppose that $\tau_{s_i}(\ell_i) > s_i \ell_i - c_i$. By definition, there is $j \in N_{s_i}$ such that $(\ell_i, s_i \ell_i - \tau_{s_i}(\ell_i))\, R_j\, (\ell_j, c_j)$ and as $c_i > s_i \ell_i - \tau_{s_i}(\ell_i)$, by monotonicity one has $(\ell_i, c_i)\, P_j\, (\ell_j, c_j)$. This is precisely what incentive compatibility excludes.

We prove condition (b) in two steps. First, by construction, no part of the graph of f_{s_i} lies in the strict upper contour set of R_i at (ℓ_i, c_i), so (ℓ_i, c_i) is among the best bundles for i if i chooses to work at s_i. Second, we need to show that it is in i's interest to work at s_i. For all $w < w' \in S$, $N_w \supseteq N_{w'}$, so for all $\ell \in [0, 1]$, $\tau_w(\ell) \geq \tau_{w'}(\ell)$ (because $\tau_w(\ell)$ is the supremum of the union of more sets than $\tau_{w'}(\ell)$). Choosing a lower w than s_i only decreases (with respect to inclusion) the budget set of labor time-consumption bundles from which to choose.

If: Let $E = (s_N, R_N) \in \mathcal{E}$. Let $z_N = (\ell_N, c_N)$ be obtained from a menu of tax functions τ_w satisfying the two conditions of the lemma. Let $i, j \in N$ be such that $s_i \leq s_j$. By condition (a), $c_i = s_i \ell_i - \tau_{s_i}(\ell_i)$. By condition (b), $(\ell_j, c_j)\, R_j\, (\ell_i, s_i \ell_i - \tau_{s_i}(\ell_i))$, the desired outcome.   ∎

The consequence of this lemma is that we can restrict our attention to allocations such that each agent i chooses to work at his or her true skill level and freely chooses labor time given how her pretax income will be taxed by function τ_{s_i}.

Let us now model the second informational context that is considered in this chapter. The policymaker observes only earnings – that is, the pretax incomes $w_i \ell_i$. Note that, in this context, it is always best for agent $i \in N$ to earn any given gross income by working at his or her maximal wage rate $w_i = s_i$, as that minimizes the agent's labor time for a fixed level of consumption. We can, therefore, focus on allocations z_N and simply assume that $w_i = s_i$ for all $i \in N$. Also observe that by working $s_j \ell_j / s_i$, agent i obtains the same earnings as agent j.

An allocation $z_N \in X^N$ is *incentive compatible* if and only if no agent envies the earnings-consumption bundle of any other agent whose level of earnings this agent could reach with his or her own skill : for all $i, j \in N$,

$$s_i \geq s_j \ell_j \Rightarrow (\ell_i, c_i)\, R_i\, \left(\frac{s_j}{s_i}\ell_j, c_j\right). \tag{11.2}$$

We denote by $\widetilde{Z}(E)$ the set of feasible incentive-compatible allocations for economy E when the policymaker observes only earnings. Allocations that are Pareto undominated in $\widetilde{Z}(E)$ are called second-best efficient for E when labor is unobservable.

It will prove useful to concentrate on bundles described by earnings rather than by labor time. Let $i \in N$. Let $\ell, \ell' \in [0, 1]$, $y, y' \in \mathbb{R}_+$ be such that $y = s_i \ell$ and $y' = s_i \ell'$. As s_i is fixed, we can slightly abuse notation and write $(y, c) R_i (y', c')$ to denote $(\ell, c) R_i (\ell', c')$.

Again, there is a very convenient way of describing $\widetilde{Z}(E)$. As the policymaker observes $y_i = s_i \ell_i$, he or she can propose a tax function on earnings $\tau : \mathbb{R}_+ \to \mathbb{R}$. Agent $i \in N$ will then choose (y_i, c_i) maximizing his or her satisfaction subject to the constraint

$$c_i \leq y_i - \tau(y_i).$$

When $c_i = y_i - \tau(y_i)$ for all $i \in N$, the allocation is feasible if and only if

$$\sum_{i \in N} \tau(y_i) \geq 0.$$

Again, if the inequality is strict, the tax function is said to generate a budget surplus.

We now claim that any incentive-compatible allocation can be generated by such a tax function. The intuition for this result is identical to that of the previous one. Again, the fact that no-envy is equivalent to the free choice of agents in an equal opportunity set is essential.

Lemma 11.2 *Let $E = (s_N, R_N) \in \mathcal{E}$. A feasible allocation $z_N = (\ell_N, c_N)$ for E is incentive compatible when the policymaker observes only earnings – that is, satisfies (11.2) – if and only if there exists a tax function $\tau : \mathbb{R}_+ \to \mathbb{R}$ such that, letting $y_i = s_i \ell_i$, for all $i \in N$:*

(a) $c_i = y_i - \tau(y_i)$,
(b) for all $y \in [0, s_i]$, $(y_i, c_i) R_i (y, y - \tau(y))$.

The proof is similar to the proof of the previous lemma and is therefore omitted.

In this chapter, we study the properties of the choice of a policymaker when he or she maximizes one of the SOFs we axiomatized in the previous chapter, and when the policymaker faces one of the informational contexts we just described. For the sake of simplicity, given that skill is always assumed to be unobservable and earnings to be observable, we characterize the two informational structures by specifying only whether labor time is observable or not.

As incentive-compatible allocations can all be described in terms of tax functions, the second-best optimality exercise we carry on here is equivalent to evaluating tax functions. This justifies the title of the chapter.

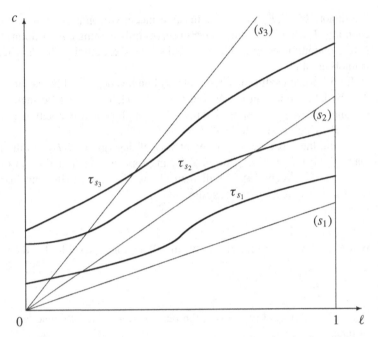

Figure 11.1. A menu of tax functions $\{\tau_s\}$ when labor time is observable

11.3 ASSESSING REFORMS

Our first second-best application deals with the evaluation of reforms. More precisely, let us assume that there is a status quo taxation scheme, and moreover, let us assume that it is not optimal for the SOF the policymaker is interested in. If the status quo must be slightly changed, where should it be changed – that is, who should pay slightly more tax, and who should pay less? We study this question here, in each of the two informational contexts identified in the previous section.

This application will again highlight the advantage of using SOFs built on the leximin aggregator. Indeed, identifying who should benefit from the reform is identical to identifying who is the worst off according to the particular well-being index embodied in the SOF.

Let us start with the case of observable labor time. Following Lemma 11.1, we assume that there exists a menu of tax functions satisfying the conditions listed previously. Figure 11.1 illustrates such a menu in a three-skill economy, with $s_1 < s_2 < s_3$. Thin lines represent the opportunity sets agents would face in the absence of any taxation. The τ_s functions are represented through the consumption functions $s_i \ell_i - \tau_{s_i}(\ell_i)$. There is a discontinuity at $\ell = 0$, as all curves must coincide at that point.

We assume that all points along the τ_s functions are relevant, that is, each point of these curves hits the indifference curve of at least one

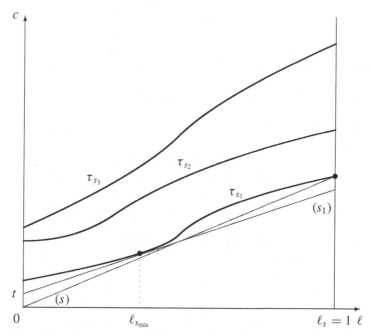

Figure 11.2. Evaluation of tax functions $\{\tau_s\}$ according to $\mathbf{R}^{s\text{lex}}$ or $\mathbf{R}^{s_{\min}\text{lex}}$.

agent.[2] Comparing the curves, we can see that all the low-skilled agents are subsidized (they end up with a higher consumption than without taxation), whereas middle- and high-skilled agents are subsidized only if their labor time is low.

Figure 11.2 illustrates how to identify the worst-off agents when the policy-maker's preferences correspond to $\mathbf{R}^{s\text{lex}}$ or $\mathbf{R}^{s_{\min}\text{lex}}$. Let us consider $\mathbf{R}^{s\text{lex}}$ first. The ray of slope s represented in the figure is the highest such ray that is below the graph of all curves. It is tangent to the consumption function associated to τ_{s_1} at $\ell_s = 1$. One can deduce that the indifference curve of agents choosing a labor time of ℓ_s is tangent to the ray of slope s. Their skill-equivalent utility is, therefore, equal to s. By a simple revealed-preferences argument, the graph shows that all other agents have a skill-equivalent utility at least as large as s. That proves that, for $\mathbf{R}^{s\text{lex}}$, low-skilled agents working full time are, in this example, the ones who should benefit from a reform. It need not be the case, in general, that hard-working low-skilled agents are the worst-off agents according to $\mathbf{R}^{s\text{lex}}$. The key parameter is the average consumption per unit of labor, $\left(s_i\ell_i - \tau_{s_i}(\ell_i)\right)/\ell_i$.

---

[2] In the case of a finite set of agents, this is achieved by assuming that the graph of the consumption function associated with τ_s functions is the lower envelope of the indifference curves of all agents with that skill.

Let us now turn to $\mathbf{R}^{s_{\min}\text{lex}}$. In Figure 11.2, we claim that the worst-off agents according to $\mathbf{R}^{s_{\min}\text{lex}}$ are the low-skilled agents choosing to work $\ell_{s_{\min}}$. Indeed, by a similar argument as previously, the indifference curve of agents choosing that labor time is tangent to the budget of slope $s_{\min}$ corresponding to a lump-sum subsidy of t. Moreover, the implicit budget of slope $s_{\min}$ of any agent choosing a different labor time is above the budget of that slope represented in the figure. That proves the claim. More generally, the worst-off agent is the low-skilled agent receiving the lowest subsidy, or equivalently, "paying" the largest tax, $\tau_{s_{\min}}(\ell)$.

Let us study the generality of two properties of the preceding example. First, both $\mathbf{R}^{s\text{lex}}$ and $\mathbf{R}^{s_{\min}\text{lex}}$ force us to conclude that worst-off agents are those with minimal skill. This property is, actually, fully general. The incentive-compatibility constraints, indeed, protect higher-skilled agents and provide them with larger opportunity sets, as proved in Lemma 11.1. It is therefore impossible for a higher-skilled agent to end up with a lower s-equivalent or $s_{\min}$-equivalent well-being level than the worst-off among the low-skilled agents.

Second, the labor time of the worst-off agents according to $\mathbf{R}^{s\text{lex}}$ is larger than that according to $\mathbf{R}^{s_{\min}\text{lex}}$. This comes from the fact that t, in the graph, is positive, so the slope of the ray that is used to identify the worst-off according to $\mathbf{R}^{s\text{lex}}$ is steeper than $s_{\min}$. It is easy to figure out that in the case $t = 0$, the two lines would coincide, so the worst-off agents would be the same. From this observation, we can conclude that if $\tau_{s_{\min}}$ is such that all the low-skilled agents are subsidized, then a policymaker maximizing $\mathbf{R}^{s\text{lex}}$ will focus on low-skilled agents working at least as much as those on which a policymaker maximizing $\mathbf{R}^{s_{\min}\text{lex}}$ would focus. If $\tau_{s_{\min}}$ is such that some low-skilled agents pay a strictly positive tax, then the conclusion is reversed.

Figure 11.3 illustrates how to identify the worst-off agents according to $\mathbf{R}^{\tilde{\ell}EW}$ for two values of $\tilde{\ell}$, $\tilde{\ell}^* < \tilde{\ell}^{**}$. First, identifying which agents, in each skill subgroup, is worse off, does not depend on $\tilde{\ell}$. Among low-skilled agents, the implicit budget of the worst-off is the same as when we apply $\mathbf{R}^{s_{\min}\text{lex}}$. In this example, they are the agents choosing a labor time of $\ell_{s_{\min}} = \tilde{\ell}^*$. Among higher-skilled agents, however, the implicit budgets are different, as $\mathbf{R}^{\tilde{\ell}EW}$ recommends to use the agents' actual skills to evaluate their well-being. In the graphical example, among s_2 and s_3 agents, the worst-off agents are those working full time.

Second, we have to compare the well-being of the worst-off across skill subgroups. The consequence of using implicit budgets of different slopes to evaluate the well-being of agents of different skills is drastic. With a low value of $\tilde{\ell}$, such as $\tilde{\ell}^*$, the worst-off agents in the economy are the high-skilled agents working full time. Their $\tilde{\ell}$-equivalent well-being index is

$$c_i - s_3\ell_i + s_3\tilde{\ell}^* = s_3\ell_i - \tau_{s_3}(\ell_i) - s_3\ell_i + s_3\tilde{\ell}^* = s_3\tilde{\ell}^* - \tau_{s_3}(\ell_i)$$

$$= s_3\tilde{\ell}^* - \tau_{s_3}(1).$$

The $\mathbf{R}^{\tilde{\ell}^*EW}$ SOF recommends in this example that the reform benefit the agents with the largest income. With a higher value of $\tilde{\ell}$, such as $\tilde{\ell}^{**}$, the ranking of

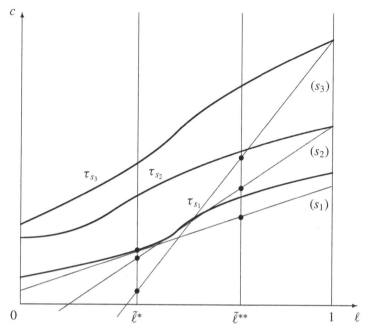

Figure 11.3. Evaluation of tax functions $\{\tau_s\}$ according to $\mathbf{R}^{\tilde{\ell}EW}$

the worst-off agents from each subgroup is different: low-skilled agents turn out to be worst-off. Their $\tilde{\ell}$-equivalent well-being index is now

$$c_i - s_1\ell_i + s_1\tilde{\ell}^{**} = s_1\ell_i - \tau_{s_1}(\ell_i) - s_1\ell_i + s_1\tilde{\ell}^{**} = s_1\tilde{\ell}^{**} - \tau_{s_1}(\ell_i)$$
$$= s_1\tilde{\ell}^{**} - \tau_{s_1}(\ell_{s_{\min}}).$$

The reform should then benefit low-skilled agents choosing a labor time of $\ell_{s_{\min}}$.

Three general features of reforms consistent with $\mathbf{R}^{\tilde{\ell}EW}$ can be derived from this example. First, it need no longer be the case that the worst-off agents in the economy are to be found among the minimal-skilled agents. It may even be the case that they are to be found among the highest-skilled agents. Second, an increase in the reference value $\tilde{\ell}$ benefits the low-skilled agents: the larger $\tilde{\ell}$, the lower the skill of the subgroup of agents on which the reform should focus. Third, the simple computation to make to identify the agents who should benefit in priority from the reform is to look for the lowest $s\tilde{\ell} - \tau_s(\ell)$ among all s and among all ℓ.

Let us now turn to the assumption of nonobservable labor time. Following Lemma 11.2, we assume that there is an income tax function τ, and we imagine that it represents the status quo from which a reform could depart. We need to identify the worst-off agents according to each of our SOFs.

Figure 11.4 illustrates a tax function in a similar three-skill economy as previously. The consumption function that is depicted has equation $y - \tau(y)$, so

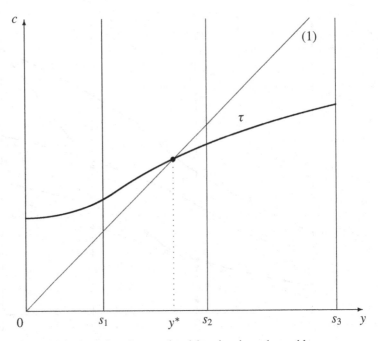

Figure 11.4. A tax function τ_s when labor time is unobservable

the tax corresponding to a level of pretax income is the difference between the line of slope 1 (that is, the no-taxation line) and the consumption level associated with that particular pretax income. Because of the incentive-compatibility constraints embedded in the figure, there is no loss of generality in assuming that this consumption function $f(y) = y - \tau(y)$ is nondecreasing. An earnings-consumption bundle in a strictly decreasing segment, indeed, could never be chosen by a rational agent, as this agent could get a larger consumption with a lower labor time.

In this example, all low-skilled agents receive a subsidy (they pay a negative tax). Among middle-skilled agents (respectively, high-skilled agents), those having a pretax income lower than y^*, that is, those working less than y^*/s_2 (respectively, y^*/s_3), receive a subsidy, and the others pay a tax. As earlier, we assume that all the points along the curve are relevant; that is, each point of the curve hits the indifference curve of at least one agent. Moreover, we assume that for each s_i, each point of the curve for incomes lower than s_i hits the indifference curve of at least one agent having this skill.

Figure 11.5 illustrates how to identify the worst-off agents when the policy-maker's objectives correspond with $\mathbf{R}^{slex}$. We need to distinguish two steps. First, the worst-off agents need to be identified in each skill subgroup. This is done in the same way as under the assumption of an observable labor time. In this example (and for the sake of clarity), it turns out that the worst-off among agents of each subgroup are the ones working full time. Second, we

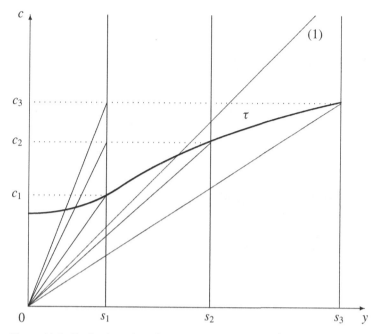

Figure 11.5. Evaluation of tax function τ according to $\mathbf{R}^{s\text{lex}}$

need to compare the s-equivalent well-being levels among the worst-off of each subgroup. In the graphical example, for each subgroup $j \in \{1, 2, 3\}$, that level is given by c_j/s_j. These numbers are not immediately comparable, as the denominators are expressed in terms of pretax income instead of labor time.

There is an easy way of comparing them, which involves rescaling them to express them in terms of a common labor time unit. This is illustrated in Figure 11.5. The ray of slope c_j/s_j for middle and high-skilled agents is rescaled so as to fit the way labor time is measured for low-skilled agents. We are left with comparing the quantities c_1/s_1, $c_2/(\frac{s_1}{s_2}s_2) = c_2/s_1$, and $c_3/(\frac{s_1}{s_3}s_3) = c_3/s_1$. Consequently, the simple observation that $c_1 \le c_2 \le c_3$ leads us to conclude that the worst-off agents among the low-skilled ones are also the worst-off in the entire population. Again, higher-skilled agents are protected by the incentive-compatibility constraints and can never end up enjoying a lower well-being level than the worst-off among the low-skilled agents.

In this example, therefore, the policymaker should reform the tax system so as to decrease the tax (increase the subsidy) of the low-skilled agents working full time. More generally, those who should benefit from a tax reform can be found by minimizing $(y - \tau(y))/y$, or simply maximizing $\tau(y)/y$, among the low-skilled agents – that is, among the pretax income levels $y \le s_{\min}$.

Figure 11.6 illustrates how to identify the worst-off agents when the policymaker's preferences correspond to $\mathbf{R}^{s_{\min}\text{lex}}$. It is again convenient to distinguish two steps. First, the worst-off agents need to be identified in each skill subgroup.

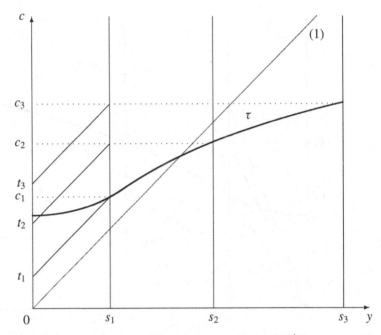

Figure 11.6. Evaluation of tax function τ according to $\mathbf{R}^{s_{\min}\text{lex}}$

This is done in the same way as under the assumption of an observable labor time, and as in the case of $\mathbf{R}^{s\text{lex}}$ in the previous paragraphs, the worst-off among agents of each subgroup, in this example, are the ones working full time. Second, we need to compare the $s_{\min}$-equivalent well-being levels among the worst-off agents from each subgroup. In each subgroup $j \in \{1, 2, 3\}$, that level is given by $c_j - s_{\min}\ell_j = c_j - s_{\min}$, as $\ell_j = 1$ for the worst-off agents. These operations are illustrated in the figure in the following way: Earnings-consumption bundles are first rescaled so they fit the low-skill consumption set. Then the three parallel lines correspond to the subtraction of $s_1 = s_{\min}$, and we get t_1, t_2, and t_3.

Again, nondecreasingness of the consumption function guarantees that $c_1 \leq c_2 \leq c_3$, which, in turn, is necessary and sufficient to get $t_1 \leq t_2 \leq t_3$. Again, the worst-off in the population must be found among low-skilled agents. In this example, therefore, the policymaker should reform the tax system to decrease the tax (increase the subsidy) of the low-skilled agents working full time. More generally, the beneficiary of a desirable tax reform can be found by minimizing $c - s_{\min}\ell = y - \tau(y) - s_{\min}(y/s_{\min}) = -\tau(y)$, or simply maximizing $\tau(y)$, among pretax income levels $y \leq s_{\min}$.

In our example, both $\mathbf{R}^{s\text{lex}}$ and $\mathbf{R}^{s_{\min}\text{lex}}$ force us to look at the shape of the tax function on low incomes. This is a fully general property, directly driven from the combination of the incentive-compatibility constraints and the fact that the well-being index we use does not depend on the agents' actual skills.

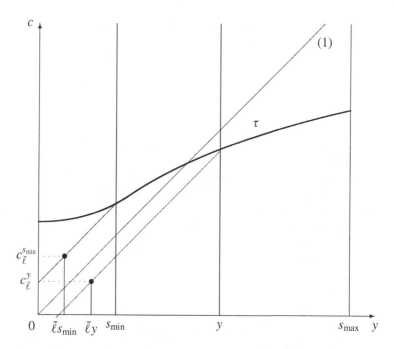

Figure 11.7. Evaluation of tax function τ according to $\mathbf{R}^{\tilde{\ell}EW}$.

The two SOFs also force us, in the examples given here, to look at low-skilled agents working full time. This, however, is not general. It may even be the case that $\mathbf{R}^{s\text{lex}}$ and $\mathbf{R}^{s_{\min}\text{lex}}$ force us to look at agents with different labor time. Again, the key condition is whether all low-skilled agents receive a subsidy. In this case, $\mathbf{R}^{s\text{lex}}$ focuses on agents working at least as much as those on which $\mathbf{R}^{s_{\min}\text{lex}}$ focuses. If some low-skilled agents pay a positive tax, then the opposite relation holds.

Let us now turn to $\mathbf{R}^{\tilde{\ell}EW}$ and show how it can be used to assess reforms. Figure 11.7 illustrates how to identify the worst-off agents when the policy-maker's preferences correspond to $\mathbf{R}^{\tilde{\ell}EW}$.

Again, in a first step, the worst-off agents need to be identified in each skill subgroup. Among the minimal-skilled agents, we need to construct implicit budgets that have a slope of $s_{\min}$. This is done in the same way as for $\mathbf{R}^{s_{\min}\text{lex}}$. In our example, the agents working full time (or being indifferent between their current bundle and working full time) have the lowest implicit budget. Should an agent, facing this budget, choose a labor time of $\tilde{\ell}$, she would enjoy a consumption level of $c_{\tilde{\ell}}^{s_{\min}} = s_{\min}\tilde{\ell} - \tau(s_{\min})$. This quantity measures the $\tilde{\ell}$-equivalent well-being index of the worst-off agents in the subgroup of minimal-skilled agents.

For any $y \in [s_{\min}, s_{\max}]$ such that there are agents with a skill level equal to y, we can compute the corresponding well-being level in a similar way,

Table 11.1. *Criteria to Evaluate Reforms, as a Function of the SOF and the Information Constraints*

	Observable labor	Unobservable labor
$\mathbf{R}^{s_{\min}\mathrm{lex}}$	$\min_{\ell\in[0,1]} -\tau_{s_{\min}}(\ell)$	$\min_{y\in[0,s_{\min}]} -\tau(y)$
$\mathbf{R}^{s\mathrm{lex}}$	$\min_{\ell\in[0,1]} \frac{-\tau_{s_{\min}}(\ell)}{\ell}$	$\min_{y\in[0,s_{\min}]} \frac{-\tau(y)}{y}$
$\mathbf{R}^{\tilde{\ell}EW}$	$\min_{s\in S,\ell\in[0,1]} \left(\tilde{\ell}s - \tau_s(\ell)\right)$	$\min_{s\in S, y\in[0,s]} \left(\tilde{\ell}s - \tau(y)\right)$

as exemplified in the figure. Among agents having a skill level equal to y, those working full time (or being indifferent between their current bundle and working full time) are the worst off. When evaluated according to $\mathbf{R}^{\tilde{\ell}EW}$, the implicit budget of agents of skill y working full time has a slope of y. That is the key difference from the previous SOFs. In the (y, c)-space, such a budget, represented from a point of y coordinate, has a slope of 1. Should an agent, facing this budget, choose a labor time of $\tilde{\ell}$, the agent would enjoy a consumption level of $c_{\tilde{\ell}}^{y} = \tilde{\ell}y - \tau(y)$. This quantity measures the $\tilde{\ell}$-equivalent well-being index of the worst-off agent in the subgroup of y-skilled agents.

Remember that it need not be the case that worst-off agents are those (indifferent to) working full time. In our example, it follows from the fact that the slope of the consumption function is lower than 1, which corresponds to a positive marginal tax rate. This is clearly the most relevant case, but it is not the only one. The most general result is that, among agents having a skill level equal to s, the worst-off have a well-being index equal to $\min_{y\in[0,s]}(\tilde{\ell}s - \tau(y))$. It is now easy to define the criterion that needs to be used to find the worst-off among the whole population: agents $i \in N$ having the lowest $\min_{y\in[0,s_i]}(\tilde{\ell}s_i - \tau(y))$ need to benefit in priority from a reform.

As it is clear from Figure 11.7, higher-skilled agents may have a lower well-being index than minimal-skilled agents: $c_{\tilde{\ell}}^{y} < c_{\tilde{\ell}}^{s_{\min}}$. This conclusion is similar to the one we reached under the assumption that labor time is observable: whereas our two SOFs grounded on the axiom of equal-preferences transfer (i.e., $\mathbf{R}^{s\mathrm{lex}}$ and $\mathbf{R}^{s_{\min}\mathrm{lex}}$) force us to find the worst-off agents among the low-skilled, the $\mathbf{R}^{\tilde{\ell}EW}$ family of SOFs, grounded on the axiom of equal-skill transfer, may lead us to claim that some higher-skilled agents pay too much income tax. Let us, again, observe that the latter conclusion depends on the value of $\tilde{\ell}$. In the example, $\tilde{\ell}$ is rather low (around $1/3$). For larger values of $\tilde{\ell}$, the well-being index values will change, and the ranking may change. For sufficiently large values of $\tilde{\ell}$, the low-skilled agents will be the worst off.

Let us now summarize the results obtained in this section about the evaluation of reforms using the SOFs characterized in the previous chapter.

- As a function of the SOF one is interested in, and as a function of the informational structure one faces, the worst-off agents are identified by minimizing the criteria in Table 11.1.
- Independent of the informational structure, both $\mathbf{R}^{s\mathrm{lex}}$ and $\mathbf{R}^{s_{\min}\mathrm{lex}}$ – that is, our SOFs satisfying equal-preferences transfer – recommend

focusing on low-skilled agents. On the contrary, $\mathbf{R}^{\tilde{\ell}EW}$, satisfying equal-skill transfer, may recommend that the reform benefit higher-skilled agents.

- Among low-skilled agents, $\mathbf{R}^{s\,\text{lex}}$ recommends that the reform benefit agents who work at least as much as those who should benefit from a reform based on $\mathbf{R}^{s_{\min}\text{lex}}$ if all low-skilled agents are currently subsidized (and, conversely, in the opposite case).

This section has illustrated that our SOFs can be used to derive simple criteria ready to be used to evaluate reforms. The exercise consists of identifying the agents who should benefit, in priority, from the reform. This exercise is made particularly easy by the fact that our SOFs are of the leximin type. Those who should benefit from a reform are those currently experiencing the lowest well-being index. Because of the constraints imposed by incentive compatibility, they are identified easily by analyzing the shape of the tax functions, which is a striking fact for the practical implementation of such criteria. No information about the distribution of characteristics of the population is needed; knowing the tax rules is enough.

11.4 OPTIMAL TAXATION SCHEMES IN A SIMPLE ECONOMY

The classical literature on optimal taxation has focused mostly on the design of the optimal tax scheme. A taxation scheme is optimal when it maximizes social preferences under incentive compatibility constraints. In this section and the next one, we derive some properties of the optimal tax schemes when social preferences are captured by the SOFs we characterized in Chapter 10 – $\mathbf{R}^{s\,\text{lex}}$, $\mathbf{R}^{s_{\min}\text{lex}}$, and $\mathbf{R}^{\tilde{\ell}EW}$. In this section, we begin our exploration with simple economies composed of four types of agents, similar to the economies we used in the previous chapter to illustrate the three SOFs in which we are interested. The study of a more general model will be tackled in the next section.

There are two possible skills, $s_1 < s_2$, and two possible preferences in the (ℓ, c) space, R_1 and R_2, such that R_1 exhibit a lower willingness to work than R_2 (that is, facing identical opportunity sets, a R_1 agent would always choose a lower labor time).[3]

Studying the optimal menu of tax functions when labor time is observable does not bring more insights and is not easier in this simple framework than in the general model. We postpone the study of this case to the next section. We therefore assume that labor time is not observable, so the tax can depend only on earned income, y_i. We have four types of agents; their preferences in the (y, c) space can be denoted R_{11}, R_{12}, R_{21}, and R_{22}, where the first index refers to skill and the second one to preferences. In the graphical illustrations, we assume that the four subgroups have the same size.

---

[3] This corresponds to the Spence–Mirrlees single-crossing condition in the (l, c) space among agents with the same skill.

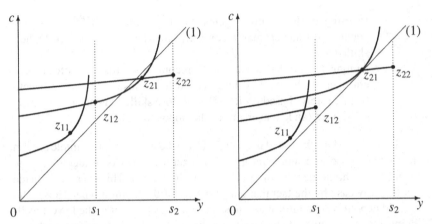

Figure 11.8. Incentive-compatible allocations in a simple economy where $z_{12} \neq z_{21}$

To make the problem of incentive compatibility more interesting, we assume that low-skilled high-willingness-to-work agents cannot be distinguished from high-skilled low-willingness-to-work ones. That is, for any bundles (y, ℓ), (y', ℓ') that are affordable to both types (that is, such that $y, y' \leq s_1$),

$$(y, \ell)\, R_{12}\, (y', \ell') \Leftrightarrow (y, \ell)\, R_{21}\, (y', \ell').$$

An allocation in that economy is a list $\left(z_{ij} = (y_{ij}, c_{ij})\right)_{i, j \in \{1,2\}}$. Figure 11.8 illustrates two incentive-compatible allocations where $z_{12} \neq z_{21}$. In the left-hand part of the figure, the two bundles are different, but agents of type 21 are indifferent between them. In the right-hand part, they strictly prefer the bundle they are assigned. The possibility of having $z_{12} \neq z_{21}$ comes from our assumption of an upper bound on labor time. In the classical literature, there is no such bound (and, therefore, nothing like a full-time job). To simplify the exposition and to be able to compare our results with the literature, we add the assumption that $z_{12} = z_{21}$.

Optimal allocations for $\mathbf{R}^{slex}$ and $\mathbf{R}^{s_{\min} lex}$ are illustrated in Figure 11.9. In the left-hand part of the figure, the allocation $(z_{11}, z_{12}, z_{21}, z_{22})$, with $z_{12} = z_{21}$, is optimal for $\mathbf{R}^{slex}$. The argument can be developed geometrically. First, the indifference curves of both types of low-skilled agents are tangent to the ray of slope s. This implies that they have the same well-being index, and it is equal to s. A ray of slope $s \frac{s_1}{s_2}$ is also drawn in the figure. It represents the implicit budget that agents of types 21 and 22 would face, should they enjoy a well-being of s as well. We see in the figure that both types of agents strictly prefer their bundle to choosing in that budget. Their well-being is therefore greater than s. The represented allocation does not succeed in equalizing the well-being indices of all the agents. One would like to further increase the well-being of types 11 and 12, at the expense of the others. However, it is impossible to decrease the well-being of type 21, as it is indistinguishable from type 12 (any deviation would

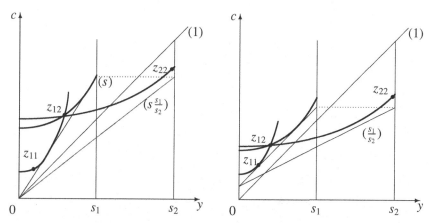

Figure 11.9. Optimal second-best allocations according to $\mathbf{R}^{s\text{lex}}$ (left) and $\mathbf{R}^{s_{\min}\text{lex}}$ (right)

violate the incentive compatibility constraint). It is also impossible to decrease the well-being of the agents of type 22. Indeed, as they are indifferent between z_{12} and z_{22}, any decrease in their well-being would give them the incentive to claim that they are of type 12. The incentive-compatibility constraint prevents us from improving the fate of the low-skilled agents. If such an allocation is second-best efficient – in the figure, it is – then it is optimal.

In the right-hand part of Figure 11.9, the allocation $(z_{11}, z_{12}, z_{21}, z_{22})$, with $z_{12} = z_{21}$, is optimal for $\mathbf{R}^{s_{\min}\text{lex}}$. Again, the indices are equalized among low-skilled agents, which is illustrated by the fact that both indifference curves are tangent to the same line of slope 1, which is equivalent to a slope of $s_{\min} = s_1$ in their (ℓ, c)-space. A similar implicit budget for the high-skilled agents is also represented in the figure, with a slope of s_1/s_2. As in the analysis relative to $\mathbf{R}^{s\text{lex}}$ in the previous paragraph, we observe that types 21 and 22 are strictly better off than if they were given the opportunity to choose from that budget. Their well-being index is therefore strictly larger than the low-skilled agents' index. We also observe that all incentive-compatibility constraints are binding, which, again, proves that if this allocation is second-best efficient – in the figure, it is – then it is optimal.

In Figure 11.10, the allocation $(z_{11}, z_{12}, z_{21}, z_{22})$, with $z_{12} = z_{21}$, is optimal for $\mathbf{R}^{\tilde{\ell}EW}$, for the represented value of $\tilde{\ell}$. Both low-skilled agents maximize over a budget of slope 1, so, again, their well-being index is equalized. The value of their well-being index is the consumption level they could afford by having a labor time of $\tilde{\ell}$ over that budget – that is, by consuming $\tilde{\ell}s_1$, represented in the figure.

Agents of type 22 are consuming z_{22}, a bundle they strictly prefer to $z_{12} = z_{21}$. The incentive compatibility constraint preventing agents of type 22 to claim they are of type 12 is not binding. That does not mean, though, that the well-being of type 12 should be increased. Indeed, agents of type 22 have exactly

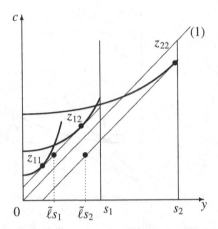

Figure 11.10. Optimal second-best allocations according to $\mathbf{R}^{\tilde{\ell}EW}$

the same well-being. This is computed by considering the implicit budget to which agents 22 are indifferent, represented in the figure. Given that budget (of slope 1), the consumption level $\tilde{\ell}s_2$ these agents would obtain by working $\tilde{\ell}$ is exactly the same as the low-skilled agents' level. Any further redistribution from high-skilled to low-skilled agents would therefore decrease the minimal well-being index in the population. Let us even observe that this allocation is first-best efficient (all slopes of the indifference curves are equal to 1 in the (y, c)-space).[4] This completes the proof that this allocation is optimal.

A larger value of $\tilde{\ell}$ would have increased the level of redistribution from agents of type 22 to low-skilled agents, with the consequence that the incentive-compatibility constraint would end up being binding. A lower value of $\tilde{\ell}$ would have decreased redistribution even more. At the limit, when $\tilde{\ell} = 0$, the policy of no redistribution – that is, laissez-faire – would be optimal for $\mathbf{R}^{\tilde{\ell}EW}$. This observation confirms that SOFs based on the leximin criterion do not necessarily call for a large redistribution.

Having identified the properties of optimal second-best allocations for our SOFs, we can deduce the following results:

- The incentive-compatibility constraints of high-skilled agents are always binding when the policymaker maximizes a SOF satisfying equal-preferences transfer. This follows from the fact that absolute priority is given to low-skilled agents. This property does not necessarily hold if the policymaker maximizes a SOF satisfying equal-skill transfer.
- Independently of which SOF is maximized, taxation is never progressive among low-skilled agents. Indeed, the amount transferred to

---

[4] With other values of $\tilde{\ell}$ or in other economies, the optimal allocation for $\mathbf{R}^{\tilde{\ell}EW}$ need not be first-best efficient.

low-skilled hardworking agents, type 12 agents, is always at least as large as the amount transferred to low-skilled low-willingness-to-work agents, type 11 agents.[5] Moreover, in the case of $\mathbf{R}^{slex}$, it is strictly larger. This result will be confirmed in the next section.

- Finally, even if our social preferences are of the leximin type, they may lead to a very limited redistribution, as exemplified by the $\mathbf{R}^{\tilde{\ell}EW}$ SOF with a small $\tilde{\ell}$. The intuition for this result is the following: The well-being index associated with the $\mathbf{R}^{\tilde{\ell}EW}$ SOF is equalized among agents when all agents working $\tilde{\ell}$ have the same consumption level, independent of their skill. For lower values of $\tilde{\ell}$, the redistribution necessary to equalize that consumption level among agents working $\tilde{\ell}$ is also lower. At the limit, if the policymaker wishes to equalize the consumption of all agents choosing not to work, then no redistribution is necessary.

Boadway et al. (2002) study the same two-skill two-preferences model under the assumptions that preferences are quasilinear in leisure and that there is no upper bound on the labor time. They study utilitarian social preferences; that is, they equip each set of preferences R_1 and R_2 with a numerical representation u_1 and u_2, linear in consumption, and social welfare is defined as a sum of individual utility levels. They show that when social preferences are utilitarian, the optimal allocations can be associated with a list of binding incentive-compatibility constraints very different from what we obtain here. In particular, it may be the case that redistribution benefits the agents of type 22. This cannot occur here because these agents always have the greatest index of well-being at the laissez-faire allocation, and we apply the maximin criterion. This proves that allocations maximizing one of the social preferences discussed in this chapter form a strict subset of the second-best efficient allocations.

Closer to what we develop here, they study the consequences of a family of utilitarian social preferences that give absolute priority to low-skilled agents in the sense that the weight assigned to the others' utility is zero, whereas the weights given to the utilities of agents with different preferences, among the low-skilled, may vary. Boadway et al. then also reach the conclusion that redistribution may be regressive among low-skilled agents. This illustrates another difference between our approach and classical taxation theory. In the latter, different conclusions are drawn about the optimal tax as a function of the weights that are assigned to different agents. These weights represent the policymaker's ethical preferences. In the former, different conclusions are drawn as a function of which SOFs is maximized – that is, as a function of which axioms capture the policymaker's ethical preferences.

---

[5] Recall that the transfers are measured by the vertical distance between the bundles agents are assigned and the no-tax 45° line.

11.5   OPTIMAL TAXATION SCHEMES

In this section we turn to the general model. All results presented here are drawn from Fleurbaey and Maniquet (2006, 2007, 2011). Formal proofs of the results can be found in those sources. We focus here on intuitive presentations.

There are two main differences between the SOFs we study in this section and the typical social preferences that are used in the classical literature on optimal taxation. The first difference comes from the aggregator. All our SOFs are of the leximin (or maximin) type, whereas the literature has concentrated on utilitarian SOFs.[6] The second difference comes from the indices that are aggregated. Our SOFs aggregate indices of well-being that are axiomatically derived from some notion of equality of resources. The classical utilitarian SOFs aggregate utility levels coming from some exogenous utility function. In the latter case, the most frequent assumption is that all agents have the same utility function (and, therefore, the same preferences). One of the main achievements of the classical literature has been to provide us with the exact formula of the optimal tax scheme under various assumptions.

As it is clear, now, a key feature of our taxation model is that agents differ in both their skill and their preferences. This double heterogeneity has a direct consequence on our objective: it becomes almost impossible to derive the formula of the optimal tax scheme analytically. Optimal tax schemes must be derived from the maximization of the criteria we defined in Section 11.3 under the proper incentive compatibility constraints. As we insisted earlier, these criteria are simple. On the other hand, characterizing the set of incentive-compatible allocations to be able to find the best allocation is an extremely difficult task. This explains why some of our results will be stated in the following format: if this or that tax scheme is second-best efficient, then it is optimal.

On the other hand, the tax schemes we will be able to point out have several properties that can be related to our objective of fairness. Identifying these properties is a key goal of second-best applications of our SOF approach. The main properties we will identify will be a zero or negative marginal tax rate on low incomes.[7]

Let us begin with the case of observable labor time. Our first formal result is that an optimal allocation for $\mathbf{R}^{\ell EW}$ or $\mathbf{R}^{s_{\min}\text{lex}}$ can be obtained by a menu $\{\tau_s\}$ such that the individuals with the lowest skill face a zero marginal tax.

---

[6] There are, however, important studies of the maximin criterion in Atkinson (1973, 1995) and Boadway and Jacquet (2008), among others.

[7] In recent developments of optimal taxation theory (Choné and Laroque 2005, Lee and Saez 2008, Kaplow 2008), the assumption of identical preferences has been dropped, and some consequences of the heterogeneity in agents' preferences on the shape of optimal tax schemes have been identified. In the models focusing on participation (the agents choosing only whether they work full time or do not work at all), it has appeared that a negative marginal tax rate may be second-best efficient (whereas the key result of Mirrlees' [1971] seminal paper was that it had to be positive or zero).

With $\mathbf{R}^{slex}(E)$, the average marginal tax for the low-skilled agents must be nonpositive.

Theorem 11.1 *Assume labor time is observable. Let* $E = (s_N, R_N) \in \mathcal{E}$. *Every second-best optimal allocation for* $\mathbf{R}^{s_{\min}lex}(E)$ *or* $\mathbf{R}^{\tilde{\ell}EW}(E)$ *can be obtained by a menu* $\{\tau_s\}$ *such that* $\tau_{s_{\min}}$ *is a nonpositive constant-valued function. Every second-best optimal allocation for* $\mathbf{R}^{slex}(E)$ *can be obtained by a menu* $\{\tau_s\}$ *such that* $\tau_{s_{\min}}$ *satisfies* $\tau_{s_{\min}}(\ell) \geq \tau_{s_{\min}}(1)$ *for all* $\ell \in [0, 1]$.

The intuition for this result goes as follows. Let z_N be an optimal allocation for $\mathbf{R}^{s_{\min}lex}(E)$. Following the proof of Lemma 11.1, one can construct the menu $\{\tau_s\}$ that implements this allocation in such a way that higher-skilled agents get better budget sets – that is, for all $\ell \in [0, 1]$, all $s > s'$, $s\ell - \tau_s(\ell) \geq s'\ell - \tau_{s'}(\ell)$, and every agent $i \in N$ picks his or her bundle from the budget defined by τ_{s_i}. Let b denote the lowest well-being level in the population at the optimal allocation.

Let us change the tax menu by simply replacing $\tau_{s_{\min}}$ with $\tau'_{s_{\min}}$, defined by: $\tau'_{s_{\min}}(\ell) = -b$, for all $\ell \in [0, 1]$. Observe that $\tau'_{s_{\min}}$ satisfies the requirement of the theorem. We claim that for all low-skilled agents, $c_i = s_{\min}\ell_i + b$, so z_N is still obtained with the new menu and the desired conclusion of the theorem is satisfied.

First, it is impossible that some low-skilled agent j has $c_j < s_{\min}\ell_j + b$ because this would imply that this agent's well-being level is less than b, contradicting the assumption that the lowest level is b. Now, suppose that there is a low-skilled agent j such that $c_j > s_{\min}\ell_j + b$. Under the new menu, there is a new allocation z'_N in which this agent "pays" $\tau'_{s_{\min}}(\ell'_j) = -b > s_{\min}\ell_j - c_j = \tau_{s_{\min}}(\ell_j)$. As $\tau'_{s_{\min}}(\ell'_i) = -b \geq \tau_{s_{\min}}(\ell_i)$ for all low-skilled i, and $z'_i = z_i$ for all higher-skilled agents, the new menu generates a budget surplus. At the new allocation z'_N the lowest well-being level is still b, and it is now attained by all low-skilled agents. One can redistribute the budget surplus of z'_N and obtain another feasible and incentive-compatible allocation z''_N that strictly Pareto-dominates z'_N. The lowest well-being level at z''_N is greater than b, which contradicts the assumption that z_N is optimal. This proves the claim of the previous paragraph.

The reasoning is identical if one looks at $\mathbf{R}^{\tilde{\ell}EW}(E)$. If c denotes the lowest well-being level at the optimal allocation, then the new tax function $\tau'_{s_{\min}}$ one should look at is $\tau'_{s_{\min}}(\ell) = -(c - s_{\min}\tilde{\ell})$, for all $\ell \in [0, 1]$. Apart from that slight change, the proof is similar.

The reasoning is also similar for $\mathbf{R}^{slex}(E)$. If s denotes the lowest well-being level at the optimal allocation, the new tax function $\tau'_{s_{\min}}$ is defined by $\tau'_{s_{\min}}(\ell) = \max\left\{\tau_{s_{\min}}(\ell), \tau_{s_{\min}}(1)\right\}$.

Theorem 11.1 is a key result of this chapter. The axioms that justify $\mathbf{R}^{s_{\min}lex}$ and $\mathbf{R}^{slex}$, on the one hand, and $\mathbf{R}^{\tilde{\ell}EW}$, on the other hand, are drastically different. The former SOFs satisfy equal-preferences transfer and, consequently, are definitely on the compensation side of the dilemma that we studied in the

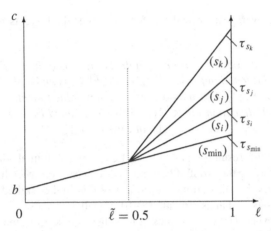

Figure 11.11. Optimal second-best allocations according to $\mathbf{R}^{\tilde{\ell}EW}$ when labor time is observable

previous chapter. The latter SOF satisfies equal-skill transfer and, consequently, is on the responsibility side of the dilemma. In spite of these opposing properties, second-best optimality, when labor time is observable, yields tax functions that exhibit a remarkable common feature: the marginal tax rate should be zero (or, on average, no greater than zero) on the earnings of low-skilled agents.

Under the assumption of observable labor time, $\mathbf{R}^{\tilde{\ell}EW}(E)$ turns out to be easier to study than the other SOFs. The next result is our first characterization of an optimal second-best allocation.

Theorem 11.2 *Assume labor time is observable. Let $E = (s_N, R_N) \in \mathcal{E}$ be such that for all $i \in N$, there is $j \in N$ such that $R_j = R_i$ and $s_j = s_{\min}$, and let $b \geq 0$. For each $s \in S$, let τ_s be defined by:*

$$\tau_s(\ell) = \begin{cases} (s - s_{\min})\ell - b & \text{if } \ell \leq \tilde{\ell} \\ (s - s_{\min})\tilde{\ell} - b & \text{if } \ell \geq \tilde{\ell}. \end{cases}$$

If an allocation obtained with the menu $\{\tau_s\}$ is second-best efficient, then it is second-best optimal for $\mathbf{R}^{\tilde{\ell}EW}(E)$.

Figure 11.11 represents a tax menu satisfying the definition given in the theorem. By construction, all low-skilled agents have an $\tilde{\ell}$-equivalent well-being level of $b + s_{\min}\tilde{\ell}$. All higher-skilled agents working more than $\tilde{\ell}$ have the same well-being level, as their actual budget coincides with their implicit budget for all labor time weakly greater than $\tilde{\ell}$. The allocation generated by this menu of tax functions has the property that all agents working more than $\tilde{\ell}$ must be considered as equally bad off as the low-skilled agents. The only agents with a well-being level larger than $b + s_{\min}\tilde{\ell}$ are among the higher-skilled agents choosing to work less than $\tilde{\ell}$.

Assume that the allocation z_N generated by $\{\tau_s\}$ is second-best efficient. The intuition of the proof that it must be optimal is the following. Suppose that there exists another feasible and incentive-compatible allocation z'_N with a lowest well-being level that is greater than $b + s_{\min}\tilde{\ell}$. As z_N is second-best efficient, necessarily some agents are worse-off in z'_N. Given the observation we made in the previous paragraph, such agents cannot be low-skilled agents or agents choosing to work more than $\tilde{\ell}$, because their well-being level is the lowest at z_N. Consequently, any agent that is worse-off in the second allocation is a higher-skilled agent working less than $\tilde{\ell}$.

Here is where the assumption of the theorem about preferences enters into play. At least one low-skilled agent has the same preferences as that higher-skilled agent, makes the same choice (from a smaller budget) at z_N, and, consequently, must also be worse-off in z'_N than in z_N. This, however, contradicts the previous paragraph, and concludes the argument.

This result may seem to have limited scope because it is generally unlikely that the menu $\{\tau_s\}$, as defined in the proposition, generates a second-best efficient allocation. One can, however, safely conjecture that if the allocation obtained with this menu is not too inefficient, the optimal tax menu is close to $\{\tau_s\}$. For $\tilde{\ell} = 0$, this menu corresponds to the laissez-faire policy (one must then have $b = 0$), which yields an efficient allocation and is indeed optimal for $\mathbf{R}^{0EW}(E)$. The likelihood that the optimal menu is close to $\{\tau_s\}$ therefore increases when $\tilde{\ell}$ is smaller.

In practice, a menu such as $\{\tau_s\}$ is easy to enforce (assuming that labor time or wage rates are observable), and one can then proceed to check whether it generates large inefficiencies.

We now turn our attention to the second informational structure – that is, we now assume that labor time is no longer observable. When labor time is not observable, the optimal tax scheme is complex to analyze when there is no restriction on the distribution of skills and preferences. For the next results of this section, we need restrictions on the distribution of types in the economy. The intuitive meaning of these restrictions is that pretax income is not too informative a signal of one's type. More precisely, the idea is that over an interval of income $[0, s]$, it is impossible, by looking only at preferences restricted to that interval of income, to identify agents with greater productivity than s and distinguish them, on the basis of their preferences, from agents with productivity s.

The first assumption applies this idea to the interval $[0, s_{\min}]$ and requires that for any agent, there exists a low-skilled agent who has the same preferences in (y, c) space over the relevant range.

Assumption 11.1 *For all $i \in N$, there is $j \in N$ such that $s_j = s_{\min}$ and for all $(y, c), (y', c') \in [0, s_{\min}] \times \mathbb{R}_+$:*

$$\left(\frac{y}{s_j}, c\right) R_j \left(\frac{y'}{s_j}, c'\right) \Leftrightarrow \left(\frac{y}{s_i}, c\right) R_i \left(\frac{y'}{s_i}, c'\right).$$

The second restriction is more demanding and extends the idea to all relevant intervals. It requires that for any agent and any skill lower than that of this agent, there exists another agent with that lower skill who is indistinguishable in the relevant range. Let $\mathcal{S}(E)$ denote the set of skills in the current profile:

$$\mathcal{S}(E) = \{s \in S \mid \exists i \in N, \ s_i = s\}.$$

Assumption 11.2 *For all $i \in N$, all $s \in \mathcal{S}(E)$ such that $s < s_i$, there is $j \in N$ such that $s_j = s$ and for all $(y, c), (y', c') \in [0, s] \times \mathbb{R}_+$:*

$$\left(\frac{y}{s_j}, c\right) R_j \left(\frac{y'}{s_j}, c'\right) \Leftrightarrow \left(\frac{y}{s_i}, c\right) R_i \left(\frac{y'}{s_i}, c'\right).$$

These assumptions are a generalization of the restriction made in the previous section, in which agents of types 12 and 21 could not be distinguished. Let us insist that even if they are restrictive, we impose them only to exclude the implausible case in which fiscal authorities can design the tax for some interval $[y, y']$ (and, in particular, apply very high tax rates over that interval) knowing that only agents having an ability to earn much greater incomes would ever end up with an income in this interval.

Our first result is reminiscent of Theorem 11.1. Even when labor time is unobservable, both $\mathbf{R}^{s_{\min}\text{lex}}$ and $\mathbf{R}^{\tilde{\ell}EW}$ recommend to assign the same subsidy to all agents earning less than $s_{\min}$.

Theorem 11.3 *Assume labor time is unobservable. Let $E = (s_N, R_N) \in \mathcal{E}$ satisfy Assumption 11.1. Every second-best optimal allocation for $\mathbf{R}^{s_{\min}\text{lex}}(E)$ or $\mathbf{R}^{\tilde{\ell}EW}(E)$ can be obtained by a tax function τ that is constant over $[0, s_{\min}]$.*

The intuition for this result is similar to the intuition of Theorem 11.1. Let z_N be an optimal allocation with lowest well-being level b. Consider a tax function such as τ represented in Figure 11.12, constructed so the budget set is the lower envelope of the indifference curves of the population. In the figure, it does not satisfy the property stated in the theorem. By Assumption 11.1, the part of the budget set corresponding to $y \in [0, s_{\min}]$ is the lower envelope of the indifference curves of the low-skilled agents. Therefore b equals the lowest value of $-\tau(y)$ for $y \in [0, s_{\min}]$.

Now, consider the new tax function τ' and the resulting allocation z'_N. It consists of applying a constant amount of subsidy, b, to all income levels y such that $-\tau(y) \geq b$. In the figure, this affects all incomes lower than y'. Beyond y', τ and τ' coincide. This rise in taxation keeps the minimal well-being level identical among agents earning less than $s_{\min}$, and it does not affect that of agents earning more than y' (those agents choose the same earnings under τ as under τ'). The agents earning between $s_{\min}$ and y' in z_N may be worse off in z'_N, but the lowest well-being level in z'_N, over the whole population, is still b.

If z_N can be obtained with τ', the conclusion of the theorem is satisfied. If z_N cannot be obtained with τ', this means that the tax paid by at least one agent has increased in z'_N. As, by construction, no agent has benefited from a tax reduction, the allocation generated by τ' generates a budget surplus. By

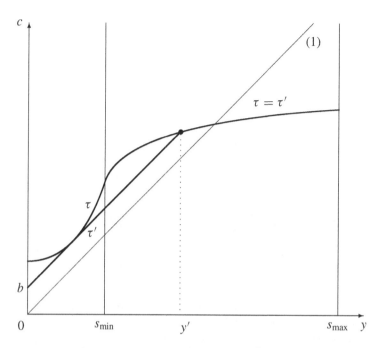

Figure 11.12. Optimal allocations for $\mathbf{R}^{s_{\min}\text{lex}}$ and $\mathbf{R}^{\tilde{\ell}EW}$ have a zero marginal rate on low incomes.

redistributing that surplus to all agents (which can be done by slightly translating τ' upward), we can obtain a new allocation that strictly Pareto dominates the previous one, thereby strictly increasing its lowest well-being level above b, and contradicting the fact that the initial allocation z_N was optimal.

Our last three results are partial characterizations of the optimal allocations according to our three SOFs. Let us now examine the optimal allocations for $\mathbf{R}^{s_{\min}\text{lex}}$. The following theorem is almost a corollary of the previous one.

Theorem 11.4 *Assume labor time is unobservable. Let $E = (s_N, R_N) \in \mathcal{E}$ satisfy Assumption 11.1. A tax function maximizing $\mathbf{R}^{s_{\min}\text{lex}}(E)$ can be computed by minimizing $\tau(s_{\min})$ under the constraints that*

$$\tau(y) = \tau(s_{\min}), \text{ for all } y \leq s_{\min}$$

$$\tau(y) \geq \tau(s_{\min}), \text{ for all } y > s_{\min}.$$

The first constraint is a repetition of the zero marginal tax result of the previous theorem. The second constraint follows from the construction given earlier.

Theorem 11.4 is illustrated in Figure 11.13. In the earnings-consumption space, computing the optimal tax amounts to maximize the height of the point

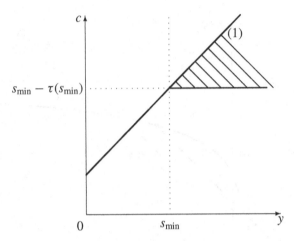

Figure 11.13. Optimal second-best allocations according to $\mathbf{R}^{s_{\min}\text{lex}}$ when labor time is unobservable

$(s_{\min}, s_{\min} - \tau(s_{\min}))$ under the constraint that the income function $y - \tau(y)$ must be located in the area delineated by the thick lines.

Let us now turn to the study of our second SOF.

Theorem 11.5 *Assume labor time is unobservable. Let $E = (s_N, R_N) \in \mathcal{E}$ satisfy Assumption 11.1. A tax function maximizing $\mathbf{R}^{s\text{lex}}$ can be computed by maximizing the net income of the hardworking poor, $s_{\min} - \tau(s_{\min})$, under the constraints that*

$$\frac{\tau(y)}{y} \leq \frac{\tau(s_{\min})}{s_{\min}} \quad \text{for all } y \in (0, s_{\min}],$$

$$\tau(y) \geq \tau(s_{\min}) \quad \text{for all } y,$$

$$\tau(0) \leq 0.$$

The three constraints mean, respectively, that the average tax rate on low incomes is always lower than at $s_{\min}$, that the tax (subsidy) is the smallest (largest) at $s_{\min}$, and that the tax (subsidy) is nonpositive (nonnegative) at 0.

Theorem 11.5 is illustrated in Figure 11.14. From the point $(s_{\min}, s_{\min} - \tau(s_{\min}))$ one can construct the hatched area delimited by an upper line of slope 1 and a lower boundary made of the ray to the origin (on the left) and a flat line (on the right). Theorem 11.5 says that computing the optimal tax may, without welfare loss, be done by maximizing the second coordinate of the point $(s_{\min}, s_{\min} - \tau(s_{\min}))$ under the constraint that the income function $y - \tau(y)$ is located in the corresponding hatched area.

The intuition of this theorem parallels that of the previous one. First, the lower bound on the amount of taxes, or, as illustrated in the figure, the upper bound on the consumption function follows the same logic as the one illustrated in Figure 11.12: if the tax scheme does not satisfy this lower bound, then it is

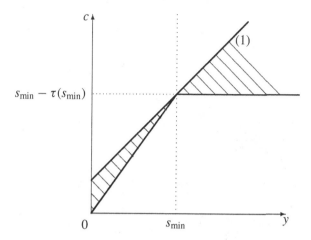

Figure 11.14. Optimal second-best allocations according to $\mathbf{R}^{slex}$ when labor time is unobservable

possible to construct another tax scheme that has this property and generates an allocation with the same associated lowest level of well-being.

Second, the upper bound on the amount of taxes, or the lower bound on the consumption function, follows from the criterion that should be maximized. As proved in the earlier section on reforms, we should try to maximize the average rate of subsidy among agents earning less than s_{min}. That amounts to maximizing the consumption level of hardworking poor agents, under the constraint that no poorer agent gets a lower average rate of subsidy, as stated in the theorem.

This result does not say that every optimal tax must satisfy these constraints, but it says, quite relevantly for the social policymaker, that there is no problem – that is, no welfare loss – in restricting attention to taxes satisfying those constraints, when looking for the optimal allocation. This result shows how the social preferences defined in this chapter lead to focusing on the hardworking poor, who should get, in the optimal allocation, the greatest *absolute amount* of subsidy, among the whole population. However, the taxes computed for those with a lower income than s_{min} also matter, as those agents must obtain at least as great a *rate of subsidy* as the hardworking poor.

Our last result is a partial characterization of the optimal tax function according to $\mathbf{R}^{\tilde{\ell}EW}$. Let $\tilde{\ell} \in [0, 1]$. Let us define the following tax function:

(a) for all $y \in [0, s_{min}]$, $\tau(y) = \tau(0) \leq 0$;
(b) for all $s, s' \in S$ such that $s < s'$ and $s < s_i < s'$ for no $i \in N$, all $y \in [s, s']$,

$$\tau(y) = \min\{\tau(0) + (s - s_{min})\tilde{\ell} + (y - s), \ \tau(0) + (s' - s_{min})\tilde{\ell}\}.$$

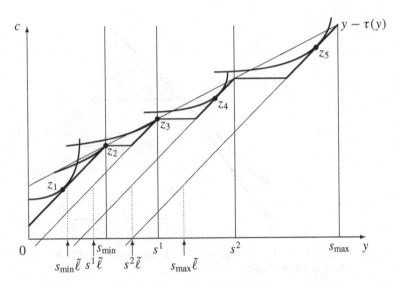

Figure 11.15. Optimal second-best allocations according to $\mathbf{R}^{\tilde{\ell}EW}$ when labor time is unobservable

A tax function of this kind will be called an $\tilde{\ell}$-type tax. This formula calls for some explanation. The tax function is piecewise linear. The segment on low incomes $[0, s_{\min}]$ is constant, with a fixed subsidy $-\tau(0)$. Then comes a segment, $[s_{\min}, y^1]$, for some y^1 between $s_{\min}$ and the next element s^1 of $\mathcal{S}(E)$, where the rate of taxation is 100 percent. Of course, no individual is expected to earn an income in this interval. The next segment covers the interval $[y^1, s^1]$, and has a zero marginal tax rate. The function continues with successive pairs of intervals, one with 100 percent marginal tax and the other with a zero marginal tax. The key feature is that the points $(s, \tau(s))$, for $s \in \mathcal{S}(E)$, are aligned, and the slope of the line is precisely $\tilde{\ell}$; that is, for all $s, s' \in \mathcal{S}(E)$,

$$\frac{\tau(s) - \tau(s')}{s - s'} = \tilde{\ell}.$$

When $\mathcal{S}(E)$ is a large set with elements spread over the interval $[s_{\min}, s_{\max}]$, the tax function is therefore approximately a flat tax (constant marginal tax rate of $\tilde{\ell}$), except for the $[0, s_{\min}]$ interval, where it is constant.

The corresponding budget set delineated by $y - \tau(y)$ is illustrated in Figure 11.15, in which the indifference curves of five individuals are also depicted. Our last result follows.

Theorem 11.6 *Assume labor time is unobservable. Let $E = (s_N, R_N) \in \mathcal{E}$ satisfy Assumption 11.2. If an allocation obtained with an $\tilde{\ell}$-type tax is second-best efficient, then it is second-best optimal for $\mathbf{R}^{\tilde{\ell}EW}(E)$.*

The proof proceeds in two steps. First, we identify the worst-off agents among agents of the same skill subgroup. As it is often the case, they will be those working full time, or, more generally, those having the largest labor time in their subgroup. Second, we compare the well-being level of the agents who are the worst-off in their subgroup. The $\tilde{\ell}$-type tax scheme is constructed in the precise way that equalizes the minimal well-being across skill subgroups. Let us go through each step in greater detail.

An interesting property of an $\tilde{\ell}$-type tax function τ is that for all $i \in N$, if i chooses a bundle that is on the segment with slope 1 (zero marginal tax) just below s_i, then

$$u_{\tilde{\ell}}(z_i, s_i, R_i) = -\tau(0) + s_{\min}\tilde{\ell}.$$

Let us illustrate this fact in the case of individual 4, assuming that $s_4 = s^2$. From the second term in the definition of τ, one has

$$\tau(y_4) = \tau(0) + (s^2 - s_{\min})\tilde{\ell},$$

Bundle z_4 is optimal for R_4 in the budget set for which this level of tax is lump-sum. Therefore one simply has

$$\begin{aligned} u_{\tilde{\ell}}(z_4, s_4, R_4) &= -\tau(y_4) + s^2\tilde{\ell} \\ &= -\tau(0) + s_{\min}\tilde{\ell}, \end{aligned}$$

which achieves the proof.

If we assume that agent 4 has a larger skill than s^2, such as $s_{\max}$, then agent 4's implicit budget is larger than that of agents with the same skill, such as agent 5. Agent 4, in that case, would have a larger implicit budget than agent 5, and, therefore, a larger well-being level. By Assumption 11.2, there exists an agent of skill s^2 who is undistinguishable from agent 4. The well-being of that agent is $-\tau(0) + s_{\min}\tilde{\ell}$. This proves that there necessarily exists an agent of skill s^2 with a well-being level of $-\tau(0) + s_{\min}\tilde{\ell}$, the lowest well-being level among agents of that skill.

The second step consists of checking that the quantity $-\tau(0) + s_{\min}\tilde{\ell}$ is independent of s_i. This tax function therefore equalizes $u_{\tilde{\ell}}$ across individuals who work full time or just below full time. This equality can be seen in Figure 11.15, in which the vertical segments at $s_{\min}\tilde{\ell}$, $s^1\tilde{\ell}$, $s^2\tilde{\ell}$, and $s_{\max}\tilde{\ell}$ between the horizontal axis and the lines of slope 1 corresponding to each of these values of s all have the same length.

Finally, suppose that there exists another feasible and incentive-compatible allocation z'_N with a greater minimal $u_{\tilde{\ell}}$. As z_N is second-best efficient, some agents must be worse-off in z'_N than in z_N. As z_N is optimal, such agents must have a greater well-being in z_N than $-\tau(0) + s_{\min}\tilde{\ell}$. However, by Assumption 11.2, for each agent of this sort there is another agent with lower skill and a well-being level in z_N at $-\tau(0) + s_{\min}\tilde{\ell}$. This was illustrated two paragraphs earlier with agent 4. In z'_N these agents must also be worse-off, falling below $-\tau(0) + s_{\min}\tilde{\ell}$. This contradiction proves that z_N is optimal.

Let us insist on the fact that an $\tilde{\ell}$-type tax is likely to be optimal only if it is second-best efficient. It is clear, for instance, that the $\tilde{\ell}$-type tax with $\tilde{\ell} = 1$ recommends a linear tax rate of 100 percent, which is obviously inefficient. The lower $\tilde{\ell}$, the more likely it is that the corresponding $\tilde{\ell}$-type tax is optimal.

11.6 CONCLUSION

Chapters 10 and 11 together illustrate how the SOF approach developed in this book can be used to evaluate social policies. The first step consists of defining axioms capturing principles of fairness in the economic situations under scrutiny. There may be conflicts between these axioms, or between fairness and efficiency axioms. After the lists of compatible axioms are identified, cross-economy robustness axioms can be added to characterize precise objectives a policymaker should try to maximize. The second step deals with the implementation of these objectives when the policymaker faces informational contraints. In this chapter, incentive-compatibility constraints are such that we can restrict our attention to tax schemes. The criteria we eventually obtain, consequently, bear directly on the shape of the tax functions.

The applications in this chapter show that the only information one needs to evaluate and compare tax schemes are the relevant tax functions – that is, the relationship between labor time or earnings on one hand and consumption on the other. That information is easy to gather; it basically involves identifying the relevant tax legislation. As we have emphasized already, it is not necessary in such evaluation to know the distribution of skills and preferences. Policymakers, with this approach, obtain evaluation criteria that are readily applicable.

We made the assumption, in this chapter, that the minimal skill is strictly positive. In our model, the skill refers to the wage rate at which one is able to find a job. In situations of high unemployment, one can argue that the skill of some agents is actually zero. Under such an assumption, the criterion corresponding to either $\mathbf{R}^{slex}$ or $\mathbf{R}^{s_{min}lex}$ boils down to maximizing the minimal consumption level. If the policymaker is interested in maximizing $\mathbf{R}^{\bar{\ell}EW}$, the zero marginal rate of taxation result disappears, but the objective is not necessarily to maximize the lowest consumption level. As the last theorem of this chapter may suggest, linear taxation (at a rate of $\bar{\ell}$) is likely to be optimal.[8]

In almost all countries, one agent's labor income tax does depend on more than the agent's earnings. The typical additional argument is the size, or, more generally, the composition of the household. There may be other arguments as well, such as the working status of the person, or the person's age. The result of this chapter can still be applied in these cases, by considering each set of agents in the same categories in turn. The results presented here do not allow us, however, to draw conclusions about the relative tax agents should pay across different categories. This problem requires a richer model.

Our last comment is about the difference between leximin and maximin types of SOFs. In the previous chapters, we saw how the combination of efficiency, fairness, and robustness axioms forces us to adopt SOFs that maximize the minimal level of some well-being index, but it was frequently the case that, among all such SOFs, the leximin was impossible to single out axiomatically. Indeed, the results said only that an allocation with a greater lowest level of

---

[8] See Fleurbaey and Maniquet (2011) for details.

well-being than another allocation was strictly better, remaining silent about pairs of allocations with the same lowest level of well-being. In this chapter, for the sake of simplicity, we always considered that the policymaker had a leximin type of SOF. We want to stress, now, that all the results we obtained in this chapter would be obtained with any kind of SOF displaying a strict preference for increasing the lowest well-being level, because this is the only element of social preferences that mattered in our proofs. In other words, the results we obtained in the axiomatic derivations of SOFs prove sufficient for second-best applications.

CHAPTER 12

Conclusions

This book presented a theory of fairness and social welfare. By fairness, we mean that economic justice is a question of fair resource allocation.[1] To be precise about what a fair resource allocation can be, we need to define the economic ingredients of the situation – that is, the available goods to allocate, the nature of the goods (whether they are private of public, divisible or not, in known or uncertain quantities, and so on), the available technology to produce new goods, and the internal and external resources owned by the agents.

What is fair, then, depends on the context; any analysis begins by identifying fairness requirements that capture basic ethical principles in that context. We have surveyed a variety of contexts in this book. Even if they all turned out to have specificities, a general picture emerges. First, fairness involves the equalization of something. Second, that thing must be related to the way agents value being given access to a given quantity of resources. To sum up, our undertaking is consistent with the notion that a society is just if and only if it equalizes the subjective value that agents give to the entire bundle of internal and external resources to which they are given access.

Our theory refers to social welfare. Defining social welfare requires aggregating the well-being of the members of a society. If the objective is to evaluate social policy, it is necessary to be able to claim that a given decline in the well-being of one agent is compensated, from the society's point of view, by an increase in the well-being of another agent. The common wisdom among the vast majority of economists on that question is that this process must involve interpersonal utility comparison. This book comes in opposition to that wisdom. Consistent with our notion of fairness, we replace utility comparison with the comparison of resource bundles, or, more accurately, with the comparison of indifference surfaces.

We end up with an approach to policy evaluation that consists of two steps. In the first step, social ordering functions are defined. They arise from the combination of efficiency, fairness, and robustness axioms. There is a hierarchy in this list of values. Efficiency is our central value. In all contexts we have

---

[1] Recall from Section 7.5 how the approach can be generalized to functionings.

been studying, we do not see any reason to recommend one policy if another policy exists that leads to higher welfare for everyone.

Fairness is our second value. Chapter 2 made clear that there may be conflicts between efficiency and fairness. Our strategy is then to weaken fairness requirements until they capture basic, sensible, and perhaps context-specific ethical objectives that are compatible with efficiency requirements. As made clear throughout the book, different fairness requirements may also conflict with one another. That is, of course, not particular to this approach, and that should not be a surprise to anyone. Does economics not keep telling us that our desires cannot be all satisfied simultaneously? When there are several conflicting requirements of fairness, there will be several conflicting ways of evaluating social policies. Our role is then to highlight the ethical choices that a policymaker needs to make before proceeding to policy evaluation.

After the ethical dilemmas are identified, robustness axioms may enter the picture. They follow the general requirement that solutions to similar problems also need to be similar. Formally, they capture the general intuition that social preference for one allocation over another should be independent of changes in some parameters of the model, when these parameters are judged irrelevant. As proved in Parts II and III of the book, the addition of robustness axioms to efficiency and fairness axioms typically results in the selection of a very limited number of acceptable social ordering functions. That is how the first step of our approach ends – namely, with the definition of acceptable social ordering functions among which a policymaker should choose as a function of his or her ethical position.

This book has been mainly about defining acceptable social ordering functions. The most striking result about it is the proof that only social ordering functions giving absolute priority to the worst-off are acceptable. The basic reasons are developed in Chapter 3, social ordering functions may apply to a variety of individual well-being indices. When one index is chosen, however, the primary concern of the policymaker should be to increase the welfare of the agents being given access to the bundles of resources associated with the lowest value of that well-being index.

Our axiomatic study of social ordering functions also revealed that there are two major families of acceptable social ordering functions. This was first exposed in Chapter 5, but is has been confirmed afterward. The first family comprises egalitarian-equivalent social ordering functions and the second gathers Walrasian social ordering functions. In the first family, the relevant indices of well-being are constructed without reference to the characteristics of the other agents. In the second family, the relevant indices are often constructed by also taking account of the prices that would be needed to decentralize an efficient allocation that bears some relationship with the allocation at which the value of the indices are computed. This implies a greater interdependence between the evaluations of well-being for different individuals.

The second step follows. Equipped with social preferences, the policymaker face a series of constraints. The typical ones are incentive-compatibility constraints. As the policymaker does not know the agents' preferences, and as preferences are a key ingredient in the definition of well-being indices (because we care about efficiency), the policymaker must limit himself or herself to policies that give the proper incentives to agents to reveal their private information about their preferences. The policymaker may face additional constraints as well. For instance, it may be the case that a status quo exists and that the only politically feasible allocations are in the neighborhood of the status quo.

Independent of the constraints, policy evaluation works by maximizing the appropriate social ordering function under the constraints the policymaker faces. As we saw throughout the book (in Chapters 5, 8, 9, and 11), such a maximization process boils down to identifying the bundle of resources chosen by the agent turning out to have the lowest well-being index value. Even if it is typically impossible to identify the well-being of all agents, agents' choices in general reveal enough information to identify the worst-off. Consequently, policy evaluation is possible and clearcut recommendations can be made.

Several recommendations have emerged, indeed, at several places in the book. In the production of a public good, for instance, one of the two acceptable social ordering functions recommends producing the public good at the level of its minimal demand, as shown in Section 8.6. In the labor income taxation problem, several social ordering functions based on different lists of axioms recommend applying a zero marginal tax rate on incomes below the lowest income corresponding to a full-time job, as shown in Section 11.5.

The next step in the development of this "fair social choice" approach to policy evaluation is to apply it to new problems, especially those in which governments are classically expected to play a role. Such a development is already in progress, especially in the field of health care provision and financing. Fleurbaey (2005a) and Valletta (2009a,b) study variants of our labor income taxation model in which the internal resource is one's health status, over which agents have preferences. The provision and financing of public education is another obvious candidate for the study of social ordering functions. Retirement benefits, family allowances, and capital income taxation could also be studied profitably using social ordering functions.

One of the assumptions that we have imposed throughout the book without questioning is the assumption that agents are rational in the classical sense; that is, their preferences are complete and transitive, and they are self-centered. We believe that this assumption is reasonable in the simple models we have studied. However, perhaps the biggest current challenge to normative economics is to take account of the fact that agents behave in ways that may depart from what these assumptions capture. We think mainly of the fact that individual behavior may depend on what the others do. In the labor income taxation model, for instance, we have assumed that agents choose their labor time by simply looking at their own budget set. It is clear, however, that the labor time and living standards of others influence many people's labor supply. For instance, some people are willing to work full time, no matter how many hours this precisely means. Studying social ordering functions when agents have other-regarding preferences is another part of the future development of this approach.

By offering a comprehensive presentation of the achievements of the theory so far, by discussing its foundations and by explaining how it can be used, we hope to have paved the way for these further developments.

APPENDIX A

Proofs

A.1 CHAPTER 3: PRIORITY TO THE WORST-OFF

Proof of Theorem 3.3. Let $\mathbf{R}$ satisfy strong Pareto, equal-split transfer, and unchanged-contour independence. Let $E = (R_N, \Omega) \in \mathcal{E}$, $z_N, z'_N \in X^N$, $j, k \in N$ be such that $z_j \gg z'_j \gg \Omega / |N| \gg z'_k \gg z_k$ and for all $i \neq j, k$, $z_i = z'_i$. Assume, by way of contradiction, that $z_N \mathbf{P}(E) z'_N$. Pick an arbitrary bundle $z_j^+ \gg z_j$ and let $R'_j, R''_j \in \mathcal{R}$ and $z_j^1, z_j^2, z_j^3, z_j^4, z_k^1, z_k^2, z_k^3 \in X$ and $\Delta \in \mathbb{R}^\ell_{++}$ be such that:

$$U(z_j^+, R'_j) = U(z_j^+, R''_j) = \left\{ x \in X \mid x \geq z_j^+ \right\},$$

$$U(z_j^4, R''_j) = \left\{ x \in X \mid x \geq z_j^4 \right\},$$

$$I(z'_j, R'_j) = I(z'_j, R''_j) = I(z'_j, R_j),$$

$$I(z_j, R'_j) = I(z_j, R_j),$$

$$z_j^2 I''_j z_j^1, \ z_j^4 I''_j z_j^3,$$

$$z_j^1 = z_j^+ - \Delta, \ z_j^3 = z_j^2 - \Delta, \ z_j^4 = z'_j + \Delta,$$

$$z_k^1 = z_k + \Delta, \ z_k^2 = z_k^1 + \Delta, \ z_k^3 = z_k^2 + \Delta \ll z'_k.$$

This construction is illustrated in Figure A.1, in which the indifference curves are those of R''_j. Observe that necessarily $z_j^1, z_j^2, z_j^3, z_j^4 \gg \Omega / |N| \gg z_k^1$, z_k^2, z_k^3.

Let $E' = ((R_{N \setminus \{j\}}, R'_j), \Omega)$, $E'' = ((R_{N \setminus \{j\}}, R''_j), \Omega) \in \mathcal{E}$. By unchanged-contour independence, $z_N \mathbf{P}(E') z'_N$. By strong Pareto, $(z_{N \setminus \{j\}}, z_j^+) \mathbf{P}(E') z_N$. By transitivity, $(z_{N \setminus \{j\}}, z_j^+) \mathbf{P}(E') z'_N$. By unchanged-contour independence, $(z_{N \setminus \{j\}}, z_j^+) \mathbf{P}(E'') z'_N$.

By equal-split transfer,

$$(z_{N \setminus \{j,k\}}, z_j^1, z_k^1) \mathbf{R}(E'') (z_{N \setminus \{j\}}, z_j^+).$$

239

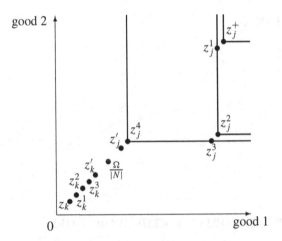

Figure A.1. Proof of Theorem 3.3

By Pareto indifference (entailed by strong Pareto),

$$(z_{N\setminus\{j,k\}}, z_j^2, z_k^1)\,\mathbf{I}(E'')\,(z_{N\setminus\{j,k\}}, z_j^1, z_k^1).$$

By equal-split transfer,

$$(z_{N\setminus\{j,k\}}, z_j^3, z_k^2)\mathbf{R}(E'')(z_{N\setminus\{j,k\}}, z_j^2, z_k^1).$$

By Pareto indifference,

$$(z_{N\setminus\{j,k\}}, z_j^4, z_k^2)\mathbf{I}(E'')(z_{N\setminus\{j,k\}}, z_j^3, z_k^2).$$

By equal-split transfer,

$$(z_{N\setminus\{j,k\}}, z_j', z_k^3)\mathbf{R}(E'')(z_{N\setminus\{j,k\}}, z_j^4, z_k^2).$$

By strong Pareto, $z_N' \ \mathbf{P}(E'') \ (z_{N\setminus\{j,k\}}, z_j', z_k^3)$. By transitivity, $z_N' \ \mathbf{P}\left(E''\right)$ $(z_{N\setminus\{j\}}, z_j^+)$, which is a contradiction.

Finally, let us check that every axiom is necessary for the conclusion of the theorem. The examples that follow are defined in the proof of Theorem 3.1.

1. Drop strong Pareto. Take $\mathbf{R}^{psum}$.
2. Drop equal-split transfer. Take $\mathbf{R}^{\Omega sum}$.
3. Drop unchanged-contour independence. Take $\mathbf{R}^{IL}$. ∎

Proof of Theorem 3.4. Let $\mathbf{R}$ satisfy Pareto indifference, equal-split transfer, separation, and replication. Let $E = (R_N, \Omega) \in \mathcal{E}$, $z_N, z_N' \in X^N$, $j, k \in N$ be such that $z_j \gg z_j' \gg \Omega/|N| \gg z_k' \gg z_k$, and for all $i \neq j, k$, $z_i = z_i'$. Let $\Delta_j = z_j - z_j'$ and $\Delta_k = z_k' - z_k$.

Let $R_0 \in \mathcal{R}$, $r, m \in \mathbb{Z}_{++}$, $z_0^1, z_0^2, z_0^3, z_0^4 \in X$ be such that

$$\frac{\Omega}{|N| + 1/r} \gg z_0^1 \, I_0 \, z_0^4 \, P_0 \, z_0^2 \, I_0 \, z_0^3 \gg \frac{\Omega}{|N| + 2/r} \gg z_k',$$

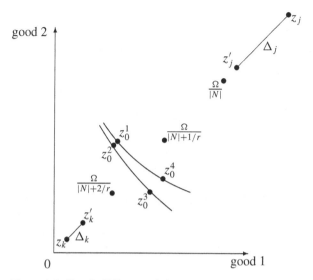

Figure A.2. Proof of Theorem 3.4

$z_0^1 = z_0^2 + \frac{\Delta_k}{m}$, and $z_0^4 = z_0^3 + \frac{\Delta_j}{m}$. The construction is illustrated in Figure A.2.

Let $E' = (R_{N'}, r\Omega) \in \mathcal{E}$ be an r-replica of E. Let $E'' = (R_{N'}, R_0, R_0, r\Omega)$, $E''' = (R_{N'}, R_0, r\Omega) \in \mathcal{E}$. By equal-split transfer,

$$\left(z_{N'\setminus\{k\}}, z_k + \frac{\Delta_k}{m}, z_0^2, z_0^1 \right) \mathbf{R} \left(E'' \right) \left(z_{N'}, z_0^1, z_0^1 \right).$$

By Pareto indifference,

$$\left(z_{N'\setminus\{k\}}, z_k + \frac{\Delta_k}{m}, z_0^3, z_0^1 \right) \mathbf{I} \left(E'' \right) \left(z_{N'\setminus\{k\}}, z_k + \frac{\Delta_k}{m}, z_0^2, z_0^1 \right).$$

By transitivity,

$$\left(z_{N'\setminus\{k\}}, z_k + \frac{\Delta_k}{m}, z_0^3, z_0^1 \right) \mathbf{R} \left(E'' \right) \left(z_{N'}, z_0^1, z_0^1 \right).$$

By separation,

$$\left(z_{N'\setminus\{k\}}, z_k + \frac{\Delta_k}{m}, z_0^3 \right) \mathbf{R} \left(E''' \right) \left(z_{N'}, z_0^1 \right).$$

By equal-split transfer,

$$\left(z_{N'\setminus\{j,k\}}, z_j - \frac{\Delta_j}{m}, z_k + \frac{\Delta_k}{m}, z_0^4 \right) \mathbf{R} \left(E''' \right) \left(z_{N'\setminus\{k\}}, z_k + \frac{\Delta_k}{m}, z_0^3 \right).$$

By Pareto indifference,

$$\left(z_{N'\setminus\{j,k\}}, z_j - \frac{\Delta_j}{m}, z_k + \frac{\Delta_k}{m}, z_0^1 \right) \mathbf{I}\left(E'''\right) \left(z_{N'\setminus\{j,k\}}, z_j - \frac{\Delta_j}{m}, z_k + \frac{\Delta_k}{m}, z_0^4 \right).$$

By transitivity,

$$\left(z_{N'\setminus\{j,k\}}, z_j - \frac{\Delta_j}{m}, z_k + \frac{\Delta_k}{m}, z_0^1 \right) \mathbf{R}\left(E'''\right) \left(z_{N'}, z_0^1 \right).$$

By separation,

$$\left(z_{N'\setminus\{j,k\}}, z_j - \frac{\Delta_j}{m}, z_k + \frac{\Delta_k}{m} \right) \mathbf{R}\left(E'\right) z_{N'}.$$

Repeating this argument $m - 1$ times, we obtain

$$\left(z_{N'\setminus\{j,k\}}, z_j', z_k' \right) \mathbf{R}\left(E'\right) z_{N'}.$$

Repeating the whole argument $r - 1$ times, we obtain

$$\left(\underbrace{z_{N\setminus\{j,k\}}}_{(r \text{ times})}, \underbrace{z_j', \dots, z_j'}_{(r)}, \underbrace{z_k', \dots, z_k'}_{(r)} \right) \mathbf{R}\left(E'\right) z_{N'}.$$

Recall that $z_{N\setminus\{j,k\}} = z'_{N\setminus\{j,k\}}$. By replication, $z_N' \mathbf{R}(E) z_N$.

Finally, let us check that every axiom is necessary for the conclusion of the theorem. The first three examples that follow are defined in the proof of Theorem 3.1.

1. Drop Pareto indifference. Take $\mathbf{R}^{p\text{sum}}$.
2. Drop equal-split transfer. Take $\mathbf{R}^{\Omega\text{sum}}$.
3. Drop separation. Take $\mathbf{R}^{IL}$.
4. Drop replication. A counterexample has yet to be found. ∎

A.2   CHAPTER 5: FAIR DISTRIBUTION OF DIVISIBLE GOODS

We first prove a variant of Theorem 3.1.

Lemma A.1 *On the domain $\mathcal{E}$, if a SOF satisfies* weak Pareto, transfer among equals, *and* unchanged-contour independence, *then for all $E = (R_N, \Omega) \in \mathcal{E}$, all $z_N, z_N' \in X^N$, if there exist $j, k \in N$ such that $R_j = R_k$,*

$$z_j \gg z_j' \gg z_k' \gg z_k,$$

and for all $i \neq j, k$, $z_i' P_i z_i$, then $z_N' \mathbf{P}(E) z_N$.

Proof. Let $\mathbf{R}$ satisfy weak Pareto, transfer among equals, and unchanged-contour independence. Let $E = (R_N, \Omega) \in \mathcal{E}$, $z_N, z_N' \in X^N$ and $j, k \in N$ be such that $R_j = R_k$, $z_j \gg z_j' \gg z_k' \gg z_k$, and for all $i \neq j, k$, $z_i' P_i z_i$. Let $\varepsilon \in \mathbb{R}_{++}^\ell$ be such that for all $i \neq j, k$, $z_i' P_i z_i + \varepsilon$.

First case: There exist $x \in U(z_j, R_j)$, $x' \in L(z'_j, R_j)$ such that $x \not\succ x'$. Let $R'_j = R'_k \in \mathcal{R}$, $z^1_j, z^2_j, z^3_j, z^4_j, z^1_k, z^2_k, z^3_k, z^4_k \in X$, $\Delta \in R^\ell_{++}$ be constructed in such a way that for $i \in \{j, k\}$,

$$I(z_i, R'_i) = I(z_i, R_i), \quad I(z'_i, R'_i) = I(z'_i, R_i),$$

$$z^1_i \, P'_i \, z_i, \quad z^3_i \, P'_i \, z^2_i, \quad z'_i \, P'_i \, z^4_i,$$

and

$$z^2_j = z^1_j - \Delta \gg z^2_k = z^1_k + \Delta,$$

$$z^4_j = z^3_j - \Delta \gg z^4_k = z^3_k + \Delta.$$

This construction is a slight modification of that illustrated in Figure 3.3.

Let $E' = \left(\left(R_{N\setminus\{j,k\}}, R'_j, R'_k \right), \Omega \right) \in \mathcal{E}$. By weak Pareto,

$$\left(z_{N\setminus\{j,k\}} + \frac{1}{2}\varepsilon, z^1_j, z^1_k \right) \mathbf{P}(E') \, z_N.$$

By transfer among equals,

$$\left(z_{N\setminus\{j,k\}} + \frac{1}{2}\varepsilon, z^2_j, z^2_k \right) \mathbf{R}(E') \left(z_{N\setminus\{j,k\}} + \frac{1}{2}\varepsilon, z^1_j, z^1_k \right).$$

By weak Pareto,

$$\left(z_{N\setminus\{j,k\}} + \varepsilon, z^3_j, z^3_k \right) \mathbf{P}(E') \left(z_{N\setminus\{j,k\}} + \frac{1}{2}\varepsilon, z^2_j, z^2_k \right).$$

By transfer among equals,

$$\left(z_{N\setminus\{j,k\}} + \varepsilon, z^4_j, z^4_k \right) \mathbf{R}(E') \left(z_{N\setminus\{j,k\}} + \varepsilon, z^3_j, z^3_k \right).$$

By weak Pareto,

$$z'_N \, \mathbf{P}(E') \left(z_{N\setminus\{j,k\}} + \varepsilon, z^4_j, z^4_k \right).$$

By transitivity, $z'_N \, \mathbf{P}(E') \, z_N$. By unchanged-contour independence, $z'_N \, \mathbf{P}(E) \, z_N$.

Second case: There are no $x \in U(z_j, R_j)$, $x' \in L(z'_j, R_j)$ such that $x \not\succ x'$. Then let $z^*_j, z^*_k, z^{**}_j, z^{**}_k, \in X$ be such that $z_j \gg z^{**}_j \gg z^*_j \gg z'_j$ and $z'_k \gg z^{**}_k \gg z^*_k \gg z_k$, and such that there exist $x \in U(z_j, R_j)$, $x^* \in L(z^*_j, R_j)$ such that $x \not\succ x^*$, as well as $x^{**} \in U(z^{**}_j, R_j)$, $x' \in L(z'_j, R_j)$ such that $x^{**} \not\succ x'$. By the argument of the first case, one shows that

$$\left(z_{N\setminus\{j,k\}} + \frac{1}{2}\varepsilon, z^*_j, z^*_k \right) \mathbf{P}(E) \, z_N$$

and that

$$z'_N \, \mathbf{P}(E) \left(z_{N\setminus\{j,k\}} + \varepsilon, z^{**}_j, z^{**}_k \right).$$

By weak Pareto,

$$\left(z_{N\setminus\{j,k\}} + \varepsilon, z_j^{**}, z_k^{**}\right) \mathbf{P}(E) \left(z_{N\setminus\{j,k\}} + \frac{1}{2}\varepsilon, z_j^{*}, z_k^{*}\right).$$

By transitivity, $z_N' \, \mathbf{P}(E) \, z_N$. ∎

Proof of Theorem 5.1. We prove the result with weak Pareto instead of strong Pareto. Let $E = (R_N, \Omega) \in \mathcal{E}$ and $z_N, z_N' \in X^N$ be such that $\min_{i \in N} u_\Omega(z_i, R_i) > \min_{i \in N} u_\Omega(z_i', R_i)$. Assume that, contrary to the result, one has $z_N' \, \mathbf{R}(E) \, z_N$. Let $i_0 \in N$ be such that $u_\Omega(z_{i_0}', R_{i_0}) = \min_{i \in N} u_\Omega(z_i', R_i)$. Let $z_N^1, z_N^2 \in \mathrm{Pr}(\Omega)$ be such that for all $i, j \in N$,

$$\left(\min_{i \in N} u_\Omega(z_i', R_i)\right) \Omega \ll z_i^2 = z_j^2 \ll \left(\min_{i \in N} u_\Omega(z_i, R_i)\right) \Omega,$$

for all $i \in N \setminus \{i_0\}$, $z_i^1 \, P_i \, z_i$, $z_i^1 \, P_i \, z_i'$, and

$$u_\Omega(z_{i_0}', R_{i_0})\Omega \ll z_{i_0}^1 \ll z_{i_0}^2.$$

Let $R_N' \in \mathcal{R}$ be such that for all $i \in N$,

$$I(R_i', z_i) = I(R_i, z_i) \text{ and } I(R_i', z_i') = I(R_i, z_i')$$

and for all $i \in N \setminus \{i_0\}$,

$$U(R_i', z_i^1) = \left\{x \in X \mid x \geq z_i^1\right\}.$$

Let $E' = (R_N', \Omega)$. By unchanged-contour independence, $z_N' \, \mathbf{R}(E') \, z_N$. By weak Pareto, $z_N^1 \, \mathbf{P}(E') \, z_N'$ and $z_N \, \mathbf{P}(E') \, z_N^2$, so that by transitivity, $z_N^1 \, \mathbf{P}(E') \, z_N^2$. Let $z_N^3 \in \mathrm{Pr}(\Omega)$ be such that for all $i \in N \setminus \{i_0\}$,

$$z_{i_0}^1 \ll z_{i_0}^3 \ll z_{i_0}^2 = z_i^2 \ll z_i^3 \ll z_i^1,$$

and

$$\frac{1}{|N|} \sum_{i \in N} z_i^3 \ll \frac{1}{|N|} \sum_{i \in N} z_i^2 = z_{i_0}^2.$$

Let $n = |N|$ and $\varepsilon \in \mathbb{R}_{++}$ be such that for all $i \in N \setminus \{i_0\}$, $\varepsilon n \Omega \ll z_i^3 - z_i^2$ and $\varepsilon n \Omega \ll z_{i_0}^3 - z_{i_0}^1$. Let $R_N'' \in \mathcal{R}$ be such that for all $i \in N$,

$$I(R_i'', z_i^1) = I(R_i', z_i^1) \text{ and } I(R_i'', z_i^2) = I(R_i', z_i^2)$$

and for all $i \in N \setminus \{i_0\}$,

$$U(R_i'', z_i^2 + \varepsilon\Omega) = \left\{x \in X \mid x \geq z_i^2 + \varepsilon\Omega\right\}.$$

Let $E'' = (R_N'', \Omega)$. By unchanged-contour independence, $z_N^1 \, \mathbf{P}(E'') \, z_N^2$.
Moreover, one has $z_N^3 \, \mathbf{P}(E'') \, z_N^1$. This is proved as follows. Let s be a bijection from $\{1, \ldots, n-1\}$ to $N \setminus \{i_0\}$. Let $z_N^{\langle 1 \rangle}, \ldots, z_N^{\langle n-1 \rangle}$ be defined as

Table A.1.

	$i = s(1)$	$i = s(2)$	$\cdots$	$i = s(n-1)$	i_0
$z^{\langle 1 \rangle}$	$z_i^2 + \varepsilon\Omega$	$z_i^1 + \varepsilon\Omega$		$z_i^1 + \varepsilon\Omega$	$z_{i_0}^1 + \varepsilon\Omega$
$z^{\langle 2 \rangle}$	$z_i^2 + 2\varepsilon\Omega$	$z_i^1 + 2\varepsilon\Omega$		$z_i^1 + 2\varepsilon\Omega$	$z_{i_0}^1 + 2\varepsilon\Omega$
$\vdots$					
$z^{\langle n-1 \rangle}$	$z_i^2 + (n-1)\varepsilon\Omega$	$z_i^2 + (n-1)\varepsilon\Omega$		$z_i^2 + (n-1)\varepsilon\Omega$	$z_{i_0}^1 + (n-1)\varepsilon\Omega$

follows: for every $t = 1, \ldots, n-1$, $z_i^{\langle t \rangle} = z_i^2 + t\varepsilon\Omega$ if $i = s(k)$ for $k \le t$; otherwise $z_i^{\langle t \rangle} = z_i^1 + t\varepsilon\Omega$. The number ε has been chosen so that for all $i \in N$, $z_i^{\langle n-1 \rangle} \ll z_i^3$. Table A.1 summarizes the construction.

Let $R_N^{\langle 1 \rangle} \in \mathcal{R}$ be such that for all $i \in N$,

$$I(R_i^{\langle 1 \rangle}, z_i^1) = I(R_i'', z_i^1) \text{ and } I(R_i^{\langle 1 \rangle}, z_i^{\langle 1 \rangle}) = I(R_i'', z_i^{\langle 1 \rangle})$$

and $R_{i_0}^{\langle 1 \rangle} = R_{s(1)}^{\langle 1 \rangle}$. The latter is possible because $U(R_{s(1)}'', z_{s(1)}^{\langle 1 \rangle}) \cap L(R_{i_0}'', z_{i_0}^{\langle 1 \rangle}) = \emptyset$ (i.e., indifference curves do not cross). By Lemma A.1, for $E^{\langle 1 \rangle} = (R_N^{\langle 1 \rangle}, \Omega)$, $z_N^{\langle 1 \rangle} \, \mathbf{P}(E^{\langle 1 \rangle}) z_N^2$. By unchanged-contour independence, $z_N^{\langle 1 \rangle} \, \mathbf{P}(E'') z_N^1$.

For $t = 2, \ldots, n-1$, let $R_N^{\langle t \rangle} \in \mathcal{R}$ be such that for all $i \in N$,

$$I(R_i^{\langle t \rangle}, z_i^{\langle t-1 \rangle}) = I(R_i'', z_i^{\langle t-1 \rangle}) \text{ and } I(R_i^{\langle t \rangle}, z_i^{\langle t \rangle}) = I(R_i'', z_i^{\langle t \rangle})$$

and $R_{i_0}^{\langle t \rangle} = R_{s(t)}^{\langle t \rangle}$. A similar argument to the previous reasoning leads to the conclusion that $z_N^{\langle t \rangle} \, \mathbf{P}(E'') z_N^{\langle t-1 \rangle}$.

By weak Pareto, $z_N^3 \, \mathbf{P}(E'') z_N^{\langle n-1 \rangle}$. By transitivity, $z_N^3 \, \mathbf{P}(E'') z_N^1$, as was to be proved.

By transitivity again, $z_N^3 \, \mathbf{P}(E'') z_N^2$. Let $z_N^4 \in \mathrm{Pr}(\Omega)$ be obtained from z_N^3 by (nonleaky) transfers, so that for all $i \in N$, $z_i^4 \ll z_i^2$. By proportional-allocations transfer, $z_N^4 \, \mathbf{R}(E'') z_N^3$. By transitivity, $z_N^4 \, \mathbf{P}(E'') z_N^2$. However, by weak Pareto, $z_N^2 \, \mathbf{P}(E'') z_N^4$, which is a contradiction. This completes the proof.

In addition, we show that if any of the conditions is relaxed, one finds a SOF that does not obey the conclusion of the theorem.

1. Drop weak Pareto. Take $\mathbf{R}^{p\text{sum}}$.
2. Drop transfer among equals. Take $\mathbf{R}^{\Omega\text{sum}}$.
3. Drop proportional-allocations transfer. Take $\mathbf{R}^{\Omega'\text{lex}}$ for Ω' not proportional to Ω.
4. Drop unchanged-contour independence. Let $\mathbf{R}^{IL}$. ∎

We present a variant of Theorem 5.2 that involves a weak version of separation. The following axiom is logically implied by the combination of separation and strong Pareto. It relies on the intuition that it would seem strange to tell an agent that the agent's own ranking of two allocations would be accepted at the social level only if the agent were not there.[1]

Axiom A.1 Opponent Separation
For all $E = (R_N, \Omega) \in \mathcal{D}$, *and* $z_N, z'_N \in X^N$, *if there is* $i \in N$ *such that* $z'_i \, P_i \, z_i$, *then*

$$z_N \, \mathbf{R}(E) \, z'_N \Rightarrow z_{N\setminus\{i\}} \, \mathbf{R}(R_{N\setminus\{i\}}, \Omega) \, z'_{N\setminus\{i\}}.$$

A valuable feature of the list of axioms in the following theorem (as well as in the variant of Theorem 5.1 proved earlier) is that they are all satisfied by the Ω-equivalent maximin SOF $\mathbf{R}^{\Omega\min}$ introduced in Section 6.3 and defined by: for all $E = (R_N, \Omega) \in \mathcal{E}$ and $z_N, z'_N \in X^N$, $z_N \, \mathbf{R}^{\Omega\min}(E) \, z'_N$ if and only if $\min_{i \in N} u_\Omega(z_i, R_i) \geq \min_{i \in N} u_\Omega(z'_i, R_i)$. This SOF does not satisfy strong Pareto and separation, but it does satisfy weak Pareto (as well as Pareto indifference) and opponent separation.

Theorem A.1 *On the domain* $\mathcal{E}$, *if a SOF satisfies* weak Pareto, equal-split transfer, opponent separation, *and* replication, *then for all* $E = (R_N, \Omega) \in \mathcal{E}$ *and* $z_N, z'_N \in X^N$,

$$\min_{i \in N} u_\Omega(z_i, R_i) > \min_{i \in N} u_\Omega(z'_i, R_i) \Rightarrow z_N \, \mathbf{P}(E) \, z'_N.$$

Its proof involves the following lemma, which is a variant of Theorem 3.4.

Lemma A.2 *On the domain* $\mathcal{E}$, *if a SOF satisfies* weak Pareto, equal-split transfer, opponent separation, *and* replication, *then it satisfies: For all* $E = (R_N, \Omega) \in \mathcal{D}$, *and* $z_N, z'_N \in X^N$, *if for all* $i \in N$, $z'_i \, P_i \, \Omega/|N|$ *and there exists* $j \in N$ *such that* $\Omega/|N| \, P_j \, z_j$, *then* $z'_N \, \mathbf{P}(E) \, z_N$.

Proof of Lemma A.2. Let $\mathbf{R}$ satisfy weak Pareto, equal split transfer, opponent separation, and replication.
Step 1. The structure of this step is similar to the proof of Theorem 3.4, to which the reader may refer for a first intuition. Let $E = (R_N, \Omega) \in \mathcal{E}, z_N, z'_N \in X^N, j, k \in N$ be such that

$$z_j \gg z'_j \gg \frac{\Omega}{|N|} \gg z'_k \gg z_k,$$

and for all $i \neq j, k, z'_i \, P_i \, z_i$. Let $\Delta_j = z_j - \Omega/|N|$ and $\Delta_k = (z'_k - z_k)/8$. We prove that $z'_N \, \mathbf{P}(E) \, z_N$. Assume, by way of contradiction, that $z_N \, \mathbf{R}(E) \, z'_N$.

---

[1] This is reminiscent of the "no-show paradox" (Brams and Fishburn 1983) in voting theory, which occurs when an agent is better off abstaining from voting than expressing his or her true preferences.

Let $R_0 \in \mathcal{R}, r, m \in \mathbb{Z}_{++}, \varepsilon \in \mathbb{R}_{++}^{\ell}, z_0^1, z_0^2, z_0^3, z_0^4 \in X$ be such that for all $t = 1, \ldots, 4$,

$$\frac{\Omega}{|N| + 1/r} \gg z_0^t + 2\varepsilon \gg z_0^t \gg \frac{\Omega}{|N| + 2/r} \gg z_k',$$

$$z_0^1 P_0 z_0^4 + \varepsilon P_0 z_0^3 + \varepsilon P_0 z_0^2 + 2\varepsilon,$$

$$z_0^1 = z_0^2 + \frac{\Delta_k}{m}, \quad z_0^4 = z_0^3 + \frac{\Delta_j}{m},$$

$$\varepsilon \ll \frac{z_j' - \Omega/|N|}{3rm}, \quad \varepsilon \ll \frac{\Delta_k}{rm},$$

and for all $i \neq j, k, z_i' P_i z_i + 3rm\varepsilon$. Let $z_N + \varepsilon$ denote $(z_i + \varepsilon)_{i \in N}$.

Let $E' = (R_{N'}, r\Omega) \in \mathcal{E}$ be an r-replica of E. By replication invariance, $z_{N'} \mathbf{R} (E') z_{N'}'$. By weak Pareto, $z_{N'} + \varepsilon \mathbf{P} (E') z_{N'}'$. Let $E'' = (R_{N'}, R_0, R_0, r\Omega)$, $E''' = (R_{N'}, R_0, r\Omega) \in \mathcal{E}$. By opponent separation,

$$\left(z_{N'} + \varepsilon, z_0^1 + \varepsilon, z_0^1 + \varepsilon \right) \mathbf{P} (E'') \left(z_{N'}', z_0^1, z_0^1 \right).$$

Because

$$z_0^2 + \varepsilon \gg \frac{r\Omega}{r|N| + 2} \gg z_k' \gg z_k + \frac{\Delta_k}{m} + \varepsilon,$$

one can apply equal-split transfer and obtain

$$\left(z_{N' \setminus \{k\}} + \varepsilon, z_k + \frac{\Delta_k}{m} + \varepsilon, z_0^2 + \varepsilon, z_0^1 + \varepsilon \right) \mathbf{R} (E'') \left(z_{N'} + \varepsilon, z_0^1 + \varepsilon, z_0^1 + \varepsilon \right).$$

By weak Pareto,

$$\left(z_{N' \setminus \{k\}} + 2\varepsilon, z_k + \frac{\Delta_k}{m} + 2\varepsilon, z_0^3 + \varepsilon, z_0^1 + 2\varepsilon \right)$$

$$\mathbf{P} (E'') \left(z_{N' \setminus \{k\}} + \varepsilon, z_k + \frac{\Delta_k}{m} + \varepsilon, z_0^2 + \varepsilon, z_0^1 + \varepsilon \right).$$

One has

$$z_0^2 + 2\varepsilon \gg \frac{r\Omega}{r|N| + 2} \gg z_k' \gg z_k + 2\frac{\Delta_k}{m} + 2\varepsilon,$$

so that by equal-split transfer,

$$\left(z_{N' \setminus \{k\}} + 2\varepsilon, z_k + 2\frac{\Delta_k}{m} + 2\varepsilon, z_0^3 + \varepsilon, z_0^2 + 2\varepsilon \right)$$

$$\mathbf{R} (E'') \left(z_{N' \setminus \{k\}} + 2\varepsilon, z_k + \frac{\Delta_k}{m} + 2\varepsilon, z_0^3 + \varepsilon, z_0^1 + 2\varepsilon \right)$$

By transitivity,

$$\left(z_{N'\setminus\{k\}} + 2\varepsilon, z_k + 2\frac{\Delta_k}{m} + 2\varepsilon, z_0^3 + \varepsilon, z_0^2 + 2\varepsilon \right)$$

$$\mathbf{P}\left(E''\right)\left(z'_{N'}, z_0^1, z_0^1\right).$$

By opponent separation,

$$\left(z_{N'\setminus\{k\}} + 2\varepsilon, z_k + 2\frac{\Delta_k}{m} + 2\varepsilon, z_0^3 + \varepsilon \right) \mathbf{R}\left(E'''\right)\left(z'_{N'}, z_0^1\right).$$

One has

$$z_j - \frac{\Delta_j}{m} \gg \frac{r\Omega}{r\,|N| + 1} \gg z_0^4 + \varepsilon$$

and by equal-split transfer,

$$\left(z_{N'\setminus\{j,k\}} + 2\varepsilon, z_j - \frac{\Delta_j}{m} + 2\varepsilon, z_k + 2\frac{\Delta_k}{m} + 2\varepsilon, z_0^4 + \varepsilon \right)$$

$$\mathbf{R}\left(E'''\right)\left(z_{N'\setminus\{k\}} + 2\varepsilon, z_k + 2\frac{\Delta_k}{m} + 2\varepsilon, z_0^3 + \varepsilon \right).$$

By weak Pareto,

$$\left(z_{N'\setminus\{j,k\}} + 3\varepsilon, z_j - \frac{\Delta_j}{m} + 3\varepsilon, z_k + 2\frac{\Delta_k}{m} + 3\varepsilon, z_0^1 + \varepsilon \right)$$

$$\mathbf{P}\left(E'''\right)\left(z_{N'\setminus\{j,k\}} + 2\varepsilon, z_j - \frac{\Delta_j}{m} + 2\varepsilon, z_k + 2\frac{\Delta_k}{m} + 2\varepsilon, z_0^4 + \varepsilon \right).$$

By transitivity,

$$\left(z_{N'\setminus\{j,k\}} + 3\varepsilon, z_j - \frac{\Delta_j}{m} + 3\varepsilon, z_k + 2\frac{\Delta_k}{m} + 3\varepsilon, z_0^1 + \varepsilon \right)$$

$$\mathbf{P}\left(E'''\right)\left(z'_{N'}, z_0^1\right).$$

By opponent separation,

$$\left(z_{N'\setminus\{j,k\}} + 3\varepsilon, z_j - \frac{\Delta_j}{m} + 3\varepsilon, z_k + 2\frac{\Delta_k}{m} + 3\varepsilon, z_0^1 + \varepsilon, z_0^1 + \varepsilon \right)$$

$$\mathbf{P}\left(E''\right)\left(z'_{N'}, z_0^1, z_0^1\right).$$

Because

$$z_0^2 + \varepsilon \gg \frac{r\Omega}{r\,|N| + 2} \gg z'_k \gg z_k + 4\frac{\Delta_k}{m} + 3\varepsilon,$$

by equal-split transfer one has

$$\left(z_{N'\setminus\{j,k\}} + 3\varepsilon, z_j - \frac{\Delta_j}{m} + 3\varepsilon, z_k + 3\frac{\Delta_k}{m} + 3\varepsilon, z_0^2 + \varepsilon, z_0^1 + \varepsilon\right)$$

$$\mathbf{R}\left(E''\right)\left(z_{N'\setminus\{j,k\}} + 3\varepsilon, z_j - \frac{\Delta_j}{m} + 3\varepsilon, z_k + 2\frac{\Delta_k}{m} + 3\varepsilon, z_0^1 + \varepsilon, z_0^1 + \varepsilon\right)$$

and

$$\left(z_{N'\setminus\{j,k\}} + 3\varepsilon, z_j - \frac{\Delta_j}{m} + 3\varepsilon, z_k + 4\frac{\Delta_k}{m} + 3\varepsilon, z_0^2 + \varepsilon, z_0^2 + \varepsilon\right)$$

$$\mathbf{R}\left(E''\right)\left(z_{N'\setminus\{j,k\}} + 3\varepsilon, z_j - \frac{\Delta_j}{m} + 3\varepsilon, z_k + 3\frac{\Delta_k}{m} + 3\varepsilon, z_0^2 + \varepsilon, z_0^1 + \varepsilon\right).$$

By transitivity,

$$\left(z_{N'\setminus\{j,k\}} + 3\varepsilon, z_j - \frac{\Delta_j}{m} + 3\varepsilon, z_k + 4\frac{\Delta_k}{m} + 3\varepsilon, z_0^2 + \varepsilon, z_0^2 + \varepsilon\right)$$

$$\mathbf{P}\left(E'''\right)\left(z_{N'}', z_0^1, z_0^1\right).$$

By opponent separation,

$$\left(z_{N'\setminus\{j,k\}} + 3\varepsilon, z_j - \frac{\Delta_j}{m} + 3\varepsilon, z_k + 4\frac{\Delta_k}{m} + 3\varepsilon\right)\mathbf{R}\left(E'\right)z_{N'}'.$$

Repeating this argument $m - 1$ times, we obtain

$$\left(z_{N'\setminus\{j,k\}} + 3m\varepsilon, z_j - \Delta_j + 3m\varepsilon, z_k + 4\Delta_k + 3m\varepsilon\right)\mathbf{R}\left(E'\right)z_{N'}'$$

This repetition of the argument requires, for the application of equal-split transfer, to have, for all $t = 1, \ldots, m$,

$$z_k' \gg z_k + 4t\frac{\Delta_k}{m} + 3t\varepsilon, \quad z_j - t\frac{\Delta_j}{m} \gg \frac{r\Omega}{r|N| + 1}.$$

This is guaranteed by the fact that

$$z_k' \gg z_k + 7\Delta_k \gg z_k + 4\Delta_k + 3m\varepsilon, \quad z_j - \Delta_j = \frac{\Omega}{|N|} \gg \frac{r\Omega}{r|N| + 1}.$$

One even has $z_k' \gg z_k + 7\Delta_k \gg z_k + 4\Delta_k + 3rm\varepsilon$. Therefore, repeating the whole argument $r - 1$ times, we obtain

$$\left(\begin{array}{c}\underbrace{z_{N\setminus\{j,k\}} + 3rm\varepsilon,}_{(r \text{ times})} \\ z_j - \Delta_j + 3m\varepsilon, z_j - \Delta_j + 6m\varepsilon, \ldots, z_j - \Delta_j + 3rm\varepsilon, \\ z_k + 4\Delta_k + 3m\varepsilon, z_k + 4\Delta_k + 6m\varepsilon, \ldots, z_k + 4\Delta_k + 3rm\varepsilon\end{array}\right)\mathbf{R}\left(E'\right)z_{N'}',$$

which contradicts weak Pareto because

$$z'_j \gg \frac{\Omega}{|N|} + 3rm\varepsilon = z_j - \Delta_j + 3rm\varepsilon,$$

$$z'_k \gg z_k + 4\Delta_k + 3rm\varepsilon,$$

and for all $i \in N \setminus \{j, k\}$, $z'_i \, P_i \, z_i + 3rm\varepsilon$.

Step 2. Let $E = (R_N, \Omega) \in \mathcal{E}$, $z_N, z'_N \in X^N$ be such that for all $i \in N$, $z'_i \, P_i \, \Omega/|N|$ and there exists $j \in N$ such that $\Omega/|N| \, P_j \, z_j$. There exist z^1_N, z^2_N such that for all $i \in N$, $z^1_i \, P_i \, z_i$, $z'_i \, P_i \, z^2_i$, and for all $i \in N \setminus \{j\}$, $z^1_i \gg z^2_i \gg \Omega/|N| \gg z^2_j \gg z^1_j$.

By weak Pareto, $z^1_N \, \mathbf{P}(E) \, z_N$. By a repeated application of step 1 (at each application, some $i \neq j$ is moved down from z^1_i to z^2_i while j is moved up from $z^1_j + t\Delta$ to $z^1_j + (t+1)\Delta$, for $t = 0, \ldots, |N| - 2$ and $\Delta = (z^2_j - z^1_j)/(|N| - 1)$), $z^2_N \, \mathbf{P}(E) \, z^1_N$. By weak Pareto, $z'_N \, \mathbf{P}(E) \, z^2_N$. By transitivity, $z'_N \, \mathbf{P}(E) \, z_N$. ∎

Proof of Theorem A.1. Let $E = (R_N, \Omega) \in \mathcal{E}$ and $z_N, z'_N \in X^N$ be such that $\min_{i \in N} u_\Omega(z_i, R_i) > \min_{i \in N} u_\Omega(z'_i, R_i)$. We must prove that $z_N \, \mathbf{P}(E) \, z'_N$.

Let $L = \{i \in N \mid z_i \, P_i \, z'_i\}$ and $L^c = N \setminus L$. By construction, $L \neq \emptyset$. If $L^c = \emptyset$, one immediately gets $z_N \, \mathbf{P}(E) \, z'_N$ by weak Pareto. We now consider the subcase $L^c \neq \emptyset$. Let $l = |L|$.

Step 1: Let $n = |N|$. We first prove that $z_N \, \mathbf{P}(E) \, z'_N$ when $\min_{i \in N} u_\Omega(z'_i, R_i) < 1/(n - l)$. Let $m, q \in \mathbb{Z}_{++}$ be such that $q > n$, $m/q < 1/(n - l)$, $m/q \neq u_\Omega(z'_i, R_i)$ for all $i \in N$ and

$$\min_{i \in N} u_\Omega(z_i, R_i) > \frac{m}{q} > \min_{i \in N} u_\Omega(z'_i, R_i).$$

Let $z^1_N, z^2_N, z^3_N, z^4_N$ be such that for all $i \in N$, $z^1_i \gg z_i \gg z^2_i \gg z^3_i$ and $z^4_i \gg z'_i$, and

$$\frac{m}{q}\Omega \, P_i \, z^4_i \Leftrightarrow \frac{m}{q}\Omega \, P_i \, z'_i$$

$$z^3_i \, P_i \, z^4_i \Leftrightarrow z_i \, P_i \, z'_i$$

$$z^3_i \, P_i \, \frac{m}{q}\Omega \text{ for all } i \in N.$$

The construction is illustrated in Figure A.3.

Case 1: $m/q \leq 1/n$. Let $E' = (R_{N'}, m\Omega)$ be a m-replica of E. Choose any $i_0 \in L$. Let $E_0 = \left(\left(R_{N'}, \underbrace{R_{i_0}, \ldots, R_{i_0}}_{q-mn} \right), m\Omega \right)$. The average endowment in E_0 is $\frac{m}{q}\Omega$. By Lemma A.2,

$$\left(z^3_{N'}, z^3_{i_0}, \ldots, z^3_{i_0} \right) \mathbf{P}(E_0) \left(z'_{N'}, z_{i_0}, \ldots, z_{i_0} \right).$$

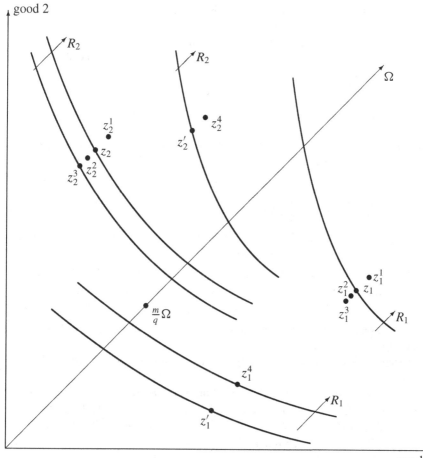

Figure A.3. Proof of Theorem A.1

By opponent separation, $z_{N'}^3 \, \mathbf{R}(E') \, z_{N'}'$. By weak Pareto, $z_{N'} \, \mathbf{P}(E') \, z_{N'}^3$ and therefore $z_{N'} \, \mathbf{P}(E') \, z_{N'}'$. By replication, $z_N \, \mathbf{P}(E) \, z_N'$.

   Case 2: $1/n < m/q < 1/(n-l)$. Let $m' \in \mathbb{Z}_{++}$ be a multiple of m such that

$$m' > \frac{m}{q} \frac{l}{\min\left\{1 - \frac{m}{q}(n-l), \frac{m}{q}n - 1\right\}},$$

and let $q' = m'q/m$. The previous inequality is equivalent to

$$l + m'(n-l) < q' < (m'-1)l + m'(n-l).$$

Let $E' = \left(R_{N'}, m'\Omega\right)$ be an m'-replica of E. Let $N(i) \subseteq N'$ be the set of agents who are "clones" of i (including i). Because of the preceding inequalities, there exists a list of subsets K_N such that for all $i \in L$, $\emptyset \neq K_i \subsetneq N(i)$ and $\sum_{i \in L} |K_i| + m'(n - l) = q'$.

Let (N_1, N_2, N_3) be a partition of N' defined by: $N_1 = \cup_{i \in L} K_i$, $N_2 = \cup_{i \in L} N(i) \setminus K_i$, $N_3 = \cup_{i \in L^c} N(i)$. To make things clearer, we define allocations with tables, so for instance, the following table

N_1	N_2	N_3
z_i^1	z_i^4	z_i^2

means that for all $i \in N$, $j \in N(i)$, if $i \in L$ and $j \in K_i$, then j consumes z_i^1; if $i \in L$ and $j \in N(i) \setminus K_i$, j consumes z_i^4; if $i \notin L$, then j consumes z_i^2. Let

	N_1	N_2	N_3
$z_{N'}^a =$	z_i^4	z_i^3	z_i^4
$z_{N'}^b =$	z_i^3	z_i^2	z_i^2

Let $E'' = (R_{N_1 \cup N_3}, m'\Omega)$. The average endowment in E'' is $\frac{m'}{q'}\Omega = \frac{m}{q}\Omega$. For all $j \in N_1 \cup N_3$, $z_j^b P_j \frac{m}{q}\Omega$, whereas for some $j \in N_1$, $\frac{m}{q}\Omega P_j z_j^a$. Therefore, by Lemma A.2, $z_{N_1 \cup N_3}^b \mathbf{P}(E'') z_{N_1 \cup N_3}^a$. Moreover, one has, for all $i \in N$, all $j \in N_2 \cap N(i)$, $z_j^b P_j z_k^a$, so that, by opponent separation, $z_{N'}^b \mathbf{P}(E') z_{N'}^a$. By weak Pareto, $z_{N'}^a \mathbf{P}(E') z_{N'}'$ and $z_{N'} \mathbf{P}(E') z_{N'}^b$. By transitivity, $z_{N'} \mathbf{P}(E') z_{N'}'$. By replication, $z_N \mathbf{P}(E) z_N'$.

Step 2: We now extend the result to the more general case, $\min_{i \in N} u_\Omega(z_i', R_i) < 1$.

Let the population of set L^c be numbered $i_1, \ldots, i_{n-l}$. We construct allocations z_N^k, for $k = 1, \ldots, n - l$. Let $j \in L$, $\lambda_0 \in (0, 1]$ be such that $u_\Omega(z_j', R_j) = \min_{i \in N} u_\Omega(z_i', R_i) < \lambda_0 < \min_{i \in N} u_\Omega(z_i, R_i)$.

The allocation z_N^1 is chosen so that

$$\lambda_0 \Omega P_j z_j^1 P_j z_j', \quad z_{i_1}^1 P y_{i_1} z_{i_1}',$$

for all $i \in L^c, i \neq i_1$, $z_i P_i z_i^1 P_i \lambda_0\Omega$,

for all $i \in L \setminus \{j\}$, $z_i P_i z_i^1 P_i z_i'$ and $z_i^1 P_i \lambda_0\Omega$.

One therefore has: $u_\Omega(z_j^1, R_j) = \min_{i \in N} u_\Omega(z_i^1, R_i) < 1$. For all $i \neq i_1$, $z_i P_i z_i^1$, whereas $z_{i_1}^1 P_{i_1} z_{i_1}' R_{i_1} z_{i_1}$. Denoting $l_1 = |\{i \in N \mid z_i P_i z_i^1\}|$, one then has $l_1 = n - 1$, and $\min_{i \in N} u_\Omega(z_i^1, R_i) < 1/(n - l_1) = 1$. Moreover, $\min_{i \in N} u_\Omega(z_i^1, R_i) < \min_{i \in N} u_\Omega(z_i, R_i)$. By a direct application of step 1 to the pair of allocations z_N, z_N^1, one concludes that $z_N \mathbf{P}(E) z_N^1$.

Similarly, for $k = 2, \ldots, n - l$, construct z_N^k such that

$$z_j^{k-1} P_j z_j^k P_j z_j', \quad z_{i_k}^k P_{i_k} z_{i_k}',$$

for $i = 1, \ldots, i_{k-1}$, $z_i^{k-1} P_i z_i^k P_i z_i'$,

for $i = i_{k+1}, \ldots, i_{n-l}$, $z_i^{k-1} P_i z_i^k P_i \lambda_0\Omega$,

for all $i \in L \setminus \{j\}$, $z_i^{k-1} P_i z_i^k P_i z_i'$ and $z_i^k P_i \lambda_0\Omega$.

This implies $u_\Omega(z_j^k, R_j) = \min_{i \in N} u_\Omega(z_i^k, R_i)$. Necessarily, $u_\Omega(z_j^k, R_j) < 1$. Denoting $l_k = \left| \{ i \in N \mid z_i^{k-1} \, P_i \, z_i^k \} \right|$, one has $l_k = n - 1$, and $\min_{i \in N} u_\Omega (z_i^k, R_i) < 1/(n - l_k) = 1$. Moreover,

$$\min_{i \in N} u_\Omega(z_i^k, R_i) = u_\Omega(z_j^k, R_j) < u_\Omega(z_j^{k-1}, R_j) = \min_{i \in N} u_\Omega(z_i^{k-1}, R_i).$$

By a direct application of step 1, $z_N^{k-1} \, \mathbf{P}(E) \, z_N^k$. Finally, by construction, for all $i \in N$, $z_i^{n-l} \, P_i \, z_i'$, so that by weak Pareto, $z_N^{n-l} \, \mathbf{P}(E) \, z_N'$. By transitivity, one concludes that $z_N \, \mathbf{P}(E) \, z_N'$.

Step 3: We extend again to the general case. Let m' be such that $\min_{i \in N} u_\Omega(z_i', R_i) < m'$, and let $E' = (R_{N'}, m'\Omega)$ be an m'-replica of E. One has $\min_{i \in N'} u_{\Omega'}(z_i', R_i) < 1$. By application of Step 2, one must have $z_{N'} \, \mathbf{P}(E') \, z_{N'}'$. By replication, $z_N \, \mathbf{P}(E) \, z_N'$. This completes the proof.

In addition, we show that each axiom is necessary.

1. Drop weak Pareto. Take $\mathbf{R}^{p\text{sum}}$.
2. Drop equal-split transfer. Take $\mathbf{R}^{\Omega\text{sum}}$.
3. Drop opponent separation. Consider $\mathbf{R}^\lambda$ defined as follows. Let $\Lambda : \mathbb{R}_+ \to X$ be defined by: $\Lambda(\lambda) = \left(\Omega_k |N|^{k-1} \lambda^k \right)_{k=1,\dots,\ell}$. This defines a monotonic path that contains 0 and $\Omega/|N|$ but is not a ray from the origin. Then for any $z_N, z_N', \lambda_N, \lambda_N'$ such that for all $i \in N$, $z_i \, I_i \, \Lambda(\lambda_i)$ and $z_i' \, I_i \, \Lambda(\lambda_i')$, let $z_N \, \mathbf{R}^\lambda(E) \, z_N'$ iff $\min_{i \in N} \lambda_i \geq \min_{i \in N} \lambda_i'$.
4. Drop replication. Consider $\mathbf{R}$ defined as follows. For any $E = (R_N, \Omega)$, let $A(E) = \{ z_N \mid \forall i \in N, \, z_i \, R_i \, \Omega \}$ and $\bar{A}(E) = X^N \setminus A(E)$. Then $\mathbf{R} = \mathbf{R}^{\Omega\text{sum}}$ over $A(E)$, $\mathbf{R} = \mathbf{R}^{\Omega\min}$ over $\bar{A}(E)$, and $z_N \, \mathbf{P}(E) \, z_N'$ whenever $z_N \in A(E)$, $z_N' \in \bar{A}(E)$. ∎

Lemma A.3 *On the domain $\mathcal{E}$, if a SOF satisfies strong Pareto and priority among equals, then for all $E = (R_N, \Omega) \in \mathcal{E}$, and $z_N, z_N' \in X^N$, if for all $i \in N$ such that $z_i \, P_i \, z_i'$, there is $j \in N$ such that $R_j = R_i$ and*

$$z_i \, P_i \, z_i' \, P_i \, z_j' \, P_i \, z_j,$$

then $z_N' \, \mathbf{R}(E) \, z_N$.

Proof. It derives directly from repeated application of the conditions. ∎

Lemma A.4 *Let $\Omega \in \mathbb{R}_{++}^\ell$, $b_1, \dots, b_n \in \mathbb{Z}_{++}$, and $x_1, \dots, x_n \in \mathbb{R}_+^\ell$. If*

$$\frac{1}{\sum_{i=1}^n b_i} \sum_{i=1}^n b_i x_i \ll \Omega,$$

then for all $p \in \Pi_\Omega$, there exist $y_1, \dots, y_n \in \mathbb{R}_+^\ell$ such that:

$$\forall i \in \{1, \dots, n\}, \; y_i \leq x_i \text{ or } y_i \gg x_i,$$

$$\forall i \in \{1, \dots, n\}, \; p y_i = 1,$$

$$\frac{1}{\sum_{i=1}^n b_i} \sum_{i=1}^n b_i y_i = \Omega.$$

Proof. Let $J = \{i \mid px_i \geq 1\}$ and $K = \{i \mid px_i < 1\}$. As $p\Omega = 1$, necessarily $K \neq \emptyset$. For all $i \in J$, define $y_i = \frac{1}{px_i}x_i$. By construction, $x_i \geq y_i$ for all $i \in J$, so that

$$\Omega' = \frac{1}{\sum_{i=1}^n b_i} \left[\sum_{i \in J} b_i y_i + \sum_{i \in K} b_i x_i \right] \ll \Omega.$$

Now, for all $i \in K$, let

$$y_i = x_i + \frac{(1 - px_i)}{(1 - p\Omega')} (\Omega - \Omega').$$

One has $y_i \gg x_i$ and $py_i = 1$ for all $i \in K$. Moreover, one computes

$$\frac{1}{\sum_{i=1}^n b_i} \sum_{i=1}^n b_i y_i = \Omega,$$

which completes the proof.   ∎

Proof of Theorem 5.5. Let $E = (R_N, \Omega) \in \mathcal{E}$ and $z_N, z'_N \in X^N$ be such that

$$z'_N \, \mathbf{R}(E) \, z_N \tag{A.1}$$

in spite of $z_N \, \mathbf{P}^{EW}(E) \, z'_N$. Let $p_z \in \arg\max_{p \in \Pi_\Omega} \min_{i \in N} u_p(z_i, R_i)$ and similarly for $p_{z'}$. There exist $m, q \in \mathbb{Z}_{++}$ such that

$$\min_{i \in N} u_{p_{z'}}(z'_i, R_i) < \frac{m}{q} < \min_{i \in N} u_{p_z}(z_i, R_i). \tag{A.2}$$

By strong Pareto, (A.1) implies that there exists $i \in N$ such that $z'_i \, R_i \, z_i$. The fact that $z_N \, \mathbf{P}^{EW}(E) \, z'_N$ implies that there exists $i \in N$ such that $z_i \, P_i \, z'_i$.

Step 1: **Construction of bundles and preferences** (see Figure A.4). Let

$$K = \{i \in N \mid u_{p_{z'}}(z'_i, R_i) = \min_{i \in N} u_{p_{z'}}(z'_i, R_i) \text{ or } z'_i \, R_i \, z_i\}.$$

In view of (A.2), there exist weights $(a_i)_{i \in N} \in \mathbb{R}^N_{++}$ with $\sum_{i \in N} a_i = 1$, and an allocation $\widehat{z}_N \in X^N$, such that for all $i \in K$, $\widehat{z}_i \, I_i \, z'_i$; for all $i \in N \setminus K$, $\widehat{z}_i \, I_i \, z_i$; $\sum_{i \in N} a_i \widehat{z}_i \ll \frac{m}{q}\Omega$.

Therefore, there exist $z^1_N, z^{1+}_N, z^{1++}_N, z^{1+++}_N$ in X^N, arbitrarily close to $\widehat{z}_N$, and $(n_i)_{i \in N} \in \mathbb{Z}^N_{++}$ such that

$$\frac{1}{\sum_{i \in N} n_i} \sum_{i \in N} n_i z^{1+++}_i \ll \frac{m}{q}\Omega \tag{A.3}$$

and such that for all $i \in N$,

$$z^1_N < z^{1+}_N < z^{1++}_N < z^{1+++}_N,$$
$$z^1_i \, P_i \, z'_i, \tag{A.4}$$
$$z_i \, P_i \, z'_i \Rightarrow z_i \, P_i \, z^{1+++}_i,$$

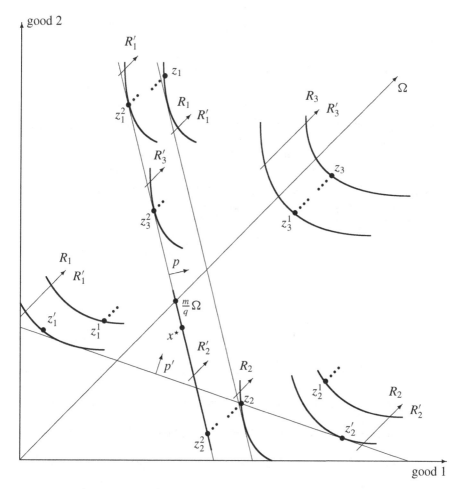

Figure A.4. Proof of Theorem 5.5

and for all $i \in N \setminus K$, $z_i^1 \, P_i \, q$ for all q such that $p_z q \le p_z \frac{m}{q} \Omega = \frac{m}{q}$. Then by Lemma A.3, one can find $z_N^2 \in X^N$ such that for all $i \in N$,

$$
\begin{aligned}
&p_z z_i^2 = \frac{m}{q} \\
&z_i^2 \le z_i^1 \text{ or } z_i^2 \gg z_i^1 \\
&\frac{1}{\sum_{i \in N} n_i} \sum_{i \in N} n_i z_i^2 = \frac{m}{q} \Omega.
\end{aligned} \tag{A.5}
$$

We now construct a new profile R_N'. Consider i such that $z_i' \, R_i \, z_i$ (agent 2 in Figure A.4 – as noted previously, some such i must exist). By (A.4), $z_i^1 \, P_i \, z_i$, so

$$
U\left(z_i^1, R_i\right) \subseteq U\left(z_i, R_i\right) \subseteq \left\{ x \in X \mid p_z x > \frac{m}{q} \right\},
$$

One can then find R_i' such that $I\left(z_i^1, R_i\right) = I\left(z_i^1, R_i'\right)$, $I\left(z_i, R_i\right) = I\left(z_i, R_i'\right)$ and

$$I\left(\frac{m}{q}\Omega, R_i'\right) = \left\{x \in X \mid p_z x = \frac{m}{q}\right\}.$$

Now consider i such that $z_i\, P_i\, z_i'$ (agent 1 in Figure A.4 – as noted previously, some such i must exist). Then, by (A.4), $z_i\, P_i\, z_i^1$. If $p_z z_i^1 < m/q$, then, by (A.5), $z_i^2 \gg z_i^1$. In addition, for all $x \in X$ such that $p_z x = m/q$, one has $z_i\, P_i\, x$. It is then easy to find R_i' such that $I\left(z_i^1, R_i\right) = I\left(z_i^1, R_i'\right)$, $I\left(z_i, R_i\right) = I\left(z_i, R_i'\right)$ and $z_i^2 \in \max|_{R_i'}\, B(\frac{m}{q}\Omega, p_z)$. If, on the other hand, $p_z z_i^1 \geq m/q$ (agent 3 in Figure A.4), then, by (A.5), $z_i^2 \leq z_i^1$. Recall that by construction, $z_i^1\, P_i\, q$ for all q such that $p_z q \leq m/q$. In that case, one can also find R_i' satisfying the preceding conditions.

Summing up, one can find R_N' such that for all $i \in N$,

$$I\left(z_i^1, R_i\right) = I\left(z_i^1, R_i'\right),$$

$$I\left(z_i, R_i\right) = I\left(z_i, R_i'\right), \tag{A.6}$$

$$z_i^2 \in \max|_{R_i'}\, B\left(\frac{m}{q}\Omega, p_z\right). \tag{A.7}$$

and such that for some j^* with $z_{j^*}^1\, P_{j^*}\, z_{j^*}$

$$I\left(\frac{m}{q}\Omega, R_{j^*}'\right) = \left\{x \in X \mid p_z x = \frac{m}{q}\right\}.$$

Note that, by (A.2), (A.6), and (A.7), for all $i \in N$ one has:

$$z_i\, P_i'\, z_i^2, \tag{A.8}$$

and $z_i\, P_i\, z_i^{1+++}$ iff $z_i\, P_i'\, z_i^{1+++}$.

By (A.5), one can find $x^* \in X$ and $\nu \in \mathbb{Z}_{++}$ such that

$$p_z x^* = \frac{m}{q}$$

$$\frac{1}{|N| + \nu}\left[\sum_{i \in N} z_i^2 + \nu x^*\right] = \frac{m}{q}\Omega. \tag{A.9}$$

Similarly, by (A.3) one can then choose $\mu, s \in \mathbb{Z}_{++}$ such that

$$|N| + \nu + \mu \sum_{i \in N} n_i = s > \frac{q}{m}$$

$$\frac{1}{s}\left[\sum_{i \in N} z_i^{1++} + \nu z_{j^*}^{1++} + \mu \sum_{i \in N} n_i z_i^{1+++}\right] \ll \frac{m}{q}\Omega. \tag{A.10}$$

By (A.5) and (A.9), one then necessarily has:

$$\frac{1}{s}\left[\sum_{i\in N} z_i^2 + \nu x^* + \mu \sum_{i\in N} n_i z_i^2\right] = \frac{m}{q}\Omega. \tag{A.11}$$

Let $L = \{i \in N \mid z_i\, P_i\, z_i^1\}$ and $L^c = N \setminus L$. Notice that one also has $L = \{i \in N \mid z_i\, P_i'\, z_i^{1+++}\}$. Indeed, by (A.4) and (A.6),

$$z_i\, P_i\, z_i^1 \Rightarrow z_i\, P_i\, z_i' \Rightarrow z_i\, P_i\, z_i^{1+++} \Rightarrow z_i\, P_i'\, z_i^{1+++},$$
$$z_i^1\, R_i\, z_i \Rightarrow z_i^1\, R_i'\, z_i \Rightarrow z_i^{1+++}\, P_i'\, z_i.$$

By (A.8), there exist $z_N^-, z_N^{--}, z_N^{---}, z_N^{2+}, z_N^{2++} \in X^N$ such that for all $i \in N$,

$$z_i > z_i^- > z_i^{--} > z_i^{---}\, P_i'\, z_i^{2++} > z_i^{2+} > z_i^2, \tag{A.12}$$

and for all $i \in L$,

$$z_i^{---}\, P_i'\, z_i^{1+++}. \tag{A.13}$$

To sum up, for all $i \in L$,

$$z_i\, P_i'\, z_i^- > z_i^{--} > z_i^{---}\, P_i'\, z_i^{1+++} > z_i^{1++} > z_i^{1+} > z_i^1\, P_i'\, z_i'$$

and

$$z_i^{---}\, P_i'\, z_i^{2++} > z_i^{2+} > z_i^2$$

whereas for all $i \in L^c$,

$$z_i^{1+++} > z_i^{1++} > z_i^{1+} > z_i^1\, P_i'\, z_i'\, R_i'\, z_i > z_i^- > z_i^{--}$$
$$> z_i^{---}\, P_i'\, z_i^{2++} > z_i^{2+} > z_i^2.$$

***Step 2*: Derivation of a contradiction.** By weak Pareto and (A.4), $z_N^1\, \mathbf{P}(E)\, z_N'$. Hence, by (A.1) and transitivity,

$$z_N^1\, \mathbf{P}(E)\, z_N. \tag{A.14}$$

Let $E' = (R_N', \Omega)$. By (A.14) and unchanged-contour independence,

$$z_N^1\, \mathbf{P}(E')\, z_N. \tag{A.15}$$

Let $E'^{ms} = (R_{N_{ms}}', ms\Omega) \in \mathcal{E}$ be an ms-replica of E'. We partition N_{ms} into four subsets: for every $i \in L$, N_1 contains (an arbitrary selection of) q clones of i and N_3 contains the remaining $ms - q$ clones; for every $i \in L^c$, N_2 contains q clones of i and N_4 contain $ms - q$ such clones. Next, we introduce three other sets of additional agents, N_5, N_6, and N_7, with sizes (the agents' indices do not matter)

$$|N_5| = q\nu, \quad |N_6| = q\mu \sum_{i\in L} n_i, \quad |N_7| = q\mu \sum_{i\in L^c} n_i.$$

By (A.15) and replication,

$$
\begin{array}{cccc}
N_1 & N_2 & N_3 & N_4 \\
z_i^1 & z_i^1 & z_i^1 & z_i^1
\end{array}
\quad \mathbf{R}(E'^{ms})
\quad
\begin{array}{cccc}
N_1 & N_2 & N_3 & N_4 \\
z_i & z_i & z_i & z_i.
\end{array}
$$

By strong Pareto,

$$
\begin{array}{cccc}
N_1 & N_2 & N_3 & N_4 \\
z_i^{1+} & z_i^{1+} & z_i^- & z_i^{1++} \\
z_i & z_i & z_i & z_i
\end{array}
\quad
\begin{array}{c}
\mathbf{P}(E'^{ms}) \\
\mathbf{P}(E'^{ms})
\end{array}
\quad
\begin{array}{cccc}
N_1 & N_2 & N_3 & N_4 \\
z_i^1 & z_i^1 & z_i^1 & z_i^1, \\
z_i^{--} & z_i^{--} & z_i^- & z_i^-.
\end{array}
$$

By Theorem 3.1, R satisfies priority among equals. Therefore, one also has

$$
\begin{array}{cccc}
N_1 & N_2 & N_3 & N_4 \\
z_i^{--} & z_i^{--} & z_i^- & z_i^-
\end{array}
\quad \mathbf{R}(E'^{ms})
\quad
\begin{array}{cccc}
N_1 & N_2 & N_3 & N_4 \\
z_i^{--} & z_i^{2++} & z_i^- & z_i^{1++},
\end{array}
$$

by Lemma A.3, because for all $j \in N_2$, $k \in N_4$ who are clones of the same $i \in L^c$, one has:

$$
\underbrace{z_i^{1++} \, P_i' \, z_i^-}_{\text{(consumed by } k)} \, P_i' \, \underbrace{z_i^{--} \, P_i' \, z_i^{2++}}_{\text{(consumed by } j)}.
$$

By transitivity:

$$
\begin{array}{cccc}
N_1 & N_2 & N_3 & N_4 \\
z_i^{1+} & z_i^{1+} & z_i^- & z_i^{1++}
\end{array}
\quad \mathbf{P}(E'^{ms})
\quad
\begin{array}{cccc}
N_1 & N_2 & N_3 & N_4 \\
z_i^{--} & z_i^{2++} & z_i^- & z_i^{1++}.
\end{array}
$$

Let $E'' = (R_{N_1 \cup N_2}', ms\Omega)$. In the last two allocations, for all $i \in L$, $z_i^- \, P_i' \, z_i^{1+}$, and for all $i \in L^c$, $z_i^{1++} \, P_i' \, z_i^{2++}$. One can then apply well-off separation and obtain:

$$
\begin{array}{cc}
N_1 & N_2 \\
z_i^{1+} & z_k^{1+}
\end{array}
\quad \mathbf{R}(E'')
\quad
\begin{array}{cc}
N_1 & N_2 \\
z_i^{--} & z_k^{2++}.
\end{array}
$$

By strong Pareto,

$$
\begin{array}{cc}
N_1 & N_2 \\
z_i^{--} & z_k^{2++}
\end{array}
\quad \mathbf{P}(E'')
\quad
\begin{array}{cc}
N_1 & N_2 \\
z_i^{---} & z_k^{2+}.
\end{array}
$$

so, by transitivity,

$$
\begin{array}{cc}
N_1 & N_2 \\
z_i^{1+} & z_k^{1+}
\end{array}
\quad \mathbf{P}(E'')
\quad
\begin{array}{cc}
N_1 & N_2 \\
z_i^{---} & z_k^{2+}.
\end{array}
$$

Let $E''' = (R_{N_1 \cup N_2 \cup N_5 \cup N_6 \cup N_7}', ms\Omega)$, with the corresponding profiles of preferences: $R_{N_5}' = (R_{j*}', \ldots, R_{j*}')$, $R_{N_6}' = (q\mu n_i R_i)_{i \in L}$ (meaning that every R_i is replicated $q\mu n_i$ times), $R_{N_7}' = (q\mu n_i R_i)_{i \in L^c}$.

We first note that $j^* \in L^c$ and that for every $i \in L^c$, $z_i^{1++} P_i' z_i^{2+}$. For every $i \in L$, $z_i P_i' z_i^{1+}$. So, by well-off separation:

N_1	N_2	N_5	N_6	N_7		N_1	N_2	N_5	N_6	N_7
z_i^{1+}	z_i^{1+}	$z_{j^*}^{1++}$	z_i	z_i^{1+++}	$\mathbf{R}(E''')$	z_i^{---}	z_i^{2+}	$z_{j^*}^{1++}$	z_i	z_i^{1+++}.

By Lemma A.3, one has

N_1	N_2	N_5	N_6	N_7		N_1	N_2	N_5	N_6	N_7
z_i^{1++}	z_i^{1+}	$z_{j^*}^{1++}$	z_i^{1+++}	z_i^{1+++}	$\mathbf{P}(E''')$	z_i^{1+}	z_i^{1+}	$z_{j^*}^{1++}$	z_i	z_i^{1+++}

because for all $j \in N_1$, $k \in N_6$ who are clones of the same $i \in L$, one has

$$\underbrace{z_i \, P_i' \, z_i^{1+++}}_{\text{(consumed by } k)} \underbrace{P_i' z_i^{1++}}_{\text{(consumed by } j)} P_i' \, z_i^{1+}.$$

By strong Pareto,

N_1	N_2	N_5	N_6	N_7		N_1	N_2	N_5	N_6	N_7
z_i^{---}	z_i^{2+}	$z_{j^*}^{1++}$	z_i	z_i^{1+++}	$\mathbf{P}(E''')$	z_i^2	z_i^2	x^*	z_i^2	z_i^2,

so by transitivity,

N_1	N_2	N_5	N_6	N_7		N_1	N_2	N_5	N_6	N_7
z_i^{1++}	z_i^{1+}	$z_{j^*}^{1++}$	z_i^{1+++}	z_i^{1+++}	$\mathbf{P}(E''')$	z_i^2	z_i^2	x^*	z_i^2	z_i^2.

Now, by (A.10),

N_1	N_2	N_5	N_6	N_7	
z_i^{1++}	z_i^{1+}	$z_{j^*}^{1++}$	z_i^{1+++}	z_i^{1+++}	$\in Z(E''')$

whereas by (A.7) and (A.11),

N_1	N_2	N_5	N_6	N_7	
z_i^2	z_i^2	x^*	z_i^2	z_i^2	$\in S^{EW}(E''')$.

As a consequence, by Theorem 5.3,

N_1	N_2	N_5	N_6	N_7		N_1	N_2	N_5	N_6	N_7
z_i^2	z_i^2	x^*	z_i^2	z_i^2	$\mathbf{R}(E''')$	z_i^{1++}	z_i^{1+}	$z_{j^*}^{1++}$	z_i^{1+++}	z_i^{1+++},

which is a contradiction.

No axiom is redundant as follows:

1. Drop strong Pareto: the SOF yielding total indifference between all allocations.
2. Drop transfer among equals: the serial dictatorship of agents (e.g., 1 is the dictator, when 1 is indifferent then 2 takes over, and so on).
3. Drop unchanged-contour independence: consider $\mathbf{R}$ defined as follows. Let $\mathcal{E}^{CD}$ be the subset of economies with Cobb–Douglas preferences. For $E \in \mathcal{E}^{CD}$ let $p(E) \in \Pi_\Omega$ denote the unique price vector of

the Walrasian allocation(s) with equal budgets. Then for all $z_N, z'_N \in X^N$, $z_N \mathbf{R}(E) z'_N$ iff $\left(u_{p(E)}(z_i, R_i)\right)_{i \in N} \geq_{lex} \left(u_{p(E)}(z'_i, R_i)\right)_{i \in N}$. For $E \in \mathcal{E} \setminus \mathcal{E}^{CD}$, $z_N \mathbf{R}(E) z'_N$ iff either $z_N \mathbf{P}^{EW}(E) z'_N$ or $z_N \mathbf{I}^{EW}(E) z'_N$ and $z_N \mathbf{R}^{\Omega lex}(E) z'_N$.

4. Drop selection monotonicity: $\mathbf{R}^{\Omega lex}$.
5. Drop well-off separation: consider $\mathbf{R}$ defined as follows. Let $p^0 \in \Pi_\Omega \cap \mathbb{R}^\ell_{++}$. For $E = (R_N, \Omega) \in \mathcal{E}$, $z_N, z'_N \in X^N$, let $z_N \mathbf{R}(E) z'_N$ iff $\left(u_p(z_i, R_i)\right)_{i \in N} \geq_{lex} \left(u_{p'}(z'_i, R_i)\right)_{i \in N}$, with $p \in \arg\max_{p \in \Pi_\Omega} \min_{i \in N} u_p(z_i, R_i)$ if there exists $z^*_N \in S^{EW}(E)$ such that for all $i \in N$, $z_i R_i z^*_i$, and $p = p^0$ otherwise; and similarly for p'.
6. Drop replication: consider $\mathbf{R}$ defined as follows. Let $E = (R_N, \Omega) \in \mathcal{E}$, $z_N, z'_N \in X^N$, and $\lambda, \lambda' \in \mathbb{R}_+$ be such that $\lambda = \max_{p \in \Pi_\Omega} \min_{i \in N} u_p(z_i, R_i)$ and $\lambda' = \max_{p \in \Pi_\Omega} \min_{i \in N} u_p(z'_i, R_i)$. If for all $k \in \mathbb{Z}_{++}$,

$$\frac{1}{k} \notin \left[\min\{\lambda, \lambda'\}, \max\{\lambda, \lambda'\}\right],$$

then $z_N \mathbf{R}(E) z'_N \Leftrightarrow z_N \mathbf{R}^{\Omega lex} z'_N$; otherwise $z_N \mathbf{R}(E) z'_N$ iff either $z_N \mathbf{P}^{EW}(E) z'_N$ or $z_N \mathbf{I}^{EW}(E) z'_N$ and $z_N \mathbf{R}^{\Omega lex}(E) z'_N$. ∎

Proof of Theorem 5.6. Let $z_N, z'_N \in X^N$ be two allocations such that $z_N \mathbf{P}^{EW}(E) z'_N$. Suppose that, contrary to the result, one has $z'_N \mathbf{R}(E) z_N$. The latter fact, by weak Pareto, implies the existence of some $i_0 \in N$ such that $z'_{i_0} R_{i_0} z_{i_0}$.

Let

$$p_z \in \arg\max_{p \in \Pi_\Omega} \min_{i \in N} u_p(z_i, R_i),$$

and $a, b, c, d, e, f, g \in \mathbb{R}$ be such that

$$\max_{p \in \Pi_\Omega} \min_{i \in N} u_p(z_i, R_i) > a > b > c > d > e$$
$$> \max_{p \in \Pi_\Omega} \min_{i \in N} u_p(z'_i, R_i),$$
$$g > f > \max\left\{\max_i u_\Omega(z_i, R_i), \max_i u_\Omega(z'_i, R_i)\right\}.$$

Let $E' = (R'_N, \Omega) \in \mathcal{E}$, with R'_N being defined as follows. First, R'_{i_0} is such that

$$U(z_{i_0}, R'_{i_0}) = U(z_{i_0}, R_{i_0}), \quad U(z'_{i_0}, R'_{i_0}) = U(z'_{i_0}, R_{i_0}),$$

for all $0 \leq \lambda \leq a$,

$$U(\lambda\Omega, R'_{i_0}) = \left\{q \in \mathbb{R}^\ell_+ \mid p_z q \geq \lambda\right\},$$

and

$$U(g\Omega, R'_{i_0}) = \left\{q \in \mathbb{R}^\ell_+ \mid q \geq g\Omega\right\}.$$

For all $i \neq i_0$, let R'_i be such that

$$U(z_i, R'_i) = U(z_i, R_i), \quad U(z'_i, R'_i) = U(z'_i, R_i),$$

and for all $f \le \lambda \le g$,

$$U(\lambda\Omega, R'_i) = \left\{ q \in \mathbb{R}^\ell_+ \mid q \ge \lambda\Omega \right\}.$$

By Hansson independence, $z'_N \, \mathbf{R}(E') \, z_N$.

Let z^1_N be such that for all $i \ne i_0$, $z_i \, P_i \, z^1_i$ and

$$U(z^1_i, R_i) \subseteq \left\{ q \in \mathbb{R}^\ell_+ \mid p_z q > a \right\},$$

whereas $z^1_{i_0} = a\Omega$. By weak Pareto, $z_N \, \mathbf{P}(E') \, z^1_N$, so by transitivity, $z'_N \, \mathbf{P}(E') \, z^1_N$.

Let z^2_N be such that for all $i \ne i_0$, $z^2_i = g\Omega$, while $z^2_{i_0} = b\Omega$. One has $z^1_{i_0} \, P_{i_0} \, z^2_{i_0}$ and for all $i \ne i_0$, $z^2_i \, P_i \, z^1_i$. In addition, for all $i \ne i_0$,

$$L(z^1_{i_0}, R'_{i_0}) \cap U(z^1_i, R'_i) = \emptyset$$

(their indifference curves do not cross). This implies that by repeated application of Lemma A.1 in combination with unchanged-contour independence and weak Pareto (the detailed argument has the same structure as the proof of "$z^3_N \, \mathbf{P}(E'') \, z^1_N$" in the proof of Theorem 5.1), one shows that $z^1_N \, \mathbf{P}(E') \, z^2_N$, and therefore, by transitivity, $z'_N \, \mathbf{P}(E') \, z^2_N$.

Because

$$\max_{p \in \Pi_\Omega} \min_{i \in N} u_p(z'_i, R_i) < e,$$

there exists an allocation z^{1*} and positive integers $a_1, \dots, a_n$ such that $g\Omega \, P'_i \, z^{1*}_i \, P'_i \, z'_i$ for all $i \in N$, and

$$\frac{1}{\sum_{i \in N} a_i} \sum_{i \in N} a_i z^{1*}_i \ll e\Omega.$$

Let $k = \sum_i a_i$, and consider a k-replica $E'^k = (R'_{N^k}, k\Omega)$ of E'. Consider the allocation $z^{2*}_{N^k}$ such that $z^{2*}_i = z^{1*}_i$ for all $i \in N$, and $z^{2*}_j = g\Omega$ for all "clones" $j \in \gamma^{-1}(i) \setminus \{i\}$ (see Section 2.3 for these notions). By weak Pareto, $z^{2*}_{N^k} \, \mathbf{P}(E'^k) \, z'_{N^k}$; therefore, by replication and transitivity, $z^{2*}_{N^k} \, \mathbf{P}(E'^k) \, z^2_{N^k}$.

Let the allocation $z^3_{N^k}$ be defined by $z^3_{i_0} = d\Omega$, $z^3_j = c\Omega$ for all $j \in \gamma^{-1}(i_0) \setminus \{i_0\}$, and $z^3_i = f\Omega$ for all $i \notin \gamma^{-1}(i_0)$. By weak Pareto, $z^2_{N^k} \, \mathbf{P}(E'^k) \, z^3_{N^k}$. Let the allocation $z^*_{N^k}$ be defined by $z^*_{i_0} = e\Omega$ and $z^*_i = g\Omega$ for all $i \ne i_0$. One has $z^3_{i_0} \, P'_i \, z^*_{i_0}$ because $z^3_{i_0} = d\Omega > e\Omega = z^*_{i_0}$, while for all $j \in \gamma^{-1}(i_0) \setminus \{i_0\}$, $z^*_j = g\Omega > c\Omega = z^3_j$, and for all $i \notin \gamma^{-1}(i_0)$, $z^*_i = g\Omega > f\Omega = z^3_i$. One also has $L(z^3_{i_0}, R'_{i_0}) \cap U(z^3_i, R'_i) = \emptyset$ for all $i \ne i_0$ (in particular, $R'_i = R'_{i_0}$ for $i \in \gamma^{-1}(i_0) \setminus \{i_0\}$). By Lemma A.1, unchanged-contour independence, and weak Pareto (same argument as earlier), $z^3_{N^k} \, \mathbf{P}(E'^k) \, z^*_{N^k}$, so, by transitivity, $z^{2*}_{N^k} \, \mathbf{P}(E'^k) \, z^*_{N^k}$.

Now, let $E''^k = (R''_{N^k}, k\Omega)$ with a new profile R''_{N^k} defined by: $R''_i = R'_i$ for all $i \in N$, and among the $(k-1)n$ remaining agents (the "clones," who all have $g\Omega$ in both $z^{2*}_{N^k}$ and $z^*_{N^k}$), $a_i n - 1$ of them have a preference relation equal to R'_i, for every $i \in N$. Because for all $i \in N^k$,

$$U(R''_i, z^{2*}_i) = U(R'_i, z^{2*}_i), \ U(R''_i, z^*_i) = U(R'_i, z^*_i),$$

by unchanged-contour independence, one has $z^{2*}_{N^k} \mathbf{P}(E''^k) z^*_{N^k}$.

Close to z^{1*}_N, in E there exist two allocations z^{3*}_N and z'^*_N such that for all $i \in N$,

$$g\Omega P'_i z'^*_i \gg z^{3*}_i \gg z^{1*}_i,$$

and

$$\frac{1}{\sum_i a_i} \sum_i a_i z'^*_i \ll e\Omega.$$

In E''^k, let $z'^{**}_{N^k}$ be the allocation defined by $z'^{**}_i = z^{3*}_i$ for all $i \in N$, and $z'^{**}_j = z'^*_i$ for all $a_i n - 1$ clones j who have $R''_j = R'_i$. One has $z'^{**}_i P'_i z^{2*}_i$ for all $i \in N$ because $z'^{**}_i = z^{3*}_i \gg z^{1*}_i = z^{2*}_i$, whereas for all clones j, $z^{2*}_j = g\Omega P'_j z'^*_j = z'^{**}_j$. One also has $L(z^{3*}_i, R'_i) \cap U(z'^*_j, R'_j) = \emptyset$ for all $i \in N$, $j \in \gamma^{-1}(i) \setminus \{i\}$ (because $R'_j = R'_i$ and $z'^*_j = z'^*_i \gg z^{3*}_i$). By Lemma A.1, unchanged-contour independence, and weak Pareto (same argument as earlier), $z'^{**}_{N^k} \mathbf{P}(E''^k) z^{2*}_{N^k}$, so $z'^{**}_{N^k} \mathbf{P}(E''^k) z^*_{N^k}$.

However, $z^*_{N^k}$ is such that for all $i \in N^k$,

$$z^*_i \geq e\Omega \gg \frac{1}{\sum_{j \in N} a_j} \sum_{j \in N} a_j z'^*_j \gg \frac{1}{nk} \sum_{j \in N^k} z'^{**}_j,$$

the latter inequality being the result of the fact that

$$\frac{1}{nk} \sum_{j \in N^k} z'^{**}_j = \frac{1}{nk} \sum_{i \in N} \left(z^{3*}_i + \sum_{j \in \gamma^{-1}(i) \setminus \{i\}} z'^*_i \right)$$

$$= \frac{1}{nk} \sum_{i \in N} \left(z^{3*}_i + (a_i n - 1) z'^*_i \right)$$

$$\ll \frac{1}{nk} \sum_{i \in N} \left(z'^*_i + (a_i n - 1) z'^*_i \right)$$

$$= \frac{1}{\sum_{i \in N} a_i} \sum_{i \in N} a_i z'^*_i.$$

Moreover, $z^*_{N^k} \in P\left(R''_{N^k}, \sum_{i \in N^k} z^*_i \right)$. This entails a contradiction with proportional-efficient dominance.

Finally, we must show that no axiom is redundant.

1. Drop weak Pareto. Take the SOF yielding total indifference.
2. Drop transfer among equals. Take $\mathbf{R}^{RU}$.
3. Drop proportional-efficient dominance. Take $\mathbf{R}^{\Omega\min}$.

4. Drop unchanged-contour independence. Take the SOF that coincides with $\mathbf{R}^{EW}$ if there are agents with identical preferences, and with $\mathbf{R}^{RU}$ otherwise.

5. Drop replication. Take the SOF $\mathbf{R}$ defined by:

$$z_N \, \mathbf{R}(E) \, z'_N \Leftrightarrow V(z_N) \geq V(z'_N),$$

with

$$V(z_N) = \min \left\{ \begin{array}{l} \lambda \in \mathbb{R}_+ \mid \exists q_N \in \prod_{i \in N} U(z_i, R_i), a_N \in \mathbb{Z}^N_+, \\ \sum_{i \in N} a_i = |N|, \; \lambda \Omega \geq \sum_{i \in N} a_i q_i \end{array} \right\}.$$

∎

A.3 CHAPTER 6: SPECIFIC DOMAINS

Proof of Theorem 6.1. We prove the result using opponent separation instead of separation. Theorem 3.2 still holds on $\mathcal{E}^R$ (even replacing separability with opponent separation; moreover, opponent separation makes the result hold for the whole domain $\mathcal{E}^R$ and not just for economies with at least three agents), so any $\mathbf{R}$ satisfying weak Pareto, nested-contour transfer, and opponent separation also satisfies a variety of nested-contour priority that says the following: For all $E = (R_N, \Omega) \in \mathcal{E}^R$, and $z_N, z'_N \in X^N$, if there exist $j, k \in N$ such that

$$z_j \gg z'_j \gg z'_k \gg z_k,$$

$$U(z'_j, R_j) \cap L(z'_k, R_k) = \emptyset$$

and for all $i \neq j, k$, $z'_i \, P_i \, z_i$, then $z'_N \, \mathbf{P}(E) \, z_N$.

Let $E = (R_N, \Omega) \in \mathcal{E}^R$ and $z_N, z'_N \in X^N$ be such that $\min_{i \in N} c(z_i, R_i) > \min_{i \in N} c(z'_i, R_i)$. Assume that, contrary to the desired result, $z'_N \, \mathbf{R}(E) \, z_N$.

Let $i_0 \in N$ be chosen so that $c(z'_{i_0}, R_{i_0}) < \min_{i \in N} c(z_i, R_i)$. Let $z^1_N, z^2_N, z^3_N, z^4_N, z^5_N, z^6_N \in X^N_c$ be such that for all $i \in N$, $z_i \, P_i \, z^3_i$, $z^1_i \, P_i \, z'_i$; for all $i \in N \setminus \{i_0\}$, $z^1_i \, P_i \, z_i$ and

$$z^1_{i_0} \ll z^2_{i_0} \ll z^6_i = z^6_{i_0} \ll z^5_i \ll z^4_i \ll z^3_i = z^3_{i_0} \ll z^2_i \ll z^1_i;$$

$$\sum_{i \in N} z^2_i + \sum_{i \neq i_0} z^3_i \ll (2|N| - 1) z^6_{i_0}. \tag{A.16}$$

By weak Pareto, $z^1_N \, \mathbf{P}(E) \, z'_N$ and $z_N \, \mathbf{P}(E) \, z^3_N$, so that $z^1_N \, \mathbf{P}(E) \, z^3_N$. For any $i \neq i_0$, let $\hat{\imath} \notin N$ be an agent such that $R_{\hat{\imath}} = R_i$. Let $M = \{\hat{\imath} \mid i \in N \setminus \{i_0\}\}$. For $t = 3, 4, 5, 6$, let z^t_M be defined by $z^t_{\hat{\imath}} = z^t_i$ for all $\hat{\imath} \in M$. By opponent separation,

$$\left(z^1_N, z^4_M \right) \, \mathbf{P}((R_N, R_M), \Omega) \, \left(z^3_N, z^5_M \right).$$

By the preceding variant of nested-contour priority,

$$\left(z^2_{i_0}, z^2_{N \setminus \{i_0\}}, z^3_M \right) \, \mathbf{P}((R_N, R_M), \Omega) \, \left(z^1_N, z^4_M \right)$$

so, by transitivity,

$$\left(z_{i_0}^2, z_{N\setminus\{i_0\}}^2, z_M^3\right) \mathbf{P}((R_N, R_M), \Omega) \left(z_N^3, z_M^5\right).$$

By weak Pareto, $\left(z_N^3, z_M^5\right) \mathbf{P}((R_N, R_M), \Omega) \left(z_N^6, z_M^6\right)$. However, certainty transfer, weak Pareto, and (A.16) imply that

$$\left(z_N^6, z_M^6\right) \mathbf{P}((R_N, R_M), \Omega) \left(z_{i_0}^2, z_{N\setminus\{i_0\}}^2, z_M^3\right),$$

which is a contradiction.

We check that no condition is redundant.

1. Drop weak Pareto. Take the SOF yielding total indifference.
2. Drop nested-contour transfer. Take $\mathbf{R}^{1_\ell \text{sum}}$, which relies on $\sum_{i \in N} c(z_i, R_i)$.
3. Drop certainty transfer. Take $\mathbf{R}^{\Omega \min}$.
4. Drop opponent separation. Take the SOF that coincides with $\mathbf{R}^{1_\ell \text{sum}}$ when preferences are identical and linear, and with $\mathbf{R}^{1_\ell \min}$ otherwise. ∎

Proof of Theorem 6.3. Let us say that the orderings R_i and R_j are strictly different if for all $x, x' \in X^N$, $I(x, R_i) \cap I(x', R_i')$ contains no manifold of dimension $\ell - 1$. Let $\mathcal{E}^{R_N}$ be the subdomain of economies with profile R_N, and consider a profile R_N such that for some $i, j \in N$, R_i and R_j are strictly different. We first show that $R = R^{\Omega \text{Nash}}$ on $\mathcal{E}^{R_N}$.

By independence of the feasible set, there is an ordering R such that $\mathbf{R}(E) = R$ for all $E \in \mathcal{E}^{R_N}$. By continuity and Pareto indifference, it is represented by a continuous function W such that for all $z_N, z_N' \in X^N$,

$$z_N \, R \, z_N' \Leftrightarrow W((u_i(z_i))_{i \in N}) \geq W\left(\left(u_i(z_i')\right)_{i \in N}\right),$$

where u_i can be taken to be an arbitrary homogeneous representation of R_i for every $i \in N$. By restricted separation and continuity, and invoking the Debreu–Gorman theorem (Debreu 1959, Gorman 1968), there exists a list of continuous functions $(\varphi_i)_{i \in N}$ such that:

$$W((u_i(z_i))_{i \in N}) = \sum_{i \in N} \varphi_i(u_i(z_i)).$$

The fact that $\max|_{\mathbf{R}(E)} Z(E) = S^{EW}(E)$ for all E entails that every φ_i is increasing. Indeed, suppose that for some $i \in N$, $\varphi_i(a) \leq \varphi_i(b)$ for $a > b$. There is $E \in \mathcal{E}^{R_N}$ such that $u_i(z_i) = a$ for $z_N \in S^{EW}(E)$. Take $z_i' = (b/a)z_i$. One then has $(z_{N\setminus\{i\}}, z_i') \mathbf{R}(E) z_N$, implying $(z_{N\setminus\{i\}}, z_i') \in \max|_{\mathbf{R}(E)} Z(E)$, which is impossible, as $(z_{N\setminus\{i\}}, z_i') \notin S^{EW}(E)$.

As every φ_i is increasing, it is differentiable almost everywhere. Let $z_N \in \max|_{\mathbf{R}(E)} Z(E)$. One has $z_N \in S^{EW}(E)$ and by Theorem 1 of Eisenberg (1961), for every $E \in \mathcal{E}^H$, the utility levels at $S^{EW}(E)$ are unique and positive. When differentiability of each φ_i holds at $(u_i(z_i))_{i \in N}$, the first-order condition of maximization of $\sum_{i \in N} \varphi_i(u_i(z_i))$ implies that for all $k = 1, \ldots, \ell$,

$$\varphi_i'(u_i(z_i)) \frac{\partial u_i}{\partial z_{ik}}(z_i) = \lambda_k(\Omega),$$

where $\lambda(\Omega)$ is the vector of Lagrange multipliers for the resource constraint $\sum_{i \in N} z_i \leq \Omega$. Because $z_N \in S^{EW}(E)$, one has $\lambda(\Omega) z_i = \lambda(\Omega) \Omega / |N|$ for all $i \in N$. Besides, u_i being homogeneous implies

$$\lambda(\Omega) z_i = \sum_{k=1}^{\ell} \varphi_i'(u_i(z_i)) \frac{\partial u_i}{\partial z_{ik}}(z_i) z_{ik} = \varphi_i'(u_i(z_i)) u_i(z_i).$$

Summarizing, one has, for almost all $\Omega \in \mathbb{R}_{++}^{\ell}$, all $z_N \in S^{EW}(R_N, \Omega)$, all $i \in N$,

$$\varphi_i'(u_i(z_i)) u_i(z_i) = \lambda(\Omega) \Omega / |N|.$$

Now, let $\Omega, \Omega' \in \mathbb{R}_{++}^{\ell}$ be such that for $z_N \in S^{EW}(R_N, \Omega)$, $z_N' \in S^{EW}(R_N, \Omega')$, there is $i \in N$ such that $u_i(z_i) = u_i(z_i')$. This implies $\lambda(\Omega) \Omega = \lambda(\Omega') \Omega'$ and therefore $\varphi_j'(u_j(z_j)) u_j(z_j) = \varphi_j'(u_j(z_j')) u_j(z_j')$ for all $j \in N$.

As utility levels at $S^{EW}(E)$ are unique, let $U_i(E) = u_i(z_i)$ for $z_N \in S^{EW}(E)$, $i \in N$. Take $i, j \in N$ such that R_i and R_j are strictly different. There exists $A \subseteq \mathbb{R}_{++}^{\ell}$ such that

$$U_i(R_N, A) = \{U_i(E) \mid E = (R_N, \Omega), \ \Omega \in A\}$$

is a singleton, whereas $U_j(R_N, A)$ is a nondegenerate interval $[\alpha, \beta] \subseteq \mathbb{R}_{++}$. This implies that $\varphi_j'(u) u$ is, almost everywhere, defined and constant for $u \in [\alpha, \beta]$.

By homotheticity, with $A' = (\beta/\alpha) A$ one obtains that $U_i(R_N, A')$ is a singleton whereas $U_j(R_N, A') = [\beta, \beta^2/\alpha]$. Therefore $\varphi_j'(u) u$ is also constant over $[\beta, \beta^2/\alpha]$. Repeating this argument, one eventually concludes that $\varphi_j'(u) u$ is constant over $\mathbb{R}_{++}$.

Because $\varphi_j'(u_j(z_j)) u_j(z_j) = \lambda(\Omega) \Omega / |N|$ for $z_N \in S^{EW}(R_N, \Omega)$, this implies that $\lambda(\Omega) \Omega / |N|$ is constant in Ω (whenever it is defined), and therefore, for all $i \in N$, $\varphi_i'(u) u$ is constant (and the same constant for all i) wherever it is defined over $\mathbb{R}_{++}$.

As a consequence, and by continuity of φ_i, for all $u \in \mathbb{R}_+$, $\varphi_i(u) = a \ln u + b_i$ for some $a \in \mathbb{R}_{++}$, $b_i \in \mathbb{R}$. This implies that $\mathbf{R}$ coincides with $\mathbf{R}^{\Omega\text{Nash}}$ on $\mathcal{E}^{R_N}$. Notice that u_i was taken to be any arbitrary homogeneous representation of R_i. The particular function $u_{\Omega}(z_i, R_i)$ is one such representation, and for this particular choice of u_i (for all $i \in N$) it is clear that the criterion $a \sum_{i \in N} \ln u_i(z_i)$ coincides with $\mathbf{R}^{\Omega\text{Nash}}$ (defined by $\prod_{i \in N} u_{\Omega}(z_i, R_i)$). However, the fact that $a \sum_{i \in N} \ln u_i(z_i)$ coincides with $\mathbf{R}^{\Omega\text{Nash}}$ holds true for any other homogeneous representations $(u_i)_{i \in N}$. This is simply because all homogeneous representations of a given homothetic R_i are proportional to each other.

Now we extend the result to $\mathcal{E}$. Let $E = (R_N, \Omega) \in \mathcal{E}$. Take $i \notin N$ such that for some $j \in N$, R_i and R_j are strictly different. Then, $\mathbf{R}(R_{N \cup \{i\}}, \Omega) = \mathbf{R}^{\Omega \text{Nash}}(R_{N \cup \{i\}}, \Omega)$ by the above argument. By restricted separation, $\mathbf{R}(E) = \mathbf{R}^{\Omega \text{Nash}}(E)$ over allocations with positive utilities. By continuity, this extends to all X^N.

We check that no condition is redundant.

1. Drop Pareto indifference. Take the SOF $\mathbf{R}$ such that $z_N \, \mathbf{R}(E) \, z'_N$ iff either $z_N \, \mathbf{P}^{\Omega \text{Nash}}(E) \, z'_N$ or $z_N \, \mathbf{I}^{\Omega \text{Nash}}(E) \, z'_N$ and $z_N \in \text{Pr}(\Omega)$.
2. Drop independence of the feasible set. For any $E = (R_N, \Omega)$, choose some p supporting price vector for $S^{EW}(E)$. Then let $z_N \, \mathbf{R}(E) \, z'_N$ iff

$$\sum_{i \in N} u_p(z_i, R_i) \geq \sum_{i \in N} u_p(z'_i, R_i).$$

3. Drop restricted separation. Let

$$EW = \left\{ z_N \in X^N \mid \exists \Omega \in \mathbb{R}_+^\ell, \ z_N \in EW(R_N, \Omega) \right\}$$

and choose an arbitrary $p_0 \in \mathbb{R}_{++}^\ell$. Then evaluate every allocation z_N by

$$\max_{z'_N \in EW \cap (\prod_{i \in N} L(z_i, R_i))} p_0 \sum_{i \in N} z'_i.$$

4. Drop $\max|_{\mathbf{R}(E)} Z(E) = S^{EW}(E)$. Take $\mathbf{R}^{\Omega_0 \text{sum}}$ for some fixed $\Omega_0 \in \mathbb{R}_{++}^\ell$.
5. Drop continuity. Take the SOF $\mathbf{R}$ such that $z_N \, \mathbf{R}(E) \, z'_N$ iff either $z_N \, \mathbf{P}^{\Omega \text{Nash}}(E) \, z'_N$, or $z_N \, \mathbf{I}^{\Omega \text{Nash}}(E) \, z'_N$ and $z_N \, \mathbf{R}^{\Omega_0 \text{lex}}(E) \, z'_N$.   ∎

Proof of Theorem 6.4. The proof is divided into four steps. In the first step, we prove the equivalence between consistency and a strong consistency axiom. In the second step, we prove that strong Pareto, independence of preferences over infeasible bundles, and consistency imply that only values of $u_m(z_i, R_i)$ matter. In the third step, we prove that the $u_m(z_i, R_i)$ need to be aggregated with infinite inequality aversion. In the fourth step, we prove that this implies the leximin.

Step 1. We begin by proving that consistency is equivalent to the following strong consistency axiom. It requires that social evaluation be unaffected by the addition of agents receiving the same bundles. Formally, it amounts to requiring that the implication of the consistency statement be replaced with an equivalence.

Axiom A.2 Strong Consistency
For all $E = (R_N, A) \in \mathcal{D}$ with $|N| \geq 3$, and $z_N, z'_N \in X^N$, if there is $i \in N$ such that $z_i = z'_i = (a_i, m_i)$, then

$$z_N \, \mathbf{R}(E) \, z'_N \Leftrightarrow z_{N \setminus \{i\}} \, \mathbf{R}(R_{N \setminus \{i\}}, A \setminus \{a_i\}) \, z'_{N \setminus \{i\}}.$$

To prove the claim, let us assume that **R** satisfies consistency but not strong consistency; that is, $z_N \mathbf{I}(E) z_N'$, whereas $z_{N \setminus \{i\}} \mathbf{P}(R_{N \setminus \{i\}}, A \setminus \{a_i\}) z_{N \setminus \{i\}}'$. As $z_N' \mathbf{R}(E) z_N$, by consistency, $z_{N \setminus \{i\}}' \mathbf{R}(R_{N \setminus \{i\}}, A \setminus \{a_i\}) z_{N \setminus \{i\}}$, the desired contradiction. The proof of the converse statement is similar.

Step 2. Let us first state the property formally.

Axiom A.3 Money Equivalence
For all $E = (R_N, A)$, $E' = (R_N', A') \in \mathcal{D}$, and $z_N, z_N', y_N, y_N' \in X^N$, if for all $i \in N$

$$u_m(z_i, R_i) = u_m(y_i, R_i') \text{ and } u_m(z_i', R_i) = u_m(y_i', R_i'),$$

then

$$z_N \mathbf{R}(E) z_N' \Leftrightarrow y_N \mathbf{R}(E') y_N'.$$

We claim that if **R** satisfies Pareto indifference, independence of preferences over infeasible bundles, and consistency, then it satisfies money equivalence. By consistency, **R** also satisfies strong consistency. Let $E = (R_N, A)$, $E' = \left(R_N', A'\right) \in \mathcal{E}^{ind}$, $z_N, z_N' \in Z(E)$, and $y_N, y_N' \in Z(E')$ be such that

$$u_m\left(z_i, R_i\right) = u_m\left(y_i, R_i'\right) \text{ and } u_m\left(z_i', R_i\right) = u_m\left(y_i', R_i'\right). \quad (A.17)$$

Let us assume that

$$z_N \mathbf{R}(E) z_N'. \quad (A.18)$$

We must prove that $y_N \mathbf{R}(E') y_N'$. Let $n = |N|$. We begin by constructing two sets of n bundles that are infeasible for E. Let $\varepsilon > 0$. Let $\tilde{m}, \tilde{m}' \in \mathbb{R}^N$ be defined by

$$\tilde{m}_i = \min \left\{-\varepsilon, u_m\left(z_i, R_i\right) - \varepsilon\right\}$$
$$\tilde{m}_i' = \tilde{m}_i \text{ if } z_i I_i z_i',$$
$$\tilde{m}_i - \varepsilon \text{ if } z_i P_i z_i',$$
$$\tilde{m}_i + \varepsilon \text{ if } z_i' P_i z_i.$$

Let $\tilde{A} \subseteq \mathcal{A}$ be such that $\tilde{A} \cap \left(A \cup A'\right) = \emptyset$ and $|\tilde{A}| = n$, so we can find a bijection $\sigma : N \to \tilde{A}$. Let $\tilde{N}$ be such that $\tilde{N} \cap N = \emptyset$ and $|\tilde{N}| = n$, so that we can find a bijection $\rho : N \to \tilde{N}$. Let $\tilde{z}_{\tilde{N}}, \tilde{z}_{\tilde{N}}' \in \left(\tilde{A} \times \mathbb{R}\right)^{\tilde{N}}$ be defined by: for all $i \in N$,

$$\tilde{z}_{\rho(i)} = \left(\sigma(i), \tilde{m}_i\right),$$
$$\tilde{z}_{\rho(i)}' = \left(\sigma(i), \tilde{m}_i'\right).$$

Let $\overline{R}_N \in \mathcal{R}^{indN}$ be such that for all $i \in N$, $a, a' \in A \cup \{v\}$, $m, m' \in \mathbb{R}$,

$$(a, m) R_i \left(a', m'\right) \Leftrightarrow (a, m) \overline{R}_i \left(a', m'\right),$$

and for all $i \in N$,

$$z_i \overline{I}_i \tilde{z}_{\rho(i)} \text{ and } z_i' \overline{I}_i \tilde{z}_{\rho(i)}'. \quad (A.19)$$

Given the way $\tilde{z}_N$ and $\tilde{z}'_N$ were constructed, such preferences exist. By independence of preferences over infeasible bundles, (A.18) implies

$$z_N \, \mathbf{R} \left(\overline{R}_N, A \right) z'_N. \tag{A.20}$$

Let $\tilde{E} = \left(\tilde{N}, \tilde{A}, \tilde{R} \right) \in \mathcal{E}^{ind}$ be defined by: for all $i \in N$,

$$\tilde{R}_{\rho(i)} = \overline{R}_i. \tag{A.21}$$

By consistency and strong consistency, (A.20) implies

$$\left(z_N, \tilde{z}_{\tilde{N}} \right) \, \mathbf{R} \left(\left(\overline{R}_N, \tilde{R}_{\tilde{N}} \right), A \cup \tilde{A} \right) \left(z'_N, \tilde{z}_{\tilde{N}} \right).$$

By Pareto indifference and (A.19) and (A.21),

$$\left(\tilde{z}_{\tilde{N}}, z_N \right) \, \mathbf{R} \left(\left(\overline{R}_N, \tilde{R}_{\tilde{N}} \right) A \cup \tilde{A} \right) \left(\tilde{z}'_{\tilde{N}}, z_N \right).$$

By consistency,

$$\tilde{z}_{\tilde{N}} \, \mathbf{R} \left(\overline{R}_N, \tilde{A} \right) \tilde{z}'_{\tilde{N}}. \tag{A.22}$$

Let $\overline{\overline{R}}_N \in \mathcal{R}^{indN}$ be the list of preferences that coincide with $\overline{R}$ on the bundles having an element of $\tilde{A} \cup \{v\}$ as first component, and with R' on the bundles having an element of $A' \cup \{v\}$ as first component; that is, for all $i \in N, a, a' \in \tilde{A} \cup \{v\}, b, b' \in A' \cup \{v\}, m, m' \in \mathbb{R}$,

$$(a, m) \, \overline{\overline{R}}_i \, (a', m') \Leftrightarrow (a, m) \, \overline{R}_i \, (a', m'), \text{ and} \tag{A.23}$$

$$(b, m) \, \overline{\overline{R}}_i \, (b', m') \Leftrightarrow (b, m) \, R'_i \, (b', m').$$

By independence of preferences over infeasible bundles, (A.22) implies

$$\tilde{z}_{\tilde{N}} \, \mathbf{R} \left(\overline{\overline{R}}_N, \tilde{A} \right) \tilde{z}'_{\tilde{N}}. \tag{A.24}$$

Let $\overset{\approx}{R}_{\tilde{N}} \in \mathcal{R}^{ind\tilde{N}}$ be defined by for all $i \in N$,

$$\overset{\approx}{R}_{\rho(i)} = \overline{\overline{R}}_i. \tag{A.25}$$

By consistency and strong consistency, (A.24) implies

$$\left(\tilde{z}_{\tilde{N}}, y_N \right) \, \mathbf{R} \left(\left(\overline{\overline{R}}_N, \overset{\approx}{R}_{\tilde{N}} \right), A' \cup \tilde{A}, \right) \left(\tilde{z}'_{\tilde{N}}, y_N \right).$$

By Pareto indifference and (A.17), (A.19), (A.21), and (A.25),

$$\left(y_N, \tilde{z}_{\tilde{N}} \right) \, \mathbf{R} \left(\left(\overline{\overline{R}}_N, \overset{\approx}{R}_{\tilde{N}} \right), A' \cup \tilde{A}, \right) \left(y'_N, \tilde{z}'_{\tilde{N}} \right).$$

By consistency,

$$y_N \, \mathbf{R} \left(\overline{\overline{R}}_N, A' \right) y'_N.$$

By independence of preferences over infeasible bundles and (A.23),

$$y_N \, \mathbf{R} \left(E' \right) y'_N,$$

the desired outcome.

Step 3. We now prove that if $\mathbf{R}$ satisfies strong Pareto, independence of preferences over infeasible bundles, consistency, and transfer among equals, then it focuses on the worst-off in terms of $u_m(z_i, R_i)$. Let $E = (R_N, A) \in \mathcal{E}^{ind}$, $z_N, z'_N \in Z(E)$, be such that

$$\min_{i \in N} \{u_m(z_i, R_i)\} > \min_{i \in N} \{u_m(z'_i, R_i)\}.$$

Assume, contrary to what needs to be proved, that $z'_N \mathbf{R}(E) z_N$. Let $E' = (R'_N, A) \in \mathcal{E}^{ind}$ be such that for all $j, k \in N$, $R'_j = R'_k$ and R'_j has the property that for all $a \in A$, $m, m' \in \mathbb{R}$, and for all $i \in N$,

$$(a, m) \; I_i \left(v, m'\right) \Rightarrow (a, m) \; R'_j \left(v, m'\right),$$

which means that the willingness to pay for any object in A is greater for R'_j than for any R_i. Given the restriction on R'_j, there exist $y_N, y'_N \in Z(E')$ such that

$$u_m(z_i, R_i) = u_m \left(y_i, R'_i\right) \text{ and } u_m \left(z'_i, R_i\right) = u_m \left(y'_i, R'_i\right). \tag{A.26}$$

By money equivalence, (A.26) implies

$$y'_N \mathbf{R}(E') y_N. \tag{A.27}$$

Let $j \in N$ be such that $u_m(y'_j, R'_j) = \min_{i \in N} u_m \left(y'_i, R'_i\right)$. Let N be partitioned into N_1, and N_2 such that $|N_1| = n_1$, $|N_2| = n_2$ and

$$\forall i \in N_1 : u_m(y_i, R'_i) \geq u_m(y'_i, R'_i),$$

$$\forall i \in N_2 : u_m(y_i, R'_i) < u_m(y'_i, R'_i).$$

Note that $j \in N_1$. If $N_2 = \emptyset$, then, by strong Pareto, $y_N \mathbf{P}(E') y'_N$, a contradiction. Thus, let us assume that $N_2 \neq \emptyset$. The remainder of the proof consists of showing that it is possible to build a new allocation y''_N, such that $y''_N \mathbf{P}(E') y_N$ and N can still be partitioned into two sets, N'_1 and N'_2, such that $|N'_1| = n_1 + 1$ and $|N'_2| = n_2 - 1$. Repeating the argument n_2 times eventually yields the contradiction with strong Pareto. Each repetition of the argument typically requires that new preferences be defined, which, by money equivalence, is always possible. Let $k \in N_2$. Let u''_j, u''_k be such that

$$u_m \left(y'_j, R'_j\right) < u''_j \leq u''_k < u_m \left(y_l, R'_l\right), \forall l = j, k.$$

Let $a, b \in A$. We may assume that $a \neq b$, because $|A| \geq 2$. Moreover, R'_j could have been defined in such a way that there is some $\Delta > 0$, and $m_j, m_k \in \mathbb{R}$, such that

$$y'_j \; I'_j \left(a, m_j\right),$$

$$(v, u''_j) \; I'_j \left(a, m_j + \Delta\right),$$

$$(v, u''_k) \; I'_k \left(b, m_k - \Delta\right),$$

$$y'_k \; I'_k \left(b, m_k\right).$$

We assume that R'_j has this property. Let $\overline{y}_N, y''_N \in Z(E')$ be such that for all $i \neq j, k, \overline{y}_i = y''_i I'_i y'_i, \overline{y}_j = (a, m_j), \overline{y}_k = (b, m_k), y''_j = (a, m_j + \Delta)$, and $y''_k = (b, m_k - \Delta)$. By Pareto indifference,

$$y'_N \, \mathbf{I}(E') \, \overline{y}_N. \tag{A.28}$$

By transfer among equals,

$$y''_N \, \mathbf{P}(E') \, \overline{y}_N. \tag{A.29}$$

By (A.27), (A.28), and (A.29),

$$y''_N \, \mathbf{P}(E') \, y_N,$$

the desired outcome.

Step 4. To complete the proof, we show that if $\mathbf{R}$ satisfies strong Pareto, independence of preferences over infeasible bundles, consistency, transfer among equals, and anonymity among equals, then it coincides with $\mathbf{R}^{m\mathrm{lex}}$.

Let $\mathbf{R}$ satisfy the axioms. It also satisfies strong consistency and money equivalence. Let $E = (R_N, A) \in \mathcal{E}^{ind}$. By money equivalence, we can assume, without loss of generality, that for all $i, j \in N, R_i = R_j$. (If this condition were not satisfied, we could change the actual profile of preferences into a new profile satisfying the condition, without affecting the social preferences over money equivalent utility vectors, as we did earlier.) Let $z_N = ((a_i, m_i))_{i \in N}, z'_N = ((a'_i, m'_i))_{i \in N} \in Z(E)$. We distinguish two cases.

Case 1: $z_N \, \mathbf{I}^{mlex}(E) \, z'_N$. Let $n = |N|$. Let $\sigma : N \to \{1, \dots, n\}$ be a bijection satisfying the property that for all $i, j \in N, \sigma(i) \geq \sigma(j) \Rightarrow u_m(z_i, R_i) \geq u(z_j, R_j)$. Let $z_{\sigma(N)} \in Z(E)$ denote the allocation obtained from z_N by permuting its component according to σ. Let σ' denote the similar bijection associated with z'_N, and $z'_{\sigma'(N)}$ the resulting allocation. By anonymity among equals, $z_N \, \mathbf{I}(E) \, z_{\sigma(N)}$ and $z'_N \, \mathbf{I}(E) \, z'_{\sigma'(N)}$. By construction, and given that $z_N \, \mathbf{I}^L(E) \, z'_N$, $z_{\sigma(i)} \, I_i \, z'_{\sigma'(i)}$ so by Pareto indifference, $z_{\sigma(N)} \, \mathbf{I}(E) \, z'_{\sigma'(N)}$. Gathering all these social indifferences yield $z_N \, \mathbf{I}(E) \, z'_N$, the desired outcome.

Case 2: $z_N \, \mathbf{P}^{mlex}(E) \, z'_N$. Assume, contrary to the statement we must prove, that

$$z'_N \, \mathbf{R}(E) \, z_N. \tag{A.30}$$

Let $n = |N|$. Let $\sigma, \sigma', z_{\sigma(N)}, z'_{\sigma'(N)}$ be defined as above. By anonymity among equals, $z_N \, \mathbf{I}(E) \, z_{\sigma(N)}$ and $z'_N \, \mathbf{I}(E) \, z'_{\sigma'(N)}$. Therefore, by (A.30),

$$z'_{\sigma'(N)} \, \mathbf{R}(E) \, z_{\sigma(N)}. \tag{A.31}$$

Given that $z_N \, \mathbf{P}^{mlex}(E) \, z'_N$, there is $j \in N$ such that for all $i \in N$ such that $\sigma(i) < \sigma(j), z_{\sigma(i)} \, I_i \, z'_{\sigma'(i)}$ and $z_{\sigma(j)} \, P_j \, z'_{\sigma'(j)}$. Then, N can be partitioned into

N_1, N_2, and N_3 such that $|N_1| = n_1, |N_2| = n_2, |N_3| = n_3$, and $j = n_1 + 1$, and

$$\forall i \in N_1 : \sigma(i) \leq n_1 \text{ and } u_m(z_{\sigma(i)}R_i) = u_m(z'_{\sigma'(i)}R_i),$$

$$\forall i \in N_2 : u_m(z_{\sigma(i)}, R_i) > u_m(z'_{\sigma'(i)}, R_i),$$

$$\forall i \in N_3 : u_m(z_{\sigma(i)}, R_i) \leq u_m(z'_{\sigma'(i)}, R_i).$$

If $N_1 = \emptyset$, then, given that **R** is infinitely inequality-averse in money-equivalent utilities, $z_{\sigma(N)} \mathbf{P}(E) z'_{\sigma'(N)}$, a contradiction. Thus, let us assume that $N_1 \neq \emptyset$. Our strategy consists of using consistency to remove agents in N_1 from the economy, so agent j has the smallest money-equivalent utility, in contradiction to **R** being infinitely inequality-averse; removing those agents, however, may yield an infeasible allocation (not enough money would be left). Let $M = \min\left\{\sum_{i \in N_1} m_{\sigma(i)}, \sum_{i \in N_1} m'_{\sigma'(i)}\right\}$. Let $\widetilde{A} \subseteq \mathcal{A}$. Let $\widetilde{N}$ be such that $\widetilde{N} \cap N = \emptyset$, $|\widetilde{N}| = n$, $\widetilde{A} \cap A = \emptyset$ and $|\widetilde{A}| = n$. Let $\widetilde{z}_{\widetilde{N}} = ((\widetilde{a}_i, \widetilde{m}_i))_{i \in \widetilde{N}} \in (\mathcal{A}^* \times \mathbb{R})^{\widetilde{N}}$, be such that $\sum_{i \in \widetilde{N}} \widetilde{m}_i < M$. Let $\widetilde{E} = (\widetilde{R}_{\widetilde{N}}, \widetilde{A}) \in \mathcal{E}^{ind}$ be such that for all $i \in \widetilde{N}$, $\widetilde{R}_i = R_j$. By money equivalence, we can assume, without loss of generality, that for all $i \in \widetilde{N}$,

$$u_m\left(\widetilde{z}_i, \widetilde{R}_i\right) > u_m\left(z'_{\sigma'(j)}, R_j\right).$$

(If this condition were not satisfied, then we could change the actual profile of preferences into a new profile satisfying the condition, without affecting the social preferences over money equivalent vectors.) Let $\overline{z}_N, \overline{z}'_N \in Z(E)$ be defined by

$$\forall i \in N_2 \cup N_3, \overline{z}_i = z_{\sigma(i)} \text{ and } \overline{z}'_i = z'_{\sigma'(i)},$$

$$\forall i \in N_1, \overline{z}_i = \overline{z}'_i = z_{\sigma(i)} \text{ if } \sum_{i \in N_1} m_{\sigma(i)} \leq \sum_{i \in N_1} m'_{\sigma'(i)},$$

$$z'_{\sigma'(i)} \text{ if } \sum_{i \in N_1} m_{\sigma(i)} > \sum_{i \in N_1} m'_{\sigma'(i)}.$$

By Pareto indifference, $z_{\sigma(N)} \mathbf{I}(E) \overline{z}_N$ and $z'_{\sigma'(N)} \mathbf{I}(E) \overline{z}'_N$, so (A.31) implies

$$\overline{z}'_N \mathbf{R}(E) \overline{z}_N.$$

By consistency and strong consistency (remember that consistency is equivalent to strong consistency),

$$\left(\overline{z}'_N, \widetilde{z}_{\widetilde{N}}\right) \mathbf{R}(E, \widetilde{E}) \left(\overline{z}_N, \widetilde{z}_{\widetilde{N}}\right).$$

By consistency,

$$\left(\overline{z}'_{N \setminus N_1}, \widetilde{z}_{\widetilde{N}}\right) \mathbf{R}\left(\left(R_{N \setminus N_1}, \widetilde{R}_{\widetilde{N}}\right), \left(A \setminus \cup_{i \in N_1} \{\overline{a}_i\}\right) \cup \widetilde{A}\right) \left(\overline{z}_{N \setminus N_1}, \widetilde{z}_{\widetilde{N}}\right),$$

which contradicts the fact that **R** is infinitely inequality-averse in money-equivalent utilities, as agent j now has the smallest money-equivalent utility in the allocation $\left(\overline{z}'_{N \setminus N_1}, \widetilde{z}_{\widetilde{N}}\right)$.

We check that no condition is redundant.

1. Drop strong Pareto. Take the SOF **R** that minimizes the largest money equivalent utility.
2. Drop independence of preferences over unfeasible bundles. Take the SOF **R** that applies the leximin to the following well-being index. Let $a^* \in \mathcal{A}$. Let index v be defined by

$$v(z_i, R_i) = m \Leftrightarrow (a^*, m) \, I_i \, z_i .$$

3. Drop consistency. Take the SOF **R** that applies the leximin to the following well-being index. For $a \in \mathcal{A}^*$, let $m^a(R_i, z_i) = m \Leftrightarrow (a, m) \, I_i \, z_i$. For all $E = (R_N, A) \in \mathcal{E}^{ind}$, index w is defined by

$$w(R_i, z_i, A) = m \Leftrightarrow m = \sum_{a \in A \cup \{v\}} m^a(R_i, z_i) .$$

4. Drop transfer among equals. Take the SOF **R** that ranks allocations to maximize the sum of agents' money equivalent.
5. Drop anonymity among equals. Let $\geq$ denote a complete ordering on the names of the agents. Take the SOF **R** that coincides with $\mathbf{R}^{mlex}$ in case of strict preference, and that prefers, in case of a tie, the allocation in which the name of agent with smallest money-equivalent utility is the smaller. ∎

A.4   CHAPTER 7: EXTENSIONS

Proof of Theorem 7.1. (1) Assume that $\bar{\mathbf{R}}(\bar{E})$ coincides with $\mathbf{R}^{\Omega lex}$ for single-profile comparisons of allocations. Let $\bar{E} = (N, \Omega) \in \bar{\mathcal{E}}$ and $z_N, z'_N \in X^N$, $R_N, R'_N \in \mathcal{R}^N$ be such that $(u_\Omega(z'_i, R'_i))_{i \in N} = (u_\Omega(z_i, R_i))_{i \in N}$, and not all the values of $(u_\Omega(z_i, R_i))_{i \in N}$ are equal. There is no loss of generality in assuming that $z_N, z'_N \in \mathrm{Pr}(\Omega)$ (which implies $z_N = z'_N$) and that $z_1 \leq \ldots \leq z_n$. Let R^*_i be such that $I(z_1, R^*_i) = I(z_1, R_i)$ and $U(z_n, R^*_i) = \{q \in X \mid q \geq z_n\}$, and R^{**}_i be such that $I(z_1, R^{**}_i) = I(z_1, R'_i)$ and $U(z_n, R^{**}_i) = \{q \in X \mid q \geq z_n\}$.

We first focus on $i = 1$. By cross-profile independence,

$$((z_1, \ldots, z_n), (R_1, \ldots, R_n)) \, \bar{I}(\bar{E}) \, ((z_1, \ldots, z_n), (R^*_1, \ldots, R_n)) .$$

By $\mathbf{R}^{\Omega lex}$,

$$((z_1, \ldots, z_n), (R^*_1, \ldots, R_n)) \, \bar{I}(\bar{E}) \, ((z_n, z_2, \ldots, z_{n-1}, z_1), (R^*_1, \ldots, R_n)) .$$

By cross-profile independence,

$$((z_n, z_2, \ldots, z_{n-1}, z_1), (R^*_1, \ldots, R_n)) \, \bar{I}(\bar{E}) \, ((z_n, z_2, \ldots, z_{n-1}, z_1),$$
$$(R^{**}_1, \ldots, R_n)) .$$

By $\mathbf{R}^{\Omega lex}$,

$$((z_n, z_2, \ldots, z_{n-1}, z_1), (R^{**}_1, \ldots, R_n)) \, \bar{I}(\bar{E}) \, ((z_1, \ldots, z_n), (R^{**}_1, \ldots, R_n)) .$$

By cross-profile independence,

$$\left((z_1, \ldots, z_n), \left(R_1^{**}, \ldots, R_n\right)\right) \bar{I}(\bar{E}) \left((z_1, \ldots, z_n), \left(R_1', \ldots, R_n\right)\right).$$

By transitivity,

$$\left((z_1, \ldots, z_n), (R_1, \ldots, R_n)\right) \bar{I}(\bar{E}) \left((z_1, \ldots, z_n), \left(R_1', \ldots, R_n\right)\right).$$

We now focus on $i = 2$. By $\mathbf{R}^{\Omega\text{lex}}$,

$$\left((z_1, z_2, \ldots, z_n), \left(R_1', R_2 \ldots, R_n\right)\right) \bar{I}(\bar{E}) \left((z_2, z_1, \ldots, z_n), \right.$$
$$\left.\left(R_1', R_2, \ldots, R_n\right)\right).$$

By the above reasoning,

$$\left((z_2, z_1, \ldots, z_n), \left(R_1', R_2, \ldots, R_n\right)\right) \bar{I}(\bar{E}) \left((z_2, z_1, \ldots, z_n), \right.$$
$$\left.\left(R_1', R_2', \ldots, R_n\right)\right).$$

By $\mathbf{R}^{\Omega\text{lex}}$,

$$\left((z_2, z_1, \ldots, z_n), \left(R_1', R_2', \ldots, R_n\right)\right) \bar{I}(\bar{E}) \left((z_1, z_2, \ldots, z_n), \right.$$
$$\left.\left(R_1', R_2', \ldots, R_n\right)\right).$$

By transitivity,

$$\left((z_1, z_2, \ldots, z_n), (R_1, R_2, \ldots, R_n)\right) \bar{I}(\bar{E}) \left((z_1, z_2, \ldots, z_n), \right.$$
$$\left.\left(R_1', R_2', \ldots, R_n\right)\right).$$

If $n > 2$, repeating the last four steps for $i = 3, \ldots, n$, one obtains

$$\left((z_1, \ldots, z_n), (R_1, \ldots, R_n)\right) \bar{I}(\bar{E}) \left((z_1, \ldots, z_n), \left(R_1', \ldots, R_n'\right)\right).$$

From this fact and by application of $\mathbf{R}^{\Omega\text{lex}}$ it follows directly that when $\left(u_\Omega \left(z_i', R_i'\right)\right)_{i \in N} >_{lex} \left(u_\Omega (z_i, R_i)\right)_{i \in N}$ one must have $\left(z_N', R_N'\right) \bar{P}(\bar{E}) (z_N, R_N)$.

(2) Assume that $\bar{\mathbf{R}}(\bar{E})$ coincides with $\mathbf{R}^{EW}$ for single-profile comparisons of allocations. Let $\bar{E} = (N, \Omega) \in \bar{\mathcal{E}}$ and $z_N, z_N' \in X^N$, $R_N, R_N' \in \mathcal{R}^N$ be such that

$$\max_{p \in \Pi_\Omega} \min_{i \in N} u_p (z_i, R_i) = \max_{p \in \Pi_\Omega} \min_{i \in N} u_p \left(z_i', R_i'\right).$$

Let $p^* \in \arg\max_{p \in \Pi_\Omega} \min_{i \in N} u_p (z_i, R_i)$ and $\lambda^* = \min_{i \in N} u_{p^*} (z_i, R_i)$.

First, assume that for all $i \in N$, R_i' is the linear ordering based on p^* and $u_{p^*} \left(z_i', R_i'\right) = \lambda^*$. Let z_N^1 be such that $z_1^1 \gg z_1$ and $\left(z_N^1, R_N\right) \bar{I}(\bar{E}) (z_N, R_N)$. Let R_N^1 be such that

$$I(z_1^1, R_1^1) = I(z_1^1, R_1),$$
$$I(\lambda^* \Omega, R_1^1) = I(\lambda^* \Omega, R_1'),$$

and $R_j^1 = R_j$ for all $j \in N$. By cross-profile independence, $\left(z_N^1, R_N^1 \right)$ $\bar{I}(\bar{E}) \left(z_N^1, R_N \right)$. By construction,

$$\left(z_N^1, R_N^1 \right) \bar{I}(\bar{E}) \left((\lambda^* \Omega, z_2, \ldots, z_n), R_N^1 \right).$$

By cross-profile independence,

$$\left((\lambda^* \Omega, z_2, \ldots, z_n), R_N^1 \right) \bar{I}(\bar{E}) \left((\lambda^* \Omega, z_2, \ldots, z_n), (R_1', R_2, \ldots, R_n) \right).$$

By transitivity,

$$(z_N, R_N) \bar{I}(\bar{E}) \left((\lambda^* \Omega, z_2, \ldots, z_n), (R_1', R_2, \ldots, R_n) \right).$$

Repeating this argument for $i = 2, \ldots, n$, one obtains

$$(z_N, R_N) \bar{I}(\bar{E}) \left((\lambda^* \Omega, \ldots, \lambda^* \Omega), R_N' \right).$$

As $(z_N', R_N') \bar{I}(\bar{E}) ((\lambda^* \Omega, \ldots, \lambda^* \Omega), R_N')$, one obtains $(z_N, R_N) \bar{I}(\bar{E})$ (z_N', R_N').

Second, assume that for all $i \in N$, R_i' is such that

$$U \left(\lambda^* \Omega, R_i' \right) = \left\{ q \in X \mid q \geq \lambda^* \Omega \right\},$$

and $z_i' = \lambda^* \Omega$. For all $i \in N$, let R_i^* be the linear ordering based on p^*. By the previous step, we know that

$$(z_N, R_N) \bar{I}(\bar{E}) \left((\lambda^* \Omega, \ldots, \lambda^* \Omega), R_N^* \right),$$

$$\left(z_N', R_N' \right) \bar{I}(\bar{E}) \left((\lambda^* \Omega, \ldots, \lambda^* \Omega), R_N^* \right).$$

By transitivity, $(z_N, R_N) \bar{I}(\bar{E}) \left(z_N', R_N' \right)$.

Finally, we prove that $(z_N, R_N) \bar{I}(\bar{E}) \left(z_N', R_N' \right)$ without making special assumptions about $\left(z_N', R_N' \right)$. Let $\left(z_N^*, R_N^* \right)$ be such that for all $i \in N$, $z_i^* = \lambda^* \Omega$ and R_i^* is such that

$$U \left(\lambda^* \Omega, R_i^* \right) = \left\{ q \in X \mid q \geq \lambda^* \Omega \right\}.$$

By the previous step, we know that $(z_N, R_N) \bar{I}(\bar{E}) \left(z_N^*, R_N^* \right)$ and that $\left(z_N', R_N' \right) \bar{I}(\bar{E}) \left(z_N^*, R_N^* \right)$. By transitivity, $(z_N, R_N) \bar{I}(\bar{E}) \left(z_N', R_N' \right)$. ∎

Proof of Theorem 7.2. (1a) Suppose that for all $i \in N$, $z_i R_i z_i'$. Then

$$\{ \lambda \in \mathbb{R}_+ \mid \exists q_N \in S(R_N, \lambda \Omega) \text{ s.t. } z_i' R_i q_i, \forall i \in N \}$$

$$\subseteq \{ \lambda \in \mathbb{R}_+ \mid \exists q_N \in S(R_N, \lambda \Omega) \text{ s.t. } z_i R_i q_i, \forall i \in N \},$$

which implies $V_S^*(z_N', E) \leq V_S^*(z_N, E)$. Similarly,

$$\{ \lambda \in \mathbb{R}_+ \mid \exists R_N' \in \mathcal{R}^N, \exists q_N \in S(R_N', \lambda \Omega)$$

$$\text{s.t. } \forall i \in N, \ z_i' R_i' q_i \text{ and } I(z_i', R_i) = I(z_i', R_i') \}$$

$$\subseteq \{ \lambda \in \mathbb{R}_+ \mid \exists R_N' \in \mathcal{R}^N, \exists q_N \in S(R_N', \lambda \Omega)$$

$$\text{s.t. } \forall i \in N, \ z_i R_i' q_i \text{ and } I(z_i, R_i) = I(z_i, R_i') \}$$

implies $V_S^{**}(z_N', E) \leq V_S^{**}(z_N, E)$. Pareto indifference follows directly.

(1b) By upper hemicontinuity, sup is in fact max in the definition of V_S^*. Indeed, by definition of sup, there is $\lambda_k \to V_S^*(z_N, E)$ such that for all k, there is $z_N^k \in S(R_N, \lambda_k \Omega)$ such that $z_i \, R_i \, z_i^k$ for all $i \in N$. As $\bigcup_k Z(R_N, \lambda_k \Omega)$ is compact, there is a subsequence of z_N^k that converges to some z_N^*. By upper hemicontinuity, $z_N^* \in S(R_N, V_S^*(z_N, E)\Omega)$ and by continuity of preferences, $z_i \, R_i \, z_i^*$ for all $i \in N$. In other words,

$$V_S^*(z_N, E) \in \{\lambda \in \mathbb{R}_+ \mid \exists q_N \in S(R_N, \lambda\Omega) \text{ s.t. } z_i \, R_i \, q_i, \forall i \in N\},$$

implying that

$$V_S^*(z_N, E) = \max\{\lambda \in \mathbb{R}_+ \mid \exists q_N \in S(R_N, \lambda\Omega) \text{ s.t. } z_i \, R_i \, q_i, \forall i \in N\}.$$

Suppose $z_i \, P_i \, z_i'$ for all $i \in N$. Then $V_S^*(z_N', E) \leq V_S^*(z_N, E)$. Suppose that $V_S^*(z_N', E) = V_S^*(z_N, E)$. By the "sup is max" argument, there is $q_N \in S(R_N, V_S^*(z_N, E)\Omega)$ such that $z_i' \, R_i \, q_i$ for all $i \in N$. One has $z_i \, P_i \, q_i$ for all $i \in N$. Let $\lambda_k \to V_S^*(z_N, E)$ such that $\lambda_k > V_S^*(z_N, E)$ for all k. By lower hemicontinuity, there is $q_N^k \in S(R_N, \lambda_k \Omega)$ such that $q_N^k \to q_N$. By continuity of preferences, there is a finite k such that $z_i \, P_i \, q_i^k, \forall i \in N$. For this particular k,

$$\lambda_k \in \{\lambda \in \mathbb{R}_+ \mid \exists q_N \in S(R_N, \lambda\Omega) \text{ s.t. } z_i \, R_i \, q_i, \forall i \in N\},$$

which implies that $V_S^*(z_N, E) \geq \lambda_k > V_S^*(z_N, E)$, a contradiction.

(2a) When S is Pareto efficient, one has $V_S^*(z_N, E), V_S^{**}(z_N, E) \leq 1$ for all $z_N \in Z(E)$. Indeed, if $V_S^*(z_N, E) > 1$, there is $\lambda > 1$ and $z_N' \in S(R_N, \lambda\Omega)$ such that $z_i \, R_i \, z_i'$ for all $i \in N$. This is impossible if $z_N' \in P(R_N, \lambda\Omega)$ and $z_N \in Z(E)$. If $V_S^{**}(z_N, E) > 1$, there is $\lambda > 1$, $R_N' \in \mathcal{R}^N$ and $z_N' \in S(R_N', \lambda\Omega)$ such that $z_i \, R_i' \, z_i'$ for all $i \in N$ (which is equivalent to $z_i \, R_i \, z_i'$ because $I(z_i, R_i) = I(z_i, R_i')$). This is impossible if $z_N' \in P(R_N', \lambda\Omega)$ and $z_N \in Z(E)$.

When $z_N \in S(E)$ or is Pareto indifferent to some $z_N^* \in S(E)$, necessarily $V_S^*(z_N, E), V_S^{**}(z_N, E) \geq 1$ and therefore $V_S^*(z_N, E) = V_S^{**}(z_N, E) = 1$.

(2b) Conversely, suppose $V_S^*(z_N, E) = 1$. There is $\lambda_k \to 1$ and $z_N^k \in S(R_N, \lambda_k \Omega)$ such that $z_i \, R_i \, z_i^k$ for all $i \in N$. There is at least a subsequence of z_N^k that tends to some z_N^*. As S is upper-hemicontinuous with respect to Ω, $z_N^* \in S(R_N, \Omega)$ and by continuity of preferences, $z_i \, R_i \, z_i^*$ for all $i \in N$. As S is Pareto efficient, necessarily $z_i \, I_i \, z_i^*$ for all $i \in N$. Therefore $V_S^*(z_N, E) = 1$ iff z_N is Pareto indifferent to some $z_N^* \in S(E)$. If all allocations that are Pareto indifferent to some $z_N^* \in S(E)$ are also in $S(E)$, then $\mathbf{R}_S^*$ rationalizes S. ∎

A.5 CHAPTER 10: UNEQUAL SKILLS

Proof of Theorem 10.5. We omit the first part and focus on the second. Let $E = (s_N, R_N)$, $z_N, z_N' \in X^N$ be such that $\min_{i \in N} u_{s_{\min}}(z_i, R_i) >$

$\min_{i \in N} u_{s_{\min}}(z'_i, R_i)$. As is now usual, we can focus on the case in which there is i_0 such that for all $i \neq i_0$,

$$u_{s_{\min}}(z'_i, R_i) > u_{s_{\min}}(z_i, R_i) > u_{s_{\min}}(z_{i_0}, R_{i_0}) > u_{s_{\min}}(z'_{i_0}, R_{i_0}).$$

Fix an arbitrary z''_{i_0} such that $z_{i_0} \, P_{i_0} \, z''_{i_0} \, P_{i_0} \, z'_{i_0}$. Let R^* be such that

$$(\ell, c) \, R^* \, (\ell', c') \Leftrightarrow c - (s_{\min} - \varepsilon) \, \ell \geq c' - (s_{\min} - \varepsilon) \, \ell',$$

where $0 < \varepsilon < \min_{i \in N \setminus \{i_0\}} u_{s_{\min}}(z_i, R_i) - u_{s_{\min}}(z_{i_0}, R_{i_0})$. As $\max|_{R^*} B(s, x) \geq \max|_R B(s, x)$ for all $R \in \mathcal{R}$, $s \in S$, $x \in X$, one has $R^* \succsim^{\text{MI}} R$ for all $R \in \mathcal{R}$.
Let t^a, t^b, t^c, t^d be such that $t^a - t^b = t^c - t^d$ and

$$\min_{i \in N} u_{s_{\min}}(z_i, R_i) - \varepsilon > t^a > t^b > t^c > t^d > u_{s_{\min}}(z_{i_0}, R_{i_0}).$$

Let us focus on i_0 and a particular $j \neq i_0$. Let R'_j be such that $I(z_j, R'_j) = I(z_j, R_j)$, $I(z'_j, R'_j) = I(z'_j, R_j)$, $I((1, t^a + s_{\min}), R'_j) = I((1, t^a + s_{\min}), R^*)$, $I((1, t^b + s_{\min}), R'_j) = I((1, t^b + s_{\min}), R^*)$. Let $z^c = \max|_{R_{i_0}} B(s_{\min}, (0, t^c))$, $z^d = \max|_{R_{i_0}} B(s_{\min}, (0, t^d))$.

As explained in Section 10.6, strong Pareto, equal-preferences transfer, and unchanged-contour independence imply equal-preferences priority. Therefore,

$$\left(z_j, (1, t^a + s_{\min}) \right) \mathbf{R} \left((s_j, s_{\min}), (R'_j, R'_j) \right) \left(z'_j, (1, t^b + s_{\min}) \right).$$

By unchanged-contour independence,

$$\left(z_j, (1, t^a + s_{\min}) \right) \mathbf{R} \left((s_j, s_{\min}), (R_j, R'_j) \right) \left(z'_j, (1, t^b + s_{\min}) \right).$$

Similarly,

$$\left(z''_{i_0}, z^d \right) \mathbf{R} \left((s_{i_0}, s_{\min}), (R_{i_0}, R_{i_0}) \right) \left(z'_{i_0}, z^c \right).$$

By $\succsim^{\text{MI}}$-equal-skill transfer,

$$\left((1, t^b + s_{\min}), z^c \right) \mathbf{R} \left((s_{\min}, s_{\min}), (R^*, R_{i_0}) \right) \left((1, t^a + s_{\min}), z^d \right).$$

By unchanged-contour independence,

$$\left((1, t^b + s_{\min}), z^c \right) \mathbf{R} \left((s_{\min}, s_{\min}), (R'_j, R_{i_0}) \right) \left((1, t^a + s_{\min}), z^d \right).$$

Let $E' = ((s_{i_0}, s_j, s_{\min}, s_{\min}), (R_{i_0}, R_j, R'_j, R_{i_0}))$. By separation, one deduces from the previous equations that

$$\left(z'_{i_0}, z_j, (1, t^a + s_{\min}), z^c \right) \mathbf{R}(E') \left(z'_{i_0}, z'_j, (1, t^b + s_{\min}), z^c \right),$$

$$\left(z''_{i_0}, z_j, (1, t^a + s_{\min}), z^d \right) \mathbf{R}(E') \left(z'_{i_0}, z_j, (1, t^a + s_{\min}), z^c \right),$$

$$\left(z''_{i_0}, z_j, (1, t^b + s_{\min}), z^c \right) \mathbf{R}(E') \left(z''_{i_0}, z_j, (1, t^a + s_{\min}), z^d \right).$$

By transitivity,

$$\left(z''_{i_0}, z_j, (1, t^b + s_{\min}), z^c \right) \mathbf{R}(E') \left(z'_{i_0}, z'_j, (1, t^b + s_{\min}), z^c \right).$$

By separation,

$$\left(z_{i_0}'', z_j\right) \mathbf{R}\left(\left(s_{i_0}, s_j\right), \left(R_{i_0}, R_j,\right)\right) \left(z_{i_0}', z_j'\right).$$

Let $E'' = \left(\left(s_{i_0}, s_j, s_{N\setminus\{i_0,j\}}\right), \left(R_{i_0}, R_j, R_{N\setminus\{i_0,j\}}\right)\right)$. By separation again,

$$\left(z_{i_0}'', z_j, z_{N\setminus\{i_0,j\}}'\right) \mathbf{R}(E'') \left(z_{i_0}', z_j', z_{N\setminus\{i_0,j\}}'\right).$$

Repeating this step for all $i \neq i_0$, one eventually obtains that for some $z_{i_0}^*$ such that $z_{i_0} \, P_{i_0} \, z_{i_0}^* \, P_{i_0} \, z_{i_0}'$,

$$\left(z_{i_0}^*, z_{N\setminus\{i_0\}}\right) \mathbf{R}(E) \, z_N'.$$

By strong Pareto, $z_N \, \mathbf{P}(E) \left(z_{i_0}^*, z_{N\setminus\{i_0\}}\right)$ and therefore, by transitivity, $z_N \, \mathbf{P}(E) \, z_N'$. ∎

Bibliography

Arrow K.J. 1963, *Social Choice and Individual Values*, 2nd ed. New York: John Wiley & Sons.

Arnsperger C. 1994, Envy-freeness and distributive justice, *Journal of Economic Surveys* 8: 155–186.

D'Aspremont C. and L. Gevers 1977, Equity and the informational basis of collective choice, *Review of Economic Studies* 44: 199–209.

D'Aspremont C. and L. Gevers 2002, Social welfare functionals and interpersonal comparability, in K.J. Arrow, A.K. Sen, and K. Suzumura (eds.), *Handbook of Social Choice and Welfare*, Vol. 2. Amsterdam: North-Holland.

Atkinson A.B. 1973, How progressive should income tax be? in M. Parkin and A.R. Nobay (eds.), *Essays in Modern Economics*. London: Longmans.

Atkinson A.B. 1995, *Public Economics in Action*. Oxford: Clarendon Press.

Atkinson A.B. and F. Bourguignon 1982, The comparison of multi-dimensioned distributions of economic status, *Review of Economic Studies* 49: 183–201.

Bergson A. 1938, A reformulation of certain aspects of welfare economics, *Quarterly Journal of Economics* 52: 310–334.

Bevia C. 1996, Identical preferences lower bound solution and consistency in economies with indivisible goods, *Social Choice and Welfare* 13: 113–126.

Blackorby C., W. Bossert, and D. Donaldson 2005, *Population Issues in Social-Choice Theory, Welfare Economics and Ethics*. New York: Cambridge University Press.

Blackorby C. and D. Donaldson 1988, Money metric utility: a harmless normalization?, *Journal of Economic Theory* 46: 120–129.

Blackorby C. and D. Donaldson 1990, A review article: the case against the use of the sum of compensating variations in cost-benefit analysis, *Canadian Journal of Economics* 23: 471–494.

Boadway R. and N. Bruce 1984, *Welfare economics*. Oxford: Basil Blackwell.

Boadway R. and L. Jacquet 2008, Optimal marginal and average income taxation under maximin, *Journal of Economic Theory* 143: 425–441.

Boadway R., M. Marchand, P. Pestieau, and M.D.M. Racionero 2002, Optimal redistribution with heterogeneous preferences for leisure, *Journal of Public Economic Theory* 4: 475–498.

Bordes G. and M. Le Breton 1989, Arrovian theorems with private alternatives domains and selfish individuals, *Journal of Economic Theory* 47: 257–281.

Bossert W. and J.A. Weymark 2004, Utility in social choice, in S. Barberà, P.J. Hammond, and C. Seidl (eds.), *Handbook of Utility Theory*, Vol. 2. Dordrecht, the Netherlands: Kluwer.

Brams S. and P. Fishburn 1983, Paradoxes of preferential voting, *Mathematical Magazine* 56: 207–214.

Broome J. 2004, *Weighing Lives*. Oxford: Oxford University Press.

Brun B.C. and B. Tungodden 2004, Non-welfaristic theories of justice: Is the intersection approach a solution to the indexing impasse?, *Social Choice and Welfare* 22: 49–60.

Chakravarty S.R. 1990, *Ethical Social Index Numbers*. New York: Springer-Verlag.

Champsaur P. and G. Laroque 1981, Fair allocations in large economies, *Journal of Economic Theory* 25: 269–282.

Chaudhuri A. 1986, Some implications of an intensity measure of envy, *Social Choice and Welfare* 3: 255–270.

Choné P. and G. Laroque 2005, Optimal incentives for labor force participation, *Journal of Public Economics* 89: 395–425.

Dalton H. 1920, The measurement of the inequality of incomes, *Economic Journal* 30: 348–361.

Deaton A. and J. Muellbauer 1980, *Economics and Consumer Behaviour*. Cambridge: Cambridge University Press.

Debreu G. 1951, The coefficient of resource utilization, *Econometrica* 19: 273–292.

Debreu G. 1959, Topological methods in cardinal utility theory, in K.J. Arrow, S. Karlin, and P. Suppes (eds.), *Mathematical Methods in the Social Sciences*. Stanford, CA: Stanford University Press.

Diamantaras E. and W. Thomson 1991, A refinement and extension of the no-envy concept, *Economics Letters* 33: 217–222.

Diamond P. 1975, A many-person Ramsey tax rule, *Journal of Public Economics* 4: 335–342.

Diamond P. and J. Mirrlees 1971, Optimal taxation and public production II: tax rules, *American Economic Review* 61: 261–278.

Dworkin R. 2000, *Sovereign Virtue. The Theory and Practice of Equality*. Cambridge, MA: Harvard University Press.

Eisenberg E. 1961, Aggregation of utility functions, *Management Science* 7: 337–350.

Fleming M. 1952, A cardinal concept of welfare, *Quarterly Journal of Economics* 66: 366–384.

Fleurbaey M. 1996, Reward patterns of fair solutions, *Journal of Public Economics* 59: 365–395.

Fleurbaey M. 2005a, Health, wealth and fairness, *Journal of Public Economic Theory* 7: 253–284.

Fleurbaey M. 2005b, The Pazner-Schmeidler social ordering: a defense, *Review of Economic Design* 9: 145–166.

Fleurbaey M. 2007a, Social choice and the indexing dilemma, *Social Choice and Welfare* 29: 633–648.

Fleurbaey M. 2007b, Two criteria for social decisions, *Journal of Economic Theory* 134: 421–447.

Fleurbaey M. 2008, *Fairness, Responsibility, and Welfare*. Oxford: Oxford University Press.

Fleurbaey M. 2010, Assessing risky social situations, *Journal of Political Economy*, 118: 649–680.

Fleurbaey M. and G. Gaulier 2009, International comparisons of living standards by equivalent incomes, *Scandinavian Journal of Economics* 111: 597–624.

Fleurbaey M. and F. Maniquet 1996a, Fair allocation with unequal production skills: the no-envy approach to compensation, *Mathematical Social Sciences* 32: 71–93.

Fleurbaey M. and F. Maniquet 1996b, The cooperative production problem: a comparison of welfare bounds, *Games and Economic Behavior* 17: 200–208.

Fleurbaey M. and F. Maniquet 1999, Fair allocation with unequal production skills: the solidarity approach to compensation, *Social Choice and Welfare* 16: 569–583.

Fleurbaey M. and F. Maniquet 2005, Fair social orderings with unequal production skills, *Social Choice and Welfare* 24: 1–35.

Fleurbaey M. and F. Maniquet 2006, Fair income tax, *Review of Economic Studies* 73: 55–83.

Fleurbaey M. and F. Maniquet 2007, Help the low skill or let the hard-working thrive: a study of fairness in optimal income taxation, *Journal of Public Economic Theory* 9: 467–500.

Fleurbaey M. and F. Maniquet 2008a, Fair social orderings, *Economic Theory* 38: 25–45.

Fleurbaey M. and F. Maniquet 2008b, Utilitarianism versus fairness in welfare economics, in M. Fleurbaey, M. Salles, and J.A. Weymark (eds.), *Justice, Political Liberalism and Utilitarianism: Themes from Harsanyi and Rawls*. Cambridge: Cambridge University Press.

Fleurbaey M. and F. Maniquet 2010, Compensation and responsibility, in K.J. Arrow, A.K. Sen, and K. Suzumura (eds.), *Handbook of Social Choice and Welfare*, Vol. 2. Amsterdam: North-Holland.

Fleurbaey M. and F. Maniquet 2011, The Kolm tax, the tax credit and the flat tax, in M. Fleurbaey, M. Salles, and J.A. Weymark (eds.), *Social Ethics and Normative Economics*. Berlin: Springer.

Fleurbaey M. and P. Mongin 2005, The news of the death of welfare economics is greatly exaggerated, *Social Choice and Welfare* 25: 381–418.

Fleurbaey M. and Y. Sprumont 2009, Sharing the cost of a public good without subsidies, *Journal of Public Economic Theory* 11: 1–8.

Fleurbaey M., K. Suzumura, and K. Tadenuma 2005a, Arrovian aggregation in economic environments: How much should we know about indifference surfaces?, *Journal of Economic Theory* 142: 22–44.

Fleurbaey M., K. Suzumura, and K. Tadenuma 2005b, The informational basis of the theory of fair allocation, *Social Choice and Welfare* 24: 311–341.

Fleurbaey M. and K. Tadenuma 2007, Do irrelevant commodities matter? *Econometrica* 75: 1143–1174.

Fleurbaey M. and A. Trannoy 2003, The impossibility of a Paretian egalitarian, *Social Choice and Welfare* 21: 243–464.

Gajdos T. and J.A. Weymark 2005, Multidimensional generalized Gini indices, *Economic Theory* 26: 471–496.

Gevers L. 1986, Walrasian social choice: some simple axiomatic approaches, in W. Heller et al. (eds.), *Social Choice and Public Decision Making. Essays in Honor of K.J. Arrow*. Cambridge: Cambridge University Press.

Gibbard A. 1979, Disparate goods and Rawls's difference principle: a social choice theoretic treatment, *Theory and Decision* 11: 267–288.

Gorman W.M. 1968, The structure of utility functions, *Review of Economic Studies* 35: 367–390.

Hammond P.J. 1976, Equity, Arrow's conditions and Rawls' difference principle, *Econometrica* 44: 793–804.

Hammond P.J. 1979, Straightforward individual incentivecompatibility in large economies, *Review of Economic Studies* 46: 263–282.

Hammond P.J. 1991, Interpersonal comparisons of utility: why they are and how they should be made, in J. Elster and J.E. Roemer (eds.), *Interpersonal Comparisons of Well-Being*. Cambridge: Cambridge University Press.

Hansson B. 1973, The independence condition in the theory of social choice, *Theory and Decision* 4: 25–49.

Hardy G.H., J.E. Littlewood, and G. Polya 1952, *Inequalities*. Cambridge: Cambridge University Press.

Kaneko M. 1977, The ratio equilibria and the core of the voting game $G(N, w)$ in a public goods economy, *Econometrica* 45: 1589–1594.

Kannai Y. 1970, Continuity properties of the core of a market, *Econometrica* 38: 791–815.

Kaplow L. 2008, *The Theory of Taxation and Public Economics*. Princeton, NJ: Princeton University Press.

King M.A. 1983, An index of inequality: with applications to horizontal equity and social mobility, *Econometrica* 51: 99–115.

Kolm S.C. 1968, The optimal production of social justice, in H. Guitton and J. Margolis (eds.), *Economie Publique*. Paris: CNRS.

Kolm S.C. 1972, *Justice et Equité*. Paris: Editions du CNRS.

Kolm S.C. 1977, Multidimensional egalitarianisms, *Quarterly Journal of Economics* 91: 1–13.

Kolm S.C. 1996, The theory of justice, *Social Choice and Welfare* 13: 151–182.

Kolm S.C. 2004, *Macrojustice. The Political Economy of Fairness*. New York: Cambridge University Press.

Koshevoy G. 1995, Multivariate Lorenz majorization, *Social Choice and Welfare* 12: 93–102.

Lange O. 1936, The place of interest in the theory of production, *Review of Economics Studies* 3: 159–192.

Le Breton M. and J. Weymark 2002, Arrovian social choice theory on economic models, in K.J. Arrow, A.K. Sen, and K. Suzumura (eds.), *Handbook of Social Choice and Welfare*, Vol. 2, Amsterdam: North-Holland.

Lee D. and E. Saez 2008, Optimal minimum wage policy in competitive labor markets, NBER WP 14320.

Maniquet F. 1998, An equal-right solution to the compensation-responsibility dilemma, *Mathematical Social Sciences* 35: 185–202.

Maniquet F. 1999, A strong incompatibility between efficiency and equity in non-convex economies, *Journal of Mathematical Economics* 32: 467–474.

Maniquet F. 2007, Social orderings and the evaluation of public policy, *Revue d'Economie Politique* 117: 37–60.

Maniquet F. 2008, Social orderings for the assignment of indivisible objects, *Journal of Economic Theory* 143: 199–215.

Maniquet F. and Y. Sprumont 2004, Fair production and allocation of a non-rival good, *Econometrica* 72: 627–640.

Maniquet F. and Y. Sprumont 2005, Welfare egalitrianism in nonrival environments, *Journal of Economic Theory* 120: 155–174.

Maniquet F. and Y. Sprumont 2010, Sharing the cost of a public good: an incentive-constrained axiomatic approach, *Games and Economic Behavior* 68: 275–302.

Mas-Colell A. 1980, Remarks on the game-theoretic analysis of a simple distribution of surplus problem, *International Journal of Game Theory* 9: 125–140.

Maskin E. 1999, Nash equilibrium and welfare optimality, *Review of Economic Studies* 66: 23–38.

Mayston D.J. 1974, *The Idea of Social Choice*. London: Macmillan.

Milleron J.C. 1970, Distribution of income, social welfare functions and the criterion of consumer surplus, *European Economic Review* 2: 45–77.

Mirrlees J. 1971, An exploration in the theory of optimum income taxation, *Review of Economic Studies* 38: 175–208.

Moulin H. 1987, Egalitarian-equivalent cost sharing of a public good, *Econometrica* 55: 963–976.

Moulin H. 1990, Uniform externalities: two axioms for fair allocation, *Journal of Public Economics* 43: 305–326.

Moulin H. 1991, Welfare bounds in the fair division problem, *Journal of Economic Theory* 54: 321–337.

Moulin H. 1992, Welfare bounds in the cooperative production problem, *Games and Economic Behaviour* 4: 373–401.

Moulin H. 1994, Serial cost sharing of excludable public goods, *Review of Economic Studies* 61: 305–325.

Moulin H. 1996, Stand alone and unanimity tests: a re-examination of fair division, in F. Farina, F. Hahn, and S. Vanucci (eds.), *Ethics, Rationality and Economic Behaviour*. Oxford: Clarendon Press.

Moulin H. and W. Thomson 1988, Can everyone benefit from growth?, *Journal of Mathematical Economics* 17: 339–345.

Moulin H. and W. Thomson 1997, Axiomatic analysis of resource allocation problems, in K.J. Arrow, A.K. Sen, and K. Suzumura (eds.), *Social Choice Re-examined*, Vol. 1. London: Macmillan and New-York: St. Martin's Press.

Parfit D. 1991, Equality or priority, Lindley Lecture. Lawrence: University of Kansas Press.

Pattanaik P.K. and Y. Xu 2007, Minimal relativism, dominance, and standard of living comparisons based on functionings, *Oxford Economic Papers* 59: 354–374.

Pazner E. 1979, Equity, nonfeasible alternatives and social choice: a reconsideration of the concept of social welfare, in J.J. Laffont (ed.), *Aggregation and Revelation of Preferences*. Amsterdam: North-Holland.

Pazner E. and D. Schmeidler 1974, A difficulty in the concept of fairness, *Review of Economic Studies* 41: 991–993.

Pazner E. and D. Schmeidler 1978a, Decentralization and income distribution in socialist economies, *Economic Inquiry* 16: 257–264.

Pazner E. and D. Schmeidler 1978b, Egalitarian equivalent allocations: A new concept of economic equity, *Quarterly Journal of Economics* 92: 671–687.

Pigou A.C. 1912, *Wealth and Welfare*. London: Macmillan.

Ramsey F.P. 1927, A contribution to the theory of taxation, *Economic Journal* 37: 47–61.

Rawls J. 1971, *A Theory of Justice*. Cambridge, MA: Harvard University Press.

Rawls J. 1982, Social unity and primary goods, in A. Sen and B. Williams (eds.), *Utilitarianism and Beyond*. Cambridge: Cambridge University Press.

Roberts K.W.S. 1980, Price independent welfare prescriptions, *Journal of Public Economics* 13: 277–298.

Robbins L. 1932, *An Essay on the Nature and Significance of Economics*. London: McMillan (2nd revised ed., 1937).

Sakai T. 2009, Walrasian social orderings in exchange economies, *Journal of Mathematical Economics* 45: 16–22.

Samuelson P.A. 1947, *Foundations of Economic Analysis*. Cambridge, MA: Harvard University Press.

Samuelson P.A. 1974, Complementarity: an essay on the 40th anniversary of the Hicks-Allen revolution in demand theory, *Journal of Economic Literature* 12: 1255–1289.

Samuelson P.A. 1977, Reaffirming the existence of "reasonable" Bergson-Samuelson social welfare functions, *Economica* 44: 81–88.

Samuelson P.A. and S. Swamy 1974, Invariant economic index numbers and canonical duality: survey and synthesis, *American Economic Review* 64: 566–593.

Sen A.K. 1970, *Collective Choice and Social Welfare*. San Francisco: Holden Day.

Sen A.K. 1979, Personal utilities and public judgements: or what's wrong with welfare economics, *Economic Journal* 89: 537–558.

Sen A.K. 1985, *Commodities and Capabilities*. Amsterdam: North-Holland.

Sen A.K. 1992, *Inequality Reexamined*. Cambridge, MA: Harvard University Press.

Sen A.K. 2009, *The Idea of Justice*. London: Allen Lane.

Shorrocks A.B. 1983, Ranking income distributions, *Economica* 50: 3–17.

Slesnick D.T. 1991, Aggregate deadweight loss and money metric social welfare, *International Economic Review* 32: 123–146.

Sprumont Y. 1998, Equal factor equivalence in economies with multiple public goods, *Social Choice and Welfare* 15: 543–558.

Sprumont Y. 2006, Resource egalitarianism with a dash of efficiency, *Journal of Economic Theory*, forthcoming.

Steinhaus H. 1948, The problem of fair division, *Econometrica* 16: 101–104.

Stiglitz J.E. 1982, Self-selection and Pareto efficient taxation, *Journal of Public Economics* 17: 213–240.

Suzumura K. 1981a, On Pareto-efficiency and the no-envy concept of equity, *Journal of Economic Theory* 25: 367–379.

Suzumura K. 1981b, On the possibility of fair" collective choice rule, *International Economic Review* 22: 351–364.

Tadenuma K. 2002, Efficiency first or equity first? Two principles and rationality of social choice, *Journal of Economic Theory* 104: 462–472.

Tadenuma K. 2005, Egalitarian-equivalence and the Pareto principle for social preferences, *Social Choice and Welfare* 24: 455–473.

Tadenuma K. and W. Thomson 1991, No-envy and consistency in economies with indivisible goods, *Econometrica* 59: 1755–1767.

Tadenuma K. and W. Thomson 1995, Refinements of the no-envy solution in economies with indivisible goods, *Theory and Decision* 39: 189–206.

Thomson W. 1996, Concepts of implementation, *Japanese Economic Review* 47: 133–143.

Thomson W. 2010, Fair allocation rules, in K. Arrow, A.K. Sen, and K. Suzumura (eds.), *Handbook of Social Choice and Welfare Volume II*. Amsterdam, New York: North-Holland.

Valletta G. 2009a, A fair solution to the compensation problem, *Social Choice and Welfare* 32: 455–470.

Valletta G. 2009b, Health, fairness and taxation, unpublished paper.

Varian H. 1974, Efficiency, equity and envy, *Journal of Economic Theory* 9: 63–91.

Varian H. 1976, Two problems in the theory of fairness, *Journal of Public Economics* 5: 249–260.

Wilson R.B. 1972, Social choice without the Pareto principle, *Journal of Economic Theory* 5: 478–486.

Index

Printed in the United States
By Bookmasters